An Interdisciplinary Approach to American History

VOLUME II

An Interdisciplinary

VOLUME II

PRENTICE-HALL, INC., ENGLEWOOD CLIFFS, N.J.

Approach
to American History

Edited by

ARI HOOGENBOOM

Brooklyn College

OLIVE HOOGENBOOM

Library of Congress Cataloging in Publication Data

HOOGENBOOM, ARI ARTHUR,   comp.
  An interdisciplinary approach to American history.

  Includes bibliographical references.
  1. United States—History—Addresses, essays,
lectures.   I. Hoogenboom, Olive, joint comp.   II. Title.
E178.1.H77   973   72-11764
ISBN   0-13-469221-7

AN INTERDISCIPLINARY APPROACH TO AMERICAN HISTORY, *Volume II*
by Ari Hoogenboom and Olive Hoogenboom

© 1973 by Prentice-Hall, Inc., Englewood Cliffs, New Jersey

Printed in the United States of America

10   9   8   7   6   5   4   3   2   1

PRENTICE-HALL INTERNATIONAL, INC., *London*
PRENTICE-HALL OF AUSTRALIA, PTY. LTD., *Sydney*
PRENTICE-HALL OF CANADA, LTD., *Toronto*
PRENTICE-HALL OF INDIA PRIVATE LIMITED, *New Delhi*
PRENTICE-HALL OF JAPAN, INC., *Tokyo*

In memory of
Willis L. King (1908–1964)
an outstanding teacher and friend

Contents

Preface

Encompassing, as it does, all human experience, history more than any other field of scholarship depends on other disciplines. Other disciplines in turn need history (out of which many of them have developed) for a better understanding of their own specialties. In recent years awareness of this mutual dependence has become pronounced, with historians utilizing concepts and methodology originally designed for examining contemporary society and with nonhistorians testing their ideas and methods against records of the past. The results have produced profound changes in the study of American history.

American history is being written differently than it was a generation ago. There is more emphasis on analysis and less on narrative, more on concepts and less on institutions, more on statistics and less on manuscripts, more on the anonymous masses and less on the articulate elite. The drift away from political, military, and diplomatic history and toward economic, social, and cultural history has continued. Much political history has been rewritten with a heavy infusion of statistics and re-evaluated with the ideas of political scientists, sociologists, and social psychologists. By applying mathematical and theoretical models to available statistical data, econometricians have created the "new" as contrasted with the "old" qualitative economic history and have wrought a revolution in that area. Social history has particularly matured, with historians moving beyond emotional involvement with the pioneer, the laborer, and the immigrant to analyses of social mobility, social stratification, and the family. Formerly neglected groups, including blacks, Indians, Mexican Americans, women, and children, are receiving attention. Intellectual and cultural historians have broadened their interests. Influenced in particular by the American studies movement, they have found revealing insights in popular culture and music as well as in the folklore, images, symbols, and myths of the American people.

The best history is being written by those who incorporate these interdisciplinary approaches with traditional methods of research. Since much that is important cannot be counted, statistics are not a substitute for, but are to be used with, manuscripts and other conventional sources. Chronology—the sequence of events—remains the key to understanding the past, but insights from other disciplines help explain past events. The best narrative history is both interesting and analytical.

The following significant and challenging interdisciplinary readings are ideal for use in basic American history courses. The term *interdisciplinary* has been construed broadly. Selections have been chosen from or inspired by not only the social sciences—anthropology, sociology, political science, geography, economics, psychology, and psychoanalysis —but also medical science, American studies, folklore, and music.

Since this work is intended for students in college survey courses, we have eliminated most footnotes and all bibliographies. Students wishing to explore further the methodology utilized by the authors are urged to consult the original sources listed beneath each headnote. The brief headnotes do not summarize selections but suggest why they are important. The readings speak for themselves.

Our greatest debt is to the authors who have permitted us to present their work. We also wish to thank Howard Harris for help in making selections and Lynn Hoogenboom, Theodore Lauer, Arthur E. Scherr, and Jerome Sternstein for help in tracking down material.

A. H.
O. H.

An Interdisciplinary Approach
to American History

White Liberals and Black Power in Negro Education, 1865–1915

JAMES M. McPHERSON

The Reconstruction period and the decades beyond defined the meaning of the Civil War. The North had won, but the effects of that victory on the politics, economics, society, and culture of the nation as a whole and of the South in particular remained to be seen. For Negroes the meaning of the war and their new freedom was unclear initially but was soon spelled out. With black civil rights circumscribed, economic opportunities restricted, and educational advantages limited, freedom meant little. To aid in black education, however, many northern-based church groups established southern schools. Ironically, these white-supported schools, which provided the best opportunity for black education, were the target of black teachers and administrators who wished to control them. Basing his work on a statistical survey of the faculties of colleges and schools established by northern mission societies, James M. McPherson evaluates the struggle for power in these schools.

Although the phrase "black power" is of recent origin and has acquired ambivalent and emotional overtones, the issue is in some respects not new. Reduced to its lowest common denominator, the concept of black power means greater control by Negroes themselves of the major institutions and processes that shape their lives. During the two generations after the Civil War there were many disputes over control of the freedmen's schools and colleges founded and supported by Northern aboli-

From *American Historical Review* 75 (1970):1357–86. Footnotes omitted. Reprinted by permission of the author.

tionists, missionaries, and other "white liberals" interested in advancing the Negro's status and improving race relations through education. Many Negroes desired a larger role in managing these schools; their demands produced clashes that foreshadowed some current racial controversies in the field of education. The earlier black-power drive did not aim toward a restructuring of the methods, content, or purposes of education; Negroes desired not to change the system but to achieve greater participation in it as teachers, deans, presidents, and trustees. While retaining considerable control over the schools they had founded, white liberal educators three-quarters of a century ago began gradually to yield most faculty and administrative posts to blacks. This article will try to describe and evaluate that transition.

The freedmen's aid societies of Northern Protestant churches established more than a hundred institutions of college and secondary education for Negroes after the Civil War (see table following text). The foremost of these societies was the American Missionary Association (AMA), organized in 1846 by abolitionists protesting the lack of anti-slavery zeal in existing Congregational mission societies. In 1861 the AMA committed most of its resources to freedmen's education; the Northern branches of the Methodist, Baptist, and Presbyterian churches soon joined the effort by setting up freedmen's aid societies or adding a freedmen's department to an established home mission body. The schools founded by these churches (plus a few supported by Quakers and minor sects) provided nearly all the college education and most of the high school training for Southern Negroes until well into the twentieth century. This was the "finest thing in American history, and one of the few things untainted by sordid greed and cheap vainglory," wrote W. E. B. Du Bois, a graduate of the AMA's Fisk University.

> The teachers in these institutions came not to keep the Negroes in their place, but to raise them out of the defilement of the places where slavery had wallowed them. The Colleges . . . were social settlements; homes where the best of the sons of the freedmen came in close and sympathetic touch with the best traditions of New England.

But all was not well in this educational Zion. Some Negroes resented the patronizing attitude often expressed in the missionary rationale for freedmen's education. "The colored people are yet children, and need to be taught every thing," proclaimed the secretary of the Methodist Freedmen's Aid Society in 1874. "They need that those more favored should take them by the hand and lead them . . . up from debasement and misery into purity and joy." Frederick Douglass was angered by such statements. "We have been injured more than we have been helped by men who have professed to be our friends," he told a black audience in

1875. "We must stop these men from begging for us. . . . We must stop begging ourselves. If we build churches don't ask white people to pay for them. If we have banks, colleges and papers, do not ask other people to support them. Be independent. . . . I am here to-day to offer and sign a declaration of independence for the colored people of these United States."

Though Douglass soon receded from this rhetorical venture into separatism, some Negro leaders turned increasingly to the concept of independent, black-owned institutions as the overthrow of Reconstruction and the onset of reaction blocked access to power and achievement in white American society. "There is not as bright and glorious a future before a Negro in a white institution as there is for him in his own," E. K. Love told the National Baptist Convention (the body representing black Baptist churches) in 1896.

> We can better marshal our forces and develop our people in enterprises manned by us. We can more thoroughly fill our people with race pride . . . by presenting to them for their support enterprises that are wholly ours. . . . The world recognizes men for the power they have to affect it. . . . Negro brain should shape and control Negro thought.

This impulse toward self-help and race pride did lead to the founding by the AME (African Methodist Episcopal) and AME Zion churches of several colleges supported and controlled entirely by Negroes. But the black community lacked the financial resources to sustain major projects, and most of these schools were poor in quality and starved for funds. The colored A & M colleges established by Southern states to provide Negroes with their share of the appropriations from the Morrill Land-Grant Act afforded another quasi-separatist outlet for black ambitions. In 1870 a district secretary of the AMA reported that some Negroes in Mississippi, dissatisfied with white control of Tougaloo College, were pressing the state legislature for the creation of a college "of *their own*" where nobody "but themselves run their machine." The legislature established Alcorn College the next year. Similar pressures were brought to bear in other states. At the South Carolina constitutional convention in 1895, black delegates urged the withdrawal of the state appropriation from Claflin University (controlled by Northern Methodists) and the creation of a school for blacks in which the "professors and instructors shall be of the negro race." Benjamin Tillman supported the proposal for a separate Negro college, and at his behest the convention authorized the establishment of the Colored Normal, Industrial, Agricultural and Mechanical College of South Carolina. By the end of the century every Southern state supported some kind of institution of higher education for Negroes. Most presidents of these schools and all but a handful of teachers were Negroes, presenting a facade of black control. The reality of black power in such institutions was dubious, however, since their faculties and administrations were beholden to state legislatures. All the state Negro colleges in this period were woefully under-financed and devoid of genuine college-level offerings. The major institutions of higher education for Negroes were and are those founded by Northern missionaries. The struggle for black power and against white paternalism in education, therefore, took place primarily within the schools established and supported largely by Northern whites, not outside them.

As the Negro colleges began turning out graduates who were denied positions of authority and influence in a Jim Crow society, the schools themselves became the focus of black ambitions. Despite their professed and, in most cases, sincere belief in racial equality, white missionaries yielded only gradually and sometimes reluctantly to black demands for greater control of schools. There were both subjective and objective reasons for this gradualism. Subjectively, some missionaries shared (perhaps subconsciously) the widespread conviction that black people were deficient in organizational and executive skills. They were especially hesitant to entrust Negroes with outright control of funds contributed by Northern philanthropy. Moreover, many teachers were slow to believe that the "grown-up children" for whom the schools were founded had matured to the point of readiness for adult responsibilities. Objectively, the first and even second generations of freedmen could not produce enough able teachers to staff the schools with personnel equal in average ability and training to Northern teachers, who came from middle-class, New England-oriented backgrounds that stressed education and achievement. A genuine concern for maintaining the highest possible standards for freedmen's schools was a major reason for the slowness to supplant white teachers and administrators with blacks. Indeed, two contemporary experts on education thought that some mission societies yielded too readily to demands for black power and that the quality of many schools suffered as a result. Black communities served by mission schools were themselves frequently divided on the question; many Negroes, especially parents of students, considered white teachers superior to black instructors and were opposed to the drive for black control of schools. The interplay of these various attitudes produced smoldering tensions in several schools.

The issue first surfaced on the question of hiring black teachers. From 1865 to 1870 the freedmen's aid societies operated several hundred elementary schools with support from the Freedmen's Bureau. Perhaps one-fourth of the teachers in these schools were black. But when the Bureau's educational work ceased in 1870, most of the common schools were absorbed into the South's new public school system and the mission societies began to concentrate their resources on a smaller number of secondary schools and colleges. At first nearly all the teachers in these higher schools were white, even though the societies often did try to employ black teachers when they were qualified. The American Missionary Association's Avery Institute in Charleston, for example, had an interracial faculty headed by a black principal in the 1860's. The trustees of Howard University made an effort to recruit black professors, and four Negroes were on the staff in the early 1870's. The Methodist Freedmen's Aid Society stated in 1878 that "as rapidly as we have been able to prepare our own students, we have introduced them . . . as teachers in our schools."

But by 1880 there was still only a handful of black teachers in the better missionary schools, a sore point in several Negro communities. A black minister in an AMA church at Mobile reported disaffection among his flock because the Association's school had no Negro teachers. "This is the great reason for all the prejudice that exists," he wrote. "The employment of a colored teacher would increase the influence of the school and the church" and "shut the mouths of those who are murmuring." A Negro educator in Virginia wrote a paper in 1876 entitled "Colored Teachers for Colored Schools," which sharply criticized Hampton Institute for its shortage of black instructors. The paper was endorsed by the Virginia Educational and Historical Association, a Negro organization. A black lawyer in South Carolina went the whole way in 1883 and demanded that "Negro teachers exclusively be employed to teach Negro schools."

This drive for more black faculty met a mixed response from white philanthropists. Some urged a crash program to recruit and train Negro teachers. The secretary of the Baptist Home Mission Society wrote to the president of Richmond Institute: "You do not know how resolutely colored leaders have pressed us to employ and pay colored teachers. . . . I pray you take your strongest and ablest students . . . and drill them, and *drill* them, and DRILL them privately" until they are competent to join the faculty. This policy was carried out, and when Richmond Institute became Virginia Union University in 1899, half the faculty was black. The white principal of the AMA's Storrs Schools in Atlanta advised the Association's secretary to yield to black pressure: "It will be well for them to try to manage the school for they will never be satisfied until they do," she wrote, and if the board "is wise in its selection of teachers I think they will do well. Certainly we are not the ones to oppose them, for it is for this work that we have been educating them. I only condemn the ungrateful spirit exhibited by many."

Other white administrators counseled a cautious policy in hiring black teachers on the ground that few Negroes were yet qualified. Laura Towne, founder of Penn School on St. Helena Island in South Carolina, wrote in 1873 that schools taught by Negroes on the sea islands "are always in confusion, grief, & utter want of everything. It is hard to imagine schools doing so little good." Miss Towne kept white teachers at Penn School until their black replacements were thoroughly trained. The president of Straight University (a forerunner of Dillard) in New Orleans urged the AMA not to employ black teachers in the law and theological departments just because of "this clamor for colored teachers. . . . We can't have any humbug about this department for the sake of color. . . . Colored teachers are not generally successful."

Some black leaders discounted the argument that educational quality would suffer if Negro teachers were employed too soon; they insisted that Anglo-Saxon academic standards should not be the only criteria for hiring teachers. Francis Grimké declared in 1885 that the development of race pride should be a major objective of Negro education. The low self-image with which the black man had emerged from slavery was perpetuated by schools with white faculties, Grimké complained. "The intellects of our young people are being educated at the expense of their manhood. In the classroom they see only white professors," which leads them "to associate these places and the idea of fitness for them only with white men." In their slowness to appoint black professors, the schools "are failing to use one of the most effective means in their power, of helping on this race." J. Willis Menard, who had been the first Negro elected to Congress, asserted in 1885 that while many white teachers were sincere and dedicated, others were selfish hypocrites, and in any case, no white teacher could achieve the rapport and empathy with black students that a Negro teacher could. "We demand educated colored teachers for colored schools," wrote Menard, "because their color identity makes them more interested in the advancement of colored children than white teachers, and because colored pupils need the social *contact* of colored teachers."

But Negroes were not united behind this viewpoint. A black woman, herself a teacher, condemned as a "peculiar error" the argument that Negroes should be given jobs "without due regard to their fitness." She did not want "the standard of excellence lowered for us. To admit the necessity is to insult the Negro. Our youth have the right to the best possible training, and we should not allow a mistaken race pride to cause us to impose upon them inferior teachers." A Negro in Atlanta pleaded with the AMA to retain control of Storrs School "with the understanding that we have Northern teachers." The school inspector for the AMA reported in 1878 that blacks in Atlanta "have again, as last year, arrayed themselves on both sides of the question and each party has petitioned . . . one for colored teachers & the other for Northern whites." There was "no doubt," the inspector stated, that in most cities where the AMA maintained schools the "parents prefer to send their children to Northern white teachers instead of colored." In a few cases after the mission socie-ties had turned their schools over to Negro teachers, the deterioration in quality prompted black leaders to ask for the return of whites. "Since the cessation of your work among us," wrote one Negro to a white educator, "the schools have degenerated, and the system as operated here is a mere farce."

Because of divided opinion among both races on the issue of black teachers, the AMA decided at a conference in 1877 to "make haste slowly in this regard." In subsequent years the AMA emphasized "slowly" more than "haste." As late as 1895 only twelve of 141 teachers in the Associa-tion's seventeen secondary schools were blacks; only four of 110 faculty members in its five colleges were Negroes. A black journalist stated in 1901 that the AMA's small percentage of Negro teachers had long been an "eyesore" to the race, and that "only the splendid work of the associa-tion has kept down an agitation of this matter."

It was not only the high quality of AMA schools but also the tiny black constituency of the Congregational Church that minimized Negro criticism of the Association. The Baptist and Methodist societies, on the other hand, were under greater pressure from the large black memberships of their denominations. By the mid-1890's approximately half the teachers in the schools of these societies were black. The Presbyterians and most of the small denominations also moved faster than the AMA in the ap-pointment of Negro teachers. In 1895 there were ninety-four schools for Negroes of nominal high school or college grade in the South established by the abolitionist-missionary impulse and largely supported by Northern Protestants. In the ninety institutions for which statistics are available there were 1,046 teachers, of whom 370 (thirty-six per cent) were black.

Viewed in one way, this represented significant progress. A race barely one generation away from slavery and illiteracy had advanced to the point of supplying more than one-third of the teachers for the higher schools founded or supported mainly by the missionary efforts of another race. Yet progress was less impressive than it appeared on the surface. Most students in the ninety-four schools, including the "universities," were in elementary grades, and at least ninety per cent of the black faculty were teaching these grades rather than secondary or college classes. Even in schools with a sizable Negro faculty, major policy decisions were nor-mally made by whites. Power flowed from the purse; Northern whites contributed most of the money, and Northern whites occupied the major administrative posts of the mission societies and colleges. Although Ne-groes were represented on the local boards of trustees of most schools and colleges, these boards usually had little power; ultimate control rested with the mission societies. Most Negroes who benefited from these schools accepted the fact that the greater administrative experience and financial resources of white philanthropists made a large degree of white control inevitable, at least for a time. Some felt differently. Virtually from 1870 on a black minority struggled behind the scenes for greater influence in the management of some schools.

Occasionally these conflicts broke into the open, as in the search for a successor to General Oliver O. Howard as president of Howard University in 1874–75. Black trustees and students supported John Mercer Langston, dean of the law school and vice-president of the university, for the job. But the white Congregationalists (most of them members of the AMA) who had founded the institution and dominated its board of trustees felt that Langston, despite his Oberlin degree and eminence as a black leader, lacked talent as a fund raiser and "was not the man to hold the institution to the religious and moral ideas on which it was founded." The board offered the presidency to three white men in succession; two of them declined and the other died before he could fully assume office. Embittered by what he considered the paternalism, prejudice, and religious narrowness of white trustees, Langston resigned from the university and denounced the AMA, which "relieve[s] the object of their sympathy of the pressure of responsibility and the honor due its efficient discharge, and thus weaken[s] him, as an over-affectionate and indulgent father does his son." The black man, concluded Langston, "seeks release from such associations and their self-assumed control of his affairs." In an editorial reply that unwittingly conceded the partial truth of Langston's charges, the AMA's monthly magazine declared that some friends of Negro education might be tempted to say, "If this is all the thanks we get, we will waste no more on such a people." But "we intend to go on with our efforts for the colored race. . . . With the abolitionists we endured persecution for the slave, and, now that he is free, we shall toil for his elevation and happiness, as undeterred by his fault-finding as we formerly were by the oposition of his foes."

While the trustees were agonizing over the selection of a president, Howard University, which had been in serious financial straits since the cessation of Freedmen's Bureau support and the panic of 1873, was on the verge of collapse. Believing that only a white man of prominence and administrative experience could tap the springs of Northern philanthropy and save the school, black and white trustees finally joined to elect William W. Patton president of Howard in 1877. Patton was a Congregational minister, a veteran abolitionist, and former district secretary of the AMA. He was a good administrator, but his relations with the black community were strained. He raised money in the North, persuaded Congress to make annual appropriations for the school, brought the university from the brink of disaster, and built it into a major institution. But Patton ran Howard with a strong and sometimes domineering hand. Some black trustees and alumni disliked his "overbearing ways," and there were periodic demands for his resignation. The *People's Advocate*, a Negro newspaper in Washington, declared in 1883 that "there are very few *white* men who possess the qualifications of a president of a college where *colored* men principally are educated," and concluded that Patton was not one of the few.

Negro criticism of Patton intensified in 1885 when the president forced through the appointment of a white professor of Greek instead of a black candidate whom Negroes on the board of trustees thought was at least as well qualified as the white man. Francis Grimké, a member of the board, published an angry article blasting Patton as a "hypocrite" and a "pseudo-friend" of the black man. "If this is philanthropy," declared Grimké, "then I, for one, think we have had quite enough of it. If this is the treatment we are to continue to receive from our friends, then it is time for us to begin to pray to be delivered from our friends."

Regarded by many Negroes as their national university, Howard continued to be a center of controversy. When Patton retired in 1889 black trustees wanted Jeremiah E. Rankin as his successor. A white man, Rankin was a former abolitionist and pastor of the integrated First Congregational Church in Washington who had won the unanimous respect of the Negro community. Frederick Douglass believed that Rankin had "done more to secure the rights of my race than all the legislation of Congress." Black leaders were pleased when Rankin was elected to the post; Richard Greener considered Rankin "the grandest type of man ever connected with the Institution." But faculty politics, rumor, and Rankin's own mistakes in judgment dissipated much of this good will and provoked a verbal attack on the president by black leaders, particularly Calvin Chase of the Washington *Bee*. Even though Rankin tripled the number of black teachers during his administration (1890–1903), Negroes were angry when he appointed his own daughter and several other whites to staff positions sought by Negroes. The president's alleged vendetta against a black professor stirred up a storm, and Calvin Chase asked angrily, "What claim has Dr. Rankin to the presidency of that institution? Is it not set apart for colored people?" But when Rankin retired in 1903 the *Bee* apologized for earlier attacks based on misinformation and praised the retiring president for having "done more . . . for the negro" than any other man in the country. "You have been a faithful public servant," Chase told Rankin, "and to you the negroes owe a debt of gratitude."

By the first decade of the twentieth century several black deans at Howard had carved out spheres of power within their colleges or departments. Rankin's successor as president, a white Presbyterian minister named John Gordon, moved to restrict the growing autonomy of the Teachers College under Dean Lewis B. Moore and the "Commercial Department" under Dean George W. Cook. The *Bee* supported Gordon because of its editor's declared conviction that inefficiency and intrigue in these departments had grown to scandalous proportions (Chase's role in this affair may also have been related to feuds among Washington's Negro leaders). The attempt to reform the departments led to a bitter power struggle that, though not specifically racial in origin, took on racial overtones as it became a showdown between a white president and two black deans. Moore and Cook rallied many students behind them, but the *Bee* continued to back Gordon and charged that "personal pique . . . selfishness, cupidity and ambition" motivated the deans' recalcitrance. When a hundred students demonstrated against Gordon and called for his resignation, the *Bee* urged the expulsion of the students and the firing of the "teachers who encouraged or inaugurated that disgraceful scene." Also supporting the white president, another black newspaper declared that "a negro mob in college looks, to the *Independent*, just like a white mob around a stake burning a negro. . . . Colleges were never intended to create and organize mobs. They were instituted for the purpose of disseminating Christian education."

Instead of expelling the students, the shaken and exhausted president submitted his own resignation. A battle for succession shaped up amid demands that a Negro be appointed to the position. In a reversal of his stand a decade earlier, Calvin Chase of the *Bee* ridiculed the intrigues among black aspirants for the presidency. Alluding to alleged power struggles, backstabbing, and corruption in the Negro public schools of Washington under a black superintendent, Chase predicted that a similar situation would prevail at Howard under a Negro president. To the advocates of a "colored president for a colored school," the *Bee* stated: "If the existence of Howard University depended upon the colored people, the institution could not exist a day. . . . White men have done far more to ameliorate the condition of the negro, and to elevate him in the social scale than negroes themselves have ever done."

After several months of discussion, the Howard board of trustees unanimously elected as president Wilbur P. Thirkield, a white Methodist minister and former secretary of the Methodist Freedman's Aid Society. An able and sensitive administrator, Thirkield retained the confidence of all parties. But when he was elected a bishop of the Methodist Episcopal Church in 1912, an "unholy scramble" for his job took place between Moore, Cook, and Kelly Miller. (Miller had been dean of the College of Arts and Sciences since 1907.) Each faction of the black community, including the *Bee* (which favored Miller), backed one of the deans. Surprisingly, only two of the eight Negro trustees supported any of the black candidates, while a majority of white trustees desired the election of a Negro president. If any two of the three deans had withdrawn from the contest in favor of the third, a black man would have been elected president of Howard in 1912. Since each of them preferred a white man to one of his rivals for the presidency, a white president was finally elected. Though two-thirds of the faculty was black by this time, another fourteen years passed before Howard had a Negro president.

Events at Howard received wide publicity in the Negro press, but the black-power struggle in Methodist and Baptist institutions was in some respects even more intense. Black militancy reached high tide in these two churches between 1880 and 1900, as the frustration born of the failure of Reconstruction and the intensification of Jim Crow produced compensatory strivings toward self-help, race pride, and separatism among Negroes and focused these strivings on two of the institutions in American society that offered some access to power, the school and the church. Since more than ninety per cent of Negro church member were Baptists or Methodists, the schools of these denominations became major arenas of conflict.

The Methodist Episcopal Church (Northern branch of the denomination) moved aggressively into the South after the war and recruited a black membership of nearly a quarter of a million by 1890. Under the leadership of Methodist abolitionists, the church established a Freedmen's Aid Society that by 1890 was maintaining twenty-two schools for freedmen, ten of them nominally colleges or professional schools. These institutions had interracial boards of trustees, and a few of the boards had a *de facto* black majority because some Northern trustees rarely attended meetings. Since real control was exercised by the Freedmen's Aid Society and white college presidents, however, tension mounted until it broke into the open after the Society overruled the trustees of Claflin University and Atlanta's Clark University in matters concerning Negro professors in 1890.

The white presidents of both schools were unpopular with a part of the black community, a situation that added fuel to the controversy. The president of Claflin, exasperated by Negro criticism, said privately: "I do not suppose that it is wrong for them to aspire to teach their own schools and manage their own concerns, but unfortunately for them not one in 1,000 has enough executive ability to manage the concerns of his own household successfully. It is not really their fault, as they had but little experience in independent management." The president feared that "an effort will be made to tear up things at our next trustee meeting. But they must not be allowed to have their own way in this matter. Until they furnish a considerable proportion of the funds necessary to conduct the school, they should be content to allow others to manage it." When a refractory black professor was fired from Clark University in 1890, a local Negro leader deplored this "attempt to crush down negro manhood" and denounced the president of Clark as a "cheap and incompetent" man who had come to Atlanta "to boss southern negroes."

Black militants urged their fellow Methodists to leave the Northern church and join the AME or AME Zion denominations. While the school controversy plus the unwillingness of the Northern church to elect a Negro bishop caused a small exodus to the black denominations, most Negro members of the Northern church rejected separatism. "The M.E. Church is doing more for the moral, educational, and religious elevation of the colored people," wrote one black minister, "than all the different colored bodies presided over by colored Bishops and all other colored churches in the United States. . . . What little I have learned was taught to me by the agencies of white people." Another moderate pointed out that most of the AME and AME Zion leaders had themselves been educated in Methodist Episcopal schools at the expense of Northern whites. The foremost Negro minister in the Methodist Episcopal Church, E. W. S. Hammond, was opposed to the drive for separatism even though his disappointment at the church's failure to elect him bishop had tempted him in that direction. "I can conceive of no calamity so appalling," said Hammond, "so calculated to blast the hopes and retard progress in the great struggle for manhood, as to be let alone," cut off from white help.

Despite the loyalty of moderates, the Freedmen's Aid Society was under increasing pressure to concede more power to Negroes. In 1891 the Society responded by appointing M. C. B. Mason, a talented black minister, as a field agent. This appointment reduced but did not end criticism. The impotence of local boards of trustees remained a festering issue. One black trustee said in 1895 that "we are no more than figure-heads. . . . It is only a question of time when there will be revolt. . . . We believe in distribution of authority, and not centralization."

"Home rule for our colored schools" had became a powerful slogan by 1895. But one Northern Methodist editor, an old abolitionist, advised caution in granting greater power to local boards. The Freedmen's Aid Society had been successful in raising money, he said, because contributors had confidence in the Society. There would be no such confidence in twenty-two separate boards of trustees. "Liberal Methodists" in the North, he asserted, "will not risk $300,000 annually to the tender mercies of the rhythmical phrase, 'Home rule for our colored schools in the south.' They will give cash confidently [only] so long as the cash is wisely expended." Decentralization might lead to "educational calamity." A black leader replied that proponents of "home rule" did not demand entire control of the schools; they wanted more authority in "the appointment of teachers and other matters pertaining to the local management of our schools," but were willing to leave financial affairs in the hands of the Freedmen's

Aid Society. Here was the troublesome point: Southern Negroes considered the mission schools "our schools" because they served the black community; Northern whites were reluctant to relinquish control of these schools, which they had founded and still supported. It was an example of the difficult, delicate relationship between benefactor and client that creates tensions not easily resolved to the complete satisfaction of both parties.

In 1895 the Freedmen's Aid Society committed itself in principle to decentralization. It decided to grant enlarged powers to local boards in proportion to increased financial support by Negroes themselves for "their" schools, with the ultimate aim of transferring ownership of the institutions to local boards when they became largely self-supporting. The amount of money contributed by black Methodists to the schools grew from about fifteen per cent of the total income (not counting tuition, room, and board) in the 1890's to one-third of the total by 1916. The authority of local boards rose in rough proportion to this growth of self-support, but in 1916 the Society still owned and controlled most of the schools. That black dissatisfaction with this situation declined after 1896 was due to the appointment of M. C. B. Mason as one of the two executive secretaries of the Society in that year and to the increasing number of black teachers and administrators in Methodist schools (see table). By 1915 six of the twelve colleges and professional schools had black presidents. Although the schools were not yet wholly under Negro leadership, the movement in that direction appeared steady enough to moderate the black-power controversy in the church.

It was in the Baptist schools that the drive for black autonomy produced the greatest discord. After the Civil War the American Baptist Home Mission Society sent missionaries to the South to help organize Negro churches and state Baptist conventions. These churches and conventions were independent of Northern control, but some were dependent upon missionary aid in the early years. The Home Mission Society also founded thirteen Negro schools of secondary or college level in the South, which were supported mainly by Northern money and owned by the Society. In addition, the local black churches and state conventions established nearly fifty schools, mostly of elementary grade, by 1895. At the same time that these institutions were owned by Negroes, fifteen of the higher-grade schools received aid and supervision from the Home Mission Society.

The younger generation of black leaders that emerged in the 1880's became restless in the leading strings of missionary and educational agencies controlled by Northern Baptists and demanded greater power in these agencies or advocated total separation for black churches and schools. As E. M. Brawley, the foremost Negro Baptist minister in South Carolina, who tried to lead a revolt against the white president of Benedict Institute in Columbia, put it in 1882: "[We] do not wish any longer to be treated like children but like men." D. Augustus Straker a lawyer and teacher, wrote in 1883 that

> we are willing to return thanks to the many friends who have assisted us in educating ourselves thus far, but we have now reached the point where we desire to endeavor to educate ourselves, to build school houses, churches, colleges and universities, by our own efforts . . . ere we sacrifice our manhood.

The issue was exacerbated by the ineptness or unpopularity of white administrators at four Home Mission Society schools between 1882 and 1891. The worst flareup occurred at Roger Williams University in Nashville, where a threatened student strike in 1887 brought the forced retirement of the president and the bursar, the expulsion of several students, and the angry resignation of four black trustees who resented the Home Mission Society's action against the students. At the height of the controversy, the hapless president and bursar received anonymous notes from students warning that "this is our house and you dirty pup we will kick your ass out if you do not act better" and informing the bursar that "[your] daughter makes love to one of us niggers."

The issue of separation versus continuing cooperation with the Home Mission Society split black Baptists into two factions. In an effort to conciliate the separatists and strengthen the cooperationists, the Society moved in 1883 to share some power with its black constituency by creating local boards of trustees for its schools to prepare for the time when Negroes "may maintain and manage these institutions for themselves." The Society also increased its support for several schools owned entirely by black Baptists. Such support involved a degree of supervision, however, and one militant separatist announced that "if Negro schools cannot get money from the Home Mission Society without making cowards and bootlicks of all the men connected with them it were far better that they never get a dime." The black-power rhetoric of such separatists as Harvey Johnson of Baltimore, Walter Brooks of Washington, and R. H. Boyd of San Antonio generated great enthusiasm in some Negro Baptist circles, but financial agents for independent schools and mission organizations complained that these institutions could not exist on enthusiasm alone. Two of the most influential cooperationists, both of them presidents of black-owned schools that survived only with help from the Home Mission Society, pointed out the perils of rejecting white help. "I state from positive knowledge that the colored people are not able to support the schools now maintained in the South," wrote William B. Simmons of Kentucky Institute. "Don't for want of discretion destroy our friends' interest in us, by biting off more than we can chew." Charles L. Purce of Selma University ridiculed the claim that blacks could sustain their own schools: "How many have we supported ourselves that have attained to anything of importance? . . . It is all nonsense for any of us to say we can support them, and then will not do it." In Georgia one of the leading Baptist advocates of black power, E. K. Love, was disillusioned by his failure to raise funds for a separate, black-owned institution to rival Atlanta Baptist Seminary, and confessed in 1887 that "we are smiply attempting too much. . . . We are poorly prepared to control and manage high schools financially and intellectually. Graduation is not a sufficient guarantee that one is prepared to manage the school from which he graduates."

The struggle between separatists and cooperationists intensified in the 1890's and was a major cause of the formal division of the Negro Baptists of Texas and Georgia into rival state conventions. The Home Mission Society came under increasing pressure from separatists and co-operationists alike, pressure that prompted the secretary of the Society, Thomas J. Morgan, a former abolitionist and commander of Negro troops in the Civil War, to explain in 1894 why the Society could not yet turn over its thirteen academies and colleges to black control. Negroes had shown commendable initiative in establishing many small schools on their own, wrote Morgan, but "it must be said . . . that the management of these schools is not in every case what it should be." Funds had been stolen, teachers were unskilled, principals incompetent. The blacks, said Morgan had not yet acquired the experience necessary to manage larger schools effectively without white assistance. Relinquishment of control by the Society, he feared, would "result in a rapid retrograde movement, if not the immediate ruin of the schools."

In an effort to head off a renewed attempt by Georgia separatists to found their own college, Morgan proposed a plan under which the two state conventions would jointly form an education association to work with the Home Mission Society in the coordination of all educational efforts in Georgia. The board of trustees of Atlanta Baptist College would then be enlarged by the addition of more black members and given increased powers. If this was unsatisfactory, Morgan suggested as an alternative the lease of the college to the state's black Baptists for one dollar per year, provided they would assume its entire financial support. This suggestion may have been a bluff; if so, the Georgia militants failed to call it. The majority of Negro Baptists did not wish to drive the Home Mission Society from the state, and the two conventions agreed to Morgan's first proposal in 1897.

The idea of an education association seemed to work out so well in Georgia that the Society helped black Baptist conventions in other states establish similar cooperative associations. But the Georgia accord almost broke down in 1899 when the separatists, resentful of the Negroes' con-

tinued subordinate position on the reorganized board of Atlanta Baptist
College and only token representation on the Spelman board, carried out
their threat to found a rival institution, Central City College at Macon.
Hailed as a grand new venture in self-help and independence, Central
City College failed to receive adequate financial support and existed essentially as a marginal secondary school. Most black Baptists in Georgia
remained loyal to the Home Mission Society and its schools. Atlanta
Baptist College (renamed Morehouse College in 1913) and Spelman grew
under the Society's guiding hand to become two of the best Negro colleges
in the South.

A dissident group of black Baptists in Virginia also denounced the
Home Mission Society as paternalistic, demanded more influence in the
running of Virginia Union University, carried a majority of the state
Baptist convention with them in 1899, and disassociated the Negro-owned
Virginia Seminary at Lynchburg from Virginia Union when the Society
declined to make the required concessions (whereupon the cooperationists
seceded to form their own convention). Shrill rhetoric by militants in
Virginia and other states caused Morgan to deplore "a spirit of unreason-
ing racism" among Negroes and to charge that a "few noisy, ignorant,
ambitious, self-seeking would-be leaders" were trying to turn the race
against its Northern friends. R. H. Boyd replied to Morgan's outburst
with an assertion that

> the race movement which you so much dread and stigmatize . . . is
> simply a determination on the part of the Negroes to assume control of
> their race life and evolve along such lines and such ways as their spirit
> and genius may dictate and unfold, and not as the Anglo-Saxon may
> outline. . . . Hitherto the Home Mission Society has led and the Negroes
> have followed; henceforth the Negroes must lead and the Home Mission
> Society may follow . . . if it will.

Fearful that anti-white tirades by black radicals would dry up Northern
support for Baptist schools, Negro moderates rallied to the defense of the
Home Mission Society. The president of a school receiving aid from the
Society said the militants were motivated only by a "greed for office. . . .
The fellow that makes the bitterest race speech gets the most applause,
and he is honored as a champion of the rights of the race." This black
educator believed in self-help, "but it is possible to separate self help
from self foolishness; it is possible to practice self help and yet receive
the generous aid of able friends." Black independence did not mean that
Negroes can "take all we can get from the whites and abuse them as much
as we please." He hoped the militants' conduct would not "discourage our
white friends who have stood by us so loyally during the dark and bitter

past." In 1902 the president of the National Baptist Convention, E. C. Morris, who had once leaned toward the separatists, expressed his desire that "all of the misunderstandings cease and all the hard sayings indulged be left in the forgotten past."

The Society reciprocated these signs of good will by stepping up efforts to bring Negroes into posts of greater responsibility. "I am not at all prepared to admit the false philosophy that a white man cannot teach a Negro," wrote Morgan in 1900, but "I recognize that race feeling is very strong, and that other things being equal, a Negro will have more influence upon his race than a white man." Atlanta Baptist College hired more black faculty and began grooming John Hope for its presidency. Hope assumed the office in 1907, the first Negro president of a Home Mission Society college. By 1915 nearly half the faculty in the Society's nine colleges was black, and three of the college presidents were Negroes.

Though the Northern Presbyterians had only a small black membership in the South, the church's Board of Missions for the Freedmen was also confronted by the black-power issue. In 1888 the white secretary of the Board, Henry N. Payne, urged a positive response to black demands for greater power and responsibility in the schools. Because of the effects of slavery, said Payne, Negroes "have been weak and dependent; only in this way can they be made strong and self-reliant." The Board decided to begin phasing out white teachers earlier than any other mission society, and in 1891 Daniel J. Sanders, born a slave, was installed as president of Biddle University (later renamed Johnson C. Smith University). Several new Negro faculty members were also appointed in 1891, and within three years the Biddle faculty was entirely black. Some Presbyterians criticized this development as a "rash experiment"; the Board of Missions for the Freedmen conceded that it was a "bold experiment," but hoped it would not turn out to be rash. In 1893 the Board pronounced the venture a success; administrative control of Biddle was thenceforth in black hands, though major financial and policy decisions were still made by the Northern Board.

The other major Presbyterian college, Lincoln University (the only white-supported Negro college outside former slave territory), took a radically different position on the issue of black teachers and administrators. Lincoln's faculty and board of trustees were virtually one hundred per cent white until the 1930's (a few Negroes were appointed earlier as instructors or assistants, but none as professors). This caused considerable dissatisfaction among Lincoln alumni and students. In 1916 Francis Grimké, an alumnus, said that Lincoln's lily-white policy was "a standing argument against the professed friendship and Christian character of the men who have permitted this condition of things to continue as long as it has." Lincoln was entirely unconnected with the Board of Missions that supervised freedmen's education in the South; it had been founded before the Civil War by the Old School Presbyterians (most of the antislavery sentiment in the denomination was concentrated in the New School faction) and was governed by an independent board of trustees.

All the mission societies rapidly increased the ratio of Negro faculty and administration in the first decade of the twentieth century, an increase that helped reduce the intensity of the black-power controversy in education. (The issue remained alive, however, and flared up again in the 1920's.) The change was most dramatic in the secondary schools of the American Missionary Association. In 1895 only nine per cent of the teachers in these institutions were black; by 1905 the proportion had risen to fifty-three per cent, and seven of the twenty-one principals of AMA high schools were Negroes. This change was in part the result of a deliberate policy decision to begin an orderly transition of "mission" schools to "native" control, but it was also a pragmatic response to continuing black pressure. In AMA schools with interracial faculties, young Negro teachers were often impatient with the continued presence of white veterans who blocked their promotions. One black male teacher wrote in a private letter: "If that old bitch from Massachusetts would ever die or get through here, I could begin to live."

Not all Negroes connected with AMA schools favored the conversion to black faculties. In fact, resistance from parents of students helped bring a virtual halt for several years to the relative increase of black teachers in AMA secondary schools, and in 1915 the percentage of Negro faculty was about the same as it had been in 1905. Many Negro parents believed that white teachers were better than black; some of them said privately, "My child shall not go to school to a nigger." The AMA's assistant superintendent of education reported that when Negro teachers replaced whites in some communities, enrollment decreased and parents complained that "their Harvard was being taken from them and they were being pushed back into the log cabin school." On more than one occasion parents formed a "Committee to Save Our School" and obtained hundreds of signatures on petitions urging retention of white teachers. This phenomenon was perhaps less an objective index of the relative quality of white and black teachers than a reflection of the self-distrust and self-hatred ingrained into many Negroes by centuries of white supremacy. In any case, the cross-pressures between younger Negroes ambitious for places in the schools and parents who wanted white teachers to stay caused many headaches for officials of the AMA.

A set of factors related to broad developments in American education had some impact on the changing ratios of white and black teachers in Negro schools. In the two decades before 1900 an "academic revolution" diminished the role of the nineteenth-century Christian college, whose curriculum emphasized the classics, moral philosophy, and theology, and led to the rise of the modern university, which has emphasized physical sciences, social sciences, vocational-professional training, and a commitment to secularism. An important part of this revolution was the increasingly self-conscious professional status of teachers at both the secondary and college level. Normal schools became teachers' colleges, which granted bachelor's degrees to prospective high school teachers; colleges were increasingly staffed by Ph.D.'s or at least M.A.'s instead of B.D.'s.

Negro colleges and secondary schools were not unaffected by these changes. By the second decade of the twentieth century the AMA (whose standards were higher than those of the other mission societies) required a college degree for its secondary school teachers and post-graduate training for its college instructors. As teaching qualifications, missionary zeal counted less and professional education more than in earlier days. Curiously, this development did not lead to an improvement in the quality of white teachers; indeed, the opposite seems to have occurred. It was generally agreed by contemporaries and alumni that the first generation of missionary teachers, who had a genuine humanitarian commitment to their work, were more effective than the later, more professional generations, who were less interested in helping the poor than in getting a job. There was an unfortunate and growing tendency among discards from Northern colleges to go South to teach in Negro colleges. As racism in white America hardened, some whites attached a stigma to teaching in a black school. Thus one reason for the partial conversion to Negro faculties was a relative decline of willing and able white teachers.

This factor should not, however, be overemphasized. Secularism and professionalism were slow to penetrate Negro education. Missionary and humanitarian motives remained the most important ones impelling Northern whites to teach at Negro schools, at least before 1915. Of course there is no necessary contradiction between thorough professional training and missionary dedication; many white teachers successfully combined both. And while the percentage of white faculty in the schools covered by this study declined between 1895 and 1915, the actual number of white teachers increased at a rate almost equal to the growth of the middle-class Protestant population from which most of these teachers came. The most important reason for the rising percentage of black teachers in the schools was not a relative shortage of white teachers, but pressure from strong segments of the black community coupled with the conscientious desire by many officials of mission societies to transfer responsibility to their former protégés.

By 1915 sixty per cent of the teachers in all secondary schools and colleges founded by or receiving support from Northern missionary sources were black. The proportion of Negro faculty in the colleges alone had nearly doubled from twenty-seven per cent in 1895 to fifty-one per cent in 1915. Nine of the thirty college presidents were black, while fifty-two of the eighty-five secondary schools had Negro principals. But most of the schools and colleges, including those with black administrations, were still governed mainly by the mission societies or by independent boards on which white trustees predominated.

In 1915, a half century after the beginnings of Negro education in the South, white influence was still paramount in the major institutions of higher learning. This was doubtless due in part to the paternalism inherent in all mission enterprises and to a reluctance by those in authority to give up power, but it was due also to a desire to maintain high standards and to a continued dependence on Northern financial support. Adam Clayton Powell, Sr., recognized the importance of this last factor in 1930 when he estimated that "Negroes have paid only 10 per cent of the cost of their [higher] education during the last sixty-five years. . . . There are only two worth-while educational institutions in America receiving their chief financial support from Negroes." Powell said that black people owed "our white friends a unanimous vote of thanks," but that "this kind of charity cannot and should not go on forever"; the Negro should do more to support his own institutions.

Of course, white sponsorship did not necessarily preclude black control of finances, though it was on precisely this point that the mission societies were most reluctant to yield authority. At the same time that the societies moved steadily forward with the appointment of Negro teachers and administrators, they maintained a close watch over funds and general policy. This was perhaps the result of an unjustified and patronizing distrust of the Negro's competence to manage things for himself. Nevertheless, several black leaders, admitting their lack of experience, urged the mission boards and white trustees to continue their supervision of Negro colleges. Kelly Miller lamented as late as 1933 the "failure of Negroes to handle successfully practical projects which they had assumed" and stated that "the race is not yet sufficiently experienced . . . to justify assuming complete guardianship of higher institutions of learning. . . . This is not a race question, nor one of discrimination, but only one of common sense and prudence."

An important government survey of Negro education in 1915 concluded that some of the mission boards had actually been premature in promoting black teachers and appointing black presidents. The Methodist and Presbyterian schools had the highest percentage of Negro faculty and administrators; the survey declared that in many of these institutions "the standards of administration and educational work" had "not been satisfactory." In several Methodist colleges the change from white to black faculties "has been too rapid for the good of the schools." At the Presbyterians' Biddle University, the first mission college to have a Negro president, "the work is poorly organized and the large plant is ineffectively used." The experience of this and other schools "shows clearly that the white boards render their best service when they send not only their money but also their capable men and women to have a vital part in the instruction of colored youth." On the whole the weakest schools, according to the survey, were those controlled entirely by Negro denominations—the Baptist state conventions and the AME and AME Zion churches—while the strongest were those founded by the American Missionary Association, in which white influence prevailed longest.

This evaluation, by a white educator, could perhaps be dismissed as the product of white racism. It was, however, echoed several years later by Kelly Miller, who asserted that the transition from white to black faculties "was too sharp and sudden. It was a misfortune barely short of a calamity." As white teachers were replaced by blacks the "colleges were shifted from a Puritan to a pagan basis" and the "moral stamina" of the first generation of Negro education declined. (E. Franklin Frazier made a similar point in *Black Bourgeoisie*.) "Painful observation," wrote Miller, "convinces us that the later crop of college output falls lamentably short of their elder brothers in this respect. The inducing process was cut short before the induction had become permanently effective."

It may be impossible to reach a consensus on whether the transition of power from white to black in Negro colleges was too fast, just right, or not fast enough. Evidence regarding administrative efficiency and the ability to impart skills and mastery of subject matter seems to indicate that white administrators and teachers were better qualified than their black colleagues, at least before 1900 or 1910. On the other hand, proficiency in these areas may have been purchased at the cost of restricting the development of black initiative, self-reliance, and pride. It is not easy to say which objectives should have been uppermost in Negro education. It can be said, however, that the schools and colleges discussed in this article could not have been sustained by pride alone. Despite discord, these institutions survived and grew, keeping Negro higher education alive through difficult times. From the viewpoint of today's black-power movement, persistent white influence in Negro education perpetuated the blacks' colonial dependence on white liberals. But without this educational "colonialism" there would have been little higher education for Negroes; there would have been no Howard, no Fisk, no Lincoln, no Morehouse, no Spelman, no Atlanta University. From the schools founded by whites were graduated many twentieth-century leaders of the black community, including W. E. B. Du Bois (Fisk), James Weldon Johnson and Walter White (Atlanta), James Farmer (Wiley), Martin Luther King (Morehouse), Thurgood Marshall (Lincoln University and Howard Law School), and Stokely Carmichael (Howard). This was their main bequest to our generation. It was no mean legacy.

Southern Negro Colleges and Secondary Schools Established by Northern Mission Societies [a]

Mission Societies and Schools	1894-95 Faculty and Administration					1894-95 Students				1914-15 Faculty and Administration [b]					1914-15 Students [c]				
	Total	Negro	White	% Negro	President or Principal	Total	Elementary	Secondary	College and Professional	Total	Negro	White	% Negro	President or Principal	Total	Attendance [d]	Elementary [d]	Secondary [d]	College and Professional [d]
American Missionary Association: Colleges																			
Fisk University, Nashville, Tenn.[e]	31	1	30	3%	White	539	221	263	55	45	14	31	31%	White	505	505	112	205	188
Straight University, New Orleans, La.	24	2	22	8%	White	569	367	152	50	30	13	17	43%	White	758	578	364	203	11
Talladega College, Talladega, Ala.	20	1	19	5%	White	581	509	66	6	41	12	29	29%	White	658	561	382	124	55
Tillotson College, Austin, Tex.	13	0	13	0%	White	193	153	40	0	20	6	14	30%	White	314	223	135	70	18
Tougaloo College, Tougaloo, Miss.	22	0	22	0%	White	377	332	45	0	31	2	29	6%	White	455	444	275	149	20
Total	110	4	106	4%	Black: 0 White: 5	2,259	1,582	566	111	167	47	126	28%	Black: 0 White: 5	2,700	2,311	1,268	751	292
AMA Secondary Schools: 1895 (17); 1915 (22) [f]	141	12	129	9%	Black: 1 White: 16	4,327	3,743	584	0	246	132	114	54%	Black: 10 White: 12	5,977	4,743	3,892	851	
Total: All AMA Schools [f]	251	16	235	6%	Black: 1 White: 21	6,586	5,325	1,150	111	413	179	234	43%	Black: 10 White: 17	8,677	7,054	5,160	1,602	292
Freedmen's Aid Society of the Methodist Episcopal Church: Colleges [f]																			
Bennett College, Greensboro, N. C.	10	10	0	100%	Black	203	198	5	0	15	12	3	80%	Black	312	312	235	67	10
Clark University, Atlanta, Ga.	19	8	11	42%	White	341	246	91	4	24	14	10	58%	Black	304	304	128	144	32

Institution																		
Claflin College, Orangeburg, S. C.	20	10	50%	White	570	473	74	23	27	21	6	78%	Black	866	814	597	191	26
Gammon Theological Seminary, Atlanta, Ga.	4	1	25%	White	84	0	0	84	6	2	4	33%	White	78	78	0	0	78
Meharry Medical College, Nashville, Tenn.f				White					30	28	2	93%	White	505	505	0	0	505
Morgan College, Baltimore, Md.	9	2	22%	White	160	96	3	61	11	4	7	36%	White	128	81	0	55	26
New Orleans University, New Orleans, La.	24	12	50%	White	603	531	65	7	24	11	13	46%	White	557	432	298	125	9
Philander Smith College, Little Rock, Ark.	15	4	27%	White	312	259	37	16	18	17	1	94%	Black	491	439	268	132	39
Rust College, Holly Springs, Miss.	10	4	40%	White	230	127	97	6	18	10	8	56%	White	378	196	128	60	8
Samuel Huston College, Austin, Tex.			Founded in 1900						20	19	1	95%	Black	405	377	267	92	18
Central Tennessee College, Nashville, Tenn.g	11	2	18%	White	326	115	158	53	17	8	9	47%	Black	107	107	30	77	0
Wiley University, Marshall, Tex.	12	3	25%	Black	284	89	139	56	30	28	2	93%	Black	439	384	176	170	38
Total	134	56	42%	Black: 2 White: 9	3,113	2,134	669	310	240	174	66	73%	Black: 6 White: 6	4,570	4,029	2,127	1,113	789
Methodist Secondary Schools: 1895 (11); 1915 (11)f	72	35	72%	Black: 4 White: 4 Un-known: 3	1,650	1,203	447		135	94	41	70%	Black: 5 White: 6	2,493	2,401	1,864	537	
Total: All Methodist Schools f	206	91	48%	Black: 6 White: 13 Un-known: 3	4,763	3,337	1,116	310	375	268	107	71%	Black: 11 White: 12	7,063	6,430	3,991	1,650	789
American Baptist Mission Society: Colleges																		
Benedict College, Columbia, S. C.	8	1	13%	White	135	0	135	0	30	12	18	40%	White	595	507	254	205	48

Southern Negro Colleges and Secondary Schools Established by Northern Mission Societies [a]

Mission Societies and Schools	1894–95 Faculty and Administration [b]					1894–95 Students				1914–15 Faculty and Administration [b]					1914–15 Students [c]				
	Total	Negro	White	% Negro	President or Principal	Total	Elementary	Secondary	College and Professional	Total	Negro	White	% Negro	President or Principal	Total	Attendance [d]	Elementary [d]	Secondary [d]	College and Professional [d]
Bishop College, Marshall, Tex.	18	7	11	39%	White	368	270	65	33	22	10	12	45%	White	421	371	176	153	42
Hartshorn Memorial College, Richmond, Va.	9	2	7	22%	White	97	22	75	0	15	3	12	20%	White	188	169	73	96	0 [h]
Morehouse College, Atlanta, Ga. [i]	11	6	5	55%	White	150	72	50	28	19	17	2	89%	Black	277	277	110	111	56
Richmond Theological Seminary, Richmond, Va.	4	2	2	50%	White	50	0	0	50	Merged with Wayland Seminary in 1899 to form Virginia Union University									
Roger Williams University, Nashville, Tenn. [j]	16	7	9	44%	White	227	141	67	19	17	17	0	100%	Black	123	107	27	80	0
Shaw University, Raleigh, N. C.	26	10	16	38%	White	362	129	175	58	30	16	14	53%	White	291	221	52	123	46
Spelman Seminary, Atlanta, Ga. [k]	38	4	34	11%	White	491	416	52	23	51	3	48	6%	White	631	595	330	254	11
Virginia Union University, Richmond, Va.	Formed in 1899 of merger between Wayland Seminary and Richmond Theological Seminary									16	7	9	44%	White	265	255	35	145	75
Total	130	39	91	30%	Black: 0 White: 8	1,880	1,050	619	211	200	85	115	43%	Black: 2 White: 6	2,791	2,502	1,057	1,167	278
Baptist Secondary Schools: 1895 (20); 1915 (16) [l]	122	97	25	80%	Black: 15 White: 5	2,483	1,951	441		208	195	13	94%	Black: 15 White: 1	4,040	3,009	2,243	766	
Total: All Baptist Schools [f]	252	136	116	54%	Black: 15 White: 13	4,363	3,001	1,060	211	408	280	128	69%	Black: 17 White: 7	6,831	5,511	3,300	1,933	278
Presbyterian College: Biddle University, Charlotte, N. C.	11	11	0	100%	Black	260	19	172	69	16	16	0	100%	Black	221	207	24	131	52

Presbyterian Secondary Schools: 1895 (7); 1915 (20) [t]	75	41	34	55%	Black: 4 / White: 3	1,515	953	562		218	173	45	75%	Black: 16 / White: 4	4,798	4,197	3,516	681	
Total: All Board of Missions for Freedmen, Presbyterian Church in the U. S. A., Schools [t]	86	52	34	60%	Black: 5 / White: 3	1,775	972	734	69	234	189	45	81%	Black: 17 / White: 4	5,019	4,404	3,540	812	52
United Presbyterian College: Knoxville, Tenn.	21	0	21	0%	White	317	186	108	23	29	5	24	17%	White	327	327	187	110	30
United Presbyterian Secondary Schools: 1895 (1); 1915 (5)	14	3	11	22%	White	686	622	64		77	57	20	74%	Black: 3 / White: 2	1,726	1,344	1,137	207	
Total: All Board of Freedmen's Missions, United Presbyterian Church, Schools	35	3	32	9%	Black: 0 / White: 2	1,003	808	172	23	106	62	44	58%	Black: 3 / White: 3	2,653	1,671	1,324	317	30
Quakers: Secondary Schools: 1895 (3); 1915 (4)	37	20	17	54%	Black: 0 / White: 2 / Un-known: 1	655	297	358		64	54	10	84%	Black: 2 / White: 2	1,464	1,243	924[m]	9.4[m]	
Other Denominations: [n] Secondary Schools: 1895 (3); 1915 (4)	16	8	8	50%	Black: 1 / White: 2	379	259	120		64	30	34	47%	Black: 1 / White: 3	917	862	614[m]	142[m]	
Independent, Nondenominational Colleges																			
Atlanta University, Atlanta, Ga.	16	0	16	0%	White	217	149	48	20	33	4	29	12%	White	586	586	182	360	44
Howard University, Washington, D. C.	64	21	43	33%	White	587	129	126	332	106	73	33	69%	White	1,401	1,401	0	373	1,028
Leland University, New Orleans, La. [o]	13	4	9	31%	White	439	357	59	23	14	4	10	29%	White	298	298	203	91	4
Total	93	25	68	27%	Black: 0 / White: 3	1,243	635	233	375	153	81	72	53%	Black: 0 / White: 3	2,285	2,285	385	824	1,076
Independent Secondary Schools (including Hampton Institute): [p] 1895 (2); 1915 (3)	70	19	51	27%	Black: 0 / White: 2	1,067	751	316		250	93	157	37%	Black: 0 / White: 3	1,167	1,115	710	405	
Total: All Independent Schools	163	44	119	27%	Black: 0 / White: 5	2,310	1,386	549	375	403	174	229	43%	Black: 0 / White: 6	3,452	3,400	1,229	1,076	1,076

Southern Negro Colleges and Secondary Schools Established by Northern Mission Societies [a]

Mission Societies and Schools	1894–95 Faculty and Administration					1894–95 Students				1914–15 Faculty and Administration [b]					1914–15 Students [c]				
	Total	Negro	White	% Negro	President or Principal	Total	Elementary	Secondary	College and Professional	Total	Negro	White	% Negro	President or Principal	Total	Attendance [d]	Elementary [d]	Secondary [d]	College and Professional [d]
All Colleges and Professional Schools [q]	499	135	364	27%	Black: 3 White: 26	9,072	5,606	2,367	1,099	805	408	397	51%	Black: 8 White: 21	12,894	11,661	5,048	4,096	2,517
All Secondary Schools [q]	547	235	294	44%	Black: 25 White: 35 (Un-known: 4)	12,762	9,779	2,892		1,262	828	434	66%	Black: 52 White: 33	22,582	18,914	14,840	3,683	
Total: All Schools [q]	1,046	370	658	36%	Black: 28 White: 61 (Un-known: 4)	21,834	15,395	5,291	1,099	2,067	1,236	831	60%	Black: 61 White: 54	35,476	30,575	19,948	7,773	2,517

[a] These statistics have been garnered from The Report of the U. S. Commissioner of Education for the Year 1894–95 (Washington, 1896), 1338–45, and from Negro Education: A Study of the Private and Higher Schools for the Colored People in the United States, ed. Thomas Jesse Jones (Washington, 1917), passim. The government figures for 1894–95 are not wholly reliable and have been checked and supplemented whenever possible by the scattered statistics available in the annual reports and other materials published by the mission societies. The statistics in this table do not include elementary schools.

[b] Includes clerical staff for a few schools.

[c] The Jones report applied stricter criteria for classifying students in secondary or college classes than the earlier reports of the Commissioner of Education, so there are fewer students listed in the higher grades than if earlier standards had been applied.

[d] Students in attendance on day of visit.

[e] Acquired on independent status in 1909.

[f] Acquired an independent status in 1909.

[g] Name changed to Walden University in 1900.

[h] Hartshorn was the girls' college of Virginia Union University; several students took college courses at Virginia Union.

[i] Named Atlanta Baptist Seminary until 1897, Atlanta Baptist College 1897–1913.

[j] Taken over by the state Negro Baptist convention in 1908; continued to receive some Home Mission Society aid.

[k] Supported mainly by the Woman's American Baptist Home Mission Society, an affiliate of the American Baptist Home Mission Society.

[l] Fifteen Baptist secondary schools in 1894–95 and fourteen in 1914–15 were owned by Negro state Baptist conventions and partly supported and supervised by the Home Mission Society.

[m] Statistics on students incomplete.

[n] Christian Missionary Society; American Christian Convention; Free Baptist Church; Reformed Presbyterian Church.

[o] Partly supported and controlled by the American Baptist Home Mission Society until 1887. Leland always maintained close ties with the Baptist Church.

[p] Hampton Institute was founded by the American Missionary Association, which continued to appropriate some funds to the school until 1894.

[q] Statistics on faculty incomplete or not available for one of the colleges and three of the secondary schools in 1894–95; statistics on students incomplete for one of the colleges and six of the secondary schools in 1894–95, and for two of the secondary schools in 1914–15.

"They Are Not Perfect, But . . ."

WILLIAM T. HAGAN

Indian adjustment to reservation life was difficult, and the task of Indian agents, called upon to administer large reservations (some as big as Connecticut) with inadequate staffs, was well nigh impossible. The appointment of Indian police in 1878, while Carl Schurz was secretary of the interior, and of Indian judges in 1883 grew out of these administrative needs in the West. Once established, Indian police and judges proved to be effective agents of acculturation. Combining the ideas and materials of anthropology with the methods of history, William T. Hagan assesses the effect of Indian participation on the process of law enforcement.

Any evaluation of the Indian police and judges must take into consideration the objectives of their originators. Although the virtue of extending a system of laws over the Indians had been discussed for many years, both police and courts seem to have been reactions to immediate problems. In the field in the 1870s, the John Clums were clamoring for help in administering their agencies, and both agents and officials in Washington were anxious for an alternative to reliance on the military. The police were the answer. The experiment was launched on a shoestring, as the pitiful salaries and initial absence of uniforms and weapons indicated.

Two years after the first police force appeared, Commissioner of Indian Affairs E. M. Marble, citing a poll of the agents, declared them an unqualified success. He stated that what "was at first undertaken as

From William T. Hagan, *Indian Police and Judges* (New Haven: Yale University Press, 1966), pp. 154–68. Footnotes omitted. Reprinted by permission of the publisher. © 1966 by Yale University.

an experiment, is now looked upon as a necessity." Schurz also noted a fringe benefit that would become one of the principal rationalizations for both police and judges: the police expedited the acculturation process by diminishing the authority of the chiefs and discouraging traditional practices deemed uncivilized by the agents. This would lead, it was hoped, to the ultimate dissolution of the tribe and the absorption of its members into the mainstream of American society.

In 1892 Commissioner T. J. Morgan maintained that the Courts of Indian Offenses, as well as the police, were established "for the purpose of relieving the anomalous conditions that existed on Indian reservations by reason of an absence of laws applicable to Indians." There had certainly been need for some tribunal before which reservation malefactors might be brought by Indian police. Nevertheless, the Courts of Indian Offenses originated not in this need but in Secretary [of the Interior Henry M.] Teller's abhorrence of certain Indian sexual and religious customs. The courts had had an even shakier beginning than the police, and five years passed before Congress appropriated money to pay judges, thus endowing them with at least a shadow of legality.

With some pride of authorship, Teller, back in the Senate in 1899, remarked: "There was only one opinion regarding the courts that I ever heard of, and that was that they were a desirable aid in keeping peace and order on the reservations." And this was the general sentiment of the personnel of the Indian Service. The agent who now had a police force to back his orders and supplement his work force, and a tribal court to relieve him of a perplexing and unpopular role, did endorse them. The degree of enthusiasim of his commendation varied in direct proportion to his ability to inspire loyalty and efficiency among his police and judges. A few agents concluded that the tribal character of their charges ruled out any possibility that either institution would work well on their reservations. But more typical were the reactions of agents administering the Standing Rock and Quapaw reservations. From Dakota Territory the first agent reported his police a "terror to the evil doers, both white and Indian." The Quapaw agent in Indian Territory saw the same quality: "perfect ferrets after criminals," he dubbed his police. His comment: "They are not perfect, but we could not get along without them at all," is probably the best summary of the agents' evaluation of the police.

The courts inspired comparable opinions, as witness a memorandum by Secretary of the Interior Hubert Work some forty years after their establishment:

> That these Indian courts have worked admirably and have proved of educational value to the Indian, there is little doubt. They have taught the Indian respect for the law. They have acquainted them with Ameri-

can jurisprudence. They have served to train them in the duties of good citizenship. . . . Needless to relate, the Indian courts are not successful on all reservations.

The most sweeping indictment of either judges or police by a member of the Indian Service was made by Special Agent H. Heth, who invoked his record of forty years among the Indians to strengthen the credibility of his statement. "I wish no better evidence of an Indian Agent's incapacity or worthlessness," Heth wrote the Indian Commissioner, "than when I read in his annual report, that he is saved much trouble by his Indian Judges." Heth was convinced that the judges would not punish anyone "rich, influential, or a friend."

While this special agent's attitude was unusual among Indian Service personnel, criticism of the judges and police was common among self-styled friends of the Indian. They were not a numerous group but quite vocal and capable of embarrassing any administration in Washington which dared ignore them. Their man in the Senate was Henry L. Dawes of Massachusetts, and they were represented on the Board of Indian Commissioners which scrutinized expenditures of the Indian Bureau and offered gratuitous advice on handling the red men. By coincidence, the same year (1883) that the Courts of Indian Offenses were inaugurated, the reformers gathered for the first meeting of the Lake Mohonk Conference. This annual outing at a hotel owned by the Quaker Albert K. Smiley would become the principal sounding board for the friends of the Indian and their opportunity to reach a consensus on policies to recommend to the government.

Whether expressed in the forum provided at Lake Mohonk, on the floor of Congress, in the minutes of the Board of Indian Commissioners, in resolutions of the American Bar Association, or in articles in periodicals, the burden of the reformers was apparent. They were most unhappy about the continued lack of a system of law for the reservations and the power this left in the hands of the agents. As the Indians' own systems of social control had deteriorated in the presence of the new conditions reservation life presented, the agent had ceased to be just the official contact between the United States and tribal chieftains. Now he often was civil administrator, police chief, judge, and jury—the source of all authority for several thousand people scattered over hundreds of square miles. Reformers attacking the system called it "evil," damned the agent as "a little king," and stigmatized the agency as an "autocracy," "a little Russia."

The problem was how to bring the Indian under state and territorial law before he became a taxpayer. Immediate citizenship was a panacea some urged. But one critic of this equated the introduction of the Indian into our political life with the influx of "adventurers of every land—the

Communists of France, the Socialists of Germany, the Nihilists of Russia, and the cut-throat murderers of Ireland." He predicted it would demoralize the Indians, who were completely unprepared for such power. He reminded his readers that the Declaration of Independence characterized the Indians as "merciless savages," and he dismissed them as "the only native sporting class in America."

Such fears of Indian bloc voting were baseless. It was discovered after the Dawes Severalty Act went into effect that citizenship and an allotment of land did not necessarily bring the Indian access to the ballot box and an accepted place in white society. As the reformers groped for a policy on law to cover the transition period, their views of the Indian police and Courts of Indian Offenses were clarified. There was less comment about the police, and most of that favorable. In 1891 Senator Dawes referred to them during debate over appropriations for Indian affairs as the "bulwark of the Government in the administration of justice and in the preservation of order on the reservation." He said the police experiment had done more than anything except the severalty law to elevate the Indian. Coming from Henry L. Dawes, this was high praise indeed! There was criticism of the police for reinforcing the agent's autocracy, but as late as 1906 the Board of Indian Commissioners judged them "indispensable if law and order are to prevail upon the reservations."

The Courts of Indian Offenses earned few such encomiums. The power of the agent to appoint the judges and overrule their decisions disturbed many observers. Bishop W. D. Walker of Dakota Territory did defend the courts before a Lake Mohonk audience, citing one he had observed functioning with a dignity equal to that of a New York police court. But the usual comment was less laudatory, although the critics admitted that the courts performed a needed function.

The hope that regular courts, administering either federal and state law or a special code, would replace the Indian courts, only gradually faded with the demise of the Thayer Bill, which was introduced into the Senate in 1888 by Dawes. The bill would have provided a special code and special courts for reservations. Despite backing from the Indian Rights Association, the Boston Indian Citizenship Committee, and the Connecticut and Massachusetts Indian Association, the bill never got out of committee. Senator Dawes himself was dubious of its constitutionality and considered that it made elaborate and expensive provisions for a situation he judged ephemeral. By 1891 Professor [James Bradley] Thayer had lost hope that the bill carrying his name would ever be enacted, although he felt there still existed a necessity to extend a system of "real courts and real law" to the reservations. Thayer acknowledged that the Courts of Indian Offenses had had a "salutary and steadying effect," but compared them to courts-martial, "really a branch of the executive department." The Indian judges, he noted, "do not administer law, but merely certain rules of the Indian Department." For Americans as yet unfamiliar with federal agencies administering their own sets of regulations in a quasi-judicial fashion, Thayer's criticism was a serious one.

But Thayer did give the Indian courts high marks for their educational function, as did others. *The Independent* carried an editorial in 1902 which summarized this attitude. The writer pronounced the courts "primary schools of law" where the Indian judges "have been learning and teaching the a b c of legal procedure." He believed they frequently had been "a real power making for righteousness." Yet the writer, like so many others, was concerned about the Indians who had become citizens but were still not provided for in state and territorial law. He exhibited very little curiosity about the reaction of the individual Indian to the legal experiments imposed on him, making the customary assumption of the white man that any evidence of abandonment of native ways constituted progress.

"The life of law has not been logic: it has been experience," Justice Oliver Wendell Holmes was saying, but few applied this dictum to the spectacle of white Americans imposing their concepts of justice on red Americans. If there had been a single Indian culture, instead of a bewildering multitude of apparently infinite variety, conceivably the native law-ways would have been treated with more respect. Or had the native Americans been concentrated, instead of scattered among a much larger and rapidly growing white population, it would have been easier and more logical to take their culture into account in formulating their legal codes. With the exception of one small reform faction headed by T. A. Bland, however, reformers and Indian Service personnel were united in the conviction that the native cultures had lost their vigor, and whatever value they might once have had for the Indian was rapidly disappearing.

It is much easier to determine the views of whites on the Indian police and judges than to speculate on how the tribesmen reacted when the institutions were installed on the reservations. Compared to other government policies, the provisions for judges and police, particularly the latter, did seem an extension of tribal institutions. Soldier societies had performed police functions; chiefs and headmen had arbitrated intratribal disputes. Only a recognition of this basis in the old culture can explain the influence the Indian police and judges did enjoy.

Other things, of course, contributed to their greater success on particular reservations. The policeman's position appears to have been more satisfying to him at the larger agencies, which had forces organized along military lines. The training he received and the feeling of being a member of a unit, which he derived from living in a police barracks instead of being the lone representative of an alien power in one of the widely scattered Indian camps, obviously contributed to a policeman's morale.

The agent's ability to select the proper personnel as judges and police was the principal key to the success of the programs. But what could persuade an Indian to align himself with the agent, and, frequently, against his tribal elders and the traditions of his people? Probably it was the power and prestige the positions carried. For a people among whom the fighting tradition was still strong, the uniforms of the police, their right to bear arms among warriors now weaponless, and the scouting missions they conducted against renegades would have been strong attractions. As policemen they visited all corners of the reservation and were the embodiment of the extratribal power that was growing yearly. The Indian policeman even commanded the grudging respect of white men residing on or visiting the reservation. An opportunity to exercise power, command such respect, and evoke some relationship with a warrior past would go a long way toward compensating for the inadequate pay and the jeers, tinged with fear and envy, of one's fellow tribesmen.

A position on the bench of the agency's Court of Indian Offenses carried power of even more impressive dimensions. The policeman might arrest the culprit, but the justices weighed the evidence and pronounced judgment. Operating near the center of the agency's power structure, the judge not only shared in it by virtue of his position but acquired a knowledge of agency administrative procedures and American law and customs, and established a personal relationship with those who now directed his people's destiny. A Sitting Bull might sulk in his cabin while his influence and prestige waned with his prowess as a medicine man and warrior. Younger, more flexible men, like Quanah [an important Comanche whose judicial career nearly spanned the life of his people's court. He was the son of the Comanche chief Peta Nocoma and the white captive Cynthia Ann Parker], recognized where the power now lay and maneuvered to grasp it. It was certainly not the pay that made a position on the Kiowa–Comanche court such a prize in the intratribal politicking.

A seat on the bench, or a badge, did not bring with it an automatic shift of loyalties. The old ties were strong and the new status difficult to understand. The Indian now was expected to cleave to an impersonal state, whereas his loyalties to his relatives and fellow tribesmen had always been much more personal. Orders to arrest a relative, or the necessity of passing judgment on a fellow clansman, created conflicts—the undoing of many a policeman or judge. Also, the old religious beliefs persisted, and some shamans successfully challenged the new order, badges and commissions paling in significance before their medicine.

The most effective police and judges of the late nineteenth century had a foot in each camp. Quanah was not a white man, as his agents pointed out. He might aspire to wealth and political power in terms any white man could comprehend, but Quanah was also a bulwark of the peyote cult. The Sioux George Sword has left us a record of his dilemma. A war leader and medicine man before he became Captain of United States Indian Police at Pine Ridge, he had scars on his chest to prove he had participated in the Sun Dance. Although Sword had forsaken this most pervasive ceremonial of the Plains Indian, and had become a deacon in a Christian church, he still feared to offend his Indian gods. Sword's explanation—"because the spirit of an Oglala may go to the spirit land of the Lakota"—must have represented the type of hedging engaged in by many Sioux of his generation. The white man's medicine appeared to have proved its superiority in combat, but . . .

It was around 1915 that Sword expressed his doubts, so it should not be surprising that a quarter century earlier there should have been many Indians who were as yet unable to grasp the new legal concepts. A particularly dramatic example of this was acted out in 1890 at the Tongue River Agency in Montana. The principal roles were played by two young Northern Cheyennes, Head Chief and Young Mule.

The Northern Cheyennes, about a thousand strong, had been located on the Tongue and Rosebud rivers since 1881. Hostile during the Sioux War of 1876, by 1890 they had been forced by circumstances to give up their nomadic life. Buffalo had grazed the valleys of the Tongue and Rosebud when the Cheyennes located there, but by 1890 they had disappeared, and the Indians, showing little inclination to turn to agriculture, were subsisting on government rations.

Their agents had set up a police force and an Indian court, but the latter was not established until 1889, and the police were undependable. Captain of Police at the time of the 1890 difficulty was White Hawk, although subsequently he was discharged for a lack of enthusiasm in returning truants to school. White Hawk then turned to religion and persuaded some of the Northern Cheyennes that he had discovered a new messiah who would resurrect the dead Indians, replacing them under a nearby mountain with the whites. This defines the quality of the police at Tongue River and indicates how little affected were the Northern Cheyennes by a decade of reservation life.

Coinciding with the tribe's flirtation with the messiah movement was trouble stemming from the intrusions of cattlemen into Cheyenne land: Indians killed an occasional steer; the cattlemen heard rumors of a new inflammatory Indian religion and demanded protection; troops were brought in. Then in May 1890 a cowboy was found murdered, and there were predictions of a war between the cattlemen and the Cheyennes. This crisis was safely passed, but in September young Hugh Boyle, recently arrived from the East to visit relatives, was found shot through the head and clubbed. Special Agent James A. Cooper, temporarily assigned to Tongue River, learned from Chief American Horse that the murderers were Head Chief and Young Mule, youths about the age of their victim.

Agent Cooper called the Cheyennes into council and demanded the murderers. After conferring, the Indians offered to pay thirty ponies for the killing. This was good Indian practice but completely unacceptable to the white man. Insisting that the letter of the law be obeyed, Cooper again demanded the persons of Head Chief and Young Mule. Unable to buy their way out of their difficulty with ponies, and unwilling to surrender themselves to trial, Head Chief and Young Mule chose to expiate their crime by dying in battle against the white troopers. The father of one of them delivered their message: "Select the place of meeting and we will come to die in your sight." This was hardly trial by combat, for the outcome was certain; it smacked more of a gladiatorial spectacle. The agent protested, but the Indians were adamant. The father returned to Head Chief and Young Mule to inform them of the verdict and help them paint and array themselves and their horses for the finale.

By the middle of the afternoon the stage was set in the valley in which the agency headquarters was located. One troop of cavalry and some Indian police were drawn up on a road running through the valley; another troop had taken up positions in hills behind the agency. The Cheyennes had turned out to see the young warriors die bravely, the male spectators occupying the best vantage points, the women farther back.

Suddenly, across the valley about a rifle shot away, the spectators saw Head Chief and Young Mule ride from a patch of timber and head for the ridge above. Painted and befeathered—one boasted a magnificent war bonnet—they sang their war songs as they rode to the top of the hill. Reaching it they circled about, meanwhile opening fire on the cavalry and police below. As the Indians advanced and retreated, keeping up an intermittent fire, the cavalry on the road moved around the hill to outflank them. Faced with this threat, the two warriors charged down the hill, yelling and firing rapidly. A hail of fire knocked down one horse, but the young Indian continued on foot until he was hit. Taking cover, he disappeared from sight only to be tracked down later and found dead from gunshot wounds. The other Cheyenne did not slow his mad dash across the valley and up the opposite slope, careening through the police and cavalry lines before being felled. He wounded three horses in breaching the cavalry's line, the only damage inflicted on the soldiers and police. The entire action lasted about an hour, and the soldiers and police fired an estimated thousand rounds in the skirmish.

As the firing died away the bodies of the Head Chief and Young Mule were recovered and brought to the agency. Echoing from the surrounding hills now was the wailing of the women as they viewed the battered young bodies. The troops, nervous and unable to comprehend what they had just participated in, were sure the women were inciting the Cheyenne men to avenge the youths. But a council called immediately by the agent brought only expressions of satisfaction from the Indians. Difficult to understand though it was for the whites, who regarded it as senseless bloodshed, the afternoon's proceedings could be reconciled with the Cheyenne concept of justice. The young warriors had acknowledged they had erred. They could not bring themselves to surrender to stand trial before strangers, perhaps to die disgracefully at the end of a rope. As had Satank [an old Kiowa war chief], Head Chief and Young Mule would go as warriors should go, singing their war songs and counting coups. No wonder the Cheyenne women had wailed the loss of such fine youths. Although born too late to have ridden with Two Moons and White Bull against Custer, they had demonstrated that their generation still cherished the traditions of a warrior people.

That the two young Cheyennes had chosen such a course of action testified to the ineffectiveness of Indian police and judges at Tongue River. A good police force would have prevented the crisis from developing. It would have kept the cattle off Indian land—Hugh Boyle was herding cattle when he was killed—and allayed the fears of the whites by keeping the Cheyenne messiah's followers under surveillance. Through their own Court of Indian Offenses the Cheyennes might have acquired some knowledge of American jurisprudence and, conceivably, some confidence in it.

Speculating about "what might have been" at Tongue River is one way of measuring the contribution Indian police and judges could make. Accepting the value judgment that change was not only inevitable but desirable, their service was obvious. Not only did they help convert reservations in a West notorious for lawlessness into "law and order havens," to use Clark Wissler's expression, they were the vanguards of a more highly developed civilization. As Americans have had to make the transition from a rural–agrarian to an urban–industrial society, the Indians also have had to adjust to a new order. Granted this premise, it is patent that their own participation in the new law and order process would be beneficial. Casually conceived, only grudgingly accepted by the reformers and Congress, Indian police and judges were the happiest developments in what was too frequently a story of unrealistic policies and inefficient, if not corrupt, administration of a subject people.

The Spanish-Americans
in the Southwest, 1848–1900

RODMAN W. PAUL

Indians were not the only inhabitants of the Southwest before the coming of Anglo-Americans. Mexicans had long been established in New Mexico, as well as in smaller and newer settlements in Texas, Arizona, and California. With little or no contact among these communities, the reaction after 1848 to the impact of an alien society differed from populous New Mexico to empty Arizona, from gold-rush California to violent Texas. Rodman W. Paul discusses the differing forms acculturation took in these societies. The following selection concentrates on New Mexico, where the Hispanic, tradition-bound society proved the most resistant to change.

At the opening of the American era, New Mexico had by far the largest Spanish-speaking population, perhaps as much as four-fifths of the total in the Southwest. Most of the New Mexicans were illiterate peasants who led an unprogressive, poverty-stricken life in small villages or as hands on great ranches. They were very much subject to the authority of the small class of rich landowners (*ricos*) or the much larger number of those who served as *patrón* or headman in each village. Only the priest approached the power of the patrón and rico over the lives of the common

From *The Frontier Challenge: Responses to the Trans-Mississippi West*, edited by John G. Clark (Lawrence: The University Press of Kansas, 1971), pp. 35–39, 52–54. Reprinted with omissions by permission of the publisher. © 1971 by the University Press of Kansas.

people. Between them, rico, patrón, and padre ruled a thoroughly paternalistic society that was medieval in the serflike dependency of the many
upon the few.

Some of the peasants of the mid-nineteenth century were held in
debt-peonage that constituted virtually permanent bondage—and through
the ignorance and helplessness of its victims this practice continued for
many years, despite the Thirteenth Amendment to the United States
Constitution and despite a specific prohibitory federal statute of 1867.
A federal territorial official asserted in 1856 that, on the whole, Southern
Negro slaves were better off than New Mexican peons.

For most peasants life centered in the village and the extended family (the *familia*). Both were organized as authoritarian structures. The
patrón was the father figure of his village. He controlled what little credit
was available, owned the store if there was one, and performed the limited
middleman functions that connected the isolated peasants with the outer
world. Politically he controlled "his" peasants, and when the Americans
introduced notions of elective government, the patrón was quick to discover the profit involved in delivering whatever popular vote had been
contracted for by higher authority. Within each family the senior married
man was not only a husband and biological father, but was also the dominant, decision-making figure whose presence gave definiteness and unity
to the extended family group.

This authoritarian pattern of village and family, when taken in con-
junction with an unchanging, labor-consuming type of crop-raising and
livestock-herding that was medieval if not biblical in inspiration, made
the life of the peasant seem to the contemporary "Anglo" observer to be
utterly devoid of incentive or opportunity for progress, while at the same
time the frequency of crop failures and stock losses in that high, dry,
and sometimes Indian-infested land seemed a guarantee of perpetual debt
or at least poverty. More discriminating observers, especially after the
social sciences began to suggest whole new frames of reference for judging alien societies, have pointed to the psychological values inherent in
this unquestionably unprogressive rural society. Life in both the family
and the village were familiar, predictable, and congenial, however pinched
in terms of income and food supply. They were based upon a highly
developed pattern of community cooperation, best illustrated by the de-
cisively communal nature of New Mexico's local irrigation systems. Together the family and the village offered a certainty in relationships and
values and a sociability unknown to the Anglo-American who, as an
individual, was aggressively trying to thrust his way into the life of the
Southwest.

The weakness of this psychologically tranquil, resigned existence
was that it prepared the villager and his children for nothing but a con-

tinuation of the same. Physically there was a margin neither for safety against bad years nor for growth and change; intellectually there was no basis for experimentation and innovation. (The federal census of 1870 reported that more than half the population over ten years of age could neither read nor write.) Natural increase of population would have put an unbearable pressure upon the scant supply of irrigable and pasture land even if no other factors had changed. But in fact the amount of land available to the villagers decreased greatly because acquisitive Anglos found ways to displace ignorant peasants by substituting new written land titles for the familiar unwritten customary use of the soil. By the end of the nineteenth century the need for additional income was so pressing that the men of the villages were absenting themselves for months at a time in order to work as transient laborers in other parts of the West. For a unit as cohesive as the familia, this meant a severe social strain, mitigated only by the role of the women, who by Hispanic tradition were supposed to remain at home, and thus were available as a force to hold the family together during the absence of the male head of the household. The practice common among Negro families of sending the wife and mother out to work as a domestic was not popular among Spanish-speaking people.

By the opening of the twentieth century the high, dry lands of rural New Mexico began to stand forth as a cultural island of poverty, illiteracy, and premodern customs—however picturesque and quaint to the eyes of Eastern visitors. While this was the fate of probably a majority of New Mexicans during their first half-century under the American flag, there were some notable exceptions that showed how alert men with the right "connections" could actually profit from the stratified and unprogressive nature of New Mexican society. The rico class of landed preprietors— masters of great estates (haciendas) whose varied economies produced most of the articles that they consumed and still had an exportable surplus —had a remarkably strong position in New Mexican life. Linked together by extensive intermarriage and united in a typically Latin American acceptance of nepotism and "influence," they were the obvious ruling class with whom the incoming Anglo-Americans must deal.

Even in the 1840s some of the great families, such as the Otero and Chavez clans, had in fact anticipated the new era by sending their sons across the plains to the Missouri frontier to be forwarded to American schools and colleges located all the way from St. Louis to New York. Other young New Mexicans, whose families wished them to have practical training, were placed in the dispatching-point headquarters of the mercantile and freighting firms that sent American-made goods to New Mexico and handled in return New Mexico's few productions, such as wool and hides. A class of English-speaking aristocrats was thus developed who soon moved still further into Anglo-American life by intermarrying and forming business partnerships with "Anglos."

The simplicity of New Mexican economic life prior to the railroads, with a stress on freighting across the plains and handling government supplies on contract, permitted a type of business in which merchandising, transportation, and finance were essentially one operation and had distinct political overtones. The abler of the American-trained Hispano aristocrats fitted easily into this undifferentiated politico-economic activity.

A similar development characterized the field of land titles. Shrewd, opportunistic Anglo lawyer-politicians found their chance in the fact that, unlike the expedient adopted for California, no special agency to handle the tangled land titles was created by Congress until 1891. For more than forty years land titles were determined by special acts of Congress and by surveys, investigations, and decisions made by appointive officials in Santa Fe and Washington. This was just the type of opening that determined lawyer-politicians wanted, and in exploiting it they formed what came to be known as the "Santa Fe Ring," an informally constituted, frequently changing group dedicated to fattening their own pocketbooks through speculation in land and land titles.

Just as Anglo businessmen and English-speaking Hispanos found it both advantageous and pleasant to form matrimonial and business alliances, so the Ring impartially drew into its transactions anyone whose influences could further the group's profits. Since Hispanos occupied most of the seats in the territorial legislature, dominated elections in the local constituencies, held some of the territorial offices, and in the beginning controlled the big landholdings, quite a few of them were able to share in the plunder.

Whether Hispanos really were the big gainers from the operations of either the Ring or the early business houses may be doubted. One suspects that their Anglo associates were too resourceful for that. And in any event, while some of the Hispano upper class were prospering, many of their cousins, through inexperience with American ways, including the intricacies of acquiring legal titles to real estate, and through a proneness to borrow and spend too freely, were losing ownership of the land that had been the traditional basis of their power. So at best only a portion of even the favored class were better off at the end of the century than they had been in 1848. Still, for them the opportunity had been there, and the prominence of a few of them, symbolized by the appointment of Miguel Antonio Otero as governor of New Mexico under McKinley and Theodore Roosevelt, suggests that so long as New Mexico remained a predominantly Hispanic, tradition-bound society, its accustomed Spanish-speaking leaders, quite unlike their peon dependents, might expect to play a role of considerable importance.

．　　．　　．

To conclude this study it would be well to look back across the whole spectrum of events in the era, so as to examine the several conclusions that stand out. First, in their initial half-century under the American flag the historical experiences of Spanish-speaking populations in the several Southwestern states were strikingly varied. In considerable part this was the result of their respective histories prior to 1848. New Mexico, by far the oldest, had built up a sufficiently substantial population base and a sufficiently cohesive society so that throughout the rest of the century the Spanish-speaking remained in the majority and rural New Mexican culture remained largely unchanged, save for the very serious loss of needed farm and pasture lands. Arizona had been so thoroughly cleaned out by Indian troubles that when revival came under American auspices, a new mixed society emerged on a basis that for two decades at least offered to all hands an equal chance to profit from the new opportunities, even though in practice it was Americans and European immigrants who took advantage of the possibilities. In California the gold rush so accelerated the process of Americanization that had already begun that thereafter the performance of the relatively small population of Hispano-Californians constituted a kind of prolonged retreat from one area to another, as the Americans and European immigrants increased in numbers and gradually took possession of the land, business, and politics. In westernmost Texas, recent history had already established an unhappy pattern of mutual antagonism, lawlessness, and violence. Retention there of a Spanish-speaking majority was not sufficient to prevent a takeover by Anglo-Americans under turbulent, angry conditions that left a heritage of bitterness.

Secondly, it is hard to see that in any of the Southwestern states Spanish-speaking cultures proved resilient or resourceful in meeting the challenge of the aggressive, acquisitive Anglo-American intruding groups. To no small degree the encounter between the two stocks was a collision between old-fashioned pastoral and agricultural societies, characterized by practices that dated back to the Renaissance if not to the Middle Ages, and an advancing society that had already experienced to the full the commercial revolution and was now well into the industrial revolution and a comparably great change in transportation and finance. A poor level of education throughout the Hispanic lands and a limited knowledge of the modern world made the contest an unequal one, but so did the one group's instinctive wish to have life continue without basic alteration, while the other was opportunistically ready either to promote change or to exploit the status quo, whichever seemed more profitable.

In New Mexico more than in any other state some members of the well-to-do upper class did show a high degree of agility in taking advantage of the economic and political opportunities brought by the invasion of Anglo-Americans. The initial status of upper-class New Mexicans was one of unusual strength, and their position was preserved by the very slowness of their state to develop or grow. To a lesser degree, upper-class Californians were able to exploit their land ownerships and otherwise favored situation so as to profit at least temporarily, although many proved unable to keep wealth once they had it, or to find for themselves a permanent place of distinction in the new society that they found arising around them.

Thirdly, the great majority of the Spanish-speaking people who were in the Southwest in 1848, or came as immigrants thereafter, were simple people who stood far down on the social and economic ladders of their own societies. Of mixed blood and often much darker-skinned than the aristocracy, they were the ones most likely to encounter racial prejudice when they came into contact with Anglo-Americans. Being illiterate or semiliterate, without capital, and possessed of only modest skills vocationally, they had little more chance of advancing in the unfamiliar, pushing world of the Anglo-Americans than they had in their own. As manual laborers, miners, cowboys, mule packers, sheepherders, sheep shearers, and agricultural workers, they made a contribution to the labor force of a region that was perennially short of manpower.

Unwittingly by so doing they prepared the way for a veritable flood of new immigration from Mexico that began at about the turn of the century, when many new job openings were created in railroad construction and repair, in the new intensive agriculture, in mining, and in some types of industry. Coming in numbers many times greater than any previous influx of Spanish-speaking people, the newcomers drowned from sight the struggling older groups, except in slow-moving rural New Mexico. In the twentieth century the "Spanish-American problem" thus became a question of how to help recently arrived immigrants who were only just beginning acculturation. The public tended to forget that hidden somewhere were older groups, composed partly of much earlier immigrants who had been long in the United States, but partly of people who should not be called immigrants at all, since they were the descendants of pioneers who were second in time only to the Indians in their occupancy of the Southwest. Perhaps the most important service this paper can contribute is to recall to our momentary attention this often-forgotten aspect of Western history.

4

Railroads . . .
Some Economic Aspects

ROBERT WILLIAM FOGEL

Alfred H. Conrad and John R. Meyer began the econometrics revolution with their article on the economics of slavery [Volume 1, No. 18], but since the 1964 publication of his *Railroads and American Economic Growth: Essays in Econometric History*, Robert William Fogel has led that revolt. It was long assumed that extensive railroad development from the mid to late nineteenth century was the basic ingredient in the rapid economic growth of America; that railroads populated western lands and eastern cities; that railroads tapped the hitherto inaccessible products of field, forest, and mine; that railroads provided manufacturers with previously unavailable raw materials and markets. By asking counter-factual questions about the nature of American economic growth without railroads and utilizing hypothetical models and statistics to answer these questions, Fogel suggests that the economic impact of the railroad was grossly exaggerated. A year after publication of his book, Fogel summarized his findings for an exploration of analogies between the railroad and the space program.

From *The Railroad and the Space Program: An Exploration in Historical Analogy,* edited by Bruce Mazlish (Cambridge: M.I.T. Press, 1965), pp. 75–83, 87–103, 104. Reprinted with omissions by permission of the publisher. © by The American Academy of Arts and Sciences.

From an economic point of view the central or primary feature of the railroad was its impact on the cost of inland transportation. Obviously, if the cost of rail service had exceeded the cost of equivalent service by alternative forms of transportation over all routes, and for all items, railroads would not have been built and all of their derived consequences would have been absent. The derived consequences of railroads can be divided into two categories. The "disembodied" consequences are those that followed from the saving in transportation costs per se and which would have been induced by any innovation that lowered transportation costs by approximately the amount attributable to railroads. The "embodied" consequences are those that are attributable to the specific form in which the railroads provided cheap transportation services.

THE EFFECT OF RAILROADS ON THE AVAILABILITY OF RESOURCES

The change in the availability of resources is perhaps the most important of the disembodied effects of the railroad. Of course, all parts of the nation would have been physically penetrable even in the absence of railroads. However, without this innovation the cost of transportation to and from some areas might have been so great that, from an economic point of view, large sections of the land mass would have been nearly as isolated as the moon is from the earth. By reducing the cost of transportation, railroads increased the *economic accessibility* of various parts of the natural endowment of the United States. The question is: Which endowments were so affected and by how much?

Agricultural Land

Agricultural land was the most valuable of the natural resources of the United States in 1890. It was also more widely dispersed than coal, iron ore, oil, and other mineral deposits. Land in farms occupied one third of the national territory in 1890. No state devoted less than 1 per cent of the area within its borders to farming, and no single state contained more than 8 percent of the nation's total farm acreage. Under these circumstances one would expect to find that railroads were more essential in obtaining access to farmland than to other resources.

Even in the case of farmland, however, certain factors suggest that the incremental contribution of railroads was limited. One of these is the experience of the half century following the ratification of the Constitution. The occupation not only of the territory east of the Appalachians but also of that lying between the Appalachians and the Mississippi River was well under way before the coming of the railroad. As Kent T. Healy has pointed out, it was "water transportation, available first on natural waterways and later on canals" which made possible the "astonishing redistribution of population and economic activity" during the first four decades of the nineteenth century. By 1840, "before a single railroad had penetrated that area from the coast, some 40 percent of the nation's people lived west of New York, Pennsylvania and the coastal states of the South."

This western population was, of course, primarily engaged in agriculture. Two decades before the Civil War, Ohio was the chief wheat-producing state of the nation. It, together with Michigan, Indiana, and Illinois accounted for 30 per cent of the nation's total wheat crop. Moreover, with one out of every four of the bushels produced in these states being sold in the East and South, it is clear that commercial agriculture was well under way in the Old Northwest long before the era of substantial railroad construction. The geographic locus of corn production provides an even more striking demonstration of the same point. Although they contained a bare total of 228 miles of disconnected railroad track, Michigan, Ohio, Kentucky, Tennessee, Indiana, Illinois, and Missouri produced 187,000,000 bushels of corn in 1840—half the nation's total. As for cotton, the westward movement of this culture was virtually completed in 1850, by which time the geographic "limits of the cotton belt were practically the same as they are at present [1900]." Yet, during the entire ante bellum period the transportation of cotton "was conducted almost exclusively by means of water." As late as 1860, about 90 per cent of all cotton shipped to New Orleans arrived by boat or barge.

The fact that the initial occupation of the trans-Appalachian lands was based almost exclusively on waterways is suggestive; but it by no means proves that waterways could have sustained later developments. The acreage of agricultural land in the North and South Central states underwent a fourfold expansion between 1850 and 1890. It is therefore necessary to devise a method of determining how much of the land settled after the advent of railroads would have been settled in their absence.

Without railroads the high cost of wagon transportation would have limited commercial agricultural production to areas of land lying within some unknown distance of navigable waterways. It is possible to use the theory of rent to establish these boundaries of feasible commercial agriculture in a nonrail society. Rent is a measure of the amount by which the return to labor and capital on a given portion of land exceeds the return the same factors could earn if they were employed at the intensive or extensive margins. Therefore, any plot of land capable of commanding a rent will be kept in productive activity. It follows that, even in the face of increased transportation costs, a given area of farmland will remain in use as long as the increased costs incurred during a given time period do not exceed the original rental value of that land.

Given information on the quantity of goods shipped between farms and their markets, the distances from farms to rail and water shipping points, the distances from such shipping points to markets, and the wagon, rail, and water rates, it is possible to compute the additional transportation costs that would have been incurred if farmers attempted to duplicate their actual shipping pattern without railroads. In such a situation shipping costs would have risen not because boat rates exceeded rail rates but because it usually required more wagon transportation to reach a boat than a rail shipping point. In other words, farms immediately adjacent to navigable waterways would have been least affected by the absence of rail service. The further a farm was from a navigable waterway the greater the amount of wagon transportation it would have required. At some distance from waterways the additional wagon haul would have increased the cost of shipping by an amount exactly equal to the original rental value of the land. Such a farm would represent a point on the boundary of feasible commercial agriculture. Consequently, the full boundary can be established by finding all those points from which the increased cost of shipping by alternative means the quantities that were actually carried by railroads is equal to the original rental value of the land.

This approach, it should be noted, leads to an overstatement of the amount of land falling beyond the "true" feasible boundary. A computation based on the actual mix of products shipped does not allow for adjustments to a nonrail technology. In the absence of railroads the mix of agricultural products would have changed in response to the altered structure of transportation rates. Such a response would have lowered shipping costs and hence extended the boundary. The computation also ignores the consequence on the level of prices of a cessation in agricultural production in areas beyond the feasible region. Given the relative inelasticity of the demand for agricultural products, the prices of such commodities would have risen in the absence of railroads. The rise in prices would have led to a more intensive exploitation of agriculture within the feasible region, thus raising land values. The rise in land values would have increased the burden of additional transportation costs that could have been borne and shifted the boundary of feasible commercial agriculture further away from water shipping points.

The method outlined above has been used to establish the boundary of feasible commercial agriculture for 1890. In this year the relative advantage of railroads over alternative forms of transportation was probably greatest. During the half century that preceded it, increases in productivity reduced the cost of railroad transportation more rapidly than that of boats and wagons. The selected year also precedes the emergence of motor vehicles as an effective alternative. It thus appears likely that the incremental contribution of railroads to the accessibility of agricultural lands was at or near its apex in 1890.

Analysis of the relevant data indicates that in the absence of railroads the boundary of feasible commercial agriculture would have been located at an average of about forty "airline" miles from navigable waterways. Forty-mile boundaries drawn around all natural waterways used for navigation in 1890, as well as all canals built prior to that date, brought less than half of the land mass of the United States into the feasible region. However, as Table 1 indicates, the feasible region includes 76 per cent of all agricultural land by value. The discrepancy is explained by the fact that over one third of the United States was located between the hundredth meridian and the Sierra Nevada Mountains. While this

TABLE 1   Farmland Lying Beyond the Feasible Region of Agriculture, 1890
(thousands of dollars)

Region †	1 Value of Farmland 1890	2 Value of Farmland Beyond Feasible Region 1890	3 Col. 2 as Percentage of Col. 1	4 Value of Land Beyond Feasible Region as Percentage of Value of All Agricultural Land
North Atlantic	1,092,281	5,637	0.5	0.07
South Atlantic	557,399	117,866	21.1	1.45
North Central	4,931,607	1,441,952	29.2	17.75
South Central	738,333	158,866	21.5	1.96
Mountain	129,655	123,016	94.9	1.51
Pacific	671,297	95,200	14.2	1.17
United States	8,120,572	1,942,537	23.9	23.91

† The states included in each of the regions are North Atlantic: Maine, New Hampshire, Vermont, Massachusetts, Rhode Island, Connecticut, New York, New Jersey, Pennsylvania; South Atlantic: Delaware, Maryland, District of Columbia, Virginia, West Virginia, North Carolina, South Carolina, Georgia, Florida; North Central: Ohio, Indiana, Illinois, Michigan, Wisconsin, Minnesota, Iowa, Missouri, North Dakota, South Dakota, Nebraska, Kansas; South Central: Kentucky, Tennessee, Alabama, Mississippi, Louisiana, Texas, Arkansas; Mountain: Montana, Wyoming, Colorado, New Mexico, Arizona, Utah, Nevada, Idaho; Pacific: Washington, Oregon, California.

vast area fell almost entirely beyond the feasible range, it was of extremely limited usefulness for agricultural purposes. By value the area represented only 2 per cent of all agricultural land in use in 1890.

Table 1 also shows that barely one quarter of 1 per cent of the lost agricultural land was located in the North Atlantic region, while only 6 per cent was in the Mountain states. About 75 per cent of the loss was concentrated in the North Central region. Indeed more than half of all the land lost by value was located in just four states: Illinois, Iowa, Nebraska, and Kansas. This finding does not support the frequently met contention that railroads were essential to the commercial exploitation of the prairies. The prairies were occupied at a time when the railroad had achieved clear technological superiority over canals. Consequently, the movement for canals that played so important a part in the development of the Eastern states was aborted in the prairies. The fact that major loss of land was concentrated in a compact area suggests an entirely different conclusion: a relatively small extension of the canal system would have brought into the feasible region most of the productive land that Table 1 puts outside of it.

Indeed, it would have been possible to build in the North and South Central states a system of thirty-seven canals and feeders totaling five thousand miles. These canals would have reduced the loss of agricultural land occasioned by the absence of railroads to just 7 per cent of the national total. The system would have been technologically feasible and economically profitable. Built across the flatlands of the middle west, the average rise and fall per mile of the proposed waterways would have been less than that which prevailed on all canals successful enough to survive railroad competition through 1890. The water supply would have been more than ample. And in the absence of railroads, the social rate of return on the cost of constructing the system would have exceeded 45 per cent per annum.

The loss in agricultural land could have been further reduced by improvements in common roads. According to estimates published by the Office of Public Roads in 1895, regrading and resurfacing of public roads could have reduced the cost of wagon transportation by 50 per cent. This implies that the boundary of feasible commercial agriculture would have fallen eighty miles from navigable waterways. Together with the proposed canals, road improvements would thus have reduced the loss of agricultural land to a mere 4 per cent of the amount actually used in 1890.

It thus appears that while railroads did increase the availability of agricultural land, their incremental contributon was—even at the apex of railroad influence—quite small.

Iron Ore and Coal

Unlike agricultural land, which in 1890 occupied nearly one million square miles of territory in over two thousand counties in every state of the nation, the mining of iron ore was highly localized. The volume on mineral industries prepared for the Eleventh Census reported that the

> ranges embraced in the Lake Superior region are none of them of great extent geographically, and if a circle was struck from a center in Lake Superior with a radius of 135 miles, all of the present iron-ore producing territory of that region would be embraced within one-half of the circle, and most of the deposits would be near the periphery. The output of this section in 1889 was 7,519,614 long tons. A parallelogram 60 miles in length and 20 miles in width would embrace all of the mines now producing in the Lake Champlain district of northern New York, whose output in 1889, aggregated 779,850 long tons. A circle of 50 miles radius, embracing portions of eastern Alabama and western Georgia, included mines which in 1889 produced 1,545,066 long tons. A single locality, Cornwall, in Lebanon county, Pennsylvania, contributed 769,020 long tons in 1889. . . . In the areas named, which are only occupied to a limited extent by iron-ore mines, there were produced in 1889 a total of 10,613,550 long tons, or 73.11 per cent of the entire output of iron-ore for the United States.

Each of these major iron-producing areas would have been economically accessible in the absence of railroads. Cornwall was within five miles of the Union Canal and could have had a direct connection with that waterway. The Coosa River, which was actually made navigable as far east as Rome, Georgia, flowed past the main iron-ore deposits of eastern Alabama and western Georgia. The red hematite deposits of central Alabama could have been reached by a relatively short canal built northward from the Alabama River to Shades Creek on the Cahawba River.

As for the Lake Superior ores, their exploitation, beginning in 1854, preceded the construction of railroads in the northern parts of Michigan and Wisconsin. Five years later, although the region was still without railroad service, its mines accounted for over 4 per cent of the national production of iron ore. Here, too, the water supply and terrain would have permitted the construction of canals that directly linked the iron deposits of Michigan, Wisconsin, and Minnesota with the Great Lakes. A canal built along the Menominee River to Florence, Wisconsin, would have traversed the iron-mining district of the Menominee Range. A canal built along the Escanaba River to Ishpeming would have pierced the center of the mining area in the Marquette range. Canals could also have been built along the Montreal River and to Vermilion Lake in Minnesota.

Many of the smaller deposits of iron ore were also well located with respect to water transportation. The main carbonate deposits of southern Ohio and northern Kentucky were located at the Ohio River; Tennessee's red hematite fields straddled the Tennessee River; and Pennsylvania had important iron ranges located along the Allegheny River, the Susquehanna River, and various of the state's canals. It is not necessary, however, to consider all of the smaller deposits in detail: if one subtracts from the total domestic production of ore in 1890 that part required for railroad iron, the residual is about equal to the ore production of the major fields singled out by the Eleventh Census. Undoubtedly, in the absence of railroads, the iron consumption of boats and other nonrail forms of transportation would have risen. But it is unlikely that such alternative demand would have accounted for more than a fraction of the ore consumed in the production of railroad iron.

The production of coal, like that of iron ore, was highly localized. Nine states accounted for about 90 per cent of all coal shipped from mines in 1890. And within these states production was further localized in a relative handful of counties. Forty-six counties shipped 76,000,000 tons— 75 per cent of all of the coal sent from mines in the nine states. Moreover, all of these counties were traversed by navigable rivers, canals actually constructed, or the proposed canals discussed above. In this case too, many of the smaller deposits were well located with respect to water transportation. Hence, it seems likely that a nonrail society could have had low-cost access to all of the coal it required.

THE POSITION OF RAILROADS IN THE MARKET
FOR MANUFACTURED PRODUCTS

While the railroad was the chief vehicle by which late nineteenth-century society actually achieved access to natural resources, other mediums could have fulfilled essentially the same function. However, the low-cost services of these alternative forms of transportation were embodied in forms of equipment and structures different from those characteristic of railroads. Hence, it is still possible that railroads profoundly affected the course of economic growth because of the specific inputs, particularly of manufactured goods, required to produce railroad services.

Railroad input requirements could have affected the productivity of manufacturing in two ways. First, the railroad's incremental consumption of the output of various industries could have been so large that it moved these industries to a level of production permitting significant economies of scale. Second, the railroads could, uniquely, have induced changes in the technology of manufacturing processes that affected the production not only of railroad goods but also of goods consumed by other sectors of the economy. This section examines the first line of possible influence. The next section deals with the nexus between railroads and technological innovation. . . .

THE POST-CIVIL WAR ERA

Since the real capital stock of railroads increased at approximately the same rate as the real output of manufacturing, a detailed survey of changes in the position of the railroad in the market of most industries between 1859 and 1899 need not be undertaken in this paper. The iron and steel industry, however, requires further consideration. It is frequently said that the introduction of the Bessemer process radically reduced the cost of producing steel and ushered that industry into a new era. As measured by value added, the production of basic steel products rose from 4 per cent of the output of the iron industry in 1859 to 23 per cent in 1880. Moreover, the consumption of steel was dominated by rails. Table 2 shows that in 1871 some 52 per cent of all steel ingots were consumed in the production of rails. The rail share rose steadily from that date until 1881, when it stood at 87 per cent, after which it declined to 50 per cent in 1890.

The fact that the rail share of steel production fluctuated between 50 and 87 per cent for a period of twenty years suggests that the market for rails was indispensable to the emergence of a modern steel industry in the United States. This opinion also seems to have been nourished by the inverse relationship between the average output of Bessemer mills and the prices of the products of these mills (see Table 3), a relationship that suggests economies of scale.

There is, however, another way of looking at the data contained in Table 2. Stress on the share of total output consumed by rails in any given year beclouds the extremely rapid rate at which nonrail steel consumption grew and the rapidity with which that type of consumption exceeded the total steel production of a given year. This feature is brought forward in Table 4. Table 4 shows that the time required for the nonrail consumption of steel to exceed the total production of a given year varied from two to nine years, the average being about six years. Consequently, if the nonrail demand for steel was inelastic over the range of prices involved, the observed scale of operations could have been achieved with an average lag of six years even in the absence of rails.

It is possible to estimate the maximum gain to the nation made possible by rail-induced economies of scale. The computation turns on the availability of the open-hearth furnace. The optimum plant size of the

TABLE 2   The Production and Consumption of Steel, 1871–1890
(thousands of net tons)

Year	1 Production of Crude Steel	2 Steel Consumed in Rails	3 Steel Consumed in All Other Production	4 Col. 2 as Percentage of Col. 1
1871	82	44	38	52
1872	160	108	52	67
1873	223	147	76	66
1874	242	166	76	69
1875	437	332	105	76
1876	597	471	126	79
1877	638	494	144	77
1878	820	640	180	78
1879	1,048	792	256	76
1880	1,397	1,107	290	79
1881	1,779	1,549	230	87
1882	1,945	1,670	275	86
1883	1,874	1,481	393	79
1884	1,737	1,279	458	74
1885	1,917	1,234	683	64
1886	2,870	2,022	848	70
1887	3,740	2,713	1,027	73
1888	3,247	1,781	1,466	55
1889	3,792	1,937	1,855	51
1890	4,790	2,396	2,394	50

TABLE 3   The Average Product of Bessemer Steel Mills and the Average Price of Steel
Rails

Year	1 Average Product of Bessemer Mills (in thousands of net tons)	2 Average Prices of Bessemer Steel Rails in Dollars of 1890 (dollars per net ton)
1870	21	73
1880	90	62
1890	99	36

Column 1: The 1870 entry refers to a calendar year while the entries for 1880 and 1890
represent production in census years. In computing average product, furnaces using the Clapp-
Griffith and Robert-Bessemer processes were excluded.
Column 2: Calendar year prices were deflated by the Warren-Pearson wholesale price
index. The current dollar prices for the three years were $120, $76, and $36 per net ton.

TABLE 4   Time Required for Nonrail Consumption of Domestic Steel to Exceed Total Production of Steel

1	2	3	4
	Nonrail	Nearest Year in	
	Consumption	Which Total Steel	
Year to Which	of Steel	Production Fell	
Nonrail Consump-	(thousands of	Short of Nonrail	Time Lag in Years
tion Applies	net tons)	Consumption	(Col. 1 — Col. 3)
1871	38	1869	2
1872	52	1869	3
1873	76	1869	4
1874	76	1869	5
1875	105	1871	4
1876	126	1871	5
1877	144	1871	6
1878	180	1872	6
1879	256	1873	6
1880	290	1874	6
1881	230	1873	8
1882	275	1874	8
1883	393	1874	9
1884	458	1875	9
1885	683	1877	8
1886	848	1878	8
1887	1,027	1878	9
1888	1,466	1880	8
1889	1,855	1881	8
1890	2,394	1885	5

open-hearth mill was about one tenth that of a Bessemer mill. In 1880, open-hearth mills had an average production of only 3,500 net tons; in 1890, the average product was 9,000 net tons.

If the absence of rails reduced the scale of operation to such a level that the cost of Bessemer steel exceeded the cost of open-hearth steel, consumers of Bessemer steel would have made their purchases from open-hearth mills. Hence the maximum gain to society from the economies of scale in Bessemer plants induced by rails was the price differential between Bessemer and open-hearth steel. In 1880, the average differential in the delivered price of Bessemer and open-hearth steel was $10.19 per net ton. Nonrail consumption of Bessemer steel was 112,200 net tons. Hence the maximum gain due to economies of scale induced by the railroad in the production of nonrail steel was only $1,144,000, or 0.01 per cent of gross national product. By 1890, the average price differential fell to $4.02 per ton, while the production of nonrail Bessemer steel rose to 1,740,000 net tons. The indicated maximum gain attributable to railroad-induced economies of scale in 1890 is thus $6,995,000, or 0.06 per cent of gross national product.

It appears that a modern steel industry would have emerged even in the absence of a demand for rails. While the increase in the scale of operations may have lagged behind that actually observed, it does not appear likely that the average lag would have exceeded six years. In any case, the maximum social loss of a slower growth in the scale of operations would have been barely one twentieth of 1 per cent of gross national product. Perhaps the most striking difference in the first quarter century of the development of a modern steel industry in the United States would have been the predominance of open-hearth over Bessemer mills.

THE EFFECT OF RAILROADS ON TECHNOLOGICAL INNOVATIONS

In discussing the effect of railroads on the introduction and diffusion of inventions, a distinction has to be drawn between innovations limited exclusively, or largely, to the operation of railroads and innovations that had a major impact outside of the railroad industry. The former category of devices will be denoted by the term "restricted," the latter by the term "transcending."

Most inventions which arose out of the operation or construction of railroads fall into the category of restricted devices. Such items as air brakes, block signals, car trucks, automatic-coupling devices, track switches, pullman cars, and equalizing bars were mere appurtenances. While they may have been important to the efficient operation of railroads, they had no significant application outside of this industry during the nineteenth century. Nor did the railroads' demand for these items induce the rise of industries or production processes of transcending economic significance. They made no independent contribution to economic growth. Rather they defined the conditions under which railroads operated—conditions that in varying degrees explain how it was that railroads were able to produce low-cost transportation service.

There are, however, certain innovations associated with railroads to which transcending significance has been attached, and which therefore require further consideration. The two that will be considered here are cheap methods of producing steel, and the telegraph.

The belief that the railroads' demand for improved rails was responsible for the inventions that led to low-cost steel production rests on shaky foundations. It was not the problem of how to produce better rails that led Henry Bessemer into the series of experiments that eventuated in the Bessemer converter. As J. S. Jeans has pointed out, Bessemer's experiments stemmed from a desire to improve the effectiveness of artillery. A major obstacle to such improvement was the inadequacy of cast iron for cannon firing heavy projectiles. Bessemer pursued his research on metallurgy with the aim of "producing a quality of metal more suitable than any other for the construction of heavy ordnance." William Kelly, who independently discovered the Bessemer process in the United States, was engaged not in the production of heavy rolled forms but in the production of cast-iron kettles. And the immediate factor that stimulated the Siemens brothers to develop the open-hearth furnace was their desire to find industrial applications for their earlier discovery, the regenerative condenser.

The point is that metallurgical research in the mid-nineteenth century was induced by the rapidly growing demand for iron in a wide variety of production processes. Cheap steel had potential marketability not only for the fabrication of rails but also for ships, boilers, bridges, buildings, ordnance, armor, springs, wire, forgings, castings, chains, cutlery, etc. Metallurgical innovators could have been, and were, lured to search for improved products and processes by the profit that was to be earned from sales in all markets for iron, and not just in the railroad market.

It is, of course, true that during the initial decades following the discovery of the Bessemer process, most of the steel that poured from converters was destined for the fabrication of rails. From 1867 to 1883, about 80 per cent of all Bessemer steel ingots were so consumed. This fact seems to suggest that railroads played an essential role in making cheap steel available on a large scale.

The problem is, however, more complex than it first appears. The fact that rails used four fifths of Bessemer steel production—in some years the share approached or exceeded 90 percent—raises the question of whether the Bessemer process was, during this period, a restricted or a transcending innovation. If Bessemer steel had been used exclusively for railroad purposes one could give an unequivocal answer to the question. Like block signals or air brakes it would fall into the category of an appurtenance that contributed to economic growth only in and through the railroads; Bessemer steel would have increased real national income only because it increased productivity in the railroad industry.

But in fact some Bessemer steel was used for nonrail products. In 1880, 8.9 per cent of all such metal was turned into bars; 5.7 per cent into rods; 0.2 per cent into structural shapes, sheets, and boiler or other plate. In total, 169,645 net tons of Bessemer steel were rolled into products other than rails. While some of these shapes were also consumed by railroads, it may be assumed that the bulk was not. Was the amount of Bessemer steel used for nonrailroad purposes large enough to warrant the classification of the Bessemer process as a transcending innovation?

While a definitive answer to this question requires more thorough research than was possible for this paper, available data suggest that the tentative answer should be: "No." In 1880, Bessemer steel accounted for only a minuscule share of the most important nonrail forms of rolled ferrous metal. Bessemer steel accounted for 9.79 per cent of rolled bar, 0.57 per cent of structural shapes, and 0.50 per cent of sheets and plates. At the time when Bessemer steel was most rapidly displacing wrought iron as the basic raw material for rails, it was unable to dislodge wrought iron from its dominance as an input in the production of other products of rolling mills. According to Peter Temin, Bessemer steel "was subject to mysterious breakages and fractures that made people prefer iron" for most nonrail purposes.

In later years the fall in the relative price of steel led to a situation in which most rolling-mill products were made from this material. By 1909, over 89 per cent of rolling-mill output other than rails was made from steel. However, most of this steel came not from converters but from open hearths. In the production of those forms for which demand was increasing most rapidly—plates, sheets, structural shapes, wire, etc.—open-hearth steel was preferred because of its superior qualities and its competitive price.

Thus superior alternatives to Bessemer steel for nonrail uses were available at comparable prices through the end of the nineteenth century. Bessemer steel does not appear to have provided the basis for the remarkable growth of productivity in other industries that it did in the railroad sector. Although the rapid expansion of Bessemer production between 1867 and 1890 is attributable to the market for rails, the Bessemer process appears to have been a restricted rather than a transcending innovation.

Unlike the case of Bessemer steel there was little connection between the railroads and the early growth of the telegraph industry in the United States. The first telegraph line was established in 1844. Just eight years later the nation was laced with lines totaling 17,000 miles. By 1852, the telegraph network connected all of the major eastern and southern cities. St. Louis, Milwaukee, Chicago, Detroit, and Toledo had telegraphic connection with the Atlantic coast well before the completion of the railroad link. In the United States, said the Superintendent of the Census, "the telegraphic system is carried to greater extent than in any other part of the world, and the numerous lines now in full operation form a network over the length and breadth of the land. They are not confined to the populous regions of the Atlantic coast, but extend far into the interior, climb the sides of the highest mountains, and cross the almost boundless prairies."

The demand that induced the remarkably rapid rate of construction emanated not from railroads but from other businesses. Bankers, stock brokers, commodity brokers, and newspapers were the largest purchasers of telegraphic service. The railroads did not try to employ the new device systematically until the basic wire network had been completed. The Erie Railroad, which began to use the telegraph for the dispatching of trains in 1851, was the first to do so. Despite its successful experience, most other railroads did not immediately become convinced of the advantages of the system. As late as 1854, a reporter for the *London Quarterly Review* could write that "the telegraph is rarely seen in America running beside the railway."

What then is the basis for the view that railroads played a fundamental role in the growth and diffusion of the telegraph? It appears to rest primarily on the operating efficiencies achieved as a result of the alliance between the two systems. Once the alliance was formed, telegraph companies could utilize railroad men "to watch the line, straighten poles, re-set them when down, mend wires and report to the telegraph company." Consequently, by making use of railroad trackwalkers and other railroad maintenance men, telegraph companies were able to reduce maintenance costs below what they would have been. Such savings were, no doubt, reflected in lower rates that probably stimulated the growth of telegraphic service. Given the existence of railroads, the telegraph was no doubt aided by the alliance. However, it by no means follows that the observed rate of growth of the telegraph industry was higher than it would have been in the absence of railroads. It must be remembered that by speeding up the distribution of mail, railroads provided consumers with a better substitute for the telegraph than would otherwise have been available. Consequently, whether railroads made the volume of telegraphic business larger or smaller than it would have been in their absence is at this point a moot question.

THE SOCIAL SAVING OF RAILROADS

It is possible to set an upper limit on the increase in national income attributable to the reduction in transportation costs made possible by railroads. The main conceptual device used in this computation is the "social saving." The social saving in any given year is defined as the difference between the actual cost of shipping goods in that year and the alternative cost of shipping exactly the same goods between exactly the same points without railroads. This cost differential is in fact larger than the "true" social saving. Forcing the pattern of shipments in a nonrail situation to conform to the pattern that actually existed is equivalent to the imposition of a restraint on society's freedom to adjust to an alternative technological situation. If society had had to ship by water and wagon without the railroad, it could have altered the geographical locus of production in a manner that would have economized on transport services. Further, the sets of primary and secondary markets through which commodities were distributed were surely influenced by conditions peculiar to rail transportation; in the absence of railroads some different cities would have entered these sets, and the relative importance of those remaining would have changed. Adjustments of this sort would have reduced the loss of national income occasioned by the absence of the railroad.

For analytical convenience the computation of the social saving is divided into several parts. We begin with the estimation of the social saving on the interregional distribution of agricultural commodities. In 1890, most agricultural goods destined for interregional shipment were first concentrated in the eleven great primary markets of the Midwest. These farm surpluses were then transshipped to some ninety secondary markets located in the East and South. After arriving in the secondary markets the commodities were distributed to retailers in the immediately surrounding territory, or exported.

Of the various forms of transportation in use in 1890, the most relevant as an alternative to railroads were the waterways. All of the eleven primary markets were on navigable waterways. Lakes, canals, rivers, and coastal waters directly linked the primary markets with secondary markets receiving 90 per cent of the interregional shipments. Consequently it is possible to compute a first approximation of the interregional social saving by finding the difference between payments actually made by shippers of agricultural products and the payments they would have made to water carriers if shippers had sent the same commodities between the same points without railroads.

The agricultural tonnage shipped interregionally, in 1890, was approximately equal to the local deficits of the trading regions of the East and South plus net exports. The local net deficits of a trading area are computed by subtracting from the consumption requirements of the area its production and its changes in inventories. The average rail and water distances of an interregional shipment are estimated from a randomly drawn sample of the routes (pairs of cities) that represent the population of connections (i.e. all possible pairings) between primary and secondary (deficit) markets. The water and rail rates per ton-mile for the various commodities are based on representative rates that prevailed in 1890 over distances and routes approximating the average condition. The application of observed water rates to a tonnage greatly in excess of that actually carried by waterways is justified by evidence which indicates that water transportation was a constant or declining-cost industry.

Using these estimates of tonnages shipped, rates, and distances it appears that the actual cost of the interregional agricultural transportation in 1890 was $87,500,000, while the cost of transporting the same goods by water would have been only $49,200,000. In other words, the first approximation of the interregional social saving is negative by about $38,000,000. This odd result is the consequence of the fact that direct payments to railroads included virtually all of the cost of interregional transportation, while direct payments to water carriers did not. In calculating the cost of shipping without the railroad one must account for six additional items of cost not included in payments to water carriers. These items are cargo losses in transit, transshipment costs, wagon-haulage costs from water points to secondary markets not on waterways, capital costs not reflected in water rates, the cost resulting from the time lost when using a slow medium of transportation, and the cost of being unable to use water routes for five months out of the year.

The first four of the neglected costs can be estimated directly from available commercial data. Insurance rates measure the average cargo loss per dollar of goods shipped by water. Transshipment rates were published. Data on the capital invested in the construction and improvement of waterways were also published. The quantity of goods required by secondary markets not on waterways is indicated in the calculation of the net deficits of trading areas. And estimates of the cost of wagon transportation are available.

It is more difficult to determine the cost of the time lost in shipping by a slow medium of transportation and the cost of being unable to use water routes for about five months during each year. Such costs were not recorded in profit-and-loss statements, the publications of trade associations, the decennial censuses, or any of the other normal sources of business information. Consequently, they must be determined indirectly through a method that links the desired information to data which are available. The solution to the problem lies in the nexus between time and inventories. If entrepreneurs could replace goods the instant they were sold, they would, *ceteris paribus,* carry zero inventories. Inventories are necessary to bridge the gap of time required to deliver a commodity from its supply source to a given point. If, on the average, interregional shipments of agricultural commodities required a month more by water than by rail, and if water routes were closed for five months out of each year, it would have been possible to compensate for the slowness of water transportation and the limited season of navigation by increasing inventories in secondary markets by an amount equal to one half of the annual receipts of these markets. Hence, the cost of the interruptions and time lost in water transportation is the 1890 cost of carrying such an inventory. The inventory cost comprises two elements: the foregone opportunity of investing the capital represented in the additional inventory (which is measured by the interest rate), and storage charges (which were published).

When account is taken of the neglected costs, the negative first approximation is transformed into a positive social saving of $73,000,000 (see Table 5). Since the actual 1890 cost of shipping the specified com-

TABLE 5   The Social Saving in the Interregional Distribution of Agricultural Commodities

First approximation	$ −38,000,000
Neglected cargo losses	6,000,000
Transshipping	16,000,000
Supplementary wagon haulage	23,000,000
Neglected capital costs	18,000,000
Additional inventory costs	48,000,000
Total	$ 73,000,000

modities was approximately $88,000,000, the absence of the railroad would have almost doubled the cost of shipping agricultural commodities interregionally. It is therefore quite easy to see why the great bulk of agricultural commodities was actually sent to the East by rail, with water transportation used only over a few favorable routes.

While the interregional social saving is large compared to the actual transportation cost, it is quite small compared to annual output of the economy—just six tenths of 1 per cent of gross national product. Hence, the computed social saving indicates that the availability of railroads for the interregional distribution of agricultural products represented only a relatively small addition to the production potential of the economy.

The estimation of the social saving is more complex in intraregional trade (movements from farms to primary markets) than in long-haul trade. Interregional transportation represented a movement between a relatively small number of points—eleven great collection centers in the Midwest and ninety secondary markets in the East and South. But intraregional transportation required the connection of an enormous number of locations. Considering each farm as a shipping point, there were not 11 but 4,565,000 interior shipping locations in 1890; the number of primary markets receiving farm commodities was well over 100. These points were not all connected by the railroad network, let alone by navigable waterways. The movement of commodities from farms to primary markets was never accomplished exclusively by water or by rail. Rather, it involved a mixture of wagon and water or wagon and train services.

A first approximation of the intraregional social saving (a) can be computed on the basis of the relationship shown in Equation 1:

$$a - x[w(D_{fb} - D_{fr}) + (BD_{bp} - RD_{rp})] \qquad (1)$$

where

x = the tonnage of agricultural produce shipped out of counties by rail

w = the average wagon rate per ton-mile

B = the average water rate per ton-mile

R = the average rail rate per ton-mile

D_{fb} = the average distance from a farm to a water shipping point

D_{fr} = the average distance from a farm to a rail shipping point

D_{bp} = the average distance from a water shipping point to a primary market

D_{rp} = the average distance from a rail shipping point to a primary market

The first term within the square bracket $w(D_{fb} - D_{fr})$ is the social saving per ton attributable to the reduction in wagon transportation; the second term $(BD_{bp} - RD_{rp})$ is the social saving per ton on payments to water and rail carriers. One of the surprising results is that only the first term is positive. In the absence of railroads, wagon transportation costs would have increased by $8.92 for each ton of agricultural produce that was shipped intraregionally by rail. However, payments to water carriers would have been $0.76 per ton less than the payments to railroads. In other words, the entire first approximation of the a estimate of the social saving—which amounts to $300,000,000—is attributable not to the fact that railroad charges were less than boat charges but to the fact that railroads reduced the amount of expensive wagon haulage that had to be combined with one of the low-cost forms of transportation.

To the $300,000,000 obtained as the first approximation it is necessary to add certain indirect costs. In the long-haul case the first approximation of the social saving omitted six charges of considerable importance. In the intraregional case, however, three of these items were covered by the first approximation. Wagon-haulage costs are included in Equation 1. Transshipment costs would have been no greater in the nonrail case than in the rail case. In both situations bulk would have been broken when the wagons reached the rail or water shipping points, and no further trans-shipments would have been required between these points and the primary markets. Since all government expenditures on rivers and canals financed out of taxes rather than tolls were assigned to interregional agricultural shipments, their inclusion in the intraregional case would represent double counting.

Three indirect costs do have to be added to the first approximation. These are cargo losses, the cost of using a slow medium of transportation, and the cost of the limited season of navigation. As is shown by Table 6

TABLE 6   The Preliminary Intraregional Social Saving
(in millions of dollars)

First approximation	$ 300.2
Cargo losses	1.3
Cost of slow transportation	1.7
Cost of the limited season of navigation	34.0
Total	$ 337.2

these neglected items amount to only $37,000,000, which, when added to the first approximation, yields a preliminary a estimate of $337,000,000, or 2.8 per cent of gross national product.

The preliminary estimate of the agricultural social saving is based on the severe assumption that in the absence of railroads all other aspects of technology would have been unaltered. It seems quite likely, however, that in the absence of railroads much of the capital and ingenuity that went into their perfection and spread would have been turned toward the development of other cheap forms of land transportation. Under these circumstances it is possible that the internal-combustion engine would have been developed years sooner than it actually was, thus permitting a reduction in transportation costs through the use of motor trucks.

While most such possibilities of a speed-up in the introduction and spread of alternative forms of transportation have not been sufficiently explored to permit meaningful quantification at the present time, there are two changes about which one can make fairly definitive statements. These are the extension of the existing system of internal waterways, and the improvement of common roads. Neither of these developments required new knowledge. They merely involved an extension of existing technology.

As has already been pointed out, in the absence of railroads it would have been technologically and commercially feasible to build canals in the North and South Central states. A five-thousand-mile system of such canals would have brought all but 7 per cent of agricultural land within forty "airline" miles of a navigable waterway. In so doing, these waterways would have reduced the combined inter- and intraregional social saving from $410,000,000, $287,000,000. Similarly, improvement of roads could have cut the cost of wagon transportation by 39 per cent, thus still further reducing the total agricultural social saving to $214,000,000.

It is possible to estimate roughly the social saving on nonagricultural commodities by extrapolating the social saving per ton-mile on agricultural commodities to nonagricultural commodities. To do so, two adjustments must be made. First, the figure of $214,000,000 presented as the agricultural social saving already includes substantial elements of the social saving on nonagricultural items. Although all of the capital costs of the improvement of waterways were charged to agricultural commodities, most of this cost should be distributed among nonagricultural items. Similarly the wagon rates used in the computations assumed zero return hauls so that these rates cover most of the additional wagon cost that would have been incurred in shipping nonagricultural commodities to farms. It is probable that 35 per cent of the $214,000,000 should be assigned to the social saving induced by railroads in transporting products of mines, forest, and factories. In other words, the "pure" agricultural social saving is about $140,000,000. Given that 20,000,000,000 ton-miles of railroad service were required for the shipment of agricultural commodities in 1890, the agricultural social saving per ton-mile of railroad service was $0.0070.

Second, available evidence suggests that the social saving per ton-mile was less on nonagricultural products than on agricultural ones. Products of mines dominated the nonagricultural commodities carried by railroads. Coal alone represented 35 per cent of the nonagricultural tonnage in 1890. Iron and other ores brought the mineral share to over 50 per cent. As has previously been shown, a relatively small extension of the canal system could have brought most mines into direct contact with waterways. Thus, very little supplementary wagon transportation would have been required on these items. Moreover, the cost of increasing inventories to compensate for the slowness of, and interruption in, water transportation would have been quite low. The total value of products of mines was well below the value of the agricultural commodities shipped from farms. As a consequence, the opportunity cost of the increased inventories of minerals would have been well below that found for agriculture. Additional storage charges, if any, would have been trivial. Minerals required neither very expensive storage facilities nor shelters. They were stored on open docks or fields.

These general considerations are supported by estimates compiled by Albert Fishlow, which reveal that in 1860 the social saving per ton-mile on nonagricultural commodities was only 46 per cent of that for agricultural goods. This ratio applied to the figure of $0.0070 indicates that in the case of nonagricultural freight the social saving per ton-mile in 1890 was $0.0032. On this basis the social saving made possible by the 59,000,000,000 ton-miles of nonagricultural freight service provided by railroads in 1890 was $189,000,000. The last figure added to the "pure" agricultural saving yields a total of $329,000,000 on all commodities. Thus, the availability of railroads for the transportation of commodities appears to have increased the production potential of the economy by about 3 per cent of gross national product. . . .

The central feature of the developmental impact of the railroads was not so much that they induced or made possible new economic activities but that by reducing transportation costs they facilitated processes and activities which were well under way prior to their advent. The cheap form of inland transportation service purveyed by railroads speeded the commercialization of agriculture, widened the market for manufactured goods, and promoted regional specialization. While the scope of these effects and the net benefit accruing to the economy from them was much less than is usually presumed, they were nonetheless large enough to warrant the investment made in railroads.

The Dimensions of
Occupational Mobility

STEPHAN THERNSTROM

The persistent rags-to-riches myth that America is a land of opportunity for the poor has been regarded as particularly relevant to the mid- to late nineteenth century. Fortunately manuscript census data enable the stouthearted researcher to determine the actual degree of social mobility during that period and to test the myth against reality. Utilizing the manuscript census of Newburyport, Massachusetts, for 1850, 1860, 1870, and 1880, Stephan Thernstrom provides precise findings on the geographic and occupational mobility of unskilled labor.

John R. Fowle was an ordinary workman of Newburyport, nothing more. Born in New Hampshire in 1802, Fowle was listed variously as "laborer," "gardener," and "porter" in the census schedules and local city directories of the 1850-1880 period. Nor did he display any great talent for saving money; the census and the tax assessor's records show him without any property holdings during these years. Fowle had five daughters and four sons; none of them received much education. Two of the sons left Newburyport while still youths. A third started work as a common laborer, but after a few years of unskilled labor, and a few more as an operative

---

From Stephan Thernstrom, *Poverty and Progress: Social Mobility in a Nineteenth Century City* (Cambridge: Harvard University Press, 1964), pp. 80–114. Reprinted with omissions by permission of the publisher. © 1964 by the President and Fellows of Harvard College.

in a shoe factory, he was able to open a small grocery; the shop was rented, and his inventory was valued at $300.

John Fowle's youngest son, Stephen, had a more striking career. Where he obtained the capital for his first venture into business is unknown. In 1856, a lad of twenty-two, he paid only a poll tax. Two years later tax records show him the owner of a house and lot valued at $1100, and the city directory lists him as a "newsdealer." His news agency prospered, and Stephen was willing to take risks. He sold the house for $1250 in 1862, and looked for new possibilities. Not long after, with the aid of $4500 borrowed from the Institution for Savings, he entered into a series of transactions which gained him a home just off the best residential street (High) and a shop on the main business thoroughfare (State). His real estate holdings reached $8000 by the time of the Census of 1870; his inventories of periodicals, fruit, and sundries approached $2000. The Fowle store is still doing well on the same site after ninety years, though the family itself has disappeared from the city.

Michael Lowry, born in Ireland in 1815, came to the New World in the great exodus following the famine. Lowry settled in Newburyport in the late forties, and worked there as a day laborer the rest of his life. His eight sons were put to work as soon as they were able, but the family remained propertyless, living in rented quarters along the waterfront. One son, James, had a minor success; he saved $450 out of his wages as a mariner to purchase a house. None of the other children appear to have advanced in the slightest; all were unskilled laborers or seamen in 1880, lacking property holdings or savings accounts. Thomas Lowry did embark on certain ventures which might have produced a considerable income, but his brief career as a housebreaker ended with five years behind bars.

Pat Moylan was one of the few laborers in Newburyport who owned his own home in 1850. Moylan too was Irish, but he had immigrated to America well before the Great Famine, and had married a native-born girl. His successes over this thirty-year period were moderate, but they were sufficient to allow his children greater career opportunities than was common at this social level. Sometime in the 1850's Moylan found the job he was to hold until his death—night watchman at a textile mill. If his daily wages were not much higher than they had been as a common laborer, he was now sure of steady employment. His Olive Street home, valued at $700, made it unnecessary to pay out a large portion of his income in rent; he reported an additional $300 in personal property on the Census of 1870. Moylan's children were freer than most of their companions from compelling pressure to enter the labor market at the earliest possible age. Two of his five daughters graduated from the Female High School, a rare achievement for a working class girl at this time. Moylan's eldest son became a factory operative at sixteen, but during the Civil War decade acquired the skills of a blacksmith. Albert and James entered more promising situations; one was employed as a clerk in a cotton mill in 1880, while the other was still studying at Brown High School.

William Hardy, like John Fowle, was a native-born day laborer; like Fowle, Hardy never succeeded in accumulating any property. Hardy's two eldest sons did little better; one became a seaman, the other a factory operative. His two younger boys, however, were able to move into a skilled manual calling. Neither James, a machinist, nor Frank, a molder, could claim any property holdings in 1880, but each had entered occupations wtih earning opportunities well above those for unskilled labor.

The families of Michael and Jeremiah Haley achieved impressive property mobility without any occupational mobility at all. Michael and Jeremiah were recorded as common laborers in the Eighth, Ninth, and Tenth United States Censuses. In 1860 Michael owned property on Monroe Street worth $700; Jeremiah had none. In 1864 Jeremiah, who had three young children working to supplement his income, bought a half share in the Monroe Street house for $400; Michael used this sum to purchase another lot. Michael added steadily to his holdings; by 1880 he paid taxes on $1700 in real estate. In 1870 Jeremiah sold his half share back to Michael, and invested in a larger place on Dove Street, valued at $900 in 1880. The two brothers between them had five sons, none of whom entered any skilled or nonmanual occupation. One of Jeremiah's sons, Pat, did save enough money to build a small house next door to his father's, but he too remained but an ordinary unskilled manual laborer.

These few sketches make one thing quite clear. The situation of the hundreds of Newburyport residents ranked common laborers on the United States Census of 1850, 1860, and 1870 had seemed bleak: these men and their families shared a common plight as members of the lowest social stratum in the community. As these cases reveal, however, not all of these families remained at the very bottom of the Newburyport social ladder. Some, like the Lowrys, were trapped in poverty and illiteracy; others were socially mobile in a variety of ways. This much can be established by examining the life histories of a few families. But a handful of instances cannot reveal what *proportion* of the laboring population of Newburyport reaped the benefits of social mobility, nor can it indicate what *avenues* of social advance were of particular significance to the working class. Perhaps the Lowry family was typical, and the Fowles a curious exception; perhaps the embittered editor of the Boston *Pilot* was right that 95 out of 100 workmen in America were fated to "live and die in the condition in which they were born." Or was Stephen Fowle a representative man, an example of the opportunities open to a wide segment of the working class? To answer the question requires a statistical analysis of social mobility.

Social mobility refers to the process by which individuals alter their social position. But to say this, unhappily, is to say nothing until social position has been defined. The terms social status and social class raise perilously complex and disputed problems of definition. A brief comment at this point will clarify the approach taken here. . . . One major sociological school—represented by W. Lloyd Warner and his followers— emphasizes the prestige dimension of class; the study of social mobility becomes the study of the subtle "climbing" tactics by which the ambitious manipulate others in an effort to improve their prestige rank. Status is measured by polling the community social elite; great emphasis is placed on the intricacies of etiquette. Whatever the merits of this subjective approach to social class and social mobility, it is of little value to the historian, for historical records rarely yield the information necessary to apply prestige categories systematically to societies of the past.

The historical study of social mobility requires the use of objective criteria of social status. The most convenient of these is occupation. Occupation may be only one variable in a comprehensive theory of class, but it is the variable which includes more, which sets more limits on the other variables than any other criterion of status. An analysis of the occupational mobility of unskilled laborers and their sons in Newburyport, therefore, is an appropriate starting point. But such an analysis must take into consideration the changing composition of the Newburyport laboring class.

MEN ON THE MOVE: THE PROBLEM OF GEOGRAPHICAL MOBILITY

Observers of cities have too often treated the modern community as a self-contained entity with a stable population core. A city like Newburyport, whose total population has varied little in the past century, is particularly conducive to such illusions. It is hardly surprising that Lloyd Warner's volumes on Newburyport social life miss the significance of migration in and out of the community and view social mobility exclusively as a reshuffling of its inhabitants into different social classes.

A careful scrutiny of the composition of the Newburyport laboring class in the 1850–1880 period suggests how misleading the myth of stability can be. The most common, if most easily overlooked, form of mobility experienced by the ordinary laborers of nineteenth century Newburyport was mobility out of the city. Slightly less than 40 percent of all the unskilled laborers and their children living in the community at midcentury were still listed there in the Census of 1860; of the 454 men in this class in 1860, but 35 percent were to be found in the city a decade later; the comparable figure for 1870–1880 was 47 percent. (Local health records indicate that deaths accounted for few of these departures.) The first generalization to make about the "typical" Newburyport laborer of this period, it appears, is that he did not live in Newburyport very long! Contemporary observers were correct in characterizing the new working class as floating. For a majority of these permanent transients, Newburyport provided no soil in which to sink roots. It was only one more place in which to carry on the struggle for existence for a few years, until driven onward again.

Even before the effects of occupational and property mobility are taken into account, therefore, it is evident that Newburyport did not develop a degraded proletarian class with fixed membership in the 1850–1880 period. The founders of Lowell had thought of the factory labor force as being made up of "a succession of learners"; to a striking extent this was true of the lowest stratum in Newburyport. A large and steady stream of working class men poured out of the community during these years. Their places were taken by masses of newcomers. Ireland was a continuing source of fresh unskilled labor throughout this period; a smaller but still important group came from the stagnant farms of Vermont, New Hampshire, and Maine. These streams of migration in and out of the community resulted in a turnover of more than half of the local unskilled labor force each decade.

Two of the chief social trends of nineteenth century America—the mass influx of immigrants from the Old World, and the drift of population from country to city—thus appear on our small stage. This volatile society made a hero of the man on the road, heading for the Great West or the Great City. And American folklore equated movement with success—the hero was on the make as well as on the move. A few shreds of evidence from recent sociological inquiries support this old belief that geographical mobility and upward social mobility are positively related, but whether the myth had any foundation in fact in nineteenth century America is unknown.

This whets our curiosity about the subsequent career patterns of the hundreds of laborers who worked in Newburyport for a short time in the 1850–1880 period and then moved on. It is quite impossible, let it be said immediately, to trace these individuals and thereby to provide a certain answer as to how many of them later won fame and fortune. Without a magical electronic device capable of sifting through tens of millions of names and locating a few hundred, there is no way of picking out former residents of Newburyport on later national censuses. We do know something, however, about the experiences of these men in Newburyport, about the circumstances in which they departed from the community, and about the New England labor market at this time. On the basis of this information we may venture certain inferences about their future with a degree of confidence.

In only a handful of all these cases was the laborer migrating from Newburyport in a particularly strategic position to take advantage of new opportunities in another community. For instance, if the son of a laborer, unencumbered as yet with family responsibilities, was fortunate enough to possess a substantial savings account and perhaps a high school education or some experience in a skilled or nonmanual occupation, his employment prospects after migration were obviously excellent. Such cases, however, were rare. The great majority of laborers who left Newburyport departed under less auspicious circumstances. Without financial resources, occupational skill, or education, frequently with heavy family responsibilities, the range of alternatives open to these men in their new destination was slender. Laborers like these were not lured to leave Newburyport by the prospect of investing their savings and skills more profitably elsewhere; they left the city when the depressed state of the local labor market made it impossible for them to subsist where they were. As a result of the collapse of 1857, for example, Newburyport suffered a population decline estimated by the *Herald* at "more than one thousand." Most of these departures, it was thought, were cases of workers moving to "locations where work is more abundant."

That the geographical mobility of such laborers dramatically improved their opportunities for upward social mobility seems highly unlikely. The telling objection which has been advanced against the famous "safety valve" theory of the frontier applies here. Migrant laborers from the city rarely had the capital or the knowledge necessary to reap the benefits of the supply of "free land" at the frontier. It seems to have been largely artisans, schoolteachers, farmers, and unsuccessful businessmen who sought their fortunes in Illinois wheat or California gold. The Newburyport newspapers of the 1850–1880 period reported but a single instance of a local laborer who successfully settled in the West, and his was not a case of which Horace Greeley could be proud. The *Herald* of June 22, 1878, carried news of a letter from one Michael Welch, then in Nevada. Welch, the son of a local laborer, had been the treasurer of one of Newburyport's volunteer fire companies; when he left for the frontier he took the treasury with him! Welch advised his parents that he was doing very well in Nevada, and would soon repay the stolen funds. Few workmen in the city, needless to say, found capital to finance a trip west so readily available.

Neither were laborers migrating from Newburyport likely to discover acres of diamonds on the urban frontier. The community fell within the orbit of Boston, which became a great industrial center in the middle decades of the century partly because of the vast reservoir of cheap labor provided by immigration. The unskilled labor market which was centered in Boston included Lowell, Lawrence, Lynn, and smaller cities like Newburyport and Chicopee. There was a high rate of labor mobility from city to city within this market, the flow varying with local fluctuations in the demand for unskilled workers. In these circumstances, differences not only in wages and working conditions but in promotion opportunities as well probably were marginal. Certainly it is doubtful that a workman without capital or skills would have found it markedly easier to advance himself in Boston than in Newburyport. The great metropolis offered alluring opportunities at the top to those with the proper requisites, but to the common laborer who drifted there from Newburyport it probably meant only more of the same. Indeed, occupational opportunities for the unskilled may have been somewhat less in a great city like Boston, where many of the most helpless and destitute members of the working class tended to cluster.

The social mobility study described below necessarily gives disproportionate attention to the settled minority of workmen who remained within the community for a decade or more and whose careers could therefore be traced. It is highly improbable, however, that our lack of precise knowledge of the later careers of migrants from Newburyport has led to an underestimation of the upward mobility eventually achieved by laborers in the sample. The circumstances in which they departed and the character of the unskilled labor market in New England make it unlikely that large numbers of these workmen were more successful in their new places of residence than were their counterparts who remained in Newburyport.

An inquiry of this kind, in fact, is biased to some degree in the opposite direction. To analyze the social adjustment of workmen who settled in a particular city long enough to be recorded on two or more censuses is to concentrate on laborers who were most resistant to pressures to migrate, and these tended to be men who had already attained a modicum of economic security in the community. Thus four fifths of the local unskilled laborers who owned real property in 1850 were still living in Newburyport in 1860, a persistence rate of 80 percent; the comparable figure for propertyless laborers in this decade was 31 percent. Migration was, in this sense, a selective process. Masses of unskilled newcomers—from rural areas and from abroad—streamed into the nineteenth century city. Large numbers of these men were unable to establish a secure place for themselves in the community. Unemployment was always a possibility, and all too often a grim reality. When jobs were too few to go around, the rumor of work in Lawrence, or Lynn, or Holyoke was enough to draw these men on. Workmen who remained in Newburyport for any length of time were therefore a somewhat select group, because to find sufficiently stable employment to maintain a settled residence in a community was itself success of a kind to the laborer. In tracing the changing social position of groups of Newburyport workmen we must keep this relationship between geographical mobility and social mobility clearly in mind. The process of internal migration within the unskilled labor market removed many of the least successful laborers from the community; the following analysis of occupational and property mobility in Newburyport applies primarily to a settled minority from the total unskilled laboring population which passed through the community between 1850 and 1880.

THE NATURE OF THE OCCUPATIONAL HIERARCHY

To speak of occupational mobility presupposes the social gradation of occupations, a gradation implied in such phrases as the social ladder and the occupational pyramid. The question we should now turn to is, in effect, how to justify the use of these metaphors in a specific historical context. The sociologist is able to go about this task more directly than the historian; by various polling devices he may ask the members of the society he studies how they rank various occupations. While the historian may extrapolate certain of these findings back into the past, he must rely chiefly on indirect evidence to support his judgments as to the nature of the occupational hierarchy.

The occupational classification scheme used in this study is simple, designed to make possible some immediate generalizations from the census data. Occupational mobility is defined as a move from one to another of the four broad categories: unskilled manual occupations, semiskilled manual occupations, skilled manual occupations, and nonmanual occupations. . . .

The superior ranking of nonmanual occupations seems incontestable. Status differences between manual and nonmanual callings have narrowed somewhat in recent years, with some overlapping between highly skilled manual jobs and certain routine nonmanual occupations. In the nineteenth century, however, the gulf between the two was wide. The annual income of the ordinary white collar worker was at least twice that of the typical laborer. Newburyport papers of the period spoke of "the general belief" that manual work was undesirable; it was often complained that far too many young men were irrationally eager to become clerks and professionals, that not enough were willing to learn a secure manual trade.

Within the broad category of manual labor, three levels of occupational status must be distinguished. If the social distance between these three was less than that between manual and nonmanual occupations as a group, status distinctions within the working class occupational world were nonetheless important. At the top of the manual laboring group stood the skilled craftsmen, artisans, and mechanics—carpenters, caulkers, sailmakers, master mariners, tailors, butchers and so forth. (Some Newburyport artisans in this period were self-employed and owned significant amounts of capital; these were considered small businessmen and placed in the nonmanual category.) Certain of these trades were prospering during these years, while others were declining from changes in technology and market structure. Even the stagnating trades, however, remained markedly superior to other sources of manual employment. The artisan possessed a special skill; he had a "vocation," a "calling," rather than a mere "job." His earnings, as Tables 1 and 2 clearly show, were much

TABLE 1   Occupational Differences in Employment and Annual Earnings, Essex County, Massachusetts, 1875

	Number in sample	Days worked [a]	Mean annual earnings
Skilled occupations			
machinist	135	272.4	$601.94
blacksmith	68	260.0	567.60
carpenter	359	218.0	534.40
mason	101	177.6	524.02
cotton spinner (male)	14	280.5	523.75
shoecutter (male)	254	243.1	521.05
painter	108	207.8	474.79
Semiskilled occupations			
shoecutter, undesignated	883	234.3	418.68
factory operative, undesignated (male)	191	249.6	379.62
Unskilled occupations			
common laborer	412	230.6	358.68

[a] On the basis of a six-day week, without considering holidays, the number of possible work days in a year is 312.

higher than those of the semiskilled or unskilled workman; his wife and children were under much less pressure to enter the labor market themselves to supplement the family income.

Status differences between unskilled and semiskilled occupations were less dramatic, but they did exist. . . . The common laborer was, to an extreme degree, at the mercy of the harsh uncertainties of the casual labor market. Without a specific economic function to perform regularly

TABLE 2 Occupational Differences in Annual Wages and Proportion of Family Income Earned by Family Head, Massachusetts, 1874 [a]

	Number in sample	Mean annual wage of family head	Percent of total family income
Skilled occupations			
machinist	41	$746.54	89.5
carpenter	44	716.57	86.6
teamster	6	646.67	86.2
Semiskilled occupations			
mill hand	13	594.31	71.9
shoemaker	22	527.41	68.4
Unskilled occupations			
laborer	43	414.42	56.8

[a] The wage levels here, it will be noted, are consistently higher than those reported for Essex County a year later (Table 1). This is largely because the 1874 sample was gathered in a way which biased the findings toward the more prosperous representatives of each occupation. We are interested in relative differentials here, so the bias is unimportant.

for a predictable reward, he was forced to take his chances daily in the competition for temporary employment. His wages were invariably below those of his fellow workmen in other occupations, and his children were the first to be forced to seek work to keep the family going.

By the criteria of earnings, skill required, and definiteness of function, semiskilled jobs were a cut above this. The ordinary operative in a shoe factory or textile mill, the gardener, or the night watchman did not perform as complex a task as the spinner, shoecutter, or mason, and his wages were correspondingly lower. But it would be a mistake to suppose that such jobs required no "skill" at all, and that they were in no way superior to common laboring positions. The semiskilled workmen of Newburyport had a somewhat more secure and respected position than the general laborers. Their function was more clearly defined, their wages were a bit higher and a bit more regular, and they were better able to support their families on their own income.

One further question about the Newburyport occupational hierarchy must be considered. The shape of a community's occupational structure is obviously a prime determinant of the range of occupational mobility opportunities there. Consider an extreme case—a city in which 95 percent of the labor force holds unskilled jobs, with only 5 percent in the higher occupational categories. Even if the occupants of these few high status positions were continually recruited from the bottom class, the majority of men in this community would remain laborers all their lives. The opposite polar type would be a city with only a small fraction of its residents in lowly occupations; here a much slower turnover of personnel in high status jobs would mean relatively greater mobility opportunities for lower class persons. The significance of data about occupational mobility in a given community cannot be grasped without some sense of the range of mobility which could be "expected" within that community.

The Newburyport occupational structure at mid-century resembled the second polar type more closely than the first. Only about 8 percent of the labor force held unskilled jobs; three times as many occupied nonmanual positions of some kind. Approximately one quarter of the employed males of the city were semiskilled workers, while almost 40 percent were skilled laborers. The diversity of skilled trades was striking—thirty-nine varieties of artisan could be counted on the local census schedules for 1850. It is misleading to classify mid-century Newburyport a "mill town"; its occupational structure was not heavily weighted toward unskilled and semiskilled callings. The community had a highly diversified craft economy, with almost two thirds of its labor force in the top two occupational categories and less than a tenth at the very bottom.

Between 1850 and 1880 the main outlines of the Newburyport occupational structure did not change drastically. A distinct shrinking of employment in the skilled trades did occur, matched by a moderate expansion of both semiskilled and nonmanual callings. But the local economy, which had reached a plateau after the rapid growth of the 1840's, did not undergo large-scale technological changes which fundamentally altered the opportunity structure. The declining proportion of skilled positions in the city, and the expansion of semiskilled and white collar occupations reflect national trends of the period, but in Newburyport these tendencies manifested themselves more slowly than in other more dynamic nineteenth century cities. The local occupational structure offered a relative abundance of high status positions in 1850; its general shape seemed equally favorable to upward occupational mobility in 1880.

INTRA-GENERATIONAL OCCUPATIONAL MOBILITY, 1850–1880

The career patterns of hundreds of unskilled laborers of nineteenth century Newburyport are summed up in Table 3. A simple generalization immediately suggests itself: less than half of the unskilled laborers listed in the city on the Census of 1850, 1860. or 1870 remained there for as much as a decade, and only a minority of those who did attained

TABLE 3 Occupational and Geographical Mobility of Three Groups of Laborers, 1850–
1880

Year	Occupational status attained			Non-manual	Rate of persistence [a]	Number in sample
	Unskilled	Semiskilled	Skilled	manual	persistence [a]	sample
	1850 Census group					
1860	64%	16%	15%	5%	32%	55
1870	36	39	9	15	64	35
1880	57	21	7	14	40	14
	1860 Census group					
1870	74	12	8	5	33	74
1880	69	19	6	6	65	48
	1870 Census group					
1880	79	6	10	5	41	102

[a] This column provides a measure of the geographical mobility of workmen in the sample. The rate of persistence of a group for a particular decade is defined as that proportion of the group recorded on the census at the start of the decade that is still present in the community at the end of the decade. Thus 32 percent of the unskilled laborers of 1850 still lived in Newburyport in 1860; 64 percent of the men in this group as of 1860 still lived in Newburyport in 1870, and so forth.

a higher status occupation.* The experiences of these obscure workmen, however, were sufficiently varied and complex to merit closer scrutiny.

Of the 171 common laborers employed in Newburyport in 1850, fully two thirds had disappeared from the city by 1860. A few of these had died; most had moved away. Of those who remained, almost two thirds were still ordinary unskilled laborers after a decade. Only 5 percent had risen into a nonmanual calling. Upward mobility was restricted almost entirely to the skilled and semiskilled occupations; a sixth of these men acquired semiskilled positions by 1860, a slightly smaller proportion found skilled employment.

During the Civil War decade, however, this group fared better. Its members were older, and more securely settled in the community; the persistence rate of the group for 1860–1870 was twice that for

* A word of warning is in order here. The discussion which follows is based on a series of tables which display in percentages the changing occupational distribution of several groups of men and boys. Scrutiny of the absolute numbers from which these percentages were calculated will reveal that, in some instances, occupational shifts by relatively few men appear as a rather dramatic percentage change. These changes in the occupational adjustment of even a small group of individuals are suggestive, but the reader must recall that this is an interpretative essay based on fragmentary data, not a large-scale, definitive statistical study.

1850–1860. Their occupational adjustment improved markedly in one respect. While two thirds of them had made no occupational gains at all between 1850 and 1860, by 1870 only one third of the group still held completely unskilled laboring jobs.

Almost all of the upward mobility attained by these men in the Civil War decade involved one small step up the occupational ladder. The dramatic shift out of the unskilled occupations was accompanied by only a small expansion of the nonmanual category and by an actual decrease in the skilled category. By far the most widespread form of upward mobility was into positions of only slightly higher status than unskilled labor—semiskilled jobs of various kinds.

Occupational opportunities for the immigrants from rural New England and abroad who arrived in Newburyport *after* 1850 were somewhat less favorable. The laborers first listed in Newburyport in the Census of 1860 remained more heavily concentrated in unskilled jobs ten and twenty years later than the men of the 1850 group. Three quarters of them attained no occupational mobility after a decade in the community, and nearly 70 percent were still common laborers after two decades. One laborer in twenty from those who stayed throughout the Civil War decade obtained a nonmanual position of some kind by 1870; no further gains of significance were made in this category during the seventies. The prospects of moving into a skilled manual job were also remote: only 8 percent held skilled positions after a decade in the city, and the proportion fell to 6 percent by 1880. The most marked difference between the attainments of the 1850 and 1860 groups, however, was in the semiskilled occupations. The unskilled laborer who came to Newburyport after 1850 had fewer prospects of attaining the very modest advance in status involved in becoming a fisherman, a factory operative, a gardener, a night watchman.

The shrinkage of semiskilled opportunities is even more evident from the experiences of the laborers first listed in the Census of 1870. Some two thirds of the men in the 1850 group remained trapped in the unskilled category after a decade; the comparable figure for the 1860 group was three fourths; in the case of the 1870 group, four out of five men remained laborers for at least a decade. This unfavorable trend, however, did not mean the appearance of new barriers against movement into the skilled and nonmanual occupations. The prospects of becoming a grocer or a mason were quite similar for members of all three groups. The chief advantage of the more successful group was that they enjoyed superior access to jobs of a semiskilled character.

It is tempting to conclude flatly that a change somewhat unfavorable to common laborers occurred in the Newburyport occupational structure during these years. But a different explanation of the pattern of declining opportunities can be conceived. We know that the industrial transformation of the Newburyport economy coincided with the arrival of masses of impoverished Irish peasants, and that the proportion of foreign-born men in the local working class rose steadily through the 1850–1880 period. It is possible that foreign laborers had fewer opportunities than their native counterparts throughout this period and that the two later groups had a larger proportion of immigrants than the 1850 group.

Did Yankee workmen climb into higher status occupations more easily than immigrant laborers in these years as many observers believed, or were ethnic differences in mobility opportunities actually negligible? The relationship between occupational mobility and ethnicity is displayed in Table 4; while the absolute numbers from which these distributions were calculated were tiny in some instances, the uniformity of the pattern which emerges is impressive. The immigrant workman in Newburyport was markedly less successful than his native counterpart in climbing out of the ranks of the unskilled in the 1850–1880 period. In each of the three groups at each census disproportionately high numbers of the foreign-born remained concentrated at the bottom of the occupational scale. The disadvantages of the newcomers were reflected, to some extent, in their underrepresentation in the skilled and nonmanual callings. But the sharpest difference in mobility opportunities was not in the two highest occupational categories but in the semiskilled field. The distribution of the 1850 group in 1870—with 77 percent of its native-born members and 14 percent of its immigrants holding semiskilled jobs—is only the most dramatic illustration of a tendency evident throughout Table 4. Evidently many local employers shared Francis Bowen's belief that "the rude labor" to which the newcomers had become accustomed had "so incapacitated them for higher tasks" that a factory could not be profitably run if more than a third of its labor force was made up of immigrants. "Foreigners generally, and the Irish in particular," wrote Bowen, "cannot be employed at all" in the factory, "except in that small proportion to the total number of hands which will make it possible to restrict them to the lower or less difficult tasks." In the Newburyport factories of this period the proportion of immigrant workmen on the payroll was kept well below that supposedly dangerous level.

The shrinking of opportunities in the semiskilled occupations, therefore, was intimately connected with the changing ethnic composition of the Newburyport laboring class. The proportion of foreign-born men in the community labor force was steadily rising, and in these years the immigrants had particularly restricted access to employment in the occupations most open to the ambitious common laborer. It is note-

TABLE 4 Ethnic Differences in Intra-generational Occupational Mobility

| Year | Occupational status attained | | | | | | | | Number in sample | |
| | Unskilled | | Semiskilled | | Skilled | | Nonmanual | | | |
	Native	Foreign	Native	Foreign	Native	Foreign	Native	Foreign	Native	Foreign
	1850 Census group									
1860	47%	72%	32%	8%	15%	14%	5%	6%	19	36
1870	15	55	77	14	0	14	8	18	13	22
1880	25	70	25	20	25	0	25	10	4	10
	1860 Census group									
1870	50	83	30	5	5	10	15	2	20	54
1880	50	74	30	15	10	5	10	5	10	38
	1870 Census group									
1880	60	84	15	4	15	9	10	4	20	82

worthy, however, that the special handicaps of immigrant laborers do not fully account for the inferior showing of the 1860 and 1870 groups. When the occupational experiences of native and foreign laborers are tabulated separately—as in Table 4—the pattern of declining mobility shows up in the figures for both groups.

A few general conclusions about the mobility patterns of common laborers in Newburyport in the 1850–1880 period can now be suggested. The composition of the community's unskilled laboring force was extremely fluid: a majority of the men registered as laborers on a United States Census in these years left the city before a second census was taken. These high rates of migration from the community significantly affected occupational adjustment; the improved occupational distribution of the three groups was partly due to the simple fact that unsuccessful laborers were quicker to leave Newburyport than successful ones.

Surprisingly, however, variations in the flow of migrants from the city were not closely related to variations in occupational opportunities there. The persistence rates of the 1850 and 1860 groups (Table 3) were almost identical—32 and 33 percent respectively the first decade, 64 and 65 percent respectively in the second decade—even though the occupational gains of the two were not. The 1870 group departed somewhat from the pattern; 41 percent of its members remained in Newburyport for at least a decade. This instance hints at a mild negative relationship between group persistence and occupational mobility, since the most stable of the three groups was also the least mobile occupationally. Ethnic differences in migration seem to have followed no consistent pattern. Foreign-born laborers were less successful occupationally than their native competitors throughout these three decades; the persistence rates of the newcomers, however, were lower in 1860 and 1870 and much higher in 1880. The rate of emigration, therefore, was an independent variable which strongly influenced the occupational adjustment of unskilled laborers; it did not vary in response to changes in occupational mobility opportunities in the community.

The common workman who remained in Newburyport in these years had only a slight chance of rising into a middle class occupation, even if "middle class" is generously defined to include the ownership of a subsistence farm. Only one laborer in twenty succeeded in making this advance during his first decade in the city. In the case of the 1850 group this proportion increased to three in twenty after two decades. but the two-decade figure for the 1860 group remained one in twenty. Moreover, neither politics nor religion, often assumed to have been important channels of upward mobility for immigrant groups, provided any opportunities for these men. Not one instance of ascent of this kind was recorded in the 1850–1880 period. The climb into a non-manual occupation was not impossible for the unskilled workman, but it was achieved by only a tiny minority.

It is perhaps not very surprising that men without capital, education, or special training of any sort should have had limited access to nonmanual occupations. More noteworthy is the fact that these laborers found so little opportunity to enter skilled manual occupations. Approximately a third of the total Newburyport labor force in this period was made up of artisans and craftsmen of various sorts, but few laborers found openings here.

In none of the groups of laborers did as much as a quarter of the men succeed in obtaining either skilled or nonmanual positions in the period studied. From 75 to 85 percent of them remained near the bottom of the social ladder in the low-skill, low-pay occupational universe. The great majority continued to work as day laborers; most of those who did change occupations became semiskilled workmen, performing simple manual tasks at slightly higher wages and with somewhat more regular employment than they had previously enjoyed.

The opportunity to take this very modest step upward into the semiskilled category varied in two significant ways—according to the laborer's nativity and to his time of arrival in the community. Compared to the Yankee, the foreign-born workman was generally under-represented at all occupational levels above unskilled labor, but his chief disadvantage was not at the top of the occupational ladder but at the second rung. Similarly, the growing tendency of laborers who arrived in Newburyport after 1850 to remain fixed in unskilled occupations involved a relatively small reduction in mobility into skilled and nonmanual positions; most of the change was due to the restriction of employment opportunities in the semiskilled category.

INTER-GENERATIONAL OCCUPATIONAL MOBILITY, 1850–1880

If nineteenth century Americans were optimistic about the laborer's chances of "pulling himself up by his own bootstraps," they were more optimistic still about his children's prospects for success. The following analysis of career patterns of sons of Newburyport laborers will help to determine to what extent such optimism was justified.

Intra-generational mobility is computed by comparing men's occupations at two or more points in their career, but the task of estimating inter-generational mobility is rather more complicated. A comparison of the status of two different individuals—father and son—is sought. At what point in the careers of the two is it appropriate to make the comparison? Half of this problem has been solved here by arranging the data on sons' occupations by age group, so that the occupational status of sons at varying stages of their careers is displayed (Table 5). Control for age is particularly important in this case because most boys entered the labor market in their early teens, and there is good reason

TABLE 5   Occupational and Geographical Mobility of Sons of Laborers, 1850–1880 [a]

| | | | Occupational status attained | | | |
Year	Unskilled	Semiskilled	Skilled	Non-manual	Rate of persistence	Number in sample
		Youths born 1830–1839				
1850	39%	56%	6%	0%	—	18
1860	10	76	7	7	29%	41
1870	11	48	30	11	56	27
1880	11	42	37	11	63	19
		Youths born 1840–1849				
1860	11	84	2	4	54	57
1870	28	45	17	10	32	58
1880	21	46	17	17	33	24
		Youths born 1850–1859				
1870	23	59	11	7	54	95
1880	33	40	20	8	44	76
		Youths born 1860–1869				
1880	25	60	7	8	56	73

[a] The reader may be surprised to see the number of youths in a group increasing from decade to decade in some instances, at the same time that the persistence rate figure indicates that half to two thirds of the group members left Newburyport each decade. The explanation is that large numbers of youths were coming *into* the city during these years as well, and that these have been included in the analysis.

to doubt that the jobs they held at that tender age provide a reasonable measure of inter-generational mobility. It is obviously important to determine how closely the adult occupations of these sons corresponded to the occupations they held while in their teens. One recent study revealed that well over half of a sample of white collar and professional workers in Oakland, California, had worked in a manual laboring position at some point in their early career, persuasive evidence of the dangers of ignoring intra-generational mobility in a study of inter-generational mobility. By utilizing age groups in analyzing the career patterns of laborers' sons this danger can be avoided.

There remains the difficulty that not all of the fathers of these men continued to be unskilled laborers through the entire period of the study. Some, we have seen, moved up the occupational ladder themselves. . . . For the present it will simplify matters to ignore occupational advances made by the father and to consider all fathers laborers. Most of them did in fact remain laborers, and, as we shall see later, those who did climb a notch or two upwards had little success in passing on their advantage to their offspring.

Perhaps the most important question to ask about the hundreds of laborers' sons whose careers are recorded in Table 5 is whether or not they customarily inherited the occupation of their fathers and themselves became unskilled day laborers. The answer is apparent in a glance. In none of the age groups at any of the four censuses between 1850 and 1880 did a majority of sons hold unskilled jobs. The most frequently chosen occupation in every instance was in the semiskilled manual category. More often than not, it has been shown, the unskilled Newburyport workman remained an unskilled laborer throughout this period; more often than not the son of such a man became a semiskilled worker.

The really dramatic opening up of semiskilled employment opportunities to laborers' sons occurred in the 1850's. Even in 1850 a slight majority of the handful of sons old enough to be employed held semiskilled positions, but the extent of direct occupational inheritance was still quite high for this group—close to 40 percent. A decade later the situation was strikingly different: almost 85 percent of the boys in the teen-age group held semiskilled jobs, and 75 percent of the youths aged 20–29; only a tenth of the members of either group were mere common laborers! Very few, on the other hand, had climbed more than one rung up the status ladder. Barely 5 percent of the teenagers working in 1860 had entered skilled or nonmanual callings. The comparable figure for youths in their twenties was higher, but even this meant no more than that one in thirteen held a skilled job and one in thirteen a nonmanual job. By far the most common form of intergenerational mobility evident by 1860 was into semiskilled occupations.

After 1860 there continued to be a heavy concentration of laborers' sons in semiskilled callings, but a significant tightening up occurred. Eighty-five percent of the teenagers in 1860 held semiskilled jobs, less than 60 percent of the teen-agers in 1870. For the group aged 20–29 in 1860 the drop was from 76 percent to 45 percent. A great wave of working class children entered the labor market during the Civil War decade, and the local employers hiring semiskilled labor did not expand their activity sufficiently to absorb all of them. Indeed, one major source of semiskilled employment began to dry up during this decade. Almost half of the laborers' sons who held semiskilled jobs at the time of the Census of 1860 listed themselves as "fisherman" or "seaman." Both the fishing industry and the coasting trade carried on out of Newburyport experienced a sharp decline during the sixties; by 1870 the maritime industries accounted for only a quarter of the semiskilled jobs held by these youths and by 1880, less than 15 percent. Semiskilled employment was coming increasingly to mean factory employment.

What happened to the boys for whom the cotton mills and shoe factories of Newburyport had no room? The narrowing of semiskilled opportunities in the sixties forced increasing numbers of the fathers of these youths to remain common laborers. This happened to some extent to the sons as well; the 1870 Census showed a rise in the concentration of sons in unskilled positions. It is striking, however, that this decade also saw a corresponding increase in mobility into the two higher occupational classes. In the case of the two younger groups in 1870, the increase in direct occupational inheritance was approximately equal to the increase in the skilled and nonmanual category. For men in the 30–39 age bracket in 1870 the construction of semiskilled opportunities during the Civil War decade resulted in a substantial rise in the proportion holding high status jobs, but virtually no increase at all in the unskilled category.

A certain number of laborers' sons gained a foothold in the white collar world after 1860—ten members of the group became clerks between 1860 and 1870, for example. But the skilled crafts were a more important source of upward mobility. The 1870 and 1880 figures show that it was uncommon for more than one in ten to cross the barrier dividing manual from nonmanual occupations, while two to three times as many youths characteristically found skilled employment. No single craft or group of crafts appears to have been unusually open to penetration from below; there was a broad scattering of upwardly mobile sons throughout the trades. The 1870 group, for example, included four blacksmiths, two carpenters, two machinists, two painters, two iron molders, a tailor, a baker, and a mason.

Two other aspects of the process of inter-generational mobility require comment—the role of ethnic differences and the influence of geographical mobility. It has already been demonstrated that the immigrant workman was markedly less successful than his native counterpart in climbing up the occupational ladder. Did the children of immigrant laborers face similar handicaps or did ethnic barriers to mobility affect only the first generation immigrant? A comparison of the occupational distribution of native and foreign sons in 1850, 1860, 1870, and 1880 is presented in Table 6. The conclusion to be drawn from it is obvious: sons of Yankee laborers obtained high status employment in Newbury-

TABLE 6   Occupational Distribution of Sons of Native and Foreign-born Laborers, 1850–
1880

Occupational category	1850		1860		1870		1880	
	Native	Foreign	Native	Foreign	Native	Foreign	Native	Foreign
Number in sample	19	14	34	76	37	148	37	158
Unskilled	26%	71%	12%	8%	8%	27%	19%	27%
Semiskilled	53	21	53	88	38	55	38	50
Skilled	21	7	18	3	27	14	24	15
Nonmanual	0	0	18	1	27	5	19	8

port much more easily than sons of foreign-born workmen in these years. The proportion of native youths in skilled and nonmanual positions was consistently higher than the proportion of foreign sons; the latter clustered heavily near the bottom of the occupational scale. But, unlike their fathers, immigrant children were not thought "incapacitated" for factory employment. The upper levels of the factory hierarchy were completely closed to them, but a high proportion found semiskilled positions in local factories.

These ethnic differences in mobility opportunities narrowed somewhat in the post–Civil War years. The censuses of 1870 and 1880 showed gains for foreign sons in both the skilled and nonmanual categories. The popular belief that second-generation Americans labored under no special handicaps in the race for occupational status was excessively optimistic, but the evidence of Table 6 hints at the beginning of a trend toward some equalization of opportunities. It is interesting to note, however, that by 1880 none of these youths had advanced through the mobility channels so often stressed in impressionistic accounts of immigrant life—politics and religion. To become a priest required education; to become a ward boss required some education too, and a well-organized, politically conscious constituency. The Irish of Newburyport, and later immigrant groups as well, eventually attained these requisites, but only after long years of struggle.

Like their fathers, these youths tended to be transient members of the community, and migration seems to have influenced their occupational adjustment in much the same way. A certain number of working class youths who had already attained some occupational mobility in the community left Newburyport during these years, but the net effect of emigration was to improve the occupational distribution of the group as a whole by removing a disproportionately large number of the least successful. The persistence of these laborers' sons (Table 5) varied roughly by age: very young children and men above thirty tended to be relatively stable members of the community; boys in their teens and twenties were most likely to move on. The persistence rates of sons of native-born laborers were generally, but not uniformly, higher than those of immigrant children. None of these variations can be clearly attributed to changes in the occupational structure.

FATHERS AND SONS

This survey of the career patterns of Newburyport laborers and their sons in the 1850–1880 period suggests the following conclusions. *

1. Unskilled manual laborers characteristically remained common laborers; the odds that an unskilled laborer living in Newburyport would hold the same lowly position ten years later were at least two to one throughout this period. The sons of these laborers, by contrast, typically became semiskilled workmen; no more than one in four inherited the exact occupation of his father and remained in it.

2. Relatively few of the adult laborers studied worked their way up into a position in a skilled craft—approximately one in ten. The sons of these men were considerably more successful in penetrating the skilled trades, at least after 1860; the 1870 and 1880 figures for sons in their twenties or older holding skilled jobs range from 17 to 37 percent.

3. The contrast between generations was less sharp at the top of the occupational scale. Entry into a nonmanual occupation was almost as difficult for the son of a common laborer as for his father. Since working class families frequently found education for their children a luxury, this is not surprising. The possibility of purchasing a farm or opening a small business existed for both generations; approximately one laborer in ten was able to do this in the three decades studied.

4. The composition of the Newburyport working class was highly unstable. Large numbers of unskilled workmen drifted into the community, but only a minority remained for long. Migration was an important mechanism of occupational adjustment in that it was selective; the successful were less likely to leave than the unsuccessful.

5. Foreign-born workmen and their sons were handicapped in the occupational competition. The sons, however, experienced fewer obstacles

---

* It must be remembered, of course, that these conclusions refer not to the entire working class population of the community but to *unskilled* laborers and their sons. Recent mobility research suggests the likelihood that an investigation of the career patterns of *skilled* families would have revealed substantially greater movement into nonmanual occupations. Presumably it would also have disclosed evidence of downward occupational mobility, since skilled workmen (unlike common laborers) have status to lose.

to occupational mobility than their fathers; ethnic differences in inter-generational occupational mobility were narrowing somewhat by 1880.

6. Adult laborers employed in Newburyport in 1850 had somewhat greater prospects for occupational advance than those who arrived after 1850. In the case of the sons of these men, however, the trend was in the opposite direction. Some four fifths of the laborers' sons who entered the labor market during the 1850's found semiskilled positions; while the shrinking of semiskilled opportunities after 1860 forced some of these youths back into unskilled jobs, an equally large group rose into skilled and nonmanual callings.

Thus we can conclude that while these laborers and their sons experienced a good deal of occupational mobility, only in rare cases was it mobility very far up the social ladder. The occupational structure was fluid to some degree, but the barriers against moving more than one notch upward were fairly high. Success of the kind achieved by Stephen Fowle was attainable, but only the few were able to grasp it.

6

Immigration and Political Life

MICHAEL PARENTI

Historians of immigration rarely play down the contributions of their subjects to American society. Traditionally they have claimed that all groups, melted down, mixed up, and stirred in, formed a durable alloy. More recently they have abandoned the melting pot and have adopted a cultural-pluralistic view that sees each group as contributing strength while maintaining its own identity. Other writers have despised immigrants as the source of radical notions, political corruption, and few positive contributions. Michael Parenti, a political scientist who takes neither a romantic nor a hostile view, assesses the impact of immigration on American life.

THE RECEPTION

There are few nations that do not experience conflicts in their belief systems or disparity between a professed ideal and existing practice. The reception the United States historically has accorded the newcomer is a case in point. From its earliest days, America never quite succeeded in making up its mind about the immigrant. Writing to a group of Irish immigrants in 1783, George Washington articulated the humane sentiment: "The bosom of America is open to receive not only the Opulent and respectable Stranger, but the oppressed and persecuted of all Nations and Religions . . ." Yet Washington proved less than consistent when

From *The Age of Industrialism in America: Essays in Social Structure and Cultural Values*, edited by Frederic Cople Jaher (New York: The Free Press, 1968), pp. 79–95. Footnotes omitted. Reprinted with permission of The Macmillan Company. © 1968 by the Free Press, a Division of The Macmillan Company.

he wrote to Adams: "My opinion, with respect to immigration, is that except of useful mechanics and some particular descriptions of men or professions, there is no need of encouragement . . . for [immigrants settled in a group] retain the language, habits and principles (good or bad) which they bring with them." A similar ambivalence was betrayed by Jefferson who on one occasion spoke of "a home for the oppressed" and another time, in far less sanguine spirit, argued that immigrants would become "a heterogeneous, incoherent, distracted mob," ready either to support despotic rulers or "imbibe principles of extreme licentiousness."

For the next century and a half, America remained the asylum for "the huddled masses" and at the same time, the breeding ground for xenophobic diatribes and exclusionist agitation. In retrospect, the virulent nativist pressures of the nineteenth century accomplished surprisingly little. A sparsely populated country, seeking fulfillment of its manifest destiny through territorial expansion and industrial production, was not yet prepared to deny itself this ready and necessary supply of manpower. Free immigration, a practice existing since the beginning of the nation's history, was not easily discarded. But before the turn of the century, as an omen of things to come, Congress had restricted Chinese laborers. By the eve of World War I, the deep South and far West had become the most vociferous restrictionist regions. The twentieth century began with eugenics and the Nordic cult very much in vogue. Racist apprehensions had spread and the South and West felt no desire to contend with large masses of immigrant voters. Southeastern Europeans, often considered less than white, were seen as only adding to the threat already posed by Japanese, Chinese, and Negroes.

Much of America found itself recoiling before the forces of a raw industrialism typified by the growth of trusts and giant corporations, the amassing of great fortunes for the few amidst continuing hardship for the many, and the spread of squalor, congestion, and poverty in old cities and new factory towns. The very tone and texture of community living, all that made life seem worthwhile, appeared to be threatened.

Well before the census of 1920 revealed that city-dwellers were the new majority, rural-white-Protestant America sought to maintain its superiority in race, religion, and politics. Highly visible because of their foreign attributes and vast numbers, the immigrants became the target for much of the rural resentment against the harsh and mindless upheavals of industrial America. Minority groups were undesirable, first, because of their alien qualities and, second, because they added to the size and power of the city and allegedly aggravated its worse features, viz., crime, corruption, and Catholicism. Within the city, itself, the immigrant's presence only seemed to increase the survival hazards faced by urban workers. The American worker, too often finding himself odd man out in a tight job market "could see alien labor, content with a lower standard of living, taking over more and more of the work which American hands had formerly performed." The immigration laws of 1921 and 1924 marked a decisive victory for exclusionist forces; the "national origins quota system" incorporated into law the popular myth of Anglo-Teutonic supremacy and southeastern European and nonwhite inferiority, reaffirmed and codified over a generation later in the Mc-Carran-Walter Act. The floodgates were locked but the problems faced by the millions of newcomers who had already entered the United States were not as simply resolved.

ETHNIC CONSCIOUSNESS

During the era of the great migrations, over 25 million people settled in this country, more than half of whom arrived between 1900 and 1914. By the end of World War I, immigrants and their children composed 38.4 per cent of the population, or more than one out of every three residents of the United States. About three-fourths of them lived in urban areas. Preemption of the land by earlier nineteenth-century settlers is the reason usually offered to explain why millions of former peasants settled in cities rather than on farms. More likely, the immigrants chose the cities because they had little liking for the land, many of them having fled the oppressive, impoverished rural life of the old world to find fortune in the great cities across the ocean. For most, the very strangeness of their new surroundings caused them to huddle together, and out of necessity and desire, they chose the urban ghettoes. Of those who had the interest, the fortitude, and the capital needed for an agrarian venture, many found the isolated life of American farms, so different from the village life of European peasantry, to be insufferable. They soon returned to the initial urban settlement.

During the early years in America, the first generation was without any real national identity, the predominant in-group feeling being *campanilismo* or provincialism. The Poznaniskers and Mazhevoers did not consider themselves natives of Poland. The Calabresians, Neapolitans, and Sicilians were more cognizant of their provincial antagonisms than of a national bond. German Jews stood aloof from the Sephardim and from the Ashkenazim who, themselves, were subdivided by various regional Yiddish identities. Provincialism was the spirit among those who came from Greece, Albania, Syria, Lithuania, Portugal, Estonia, Armenia, Serbia, Bohemia, and almost all other regions in Europe. Neighborhoods and fraternal societies were organized along lines of provincial consanguinity. Writing of the Greeks, Theodor Saloutos describes a situation characteristic of most immigrant groups: "It appeared that every village and minute parish in Greece was represented in the United States by a society with an impressive array of banners, lengthy constitutions and high sounding names. . . . This plethora of organizations unfortunately tended to breed suspicion, mutual antagonism, aloofness, stubbornness, and 'do it alone' attitude. They helped to isolate members from strangers and to divide Greek from Greek."

With the passage of time, regional prejudices were slowly submerged in the common problems of acculturation. Thrown together in crowded urban neighborhoods, the former provincials experienced a degree of intermingling unknown in the far-flung regions of the old world. Foreign language newspapers appeared written in the national tongue rather than in some regional dialect. Contacts with the American world emphasized to the immigrant his kinship with compatriots who, regardless of provincial differences, were in many ways closer to him than were other people. Defamatory epithets and discriminatory practices were applied democratically to all the group's members by a host society indifferent to provincial distinctions.

While ethnic identity expanded to include broader reference groups, ethnic subculture shrank in the face of new world conditions and exigencies. The immigrant cultures are said to have become part of a unique American blend. If, in fact, there was a "melting pot," it more often was intended to operate as a "smelting furnace . . . to burn out the alien culture elements like slag from the pure metal of American culture." The contributions of the newcomers were substantial when measured in terms of manpower, talent, and occupational skills, but there seems little reason to assume they contributed greatly of their original cultures. A distinction should be drawn between the considerable impact made by ethnics as individuals and the extremely modest impact of minority cultures on established Anglo-American norms. Since the early days of the Republic, the dominion of Anglo-American cultural styles, roles, values, law, and language has never seriously been threatened. Certainly a structured, ongoing American culture was clearly visible to de Tocqueville in the 1830s. With few exceptions, as the immigrants and their children made their contributions as laborers, farmers, doctors, lawyers, and educators, they did so on terms set by the dominant culture. The inability to acculturate, that is, to adopt the necessary social and linguistic skills of the Anglo-American world, severely limited any advancement or participation within that world.

Not only were the immigrants unable to exert substantial influence on American culture, they failed to preserve their own cultures. America has never been a patchwork of autonomous cultural enclaves. Nearly every group arriving in this country attempted to reconstruct their old-world communities. With the exception of a few isolated sectarian groups, such as the Amish they failed. If culture is to be represented as the accumulated styles, solutions, and practices that represent a society's total adjustment to its physical and social environment, then it would follow that no specific cultural system can be uprooted and transplanted to another environment without some substantial change. After the shock of departing from old-world communities immigrants were confronted with an established American culture possessing indigenous forms differing in many respects from their own. The newcomers faced heavy social pressure to conform, the instruments of conformity becoming ever more efficient with the growth of industrialization, mass communication, and public education. Some in-group norms and residual subcultural patterns have survived, but immigrant cultures as self-contained systemic entities began to disintegrate soon after the initial settlement. Certainly by the second generation, valuations, work habits, family life, consumption and recreational patterns, material goals, language and political loyalties assumed an unmistakably American stamp, reflecting the new-world diversity of class, income, and locale more faithfully than the old-world diversity of cultures.

If the national minorities were unable to preserve their respective cultural autonomies, does this mean they were indistinguishably absorbed into American society? Were such the case, ethnic groups would have hardly earned the attention accorded them by historians, sociologists, and politicians. Industrialization, the mass media, public education, urbanization, and suburbanization imposed a uniform imprint on the lives of nationality groups, but ethnic feelings persisted. Thus half a century after immigration, distinct minority ecological and identificational patterns are still discernible. The national minorities may have adapted themselves to the Amercan practices available to them within the boundaries of their class and locale, but they usually have remained in close associational and social contact with others of their kind. In neighborhood, marriage, extended kinship relations, recreational and peer group activities, church and formal organizations, even at work or school or in the sectarian hospital, old age home and, finally, the sectarian cemetery, the ethnic could live and die within the confines of his group, and many of them did. Whereas acculturation moved rapidly toward American norms, assimilation—that is, actual interpersonal social integration—developed much less certainly.

There are several explanations for the tenacity of in-group awareness. The limitations of social distance and the natural range of interpersonal exposure inevitably brought the immigrant and the second-generation offspring into closer and more frequent contact with other group members. Early life experiences and contacts with the wider world often left ethnics with a preference for those of similar backgrounds. Frequently the group, itself, as personified by family and friends, discouraged intimate associations with people of different stock. At one time or another, spokesmen for most minority groups have expressed their fear of extinction through assimilation. Frequently, even the socially mobile member, because of family attachments and other such positive sentiments, preserved a strong identification with his group even though he had no contact with, and little knowledge of, the old culture. In a mass society often described as threatened by a "lack of belongingness" and "alienation," an ethnic identity, something larger than the self yet smaller than the nation, is not without its attractions. Finally, and most importantly, the native population, whilst insisting that nationality groups "Americanize," a process entailing the destruction of customs and appearances offensive to native sensibilities, never manifested an equally persistent desire to see the ethnics enter Anglo-American primary group life. And few things so effectively assured the persistency of in-group awareness as out-group rejection. "When the natives combined to crush what they considered the undue influence of alien groups," Hansen observes, "they committed a tactical error, for the newcomers, far from being crushed, were prompted to consolidate their hitherto scattered forces."

Frequently the intolerant host society was not composed of native white Protestants but of other ethnic groups, especially in the urban centers. Generally the old-stock Yankee opinion of the Irish became very much the Irish opinion of the Italians and the Italian opinion of the Puerto Ricans. Each group saw the succeeding newcomers as "trying to take over," "lowering our standards," and "refusing to Americanize." This willingness to embrace the conventional discriminatory attitudes toward other groups is partly an expected consequence of becoming American, or wanting to become American by assuming the posture of the dominant culture and identifying with those who "belong," even at the expense of less fortunate groups. Bigotry among minorities reflected with disheartening accuracy an awareness of the pecking order accorded minority groups in American society. In their treatment of each other, minorities proved themselves to be no more virtuous and no less American than the native-born.

CLASS CONSCIOUSNESS

The immigrants and their children provided much of the market and the labor for the increasing services, trades, and crafts and for the titanic industrial growth America has experienced since the late nineteenth century. "We built this country" has been claimed, at one time or another, by almost every group of substantial size, and perhaps with good cause. For those who crossed the Atlantic soon became grist for the industrial mill, paying more than their full measure of misery and deprivation. Crowded into filthy and dilapidated tenements, living without privacy, sunlight, or elemental sanitary conditions, the immigrant and his children toiled from dawn to dusk in sweatshops, "crouched over their work, in a fetid air . . . hunger-hollowed faces" and "shoulders narrowed with consumption, girls of fifteen as old as grandmothers, who had never eaten a bit of meat in their lives;" ". . . heavy brooding men, tired anxious women, thinly dressed, unkempt little girls, and frail, joyless lads passed along, half awake, not uttering a word, as they hurried to the factories." The work was filthy, exhausting, noisy, mindless, endless and often dangerous; rarely a day passed in large factories when a man was not killed or severely maimed because of inadequate safety conditions.

Yet if proletariat misery was the lot of most, a militant proletariat consciousness was not the corresponding ideological response. Nor was there much trace of reforming zeal in the ethnic population. The same barriers that made the native-born eschew contacts with the immigrants left the latter indifferent to social action programs. Indeed, the immigrants were more often the victims than the benefactors, more often the targets than the allies of reform movements. Middle-class reformers concerned with moral uplifting of public and private life, the abolition of corruption, the extension of civil service, and the destruction of the urban party machine offered little to the nationality groups. The immigrant communities and most of the foreign language press were lukewarm or even hostile toward Populism, urban Progressivism, women's suffrage, Negro rights, Prohibition, and in many instances, trade unionism.

Even when, as with socialism, intentions were of the best and protest directed itself to the objective material conditions of urban workers, other sociocultural and psychological forces militated against change. The socialist movement of the early twentieth century, a melange of reformers, muckrakers, populists, Marxists, syndicalists, and a handful of Social Gospel Christians and millionaire converts, was brought to the height of its appeal—and 897,000 votes—in 1912 by Eugene Victor Debs. "Far from being an exotic aberration or an imported disease like parrot fever," socialism was an indigenous movement. There is no denying that some immigrants played a prominent role in the radical protest. Of the socialist publications before World War I, there were five English and eight foreign-language dailies, 262 English weeklies, and thirty-six foreign-language weeklies. The left wing of the movement found much of its support in the Bolshevik-oriented foreign language federation, especially among coteries of Jews, Russians, and other Slavs.

But those who did respond to the left were a minority of the great mass of immigrants and their children. The linguistic, ethnic, and social distances between the native-born socialist and the ghetto worker were not easily overcome. While pertinent to the ethnic's class condition, the ideology of the left did not easily fit into his *Weltanschauung*. Suspicious of much beyond the home or beyond the ethnic community, tradition-bound and fearful of authority, sometimes entrepreneurial in his aspirations if proletariat in his predicament, longing for security, stability, and gain rather than sacrifice and agitation, the immigrant peasant from Europe was not the best political material.

Furthermore the immigrants, largely Catholic, often shared the hierarchy's suspicion and hostility toward all workers' movements. "Several bishops grew to think of labor unions as socialistic and therefore to be condemned as subversive of the Church and society." While the Church eventually did condone membership in nonsocialistic trade unions, Catholic thought at the turn of the century reflected a "great terror of socialism." Far from intensifying class consciousness with injections of alien radicalism, a favorite xenophobic nightmare of the native stock, the minorities gave the American left little cause for its earlier high anticipations. The failure of American working-class radicalism is at least partly ascribable to the unresponsiveness of the ethnic masses.

According to Marxist theory, the necessary prerequisite of a proletariat movement is some sense of class interest and identification, which eventually leads to cohesive and militant class action. But such a theory anticipates a working class enjoying a common national culture and common history. In the pluralistic cacophany that developed in America, nativist workers opposed immigrants, and immigrants opposed other immigrants. Just as warfare in Europe turned more on struggles between nations and between national groups than upon a class conflict transcending national boundaries, so in America, more thought and energy were expended on divisive interethnic competitions for jobs, neighborhoods, social standing, and group recognition than was ever directed toward the development of a common class identity. Another man was more likely to be seen as a Polak, kike, dago, mick, or hunkie than as a fellow worker in the proletariat cause. (It might be noted parenthetically that in the nativist South, relatively untouched by immigration, racial animosities served a similar and perhaps even more decisive regressive function by playing off lower class whites against blacks, thereby aborting Southern Populism.)

Not only did the various national groups conflict with each other, but, as noted earlier, the provincial segmentations that obtained with any one group through much of the first generation made concerted effort that much more unlikely. Old world animosities were reenacted on the new soil, newly developed intergroup bigotries arose, and ethnic associational differences persisted making for a highly vertically stratified urban population. Under such conditions of intra- and inter-ethnic cleavage, the forces of industrialization, urbanization, and political protest were not sufficiently potent to achieve a militant class consciousness. Indeed, to the extent that the minorities Americanized, it was in the direction of American bourgeois standards and valuations.

Finally, to borrow a phrase from psychology, it might be said that the immigrant worker lacked a sufficient "future-orientation." Under the socialist state to come, social equality and material well-being would be secured, but meanwhile, who would alleviate the urgent plight of the immigrant family? Who would give a helping hand now? It may be for this reason alone that the minorities bypassed the future glories of the Internationale for the more immediate emoluments of Tammany Hall.

POLITICAL LIFE

In the period from 1875 to 1940, millions migrated to these shores, became regular voters, and raised millions of children who also became regular voters. In this same period the urban political machine flourished as never before, or since. "Once the immigrant base finally began to disappear," Cornwell observes, "so did most of the bosses of the classic model. In a very real sense then, the one phenomenon was dependent upon the other." Immigration is not the sole factor in the rise and decline of urban political machines but it is doubtful that the old-style bosses, dependent as they were on an acquiescent and pliable mass base, could have prevailed for so long without a supply of succeeding waves of impoverished culturally alienated, socially unequipped, non-ideological—but swiftly enfranchised—immigrants.

Although most students of urban politics recognize the contributions made by the city machines popular perception to this day is still largely colored by the excoriations of muckrakers and early civic reformers. In E. E. Schattschneider's words "power, patronage and plunder" were the boss's exclusive *raison d'être*. Proponents of this view either pity the nationality groups for being dupes or chastise them for being the accomplices of a corrupt system. Moral judgments, however, should not preclude analytic explanations. That the immigrant became the boss's ready collaborator was due less to venality than to necessity. We must remind ourselves of that extraordinary time in American history, when millions of indigent aliens were literally dumped onto our city streets without the barest provision made for their settlement, employment, or survival. Inadequate or, more often, nonexistent public services and chaotic antiquated governmental structure were the most distinguishing features of earlier municipalities.

In an era of ruthless, boundless capitalism, enfeebled unionism, limited and often discriminatory private charity, and indifferent and insufficient government, the only social agency that filled the vacuum and answered to the pressing needs of a large dependent population was the political machine. Jobs, housing, emergency relief, minor welfare services, personal favors, outings and other recreational activities, and instant naturalization were among the services performed by the party organization. In return the immigrant only too gratefully lent his support to organization candidates. In terms of the services performed, the fee exacted was not an unreasonable one. The relationship was more symbiotic than exploitative.

If the party's voting resources came from the ethnic population, its financial resources were siphoned from the public treasury and from the sale of municipal properties, permits, licenses, and contracts to the business community for a variety of legal and sometimes illegal enterprises. As broker for the businessman and patron of the ethnic, the political machine used its political power to extract financial support, and its financial power to win political support. It was probably this system that prompted Frederic Schuman to describe politics as that process whereby the politician gets money from the rich and votes from the poor on the promise that he will protect each from the other.

The result was a crude, inefficient, and frequently corrupt improvization of a social welfare system, involving a minor redistribution of income. As in most welfare systems, the lower-strata groups paid a good part of the expenses in the form of widely diffused taxes and in the costs that business passed on to the consumer. But such cost was not readily discernible, whereas the particular and personalized benefits allocated by the district captain were highly visible and readily appreciated.

To treat only the material services, however, is to overlook other important functions performed by the local political system. In a world of threatening, faceless forces, the political club was a friend. Even for those individuals who did not materially benefit, and even in instances when the local politician could not perform a miracle, the fact that there was someone to go to who cared enough to listen and "look into it" was no small comfort. Most of the activities that district leaders considered of the utmost importance, such as attending funerals, putting in a good word with the judge, offering moral support, knowing people personally, complimenting people, inquiring about family illnesses, reminding constituents that you are available if ever needed and keeping "your door open at all times," were explicitly designed to maximize this sheltering, comforting role of the politico. Many social institutions afford a sense of security by "just being there" and enjoy a good portion of their support on this account; the political club was—and in some areas still is—a case in point.

Furthermore, in facilitating naturalization, inducing electoral participation, and conferring a citizen's identity upon the immigrant and his children, the party hastened political acculturation. The politico, himself, was sometimes aware of this function, as erstwhile Tammany chieftain, Richard Crocker, testified:

> More than one half [of the people of New York] are of foreign birth. . . . They do not speak our language, they do not know our laws, they are the raw material with which we have to build up the state. . . . There is no denying the service which Tammany has rendered to the Republic. There is no such organization for taking hold of the untrained, friendless man and converting him into a citizen. Who else would do it if we did not? . . . There is not a mugwump in the city who would shake hands with him.

Election campaigns, voting, and friendly contacts with the political club gave the ethnic some small sense of participation and practice as an American, some tenuous feeling that his voice counted with the powers that be, and some claim to legitimacy and equal status.

For over a century, nativists' anxieties rested on the unexamined presumption that immigrants and their offspring would be slow to discard foreign loyalties and unwilling to attach themselves to American symbols and institutions. As late as 1914, there were officials who believed that the United States could never intervene in the European conflict without bringing on a civil war between the large German and English elements in our population. In war or peace, the minorities were suspect. The danger of contamination and subversion from alien ideologies remained an historical preoccupation. Palmer raids, alien deportation, denaturalization, surveillance, detention, and culturally intolerant federal, state, and local programs for the propagation of "100 per cent Americanism" were symptomatic of this phobia. Yet, ironically enough, no other nation has ever absorbed such a vast number of foreigners and their children with so little challenge to its basic unity. The ethnics internalized a loyalty to the core political symbols, values, and institutions of the American polity. One of the factors determining the positive identification to the political system was the political system itself. Political life is seldom a merely dependent variable. Without the grass roots, egalitarian, and inclusive features of American politics it is difficult to imagine what course minority loyalties and political activity might have taken.

As part of its assimilative function, the political club served as an avenue of upward mobility for some of the more ambitious sons of immigrants. Andrew Hacker reminds us that "it is only since 1940 that banks, investment houses, the diplomatic service and established industries and universities have opened their positions of power and responsibility to others than those of old American antecedents. Twenty years ago Americans of Irish, Italian, Slav and Jewish antecedents were simply not recruited, admitted or welcomed." Until these new social areas were opened, opportunities for ethnic upward mobility were largely confined to the worlds of sports, entertainment, marginal service trades, the rackets, and politics. Seen in this light, the "balanced ticket," so often bemoaned as un-American because it gave more weight to the candidate's tribal identity than to his other qualifications, could not have been more American. What better way of getting ahead? And what firmer assurance of the group's Americanism, social respectability, legitimacy, and worth than accession to positions of power, prominence, and public responsibility. If the old stock did not see it that way, at least the nationality groups did.

An analysis of immigrant political life usually begins and ends with a discussion of the big-city machine. Nationality groups, however, played a crucial role in national politics by lending massive support to federal decision-makers who were more responsive to the problems of an urban industrialized society than to the images and myths of an agrarian or laissez-faire past. The 1928 election gave the first clear sign that something new was happening in national politics. The defeat, in the Democratic party, of the forces of prohibitionism, western ruralism, and Protestant old-stock respectability, and fundamentalist bigotry, by the big-city, wet, Irish-Catholic Al Smith, a lower East Side emissary of the sidewalk masses, was symbolic of the emergence of a new generation, and was the inevitable reflection of "a little matter of birth rates."

The thirteen million foreigners who arrived in America between 1900 and 1914 began their political participation in growing numbers after the first world war. Their children, whose numbers were substantially greater, were to reach voting age in full force between 1930 and

1940. Smith gleaned the early benefits of this demographic upsurge. He laid the foundation for a new coalition within the Democratic party, shifting the center of gravity from the rural South and West to the big cities of the industrial North. Until 1928, the Northeast had the most consistent Republican record and the greatest number of foreign-born. After 1928, this same region harbored many of the most heavily concentrated Democratic counties in the nation. Smith was a catalyst for that "other half" of America. His emergence as a presidential candidate stirred a new sense of political consciousness in millions of minority-group members, and was for them a symbolic affirmation of their own personal worth and a refutation of their marginal status.

If the personal appeal of Al Smith was not enough in 1928, the expanding ranks of second-generation voters and a catastrophic depression were sufficient to bring the Democratic party to power four years later. The New Deal era saw a changing social temper in the nation: a new class militancy born of despair and depression coupled with a widespread hostility toward the financial-industrial powers that seemed to have brought America to ruin. It was during this time that the first significant steps were taken toward ending the long-standing ethnic divisions among American workers. The day was passing when mining companies could place groups of different nationalities in each mine in the correct assumption that a work force segmented along ethnic lines would be difficult to organize. "Much of the A. F. of L.'s reluctance to embark on a real organizing drive in the mass production industries," Lubell notes, "reflected the dislike of the 'aristocrats of labor' in the skilled crafts for the immigrant 'rubbish'." With the encouragement of a friendly Administration in Washington, and the passage of the NRA, particularly section 7a recognizing the workers' right to organize, industry-wide unionization of unskilled workers began. The conservative craft unions, which had so long monopolized and constricted the field of organized labor, now had to contend with an industrial unionism that brought large numbers of native and ethnic workers under the same banner. The acculturated second generation was coming into its own; in earlier years immigrants might have been used as strikebreakers, but more and more of their American-born sons were joining the CIO.

The regional and ethnic considerations of previous elections now shared the political stage with a growing class feeling. The 1936 election saw a realignment in both parties. Always more favorably disposed toward the party of Coolidge and Hoover, large propertied and financial interests moved with even greater solidarity than usual into the Republican camp, while urban workers of all regions and ethnic identities rallied in still greater numbers to Roosevelt's support. But the heavy pluralities of the urban-ethnic masses in the great cities formed the center phalanx of the Democratic coalition. In retrospect, the year 1928 marks the last victory of small-town, old-stock Protestant America.

CONCLUSION

This essay has attempted to investigate the ways in which the late immigration was and was not consequential to American life. Here we might summarize some of the central propositions:

Contrary to popular thought, immigrants contributed only a negligible element of their original cultures to an ongoing cultural system established well before their arrival. There is little evidence to support the myth of a "melting pot." The "alien cultural challenge" existed more in the fearful anticipations of the native population than in reality. By the same token, contrary to nativist phobic preoccupations, the newcomers did not contaminate America with alien political radicalism. During their acculturation, they developed a positive identity to American core political symbols and institutions, and a loyalty to the American nation, demonstrated in both war and peace. Their general political orientation betrayed a marked social conservatism. While popular anxiety has concentrated on the potentially centrifugal effects of aliens and alien loyalties, the remarkable fact is that this nation did absorb so many millions in the span of a generation with no serious challenge to its basic unity.

Although the old world cultures did not survive as systemic entities much beyond the immigrant first generation, identificational pluralism persisted into the second and even the third generations. Even as the minorities considered themselves loyal Americans, they retained their ethnic identifications with a tenacity that may be as much attributable to the bigotry encountered beyond the group as to the attachments and enjoyments experienced within the group. At the very time exploitation of immigrant labor was most ruthlessly practiced, intergroup conflicts with the native-born or with other minority groups had the effect of retarding the ethnic's class consciousness and class protest. In short, ethnic in-group attachments and intergroup rivalries worked to the detriment of lower-strata material interests.

The popular view that the nationality groups were to blame for the political strength of urban political machines is correct insofar as any group might be "blamed" for lending massive support to the one agency that performed a variety of material and psychological functions on its behalf. The view that the city machines retarded the Americanization of the nationality groups seems to have little basis in fact and rests mainly on unexamined moral judgments. What evidence we have indicates that the local clubs fostered the political acculturation of minority groups in a variety of ways. The political parties hastened the political education and experience of the minorities, while the political system in general became an arena for the maximization of ethnic interests, and the realm in which the marginal minorities could challenge the hegemony of established Protestant America.

We are left with the conclusion that the major impact the immigrants and their children have had on American life is to be measured in terms of their numbers, labor, and votes rather than in terms of their alleged old world ideologies or new world corruptions. As workers, consumers, and city-dwellers, the minorities contributed massively to an industrialization that transformed America from a rural to an urban civilization. As voters they gave strategic support to an era of federal activism, thereby helping to move the nation toward new public commitments. The transition from antiquated laissez faire capitalism to the reality of social welfare programs is not over; in many ways it is only beginning.

7

Middle-Class Families and Urban Violence: The Experience of a Chicago Community in the Nineteenth Century

RICHARD SENNETT

Late nineteenth-century Americans who lived in the rapidly expanding cities often confronted violence. Richard Sennett has studied their reaction to it. For his book *Families Against the City: Middle Class Homes of Industrial Chicago, 1872–1890* (1970), Sennett, a sociologist, carefully analyzed the 1880 manuscript census for the forty-block area of Union Park. Utilizing that study as a base and also using concepts from social psychology, Sennett suggests that Union Park residents' over-reaction to violence was rooted in their intensive family life.

This study seeks the hidden connections between two seemingly disparate phenomena in a quiet middle-class neighborhood of Chicago in the late nineteenth century: the family patterns of the people of the community and the peculiar response made by men living there to the eruption of

From *Nineteenth-Century Cities: Essays in the New Urban History,* edited by Stephan Thernstrom and Richard Sennett (New Haven: Yale University Press, 1969), pp. 386–87, 388, 397, 399–418. Reprinted with omissions by permission of the publisher. © 1969 by Yale University.

violence in their midst. In imagining how the structure of family life was related to the character of men's reaction to violence, I have tried to recapture some of the subtlety of what it was like to be a middle-class city dweller during this era of rapid urban growth.

In the years 1886 and 1888 an epidemic of violence broke out in this quiet neighborhood of Chicago. The striking feature of this epidemic lay not in the violent events themselves but in the reaction of shopkeepers, store clerks, accountants, and highly skilled laborers to the disorder suddenly rampant among their sedate homes. Their reaction to violence was impassioned to an extent that in retrospect seems unwarranted by events; indeed, it is the contrast between the limited character of the disorder and the sense residents had of being overwhelmingly threatened by anarchy that suggests that the response could have been a product of larger, seemingly unrelated social forces, such as the structure of family life. . . .

During the middle 1880s, it was in modest, cheerless Union Park that a series of unexpected events broke out. A bloody encounter between laborers and police took place on its borders during the Haymarket Riot of 1886, to be followed eighteen months later by a series of highly expert robberies in the community, a crime wave that culminated in the murder of a leading Union Park resident. Union Park reacted by holding a whole class—the poor, and especially the immigrant poor—responsible for the course of unique and rather narrow events. . . .

The effect of the riot and the train of burglaries and murder was to put the citizens in a frame of mind where only the closure of the community through constant surveillance and patrolling would reassure them. Indeed, the characteristics of their reaction to violence could only lead to such a voluntary isolation: everyone "knew" immediately what was wrong; and what was wrong was overwhelming; it was nothing less than the power of the "foreigner," the outsider who had suddenly become dominant in the city. Isolation, through garrisons and police patrols, was the only solution.

Union Park held onto its middle-class character until the middle of the 1890s; there was no immediate desertion by respectable people of the area in the wake of the violence: where else in a great city, asked one citizen, was it safe to go? Everywhere the same terror was possible.

The contrast between the limited character of civil disturbance and the immediate perception of that disturbance as the harbinger of an unnameable threat coming from a generalized enemy is a theme that binds together much research on urban disorders. . . .

The problem of the Union Park experience was the citizenry's inability to connect the facts seen to the facts as elements of what people knew was a correct interpretation. Expecting "seething passions" to erupt hysterically, the middle-class people of Chicago and their police were somehow immune to the spectacle they should have enjoyed, that of the workers becoming bored with the inflammatory talk of their supposed leaders [at Haymarket Square]. The expectations of a seething rabble had somehow to be fulfilled, and so the police themselves took the first step. After the shooting was over, the respectable people of Chicago became in turn inflamed. This blind passion in the name of defending the city from blind passion is the phenomenon that needs to be explained. A similar contradiction occurred in the series of robberies a half year later as well. As in the riot, the facts of the rationality of the enemy and his limited purpose, although acknowledged, were not absorbed; he was felt to be something else, a nameless, elusive terror, all-threatening. And the people reacted with a passion equal to his.

This mystifying condition, familiar now in the voices heard from the "New Right," is what I should like to explain, not through a sweeping theory that binds the past to the present, but through a theory that explains this peculiar reaction in terms of strains in the family life of the Union Park people. What I would like to explore—and I certainly do not pretend to prove it—is how, in an early industrial city, the fears of the foreign masses by a middle-class group may have reflected something other than the actual state of interaction between bourgeoisie and proletariat. These fears may have reflected instead the impact of family life on the way the people like those in Union Park understood their places in the city society.

Studies of overreaction to limited stimuli have centered, for the most part, on the idea of a "frustration-aggression syndrome." This ungainly phrase was given a clear definition in one of the early classic works of American social psychology, *Frustration and Aggression* (1939). The authors wrote that

> aggression is always a consequence of frustration. More specifically . . . the occurrence of aggressive behavior always presupposes the existence of frustration and, contrariwise, the existence of frustration always leads to some form of aggression.

Applied in terms of social class, this frustration-aggression syndrome implies that when a group fails to achieve goals it desires, or when it is unable to maintain a position it covets, it becomes aggressive, and searches out objects on which it can blame its failure. This simple, clear idea [Talcott] Parsons has applied to the formation of the Nazi party in Germany: the fall in status in the 1920s of fixed-income, middle-class groups breeding an aggressive desire to get back at their enemies, without knowing, or really caring, who they were. [Seymour Martin] Lipset has incorporated elements of the same idea in his essay on working-class authoritarianism in the United States after the Second World War. And of course the concept is now used to explain the hostility of lower middle-class whites toward blacks: the whites who have failed to rise high in the economic system they believe in are said to make blacks "aggression objects" of the frustration they themselves have suffered.

If it is true, as this syndrome of frustration-aggression suggests, that in the character one ascribes to one's enemy lies a description of something in one's own experience, the nature of the fear of lower-class foreigners among Union Park families might tell something about the Union Park community itself. The Union Park men, during the time of the riot and robberies, accused their chosen enemies of being, first, lawless anarchists, which was transmuted, secondly, to being pushed by their base passions outside the bounds of acceptable behavior, which resolved itself, finally, to being emotionally out of control. If the poor were reasonable, if they were temperate, ran the argument, these violent things would not have come to pass.

What about the Union Park people themselves, then? Were they masters of themselves? A study I have recently completed on the family patterns of the Union Park people during the decades of the 1870s and '80s may throw some light on the question of stability and purposefulness in their lives: it is the dimension of stability in these family patterns, I believe, that shaped sources of the reaction to violence.

INTENSIVE FAMILY LIFE

In 1880, on a forty-square-block territory of Union Park, there lived 12,000 individuals in approximately 3,000 family units. These family units were of three kinship types: single-member families, where one person lived alone without any other kin; nuclear families, consisting of a husband, wife, and their unmarried children; and extended families, where to the nuclear unit was added some other relative—a brother or sister of the parents, a member of a third generation, or a son or daughter who was married and lived with his spouse in the parental home. The most common form of the extended family in Union Park was that containing "collateral kin," that is, unmarried relatives of the same generation as the husband or wife.

The dominant form of family life in Union Park was nuclear, for 80% of the population lived in such homes, with 10% of the population living alone in single-member families, and the remaining 10% living in extended family situations. A father and mother living alone with their growing children in an apartment or house was the pervasive household condition. There were few widowed parents living with their children in either nuclear or extended homes, and though the census manuscripts on which my study of the year 1880 is based were inexact at this point, there appeared to be few groups of related families living in separate dwellings but in the same neighborhood.

Is this nuclear-family dominance a special characteristic of middle-class life in this era? At the Joint Center for Urban Studies, I was fortunate in working with other researchers in this field to coordinate census measures of class and family form that could be used comparatively across different studies. Comparison with these other studies, as well as within the limited range of social groups in Union Park, convinces me that this kind of family form was not a middle-class phenomenon. Within Union Park, the 80% dominance of the nuclear families held in lower social strata (of which enough existed to measure and test statistically, since the population as a whole was so large—about 25% of the community fell into a working-class category, excluding the servants in the homes of the other 75%) and throughout the range of middle-class groups. In Lynn Lees' data on an Irish working-class district in London in 1860, it similarly appeared that about 80% of her community's population lived in nuclear family configurations, 10% in single-member families, and 10% in extended families, virtually the same distribution as was found in Chicago's Union Park in 1880.

Again, the *outer* limits on the size of families in Union Park did seem to be the product of a special class condition. Contrary to the stereotype of the sprawling families of the poor, in Union Park the size of poor families was in its contours similar to the size of the wealthier ones: few families were larger than six members, among rich or poor. Similarly, comparison of family sizes in Union Park to the poor Irish of Lynn Lees' study or to the middle-class area of St. Pancras in London reveals the limits on family size in the three areas to have been the same.

Since family studies of nineteenth-century cities are at this date in a primitive stage, the body of future research may show these present examples to be "sports" or explainable by circumstances researchers do not now understand. Yet it does now seem more fruitful to concentrate on the *function* of nuclear families or on the *function* of families of restricted size in middle-class communities in the great cities of the nineteenth century, rather than to try to locate the conditions of peculiarly middle-class life in the *structural* existence of these family types.

What I did find to be true in Union Park was the following: over the course of time internal conditions of family structure and of family size tended to lead to similar family histories. Nuclear families had characteristic histories similar to the experience of smaller families having from two to four kin members in the 1870s and '80s. Extended families, on the other hand, had histories similar to the experience of the minority of families with four to six kin members during these decades. What made this process subtle was that nuclear families did not tend to be smaller, or extended larger. Family size and family kinship structure seemed rather to be independent structures with parallel internal differences in functioning.

Why and how this was so can be understood by assessing the patterns of the generations of the dominant group of nuclear, small-size families during the year 1880. These families were marked, in the relations between husbands and wives, parents and children, by strong patterns of family cohesion. Whether rich or poor, the young men and women from such homes rarely broke away to live on their own until they themselves were ready to marry and found families, an event that usually occurred when the man was in his early thirties. The families of Union Park, observers of the time noted, were extremely self-contained, did little entertaining, and rarely left the home to enjoy even such modest pleasures as a church social or, for the men, a beer at the local tavern. The small family, containing only parents and their immediate children, resisted the diverse influences of either other kin associations or extensive community contacts. This was the mode of family life that dominated Union Park numerically. These families can be called "intensive families," and their life histories contrasted to families of larger size or more complex kinship. The intensive families would seem to epitomize a defined order of stability among the people of Union Park. Yet, Lynn Lees and I have found some functional differences between Chicago and London in families of this general character.

INSTABILITY THROUGH SEPARATION OR DESERTION

In most census collections in the United States and Britain, the official tabulations of divorce are very low, because the formal breaking of the marital tie was considered a personal disgrace to both partners. But, as Talcott Parsons has demonstrated, these official figures are misleading, since a great deal of unofficial divorce through separation or desertion occurred, at a higher rate, Parsons thinks, than in our own time. One means of detecting this hidden marital disorder in the census is to locate the individuals who were officially married but living without a spouse in the family. This measurement lets in a certain number of "beachhead migrants," men who have come to the city in advance of their families to establish a job and find a house, but in Union Park such men were less common in this category than spouses who were married, living with their children, but not with their husbands (or wives).

In Union Park the number of families involved in such a break was about 10%. But in London, in the middle-class district of St. Pancras, the incidence of such marital separation was one-half of this, or 5%; in the lower-class Irish district Lynn Lees studied, there were less than a third as many marital separations of this type. In all three communities, of course, the official rate of divorce was nearly zero.

The explanation for this comparatively high incidence of marital break in Union Park is obscure, since there are now so few other comparative measures of family conditions behind the official statistics to use. In terms of these Chicago and London communities themselves perhaps the best thing to be said is the simplest: the higher incidence of marital break occurred in a city whose development was exclusively in the industrial era; the lower incidence of such a break occurred in a city for whom industrial production and large bureaucratic enterprises were but one chapter in a very long history.

WORK MOBILITY AND FAMILY STABILITY

Added to this kind of family instability in the community as a whole, my study of intergenerational mobility in work and residence from 1872 to 1890 revealed a complicated, but highly significant pattern of insecurity in the dominant intensive families when compared to the smaller group of less intensive families.

In the nuclear-family homes and in the smaller families the fathers were stable in their patterns of job holding, as a group, over the course of the eighteen years studied; roughly the same proportions of unskilled, skilled, and white-collar workers of various kinds composed the labor force of these nuclear fathers in 1890 as in 1872. Given the enormous growth of Chicago's industrial production, its banking and financial capital, retail trade volume, as well as the proliferation of the population (100% increase each ten years) and the greatly increasing proportion of white-collar pursuits during this time, such stability in job distribution is truly puzzling. Further, this pattern of job holding among the fathers of intensive families was not shared by the fathers in extended families or fathers of larger families living in Union Park. They were mobile up into exclusively bureaucratic, white-collar pursuits, so that by 1890 virtually none of these fathers worked with their hands. Within the range of white-collar occupations, the extended-family fathers and the large-family fathers gradually concentrated in executive and other lesser management pursuits and decreased their numbers in shopkeeping, toward which, stereotypically, they are supposed to gravitate.

Now the differences between fathers and sons in each of these family groups were even more striking. I found the sons in the dominant family homes to be, unlike their fathers, very unstable in their patterns of job holding, with as much movement down into manual pursuits over the course of the eighteen years as movement up within the white-collar occupations. Following the lead of [P.] Blau and [O. D.] Duncan, we might be tempted to explain this pattern of dispersion simply as regression-toward-the-mean of higher status groups intergenerationally. But the sons of extended and large families did not move in this mixed direction. Rather, they followed in the footsteps of their fathers into good white-collar positions, with almost total elimination of manual labor in their ranks over the course of time. This pattern occurred in small-family sons versus large-family sons and in nuclear-family sons versus extended-family sons. The difference in the groups of sons was especially striking in that the starting distribution of the sons in the occupational work force was virtually the *same,* in the measure of family form and in those of family size. [Stephan] Thernstrom has pointed out in the conference discussions for this volume that economic aid between generations of workers ought to manifest itself more at the beginning point in the careers of the young rather than when the older generation has retired and the young have become the principal breadwinners. In Union Park, the fact that both extended-family and nuclear-family sons, both large- and small-family sons, began to work in virtually the same pursuits as their fathers, but then became distinctively different in their patterns of achievement, strongly suggests that something *beyond* monetary help was at work in these families to produce divergences in work experience in the city.

The residence patterns of the generations of the intensive and less intensive families also bear on the issues of stability and instability in the lives of the people of Union Park. Up to the time of violence in the Union Park area, the residence patterns of the two kinds of families, in both the parents' and the sons' generations, were rather similar. In the wake of the violence it appears that, within the parents' generation, there was significant movement back into the Union Park area, whereas for the half decade preceding the disturbances there was a general movement out to other parts of Chicago. It is in the generation of the sons that differences between the two family groups appeared. In the wake of the violence, the sons of large families and of extended families continued the processes of residential break from Union Park initiated during the early years of the 1880 decade. The sons from intensive families did not; in the years following the violence they stopped migrating beyond the boundaries of the community they had known as children, and instead kept closer to their first homes.

TWO THEORIES OF INTENSIVE FAMILY STABILITY

In my study of Union Park, I tried to explain these differences in work experience and in residence in terms of patterns of family life and child nurturance for bourgeois people in a new, immensely dynamic, disordered city. In so doing, my researches led me into a debate that exists between the work of the sociologist Talcott Parsons and the cultural historian Phillippe Aries. For Parsons has argued that the small nuclear family is an adaptive kinship form to the industrial order; the lack of extensive kin obligations and a wide kin circle in this family type means, Parsons has contended, that the kinship unit does not serve as a binding private world of its own, but rather frees the individual to participate in "universalized" bureaucratic structures that are urban-wide and dynamic. Aries has challenged this theory by amassing a body of historical evidence to show that the extended kinship relationships in large families, at least during the period he studied, were actually less sheltering, more likely to push the individual out into the world where he would have to act like a full man on his own at an early age, than the intense, intimate conditions of the nineteenth-century home. In intensive homes, the young person spent a long time in a state of independence under the protection and guidance of his elders. Consequently, argues Aries, the capacity of the young adult from small nuclear homes to deal with the world about him was blunted, for he passed from a period of total shelter to a state in which he was expected to be entirely competent on his own. Aries' attack has been supported for contemporary American urban communities by a variety of studies, the most notable being those of Eugene Litwak and Marvin Sussman, and it has been supported for English cities by the work of Peter Wilmott and Elizabeth Bott.

The data I have collected on Union Park during the early stages of Chicago's industrial-bureaucratic expansion clearly are in line with the argument made by Aries. The young from homes of small scale or from homes where the structure of the family was nuclear and "privatistic," in Aries' phrase, had an ineptness in the work world, and a rootedness to the place of their childhood not found to the same degree among the more complex, or larger-family situations. (I have no desire to argue the moral virtues of this rootedness to community or failure to "make it" in the city; these simply happened to be the conditions that existed.) But the context of these Union Park families as new urbanites, in a new kind of city form, alters the meaning of stability and shelter leading to instability in the next generation among the intense family households. For it is clear that the nineteenth-century, privatistic, sheltering homes

Aries depicts, homes Frank Lloyd Wright describes in his *Autobiography* for his early years in Chicago, homes that observers of the time pointed to as a basic element in the composition of the "dull respectability" of Union Park, could easily have served as a refuge themselves from the confusing, dynamic city that was taking shape all around the confines of Union Park. It indeed seems natural that middle-class people should try to hold onto the status position they had in such a disrupting, growing milieu, make little entrepreneurial ventures outside their established jobs, and withdraw themselves into the comfort and intimacy of their families. Here is the source of that job "freeze" to be seen in the mobility patterns of fathers in intense-family situations; the bourgeois intensive family in this way became a shelter from the work pressures of the industrial city, a place where men tried to institute some control and establish some comforting intimacies in the shape of their lives, while withdrawing to the sidelines as the new opportunities of the city industries opened up. Such an interpretation of these middle-class families complements, on the side of the home, the interpretation Richard Hofstadter has made of the middle classes politically, in the latter part of the nineteenth century. He characterizes them as feeling that the new industrial order was not theirs, but had passed them by and left them powerless. It is this peculiar feeling of social helplessness on the part of the fathers that explains what use they made of their family lives.

CONFUSION IN THE DESIRE FOR STABILITY

What makes this complex pattern of family stability-instability significant for wider social orientations are the values about work to be found in the middle classes of this era. For here the idea of seizing opportunities, the idea of instability of job tenure for the sake of rising higher and higher, constituted, as John Cawelti has described it, the commonly agreed-upon notion of how sure success could be achieved at this time among respectable people; in the same way, this chance-taking path was presented, in the Horatio Alger novels and the like, as the road into the middle class itself. One should have been mobile in work, then, for this was the meaning of "opportunity" and "free enterprise," but in fact the overwhelming dislocations of the giant cities seem to have urged many men to retreat into the circle of their own families, to try simply to hold onto what they knew they could perform as tasks to support themselves, in the midst of the upheaval of urban expansion.

This is deduction, to be sure, and perhaps it is characteristic of sociologists dealing with history that they speculate where historians would prefer to remain silent and let the ambiguities stand. Yet the body not only of Union Park data, but the memoirs, fictional portraits, and secondary studies of this period seem to me to indicate that such an internally contradictory response to urbanization among the heads of middle-class families is the means by which the differences in social mobility between kinds of families can be explained. Conditions of privacy and comfort in the home weakened the desire to get ahead in the world, to conquer it; since the fathers of the intensive families were retreating from the confusions of city life, their preparation of their sons for work in Chicago became ambiguous, in that they wanted, surely, success for their sons, yet shielded the young, and did not themselves serve as models of successful adaptation. The result of these ambiguities can be seen directly in the work experience of the sons, when contrasted to the group of sons from families which, by virtue either of family form or size, were more complex or less intense. Overlaid on these family patterns was a relatively high rate of hidden marital breakdown in Union Park—one in every ten homes—while the expectation was, again, that such breakdown must not occur, that it was a disgrace morally.

These contradictions in family process gave rise, I believe, to the characteristics of Union Park's reaction to violence during the years 1886 to 1888.

THE FEELING OF THREAT GENERATED BY THE FAMILY EXPERIENCE

In the older version of the "frustration-aggression" syndrome it was assumed that if a social group failed to achieve a certain goal, it searched for an enemy to punish. But the goals of these middle-class people in Union Park were themselves self-contradictory: they wanted success in the work of the city and yet they didn't want it, given the definition of success at that time as an entrepreneurial grasping of opportunities rather than the fruit of plodding and routine service. The goals for the home were also contradictory: they wanted a stable shelter from the confusion and terror of the city, yet somehow they expected their sons, growing up sheltered, to be able to make it in that city world, and the sons of the dominant family groups seemed unable to do so. Divorce was a disgrace, yet there is evidence that one out of every ten of the neighborhood families were involved in a marital separation or desertion, a voluntary condition as opposed to the involuntary break of widowhood. Thus, because the goals of these middle-class people were bred of an equal desire to escape from and succeed in the city, the possibility of a wholly satisfying pattern of achievement for them was denied. The contradictory nature of the family purpose and products was innately frustrating so that a family impulse in one direction inevitably defeated another image of what was wanted. This meant that the sources of defeat were nameless for the families involved; surely these families were not aware of the web of self-contradictions in which in retrospect they seem to have been enmeshed; they knew only that things never seemed to work out to the end planned, that they suffered defeats in a systematic way. It is this specific kind of frustration that would lead to a sense of being overwhelmed, which, in this community's family system, led easily to a hysterical belief in hidden, unknown threats ready to strike at a man at almost any time.

FEELING OF THREAT AND PERCEPTIONS OF VIOLENCE

What I would like to suggest is that this complex pattern of self-defeat explains the character of the Union Park reaction to violence. For the dread of the unknown that the middle classes projected onto their supposed enemies among the poor expressed exactly the condition of self-instituted defeat that was the central feature of the family system in Union Park. And this dread was overwhelming precisely because men's own contradictory responses to living in such a city were overwhelming. They had defined a set of conditions for their lives that inevitably left them out of control. The fact that there was in Union Park a desire to destroy the "immigrant anarchists" or to garrison the neighborhood against them, as a result of the incidents of violence, was important in that it offered an outlet for personal defeats, not just for anger against lawbreakers. This response to violence refused to center on particular people, but rather followed the "path of hysterical reaction," in Freud's phrase, and centered on an abstract class of evildoers. For the fear of being suddenly overwhelmed from the outside was really a sign that one was in fact in one's own life being continually overwhelmed by the unintended consequences, or "latent consequences" as [Robert K.] Merton calls them, of what one did. By blaming the urban poor for their lawlessness, these middle-class people were expressing a passion for retribution that had little to do with riots or thefts. The retribution was rather in the nature of what [Erik] Erikson calls a "cover object" for hostility, an expression of inability to deal with the issues of one's own life, of mobility and stability in the city: the fear in these middle-class people was that if they were to act entrepreneurially in the work world they might be destroyed, yet their desire was to make it big suddenly. The desire to escape to the safety of the simple home of father, mother, and children became, unexpectedly, a crippling shield when the sons went out into the world.

This dilemma, expressed in the terrible fear of attack from the unbridled masses, was also related to the fear of falling into deep poverty that grew up in urban middle-class families of this time. To judge from a wide range of novels in the latter half of the nineteenth century there was a dread among respectable people of suddenly and uncontrollably falling into abject poverty; the Sidwells in Thackeray's *Vanity Fair* plummet from wealth to disorganized penury in a short space of time; Lily Bart's father, in Edith Wharton's *Age of Innocence,* is similarly struck down by the symbol of entrepreneurial chance in the industrial city, the stock market. This feeling of threat from the impersonal, unpredictable workings of the city economy was much like the sense of threat that existed in the Union Park families, because the dangers encountered in both cases were not a person or persons one could grapple with, but an abstract condition, poverty, or family disorder that was unintended, impersonal, and swift to come if the family should once falter. Yet what one *should* do was framed in such a self-contradictory way that it seemed oneself and one's family were always on the edge of survival. In this way, the growth of the new industrial city, with its uncertainties and immense wastes of human poverty not all to be dismissed as personal failures, could surely produce in the minds of middle-class citizens, uneasy about their own class position, living out from the center of town, the feeling that some terrible force from below symbolized by the poor, the foreigner, was about to strike out and destroy them unless they did something drastic.

The demographic reaction among most of the families to the eruption of violence bears out this interpretation of events. With the exception of the upwardly mobile, extended-family sons, most family members did not try to flee the community as a response to the threats of riot and the organized wave of crime. The demographic movement mirrored a renewed feeling of community solidarity in the face of violence, a solidarity created by fear and a common dread of those below. Again, it is significant that the group that did not show this pattern of "sticking out the trouble" is the generation of young family members who lived in more complex family circumstances than the majority, and who achieved, on the whole, greater occupational gains than the majority.

The relations between family life and the perception of violence in this Chicago community could be formed into the following general propositions. These were middle-class families enormously confused in what they wanted for themselves in the city, considered in terms of their achievements in the society at large and in terms of their emotional needs for shelter and intimacy; their schema of values and life goals was in fact formed around the issues of stability and instability as goals in a self-contradictory way. The result of this inner contradiction was a feeling of frustration, of not really being satisfied, in the activities of family members to achieve *either* patterns of stability or mobility for themselves. The self-defeat involved in this process led these families naturally to feel themselves threatened by overwhelming, nameless forces they could not control, no matter what they did. The outbreak of violence was a catalyst for them, giving them in the figure of the "other," the stranger, the foreigner, a generalized agent of disorder and disruption.

It is this process that explains logically why the people of Union Park so quickly found a communally acceptable villain responsible for violence, despite all the ambiguities perceived in the actual outbreaks of the disorders themselves; this is why the villain so quickly identified was a generalized, nonspecific human force, the embodiment of the unknown, the outside, the foreign. This is why the people of Union Park clung so tenaciously to their interpretation, seemed so willing to be terrorized and distraught.

If the complex processes of family and social mobility in Union Park are of any use in understanding the great fear of disorder among respectable, middle-class urbanites of our own time, their import is surely disturbing. For the nature of the disease that produced this reaction to violence among the industrial middle classes was not simply a matter of "ignorance" or failure to understand the problems of the poor; the fear was the consequence, rather, of structural processes in the lives of the Union Park families themselves. Thus for attitudes of people like the Union Park dwellers to change, and a more tolerant view of those below to be achieved, nothing so simple as more education about poor people, or to put the matter in contemporary terms, more knowledge about Negroes, would have sufficed. The whole fabric of the city, in its impact on staid white-collar workers, would have to have been changed. The complexity and the diversity of the city itself would need to have been stilled for events to take another course. But were the disorder of the city absent, the principal characteristic of the industrial city as we know it would also have been absent. These cities were powerful agents of change, precisely because they replaced the controlled social space of village and farm life with a kind of human settlement too dense and too various to be controlled.

And it comes to mind that the New Right fears of the present time are as deeply endemic to the structure of complex city life as was the violent reaction to violence in Union Park. Perhaps, out of patterns of self-defeat in the modern middle classes, it is bootless to expect right-wing, middle-class repression to abate simply through resolves of goodwill, "education about Negroes," or a change of heart. The experience of these bourgeois people of Chicago one hundred years ago may finally serve to make us a great deal more pessimistic about the chances for reason and tolerance to survive in a complex and pluralistic urban society.

8

The Nursery Tales
of Horatio Alger

MICHAEL ZUCKERMAN

No American author is cited more and read less than Horatio Alger. Virtually all discussions of late nineteenth-century social mobility begin by invoking his name in connection with the phrase "rags-to-riches" before the writer either proves or disproves
the Horatio Alger myth. Michael Zuckerman does not question whether the Alger myth
squares with social reality, but whether the myth squares with Horatio Alger. Did
Alger in fact celebrate the rise of the frugal, acquisitive, self-made, rugged indi-
vidualist?

D. H. Lawrence taught us long ago how to approach American literature.
"Never trust the artist," he warned. "Trust the tale."

But Lawrence never extended his edict or his analysis to our popular
culture, and subsequent students of the subject have often been at such
pains to be condescending that they could not be bothered comprehending. Accordingly, we have hardly conceived that the very pressures of
propriety that made our major writers such darlings of duplicity must
have been even more intense for authors with still broader audiences.
We have been inclined to discount all possibility of depth and disingenu-
ousness in our hack writers, seeing them simply at their own stated estima-

From *American Quarterly* 24 (1972): 191–209. Footnotes omitted. Reprinted by permission of the author and *American Quarterly*. Copyright, 1972, Trustees of the
University of Pennsylvania.

tion. And in the case of Horatio Alger, we thereby make a serious mistake.

We have imagined Alger our dreamer of success, our rhapsodist of rags-to-riches, our avatar of the self-made man—and it is true that Alger knew that tune and announced it unfailingly. He just never played it. In his tales success was but a subterfuge, and self-made men were nowhere to be found. Yet Alger was profoundly, even prophetically, American, and the deflected drive of his stories is essential to an understanding of the emergence of American industrial society.

Alger wrote more than one hundred novels, but he remained so completely within the compass of a few recurrent themes that there is no need to engage his entire corpus. Almost any of his story cycles gives access to his sentiments and obsessions. The most interesting of them is perhaps his first and most famous, the Ragged Dick series, whose six novels established the Alger formula.

The tales themselves may be speedily summarized. The first, *Ragged Dick,* is a story of the early adolescence of a New York City bootblack, Dick Hunter; it follows him in alternating episodes of fostering friendship and threatening enmity to a culmination in his dive from a ferry to rescue a drowning boy who proves to be the only child of the wealthy Mr. Rockwell. Its sequel, *Fame and Fortune,* finds the young bootblack ensconced in a privileged position in Rockwell's counting room and assured of the further favors of the rich man, who helps him survive an attempted frameup by his disappointed rivals. In *Mark, the Match Boy* Dick himself becomes a patron, succoring and sheltering the ineffectual little matchboy when he runs away from his exploitive guardian, Mother Watson, until Mark is suddenly discovered to be the long-lost grandson of a prosperous Milwaukee businessman who is only too delighted to relieve Dick of the young boy's care. *Rough and Ready* introduces another hero, a New York newsboy named Rufus, and traces his flight with his sister Rose from their bibulous stepfather, James Martin; its action is dominated by Rufus' successful struggle with Martin for custody of the little girl and, more briefly, by the newsboy's prevention of the armed robbery of a stockbroker, Mr. Turner, who rewards him with a job in the brokerage. In *Rufus and Rose* the lad foils another robbery of yet another rich man, Mr. Vanderpool, who adopts him and bequeaths him a small fortune in stocks. *Ben, the Luggage Boy* recounts the runaway of a boy of ten from his stern father and splendid home outside Philadelphia, his six years as a porter in the streets of New York, his chance encounter with a rich cousin which ignites a new determination to return to the swell life, and his triumphant welcome home.

If such summaries seem overdependent on luck, patronage and the deus ex machina, it is because Alger was too. And if they do not emphasize free enterprise, it is because Alger did not do so either. Despite his homilies and preachments, he was simply not very interested in business, and he was certainly no exponent of entrepreneurial individualism. His heroes neither possess nor prosper by the virtues of self-seeking, and Alger never espoused them. To call him a social Darwinist, as so many have done, is an inconceivable canard.

Alger did not even think comfortably in capitalistic terms. Some of his characters are "ashamed" to use credit, others do not see in money an impersonal measure of value, and none are enmeshed utterly in the mechanisms of the marketplace. The prices they pay and the wages they receive are as often determined by consideration and decency as by supply and demand. Bargains are struck solely on equity between the boys. Rents are set by people who "don't want to make money" and are renegotiable "if you find it is too hard on you to pay so much." Alger's heroes are all allowed incomes by their benefactors that are sufficient contradictions in themselves of the primacy of profit in the motives of those worthies. Indeed, Alger in his own voice quite condemned those who charge what the market will bear, insisting instead that "fair prices in the long run are the best for all parties."

His comprehension of capitalistic individuals was no clearer than his conception of capitalist institutions. Figures of frugality pass through his pages with "thin lips and pinched expression," and though they are flourishing merchants they have "an outward appearance of meanness, which, by the way, did not belie [their] real character." Men make great fortunes and find that money alone buys no contentment. People of surpassing villainy "look out for number one" or mind only their own business, and in every volume it is the hero's enemy who is "intent only upon his own selfish gratifications."

Alger's favorites, on the contrary, are strangers to such strategies of self-maximization. For them "the best use of money" is in helping others. Dick never gets "so much satisfaction" as when he depletes his own savings to assist a fellow bootblack who has "supported his sick mother and sister for more'n a year," which Dick takes to be "more good than [he himself] ever did." Rufus puts his money where his morals are, buying a baseball bat from his own earnings to stave off a robbery of a man he does not even know. And all alike lavish charities on the needy, whether worthy or unworthy.

In fact, profligacy prevails over parsimony at every turn. All six stories open on a note of heedless indulgence—for the theater, an apartment or food—and all six sustain that note thereafter. Boys who are fortunate splurge immediately and to the limit of their luck, sharing their strike with friends if they cannot spend it alone. Others who are down to their last pennies yet yield to "temptation" and buy apples and ice cream. And few of the boys are any more frugal than Ben, who feels "very well satisfied" if he comes out "even at the end of the day." By and large they all place their bellies before their bank accounts and otherwise set gratification above accumulation.

Nor could their self-indulgence have horrified Alger, for he often allowed it to lead to decisive transformations in their destinies. Mark gets his grubstake while sleeping on an all-night ferry. Rufus first gains solid ground financially when he finds five dollars in a barroom he enters on an "idle impulse," and he overhears the plans for the robbery he prevents in still another saloon to which he repairs upon "the promptings of appetite." Miss Manning, the kind woman who takes care of Rose after the children flee their stepfather, discovers the perfect lodging for herself and the little girl on "an impulse which she did not attempt to resist" even though the room seemed obviously "beyond her means."

In fact, Alger's favorites are almost always impetuously improvident. Prudent calculation of prospects, so crucial for the capitalist entrepreneur, is simply not their style. Dick springs with such "alacrity" to the relief of the drowning boy that he does not even hear the father's shouted offer of reward. Mark, waking to find a dollar in his pocket, sets out on his own without once looking "forward to the time when this supply would be exhausted." Rufus flies from Martin "without any well-defined plan in his mind" and with no idea where he and Rose "should live in the future." And Ben runs away from his father so precipitately that he arrives in New York "an utter stranger with very indefinite ideas as to how he was to make a living." Indeed, even when Ben finds himself but two cents from starvation, "the time had not yet come to trouble himself" about his prospects; and after six years in New York he still does "not think much about the future" for, "like street boys in general, his horizon [is] limited by the present."

Unconcerned for the future, Alger's vagabonds could hardly pursue goals with the perseverance so celebrated in the success manuals of the 19th century. Alger did deliver an occasional descant on diligence, but in the tales themselves his heroes are hares, not tortoises. They work sporadically rather than steadily, and they work when they need money rather than for work's own sake. They are more nearly Galahads than Gradgrinds, giving up their own gainful opportunities on a moment's notice to protect the helpless or follow the action. And it is by just that temperamental disposition to knight-errantry rather than discipline or steady application that poor boys prosper. Dick is on the ferry to dive for Rockwell's son only because he takes "half holidays" to go on "excursions." Rufus finds economic security only as a consequence of quitting work early one day to wander around Battery Park.

All six stories are studded with kidnaps, captures, and escapes, robberies and false arrests, detection and derring-do. Some of them are strung entirely on such narrative threads. *Mark, the Match Boy* derives its design from the search for Hiram Bates' missing grandson. *Rough and Ready* is an account of abduction and recapture. And the others are laced with chapters such as "Tracking the Thief," "A Parley with the Enemy" and "Suspense." In all, less than one-fourth of the chapters even pretend to show the protagonists at work, while the rest show them established at home or embroiled in adventure.

Only when the boys are thus beset by danger do they disclose concern for what they do. At their employment they evince no emotion at all, betraying not the slightest sign that they like or dislike their assigned tasks. Unlike Weber's Protestant capitalists, for whom the moral worth of work was so central, they find neither purpose nor personal fulfillment in their jobs. They just do what the work requires, gaining no intrinsic satisfaction from it, and they identify the good life with consumption and gratification far more than with production.

Disdaining the ascetic capitalist and the entrepreneurial self-seeker, Alger inevitably anathematized the social Darwinians. Against their assertions of the prerogatives of strength, he held the obligation of the powerful to protect the weak. Against Sumnerian standards of self-reliance, he suggested an endless round of charitable reciprocation. And against the Spencerian insistence on laissez-faire individualism, he urged that "we ought all to help each other."

Alger admitted quite openly his environmental reformism and his hopes of stirring "a deeper and more widespread sympathy" for the "waifs of the city." He never forgot that they too were "somebody's children, and that cold, and harshness, and want were as hard for them to bear as for those in a higher rank of life." He made endless excuses for them because they "had never had a fair chance" or "a very good bringin' up" on the streets: for him, even armed robbers "might have been capable of better things, had circumstances been different." Poverty was not, in his eyes, a measure of personal failings. Many poor boys, he insisted, "have good tendencies and aspirations, and only need to be encouraged and placed under right influences to develop into worthy and respectable men"; more fortunate people might have it in their "power to give some one the chance that may redeem him."

Accordingly, Alger's heroes succeed, to the extent that their own attributes have anything to do with their success, because they are good, not because they have sharper fangs and longer claws than anyone else. Like Rufus, who pinches pennies to buy decent clothes for his sister, their economies and ambitions are as often for another as for themselves. Like Mark, they are frequently "bolder in behalf of [a] friend than [they] would have been for" themselves. Like Dick, they can be even "more pleased at the prospective good fortune of [a] friend than if it had fallen to" their own benefit, and like Rose they can be moved more readily by concern for another than by self-interest. They are all, presumably, destined to develop like the successful stockbroker Alger so admired, who was

> a large-hearted man, inclined to think well of his fellow-men, and though in his business life he had seen a good deal that was mean and selfish in the conduct of others, he had never lost his confidence in human nature, and never would. It is better to have such a disposition, even if it does expose the possessor to being imposed upon at times, than to regard everybody with distrust and suspicion. At any rate it promotes happiness, and conciliates good will, and these will offset an occasional deception.

Such sentimental reliance on men's kindness made aggressive imposition unnecessary and even undesirable. It is only the Micky Maguires and the James Martins, the young toughs and the manipulators, and the counterfeitors, confidence-men and others of "few redeeming qualities," who use force and cunning for personal gain. Lads like Dick and Rufus have "a certain chivalrous feeling," that does not "allow" them to exploit anyone weaker, while other boys such as Mark and Dick's friend Fosdick are so "timid" that they require the protection of their sturdier allies. Alger never glorified strength or shrewdness in the struggle for success because he did not believe it was that sort of struggle.

The virtues Alger did exalt, revealingly enough, were the virtues of the employee, not the employer. Since his heroes do not succeed at the expense of others, it is not essential that they build better mousetraps, cut costs or innovate in any way. They have little enough initiative even in the streets, and less in the shop. Indeed, when they enter upon their white-collar careers, they promise their new bosses primarily to "try to make you as little trouble as possible." Dick will do "anything that is required" in the line of duty, but neither he nor any of the others ever re-think such duties. And no one ever asks them to. Employers themselves assure the boys that they "have only to continue steady and faithful" to be "sure to rise." None but the heroes' rivals—the preening pretenders to superiority by birth, such as Roswell Crawford—fail to content themselves with service in subordinate places, and the Roswell Crawfords come to bad ends.

As Alger would have it, then, success follows dependability and a desire to serve others. It attends those who obey orders cheerfully and serve others willingly. And it is available to all, for Alger posited no pinnacle of preeminence for which many compete and a few prove fit. The Alger stories were never about the fabulous few who rose from poverty to great riches; they were, at best, tales of a much more accessible ascent from rags to respectability. His nonpareils do not wax wealthy so much as they grow reputable, leaving the promiscuity of the streets for the propriety of a desk job. Dick is barely begun upon a clerical career at the conclusion of *Ragged Dick*, still six months away from promotion to bookkeeper at the end of *Fame and Fortune,* and headed no higher than a junior partnership in a good mercantile house even at the termination of *Mark, the Match Boy*. Rufus can claim only an eight-dollar-a-week clerkship at the climax of *Rough and Ready*, is still on "the lowest rung of the ladder" halfway through *Rufus and Rose*, and is destined only for an undescribed junior partnership when all is done. Mark is restored to his grandfather, a moderately wealthy broker in Milwaukee, and Ben is reclaimed by his father, a coal dealer outside Philadelphia. There is not a robber baron in the bunch, nor even any remarkable fortune. The boys gain only "the fame of an honorable and enterprising man of business," which was all they ever aimed at anyway. "I'd like to be a office boy, and learn business, and grow up 'spectable," Dick confides at his first stirring of ambition; and even as he nears the end of his odyssey he sets his sights no higher. "Take my advice," he urges Mark, "and you'll grow up respectable and respected."

Such commitment to respectability implied also a commitment to others rather than to selfish aspiration. Respectability, in Alger's idea of it, could not come from within, but could only be conferred by others. Accordingly, his heroes require the good opinion of the herd for their own sense of success and for their very sense of self. And they seem to believe they can gain it by behaving the way the herd behaves or would want them to behave. Dick, for example, acquires clothes so modish as he moves out into "society" that Fosdick accuses him of dandyism; Dick answers that he wants "to look respectable. . . . When I visit Turkey I want to look as the turkeys do." Rufus shows a comparable concern for respectable appearance and a similar identification of such respectability with doing as others do when he goes to the theater. At expense he can ill afford, he buys a pair of white kid gloves which he twirls about "in rather an embarrassed way" because he can hardly get them on; "I'd enough sight rather go without any," he admits, "but I suppose, if I'm going to sit in a fashionable seat, I must try to look fashionable." Later, though the gloves still do not "feel comfortable," he looks at his hands "with satisfaction," for "step by step he was getting into the ways of civilized life." (The performance itself he enjoys "almost as well" as the less classy ones he had haunted as a newsboy, which he would have attended even that night had he not suspected that the Old Bowery "was not exactly a fashionable place of amusement," one which he would "hardly have liked to mention" at the boardinghouse table the next day.)

Rufus' integrity counts for no more than his entertainment in matters of reputation, giving him no pause whatever in telling a lie before his sister sooner than lose face with a total stranger. When he finds a fine new house in which to room, he offhandedly informs the landlady that he will send his trunk up later. Rose lets slip that she "didn't know [he] had a trunk," and though he replies smoothly that he does not "carry [his] trunk round all the time like an elephant," he is "a little embarrassed" because "he wanted to keep up appearances in his new character as a boarder at an up-town boarding-house." And appearance is so central for Ben that he bases his entire estimate of his acceptability at home on his outward aspect, building the strategy of his return solely on a plan to "purchase a suit as handsome as that which his cousin wore." The thought that he might be as welcome without the suit, simply for himself, never enters his mind.

Even the most elemental virtues of individual character acquire an other-oriented flavor in Alger's hands. Dick may be honest when he informs a fellow boarder that he once shined the man's shoes, but the author admits that Dick "wouldn't have said so" if he thought the man might believe him. Ben may decline to steal, but only because "he still felt that he should not like to have a report reach home"; and on the one occasion he does swipe an apple he feels only a fear for what "his friends at home [would] think of it" if they heard. Rufus may have a superfluity of intrinsic reasons to reject the company of his stepfather, but he spurns him solely from anxiety over what others might think when that "not very respectable-looking object" tries to walk alongside him. And almost all the principal characters pursue education simply because they recognize that there is "something more than money needed to win a respectable position in the world."

The Alger hero's very notion of his own nature depended, ineluctably, upon others. If Alger's world was a Carnegie world, it was surely not Andrew's but Dale's. Alger could not create self-impelled individuals because his stalwarts required a crowd for their sense of self. The quest for respectability imposed a communal derivation of identity, and a communal dedication of the self as well. Accordingly, when Alger offered examples outside fiction of the newsboy success story, he cited politicians, journalists, judges, a district attorney and a clergyman before arriving finally at "still others prosperous and even wealthy businessmen." Businessmen brought up the rear while public figures led because it was primarily the redemption of respectable citizens Alger sought. His aims were social and moral more than they were ever economic.

Alger's inability to conceive convincingly his heroes' inner resources made it quite impossible for him to maintain the traditional connection of character and success. He could—and did, occasionally—claim it, but he could not bring it to life. His tales contradicted him at every such turn. The path to wealth was not, as it had been for Franklin, "as plain as the way to market." Instead there intervened always between constitution and conquest the sudden stroke of luck.

The typical Alger story, therefore, was one of casual contingency, not causal necessity. Bootblacks rise by diving for the drowning son of a rich man, newsboys by foiling attempted robbery, matchboys by the belated beneficence of a grandfather a thousand miles away. None ever attain eminence by diligent application; none are ever on a course of notable advancement before their big break. Alger knew the litany of industry and frugality as well as most men, but for him and his characters the failure of firm selfhood and the facts of late-19th century life kept getting in the way.

Primarily the problems were that these gamins of Gotham could not get the kind of work Alger wished for them and that, even if they could, they could not afford to take it. In the Algerine cosmos, nothing but a white-collar career would do, finally—protagonists had somehow to quit the street for a store—and in the Ragged Dick series not a single favorite ever secures a clerical position purely on personal initiative. Dick makes "several ineffectual applications" and surrenders for the season. His friend Fosdick solicits 50 appointments and suffers "as many failures." Ben gives up entirely after a few rebuffs; Rufus never even tries. And the reason is always the same: "it was generally desired that the boy wanted should reside with his parents" or "bring good references." Fosdick finds that to confess himself "a boy of the street" is usually "sufficient of itself to insure a refusal," and the others all share his discouragement in a system that supports no self-made men. They hustle on the streets precisely because they are alone and unaided and consequently can do no better, for they have no access to a countinghouse unless they can claim a place in a household. Unsponsored and unspoken for, their success can only be extra-systemic. In the very structure of the situation they can advance by no means but the lucky acquisition of a patron who will provide the protection they require.

In the very structure of the situation too, young men on their own are all but obliged to remain independent rather than seek employment, because the financial price of propriety is too steep. Energetic newsboys and bootblacks in Alger's New York make far more money than beginning clerks do—Dick, for instance, sees at once that on an office salary he would "be nothin' but skin and bones" within a year—and such stalwarts of the street have far fewer expenses besides. They worry little about lodging, less about clothes and cleanliness, and not at all about education. It is all the same to them if they sleep in a box, an illegal hideout between the wharves or a suitably impressive address. An aspiring bookkeeper, on the other hand, cannot afford to be so cavalier. He has a position to up-hold, so he has to incur the costs of a regular room, presentable clothes and perhaps even a few luxuries for the sake of such respectability. His office job, if he is but beginning, nets him less than the expenses of his own support; and even Dick recognizes this for bad budgeting, assert-ing as he does his disinclination "to give up a independent and loocra-tive purfession" for the pittance he would be paid in a store.

Luck, then, does not simply seal the success of those on the proper path. On the contrary, fortune's favor is indispensable to lift poor boys out of the ditch. Ragged Dick is not on his way before he saves Mr. Rockwell's son, for there is no way. Orphans of the city cannot afford an apprenticeship in respectability, since they have no parental subsidy to tide them over and can hardly survive on status alone. Only by benevolent patronage can they manage their entry upon a white-collar walk of life. Only from parental surrogates who set defiance of the market's determination of wages at "no consequence" can they extract salaries they cannot economically earn. Dick speaks for them all when he admits that he "was lucky" to have "found some good friends who helped [him] along."

So far from telling of a system so bountiful that any earnest lad could succeed if he tried, Alger's tales implied one that held the dis-privileged down so securely that only by the unlikely advent of chance and championship could the impoverished even set foot on the social ladder. In the Alger novels of New York a steady undertone of despera-tion resonated beneath the scattered cries of lucky triumph.

As essential as luck was to the manifest social action of the stories, it was still more imperative at their latent levels of intimate familial relationships and personal fantasies of fulfillment. For if Alger could not in the end cleave a straightforward course from character to suc-cess, it was because he could not from the first conceive of any satisfac-tory character at all. In an era whose leading spokesmen defined character—at least male character—in terms of will, Alger's deepest desire was persistently for a denial of the will.

At first, of course, it does not seem so. His heroes have always to fend for themselves, often in adversity, and generally they enjoy their lot. Dick delights in being his "own boss," trumpeting it as "the dif-ference" between himself and his storeboy sidekick. Mark exults in being "free and independent." Rufus, disdaining another boy's servility, announces that he does not "want anybody to give [him] money." And Ben becomes "so accustomed to the freedom and independence of his street life, with its constant variety, that he would have been unwilling to return, even if the original cause of his leaving home were removed.

Life in a Pennsylvania village seemed 'slow' compared with the excitement of his present life."

But such bold sentiments are the artist's asseveration, not the tale's truth, and they are always spoken before opportunity offers. As soon as it does, Dick decides he would rather be Mr. Rockwell's hireling, Mark accepts his grandfather's guidance, Rufus takes Mr. Turner's money and Mr. Vanderpool's too, and Ben goes back home. In every case their independence is only for the interim. In the end they abandon all autonomy, willingly. Ben declares it "a good deal pleasanter resting in the luxurious bedchamber . . . than the chance accommodations to which he had been accustomed." Dick is "rather pleased" that his old rags are stolen, since their loss seems "to cut him off from the old vagabond life which he hoped never to resume."

Not one of Alger's elect is ever self-employed at the end of a novel, nor do any of them ever really wish to be. Mark most obviously needs "somebody to lean on," but even Dick admits that his deepest dreams involve "some rich man" who "would adopt me, and give me plenty to eat and drink and wear, without my havin' to look so sharp after it.'" It is not with his usual levity that he adds that he would "like to have somebody to care for me," and later, when he wishes explicitly for a mother, there is the same "tinge of sadness in his tone."

Dick's fantasied confusion of men and mothers comes very close to the emotional core of the Alger stories, for though the boys all crave caretaking, they are quite particular about its provenance. Not any parent will do. Each of Alger's prodigies is seeking something very special, and it is no accident that in a nation still two-thirds rural and presumably patriarchal, every story in the series is conditioned on father-absence. Only one of the six tales even admits a flesh-and-blood father, and Ben runs away from him. In the others there are a few self-sacrificing mothers, an indulgent grandfather, a stern stepfather and a monstrous mother-substitute; and only those among them who abdicate their authority succeed in sustaining a relation with their wards. All who play the traditional masculine part—demanding and commanding —discover one day that their fledgings have flown the coop.

Over and over again in these stories, Alger returned to the problem of proper parentage. His fixation was overt in *Mark, the Match Boy* and *Ben the Luggage Boy*, more muffled in the others—the first two tell quite focally of falls from family and re-entry into its bosom, the rest dwell less on literal than on figurative kinships that are reclaimed as the protagonists find their patrons—but it pervaded the entire series. In every novel the hero experiences the unsettling sense that his own parents have failed him, that somewhere else his true parents are waiting to be found by accident and good luck.

Proper parents such as these are invariably defined in terms of nurturance and even indulgence, not discipline and hard knocks. It is because his stepfather "couldn't take care of [him]self, much less of anyone else" that Rufus so often reminds him, "I am not your son." It is because Mother Watson assumed charge of him "rather for her own advantage than his" that Mark finally realizes that she "had no claim on him" and pronounces her "no relation." And it is because his father, though a good provider, is intolerant of impulse and unbending in righteousness that Ben runs away and refuses to return:

> knowing his father's sternness, he knew that he would be severely punished. Unfortunately for Ben, his father had a stern, unforgiving disposition, that never made allowances for the impulses of boyhood. He had never condescended to study his own son, and the method of training he had adopted with him was in some respects very pernicious. His system hardened, instead of softening. . . .

Proper parents, then, are permissive. Like Ben's mother, who is "quite different from her husband, being gentle and kind," such parents are sweet but not strong. They give, and they ask little or nothing in return. Every Alger favorite finds a few of them on his way, and the occasions of these encounters are the hinges on which his history turns.

Dick's advancement, for example, can be traced quite completely through his successive sponsors, who provide him the incentives and resources for his rehabilitation. Mark's merest survival, to say nothing of his brief flight to freedom, is conditioned on the support, first, of an older street urchin who fends off Mark's former guardian by claiming to have "adopted that boy," and then, of course, by Dick himself, who declares Mark his ward and explains that he will "look after" the little boy "just as if I was your uncle or grandfather." Ben is squired by a series of street people who provide him present comfort and promises of future assistance at any time he is "in need" of them, and later he is assured by a wealthy merchant that "when you need a friend, you will know where to find me." Rufus alone requires scant succor before his decisive break, but only because the focal roles are reversed so that he protects his sister, sheltering her from any obligation "to go out into the street to earn anything" though "many girls, no older than she," do work; and even Rufus dreams of the day Rose "grows up, and can keep house for me."

In truth, almost every character establishes his connection to others on an axis of caring or being cared for, or defaulting on such fostering duties. And the narratives move almost wholly on these matters of maintenance. *Rough and Ready*, for instance, is at its core an adventure of abduction and recovery, of nurture ruptured and restored. Success is so peripheral to the story that Rufus quite literally thwarts the thieves and gains his clerkship in an interlude while waiting to save his sister. His own advancement never does concern him so much as her sustenance, which is why her stepfather steals her in the first place, knowing "that nothing would strike the newsboy a severer blow than to deprive him of his sister." In *Rufus and Rose,* the former newsboy himself escapes from his stepfather and the criminals Martin has fallen in league with; and he is able to do so because one of them unjustly beats the hunch-back guard Humpy, whose "rude sense of honor" had previously held him "faithful to his employer." Humpy determines to betray his masters for that failure—regretting that he "wouldn't have gone ag'inst' them had they been more supportive—and he single-handedly engineers Rufus' rescue. In *Mark, the Match Boy* Hiram Bates triggers the action not merely by setting Dick to search for his grandson but also by having failed, years before, to accept his daughter's love for his clerk. She married the man anyway, Bates "disowned her" and "hardened [his] heart against her," and it is his remorse that drives him to try to make amends when he learns that his daughter and her husband are dead. "I cannot forgive myself," he swears, "when I think of my unfeeling severity." And in *Ragged Dick* and *Ben, the Luggage Boy* alike, the young hero's ascent is fired by first fostering, Dick's when he is encouraged as "nobody ever talked to [him] so before," Ben's when he is assured that his cousin's love for him is unconditional, "no matter how he looked, or how poor he might be."

Ultimately, then, Alger's every novel was a novel of nurturance, a novel whose dearest ideal was to be cared for and indulged, not to be self-sufficient and self-reliant. Each of them begins with a boy alone and on his own, but each of them concludes with that boy safely sheltered in some secure niche where his future is assured because his protector will look after him forevermore. Alger allowed his every hero and half his supporting cast this movement from the streets to easy street, and it afforded him the essential drama and the irresistible consummation of all his narratives. Dick gains Mr. Rockwell's undying gratitude, Mark secures "a comfortable and even luxurious home, and a relative whose great object in life is to study his happiness," Rufus has Mr. Turner's pledge that there will be many ways "in which I shall find an opportunity to serve you" while Rose has Rufus' reassurance that she is "safe now, and nobody shall trouble" her, and Ben is welcomed home by all to take over the family firm. In every case the womb is warm; in no case will the hero have to struggle any longer.

At this level the public and the private themes of the tales merge and reinforce each other superbly. The quest for a patron that provides much of the explicit action of the stories parallels—and is finally the very same as—the quest for a new and more nurturant parent that provides the covert action. The social and the personal themes are one and the same, and they are both fantasies of fosterage. The hero eludes stern parental authority and secures a more supportive champion who supplies rather than demands. His lot is unconditional love, from a guardian much like the father Ben goes back to, who "seems to have changed greatly" and "is no longer stern and hard, but gentle and forbearing." The thrust of the stories is not the growth of the heroes but the alteration of their environments; Ben can return because his father and his home have changed.

All the stories are, in a similar sense, tales of a return to respectable estate. Their movement is not even from rags to respectability, for their subjects never really start in rags. They pass their formative years in the bosom of a family, and they are quite familiar with its comforts before they run away or are orphaned. In their success, they simply recover a condition that was originally theirs. Like Mark and Ben, they reclaim a literal birthright with a reformed relative; or, like Rufus and Fosdick, they find a fonder patron altogether. In either case their progression is the same: from respectability to rags to respectability, from home to street to a new and more nurturant home.

Indeed, homes are crucial concerns for Alger even before his heroes consummate their quest, for such lodgings symbolize superbly the fusion of public and private aspiration to passive security and indulgence in their desires. The boys move constantly to more expensive and commodious quarters, even though they can scarcely afford to feed themselves and cannot save a penny after they have paid their rent, because they need both to signify the stations of their advancement to social respectability and to simulate the safety of the cradle. As Alger explained, "those young men who out of economy contented themselves with small and cheerless rooms . . . were driven in the evening to the streets, theatres, and hotels, for the comfort which they could not find at home." An ample home is, in Alger, the alternative to the real independence and loneliness of the large city, and none of the boys want such self-reliance if they can avoid it. They pay so excessively for a room because it is so much more important to them than saving. It is a sanctuary, a veritable womb.

So too, in the end, do the dependence on luck and the cultivation of the employee virtues conduce to the same comfort. The reliance on chance issues from a passivity before the environment, an impingement of favorable circumstance upon the individual; the sanction of subordinacy clarifies the heroes' progress by patronage, since the very virtues the boys acquire represent efforts to come to the attention of their superiors and gain such support. And success itself is attained not by fighting to the top in constant, clawing struggle, but precisely by moving out of the fray entirely, into another's custody.

If Horatio Alger was the mentor of an emergent industrial society, then the Americans who grew up under his tutelage were surely schooled for service in the corporate bureaucracies which would in time transform the culture. For Alger never encouraged his audience to care so much for work as for the gratifications of income, and he never dared his readers to be as they might be so much as to do as their neighbors did. Beneath his explicit emphasis on striving upward ran a deeper desire for stability and security; beneath his paeans to manly vigor, a lust for effeminate indulgence; beneath his celebration of self-reliance, a craving to be taken care of and a yearning to surrender the terrible burden of independence.

9

From Prairie to Corn Belt: Farming on the Illinois and Iowa Prairies in the Nineteenth Century

ALLAN G. BOGUE

Although historians generally differentiate among businessmen according to the size and type of their enterprises, they usually think of a typical or average farmer. Mentioned in discussions of Granger, Farmers' Alliance, and Populist unrest, this typical farmer is seen suffering through a long depression from the 1870s to the 1890s, during which he is victimized by railroads, bankers, middlemen, manufacturers, and politicians. Using manuscript census records, letters, diaries, account books, and records of mortgage foreclosures of the Illinois and Iowa corn belt for illustration, Allan G. Bogue emphasizes the diversity among and the frequent success of prairie farmers.

During the last half of the nineteenth century . . . the production plans of farmers throughout Illinois and Iowa were different enough so that we can detect areas of high and low production of the various farm crops and farm animals. But what of neighboring farmers? How great was the change when John Smith clambered over his line fence?

From Allan G. Bogue, *From Prairie to Corn Belt: Farming on the Illinois and Iowa Prairies in the Nineteenth Century* (Chicago: The University of Chicago Press, 1963), pp. 241–43, 253–66, 280, 283–87. Reprinted with omissions by permission of the publisher. © 1963 by The University of Chicago.

Let us follow the census marshal as he travels from farm to farm in Center and Rochester townships of Cedar County, Iowa, in the late spring days of 1850. What did his enumeration show when he emerged from the roughly-hewn door of the one hundred and first farmhouse and mounted his horse to move on through the openings?

Table 23 summarizes the findings of our census-taker. The most

TABLE 23   Production Statistics 101 Cedar County Farmers Census Years 1850–80

	Farms Reporting		Medians		Maximums	
	1850	1880	1850	1880	1850	1880
Acres per farm ...	101	101	120 acres	160 acres	640 acres	1,120 acres
Improved acres ...	101	101	50 acres	150 acres	320 acres	1,100 acres
Farm values	101	101	$700	$5,200	$6,000	$31,200
Value of livestock .	101	101	$220	$900	$1,960	$15,250
Horses and mules .	97	100	2	6	12	26
Work oxen	25	0	0	0	26	0
Milk cows	99	98	3	4	15	42
Other cattle	78	75	3	5	50	330
Sheep	59	7	7	0	50	185
Swine	98	97	16	72	100	350
Wheat †	98	71	180 bus.	30 bus.	1,000 bus.	500 bus.
Indian corn	98	96	400 bus.	2,800 bus.	3,000 bus.	9,000 bus.
Rye	1	8	0	0	30 bus.	0
Flax	4	0	0	360 bus.	100 lbs.	580 bus.
Oats	69	83	50 bus.	0	500 bus.	1,500 bus.
Barley	6	15	0	0	80 bus.	450 bus.
Buckwheat	14	8	0	0	200 bus.	122 bus.
Clover seed	2	5	0	0	3 bus.	22 bus.
Grass seed	4	14	0	0	5 bus.	185 bus.
Hay	99	90	8 tons	2 tons	60 tons	160 tons
Butter	89	98	100 lbs.	350 lbs.	1,200 lbs.	1,550 lbs.
Cheese	13	0	0	0	300 lbs.	0

† In 1880 twenty-one farmers reported wheat "not cut"—an obvious misunderstanding of his duties on the part of the census marshal.

striking contrast from neighbor to neighbor was one of scale. Acres per farm, improved acres, farm value, and value of livestock are all indexes of the size of farming operations. The median farmer of our 101 listed a holding of 120 acres, but one of his neighbors owned 640 acres. The median farmer had improved 50 acres, but one man in the community had broken 320 acres to the plow. The median farmer valued his holding at $700, but the most affluent of the group believed that his farm was worth $6,000. The livestock of the median farmer was worth $220, that of the most committed stockman, $1,960.

Obviously, neighboring farmers differed somewhat in their combination of farm enterprises and methods of farming. Almost all the 101 farmers owned horses, milk cows, and swine but only 59 owned sheep. Twenty-five owned oxen, and 23 listed no "other cattle." Almost all the farmers raised wheat and corn and cured hay, but only 69 reported that they had harvested oats in the previous crop year. A scattering of farmers grew minor field crops of which the most important was buckwheat—raised by 14 of 101 farmers in 1849. Only two had harvested clover seed. Eighty-nine households made butter, but only 13 reported the manufacture of cheese. The individual census figures may of themselves, of course, have masked fundamental differences in farming patterns. Twenty-three farmers for instance reported that they owned no "other cattle." Some members of this group were small farmers, owning but a cow or two and selling or butchering the calves at an early age. But even at this early date a few of them may well have been feeding stock and received the census marshal after they had disposed of their steers and before they had purchased their next lot of feeders.

In the categories of Table 23 the median farmer was always much closer to the smallest operator than to the largest in the scale of his operations. Looking behind the measures of tendency in Table 23 to the actual figures in the various categories of production, one discovers usually that a handful of farmers—from three or four to as many as ten in some instances—listed production or livestock numbers that were three times or more greater than those of the median farmer. This was probably the case throughout Iowa and Illinois and is important to our understanding of the local economy, because the large business and the small were interrelated. The smaller farmer frequently looked to the larger as a market both for some of his production and for some of his labor. The larger looked to the smaller for labor in times of extra need, for stock cattle and pigs, and for an extra crib of corn or stack of hay that he might buy when his own supplies ran short.

As Table 23 also shows, the picture had changed somewhat in Center Township by 1880. The first 101 farms that the census-enumerator visited in 1880 were larger, more highly improved, more valuable, and, understandably, more productive than in 1850. The farmers of the region generally were putting greater dependence on a smaller number of farm enterprises. But the individual differences from farm to farm were still there. And indeed, to the surprise of the newcomer to the Corn Belt today, they still are to some extent today, when one may see a herd of Holsteins grazing in lush pasturage around a sign reading "Dairy Farming Pays" located in the very heart of the cash-grain region of north-central Iowa.

The reasons underlying contrasts from farm to farm include many of the factors that account for regional or subregional farming patterns. Soils, topography, even climate changed from farm to farm. In the nineteenth century differences due to cultural factors were doubtless more apparent in the neighborhood than in the statistics that blended the production programs of a county of farmers. Probably, however, differences from neighbor to neighbor most often reflected the capital resources available to the individual farmer, and these, of course, were linked in part to the age of the operator.

If we would understand the way in which the pioneer farmer combined his varied farm enterprises to make a farm business, we must, of course, go beyond the census materials and consider actual farm records.

.   .   .

Now we can visit the farm of Ole and Gro Svendsen in north-western Iowa. In this case, too, we would like to know more about the farm than we ever can, but Gro Svendsen's letters to her family in Norway picture it with some clarity. Arriving in America in 1862, this young Norwegian couple lived for a short time among their countrymen at St. Ansgar, Iowa. During the next spring Ole journeyed west and staked a claim to a fractional quarter section of land near Estherville in Emmet County. Close by lay the claims of other Norwegians. Leaving Gro with his father and mother for the summer, Ole worked for an American in Emmet County. The wages were good—$15.00 per month was a common wage, perhaps he earned more—and he could guard the claim that he hoped to homestead. During the fall of 1863 he brought Gro to the claim, and they began the tasks of farm-making. The Svendsen's land was prairie with few trees. So few trees were there, indeed, that Ole purchased 12½ acres of wooded land that lay six miles away. Here was the raw stuff of house, stable, and fences for an outlay of $100 that Ole borrowed from his father at 7 per cent interest, with five years in which to repay.

The Svendsens lived on their claim for ten years before they obtained a title to it. Lest failure to become a citizen should compromise his homestead entry, Ole began naturalization proceedings as rapidly as possible. As a result, or so the Svendsens believed, he was drafted in 1864 and enjoyed the dubious pleasure of serving under General Sherman in the closing days of the war. And in the end they failed to secure their claim under the homestead law. They discovered instead that they must buy it because it was adjudged to lie in a railroad land grant.

During 1873 they borrowed $500 from a loan office in Estherville and bought the farm for $480, mortaging it immediately as security for the loan. Ole Svendsen acquired no additional land in Iowa. Gro died in childbirth during 1878, and in the following year Ole quitclaimed his farm for $1.00. Following his brother's trail to the Goose River region of Dakota Territory, he once more began to cut a farm from the virgin prairie.

Ole Svendsen purchased a yoke of oxen for $30 in 1862 and never thereafter lacked the animal power necessary to work a farm. Yet improvement of the holding went slowly. He had broken only a few acres of land when he went to war, and his younger brother broke just three acres during the season of 1865. With the soldier safely home, farm-making moved more rapidly; Gro reported 21½ acres under the plow in 1867. Although Svendsen did not apparently break large acreages at any time thereafter, the arable grew slowly over time.

The dwelling that Ole built in the fall of 1863 was "very small and humble," but Gro reported in 1867 that they were now well housed "both man and beast." Near the house were two wooden stables, large enough to shelter more than 24 head of cattle, with a shed between "for the bulls." By 1867, also, they had dug a well to provide a supply of water close at hand. Svendsen cut the wood for his improvements from his timber lot during the winter and had it sawed to dimensions, when necessary, at a nearby mill. From the woodlot also he hauled the rails to protect his crops from the livestock that ranged the unimproved land of the neighborhood.

While the arable on the Svendsen claim still numbered only a few acres of land in 1865, Gro Svendsen described crops of corn, sorghum, potatoes, and watermelons. After the veteran had enlarged the breaking, he placed his major dependence on wheat. In 1866 and 1867 he had some ten acres of this crop; by 1869 the land devoted to it was eighteen acres. In the latter year he sowed three acres of oats also and had a few acres of corn and sorghum in addition to the inevitable potato patch. A year later he sowed a little barley as well. Gro would speak gratefully of the sorghum molasses, extracted and refined on the equipment of a neighbor for half the product. Since Ole Svendsen ordinarily grew little corn and kept a fair number of livestock, he must have cut considerable prairie hay each August and September.

Year after year the young Norwegian couple planted their crops and hoped for the best. Svendsen harvested 320 and 340 bushels of wheat in 1868 and 1869—years of bountiful crops and good prices. The years of the 1870's were apparently hard in Emmet County. Grasshoppers had appeared in 1868 without damaging the Svendsen crops to any extent, but in 1873 Gro reported, "In many places there will be no harvest. We did get a little, enough for our own living, but none to sell." A year later she wrote, "The pests . . . consumed everything except a little of the corn and the potatoes." In July of 1876 the pests returned again, "causing a great deal of damage." Although the Svendsens and their neighbors agreed to burn their prairie grass at the same time during the spring of 1877 in order to destroy the eggs of the grasshoppers, the insects worked considerable damage in that year as well. Anticipating their ravages, the Svendsens planted only corn in 1877 and harvested an indifferent crop. Still there was an abundant crop of grass for the livestock, and the Svendsens made twenty-nine gallons of syrup from sorghum that they saved from the locusts. They had not yet suffered, Gro informed her family in Norway, and the grasshoppers had left no eggs. Surely they were delivered from this plague.

If others did as the Svendsens, the pioneers of northwestern Iowa adjusted to the hopper invasion by putting more stress on the corn crop. But evidently corn was not highly successful in this region during the 1870's. The farmers of northwestern Iowa did not renounce their commitment to wheat for some time yet, although those in older settlements to the south and east were doing so during this decade. The corn planted in northwestern Iowa by the new settlers evidently was not adapted to the shorter seasons of that area; greater emphasis on the crop had to wait until the farmers found strains that would ripen more rapidly.

In a letter to her family in 1863, Gro Svendsen included a little sermon in practical economics. Discussing the yoke of young oxen that her husband had purchased in the previous year for $30.00 she wrote:

> You ask me why we use oxen. . . . In the first place, it is better to have cattle than cash. Currency fluctuates constantly. . . . We actually have nothing but paper money. There is no sign of gold or silver money. So you see it's far better to have cattle than the practically worthless paper money. . . . The price of cattle . . . does not fluctuate so much, and the young oxen will rise in value each year. If we were to sell them in the fall, we would surely get 45 or 50 dollars a yoke, good returns for the winter fodder. They continue to rise in value till they are eight years old, when they will bring anywhere from 80 to 100 dollars. When they are fully grown, they can do all the work. Therefore, anyone who intends to buy land should buy and raise young oxen. They are easy to care for, hay is plentiful, and in a very short time they are old enough to work. Then, too one can hire them out by the day. Even if one doesn't plan to buy land, it is wise to raise oxen and sell them, because of the profit.

In part for these reasons no doubt, and probably in part, also, because the distance to the nearest railroad limited the amount of grain that could be sold from the farm, the Svendsens consistently kept more livestock than one might have expected. In December, 1865, they were feeding twenty-three head of cattle, although a few of these were boarders belonging to other members of the family. During that fall Gro sold $35.00 worth of butter. Ordinarily thereafter the Svendsens kept between twelve and twenty head of cattle on their farm. During the 1870's Gro consistently reported six cows and a variety of younger stock. From a herd of this size the Svendsens were probably able to sell three or four animals each year and slaughter the occasional beef or old cow for family use. Six cows, doubtless, also provided Gro with sufficient cream so that she could make butter in amounts beyond the needs of her growing family.

Despite Gro Svendsen's endorsement of oxen in 1863, her husband was not permanently committed to them. By 1871 he owned a team of bay horses, "fine looking—the finest in the countryside," and had sold his work oxen. By 1877 the number of horses on the farm had grown to five although Ole owned a yoke of five-year-old oxen in addition. But the fine bays were now gone. The horses instead were "ponies" that the members of the family used mainly for driving and riding. When Gro enumerated the farm census for the last time in November of 1877, she listed five horses and sixteen head of cattle, including two "driving oxen," six cows, three heifers soon due to calve, two that would not, and three calves. There were in addition, twenty sheep, two pigs, twenty-five chickens, one dog, and one cat. The flock of sheep was a development mainly of the 1870's, although the Svendsens had owned a few during the 1860's. The Svendsens had apparently little liking for hogs. Gro never reported more than four pigs in any of her letters, and generally the number was less. This was no corn-hog farm. Evidently, Ole Svendsen fattened a litter each year for family use, and there his interest in porkers stopped.

When writing to her relatives in Norway, Gro Svendsen told little that was specific about farm income. But from the crops and stock and the few comments that she did make, it is easy to reconstruct the general outlines of the Svendsen farm business. Each year they sold a few head of cattle—often young oxen already broken to the yoke. During the late spring and summer, the milk cows produced sufficient milk so that Gro could churn a surplus of butter for sale in Estherville. The price per pound was low—between five and ten cents in all probability—but she reported proudly that she had sold $35.00 worth in 1865. Since the Svendsens increased the number of their cows shortly from four to six, Gro doubtless produced larger quantities of butter in subsequent years. This increase in output was balanced, to some extent, by the growth in size of her family and by lower prices. When the small-grain harvest was good, it added considerably to farm income. If we use the state average price for these years, the 320 bushels of wheat produced in 1868 and the 340 of 1869 were roughly worth $440 and $310, although the Svendsens may have received much less. Some of the wheat was retained for family use and seed; much of it was sold. In 1868 Ole drew wheat to the railroad at Waseca, Minnesota, and undoubtedly the local community in Emmet County absorbed considerable grain as a stream of new farm-makers flowed in during the late 1860's.

Even in 1868 and 1869 the cash income of the Svendsen farm could hardly have been much more than $400, if that, and in earlier and later years it was undoubtedly much less. In several locust years the grain crop was a flat failure, and the Svendsens could look only to the live-stock for cash income. At all times they avoided the purchase of store goods with an ingenuity that would amaze a modern farm family. In one of the early years in Emmet County, Gro sheared their lone sheep twice. We find in her letters the purchases that the Svendsens must have considered to be major milestones in the history of their farm. During 1864 they purchased a wagon for $35 and a stove for $25. This money they borrowed at interest from Ole's father. During 1867 they acquired a new harrow—price unknown but considered costly—and in 1868 Ole paid $26 for a new plow. The next year he purchased a new wagon for $90. In 1871 a new harness cost $40. Two years later one of the horses developed a sore leg during the summer working season and Ole must buy "Jack" at a cost of $150.

The year 1873 was a particularly discouraging one for the Svend-sens. The grasshoppers preyed upon the fields in the spring so that the crop was meager, they found that they must buy the land that they had hoped to homestead, and there was the expense of the new horse. This last outlay was all the more frustrating because the sick animal had recovered by autumn. "Times," wrote Gro, "have been hard this fall—much harder than any since we came to this land. The future is uncertain. . . . We have been thinking not a little of selling this land."

The Svendsens were appalled, at times, by the prices that they must pay for labor. The picture was by no means one in which co-operative pioneers traded their labor freely. Some labor exchange there undoubtedly was, but the Svendsen's kept a hired man intermittently— no less hired because sometimes a relative—and they paid cash for labor at harvest and threshing times. In 1868 a neighbor cut their eighteen acres of wheat with a reaper while five men bound the sheaves and one shocked. Ole and "our handy man, old man Hagen," were sufficient force to stack the grain. In the next year the "cost of reaping, binding, shock-ing, and stacking came to exactly fifty dollars. (Fifteen dollars for reaping alone.)" Threshing amounted to a further $42.00, which in-cluded the "wages of three men and the use of three teams of horses that accompanied the threshing machine," as well as the wages of eight extra men and the cost of two additional teams of horses needed to run the five-team horsepower. To Gro this was a considerable sum to set against a crop of 340 bushels on which the price ultimately fell to 50¢ a bushel. In August, 1872, she estimated that their debt at the end of the summer would be over one hundred dollars of which the greater part was owing "to brother Sevat for wages."

"When one begins to farm, it takes a great deal to get started— especially when one must begin with nothing and must go into debt besides." So wrote Gro Svendsen in 1864. The Svendsens occupied their claim on railroad land in Emmet County for ten years before they finally purchased it. Although the land had stood tax free in all probability, they still lacked savings that they could apply on the cost of the land. When Ole Svendsen decided to move to Dakota in 1879, the land was still encumbered. The sixteen years in Emmet County were not completely wasted years for the Svendsens, however. They wrested a living from the land and fed a constantly growing family. Nine children were living when Gro died in 1879. Despite these facts, the Svendsen story was one of painfully slow progress toward unencumbered ownership and security. The grasshopper years and the low prices of the 1870's undoubtedly explain the pattern to a considerable extent. These were the years also that constituted the first period of labor scarcity in the labor cycle of this farm family. Only in the mid-1870's did Ole's oldest sons become large enough to help him materially on the farm. Ole Svendsen was not a poor manager. . . . Ultimately he became a prosperous farmer in North Dakota. Unquestionably, however, he must have looked back upon the 1870's in Iowa as hard years, and so would many other farm-makers of northwestern Iowa.

Only a relatively few farmers knew pioneering at its rudest in the prairie communities. Croft Pilgrim . . . began . . . farming . . . after the settlements had taken shape.

Croft Pilgrim was born in England during 1834 and emigrated with his father and family to Peoria County, Illinois, in 1852. Three years after arriving in America, young Pilgrim married Susan Swank. The young couple evidently sought their fortunes in troubled Kansas during the late 1850's or early 1860's because Croft Pilgrim's first diary and account book lists the receipt of $414 on September 8, 1863, "from Kansas of Isac Hiner for land." How the young man had obtained money to buy land in Kansas we do not know, and we can only guess why he and his young wife left that embattled state. When Pilgrim started his journal in 1862, he had recently purchased an 85-acre farm in Stark County, Illinois. Six days after receiving the money from Kansas, he paid $184.95 to the attorney of the Egbert estate in partial payment for this Illinois farm. Pilgrim's deed listed a consideration of $376. Although Croft Pilgrim's diaries and accounts provide only a fragmentary record of his farming operations during the 1860's and have regrettable gaps in the next two decades also, they do present an informative picture of Corn Belt agriculture in evolution.

Croft Pilgrim's farm business was undoubtedly a small one during the early 1860's. His crops of grain in 1862 yielded 343 bushels of wheat and 252 bushels of oats, harvested, probably, from no more than thirty acres of cropland. His livestock consisted of a few pigs and cattle and probably a team of horses. The agricultural census-taker in 1880 would discover Croft Pilgrim established on a large farm of 310 acres in Poweshiek County, Iowa. The valuation of this farm was $11,100, ranking it as the seventh most valuable of the 176 farms in Grinnell Township. At the same time Pilgrim's two eldest sons were buying other farms from their father. Croft Pilgrim had won this comparative affluence in a period that agricultural historians portray as one of agricultural depression.

The major steps in the emergence of Croft Pilgrim as a successful farmer seem clear. During the 1860's he apparently paid off the debts on his original farm in Illinois, improved it by breaking and fencing, and began to accumulate additional capital. Wheat, at war prices, was evidently his largest source of income, although the share that he and his wife received of her father's estate may have smoothed the path materially. By the late 1860's he wanted more land. During 1869 he rented an additional forty acres of land, concluding, after keeping a meticulous record of labor and seed expended on it, that he had lost $82.00 by the transaction. In 1870 he tried to borrow on trust deed from a widow in Peoria in order to buy the farm of his brother John. At this point Susan Pilgrim, ordinarily referred to in the diaries cryptically as "the wife," takes on character and personality for the reader. She refused to sign the trust deed, although her husband had already paid down several hundred dollars on the purchase. By 1873, however, Susan's reluctance to buy land had apparently diminished, and Croft Pilgrim purchased an 80-acre farm from a neighbor for $3500. During 1876 he made his last payment and received the deed for this land, which lay in Bureau County.

In February, 1877, Croft Pilgrim spent two weeks in Iowa where he examined farms in Fayette, Buchanan, and Poweshiek counties. Later in 1877, he purchased 320 acres from J. K. James in Grinnell Township, Poweshiek County. At this point he sold the Illinois farm to the tax-collector in Stark County for $10,500. This young man, however, had second thoughts about the transaction, and Pilgrim agreed to cancel the contract in return for some $400 of damages. Despite the loss of anticipated income from the Illinois sale, Pilgrim could still tender the initial payment of $3500 for his new farm in Iowa. When the rest of the family moved to Poweshiek County during the spring of 1878, he left the farm in Illinois under the management of his eldest son, Charles Morey, who soon contracted to purchase the portion lying in Bureau County. In 1881 Croft Pilgrim sold the old home place to his brother William for $4500.

Why would a successful Illinois farmer sell his farm, break his community ties, and transfer his family and business to Iowa? More important still, what was there about Croft Pilgrim's farm business that allowed him to accumulate land and capital through the depression-torn 1870's? The implications of these questions spread far beyond the story of Croft Pilgrim, because he was not unique in the emergent Corn Belt. A detailed analysis of Pilgrim's accounts and diaries provide some tentative answers.

Through the twenty years of this study, Croft Pilgrim depended mainly on the sale of grain and hogs for his income. One might call his farm a cash-grain-and-hogs operation. During the Civil War he evidently grew and sold considerable amounts of wheat; by the early 1870's his wheat crop was intended primarily as a source of flour for the kitchen and of chicken feed. Consistently he raised comparatively large quantities of oats—mainly for sale rather than for feed on the farm. Consistently, also, he kept a few cows. From the milk the family churned butter that was mostly consumed at home, although Pilgrim traded some at the local store. He might raise and sell a few animals for veal or beef, but he was short of pasture despite the purchase of additional acreage. In 1876 he rented pasture for ten head of young stock. Ordinarily his major income from stock came from hogs. Of these he was selling several carloads a year by the late 1870's. To feed the hogs and also, to some degree, for cash sale, he grew corn. In 1879 he reported 150 acres of corn—an acreage equal to that in all other crops and hay. At first Pilgrim sold all his products locally. He continued to dispose of his grain in this way by dealing with local grain merchants. His cattle, too, he sold to local drovers or farmers. By 1873 he was accompanying his hogs to the stockyards in Chicago.

In even the small farm operation of the early 1860's there were periods when the farm-operator needed assistance if he was to work efficiently. When his diaries begin, Pilgrim was a member of a small group of seven neighbors who helped each other in haying, grain harvest, stacking, and threshing. Within the group minor patterns of exchange occurred at corn-planting time or when Pilgrim or a neighbor butchered a beef or one or two hogs. The first record that Croft Pilgrim kept was a harvest account in which he tabulated the amount of labor given and received within the work ring. Here, labor was a commodity that was used to pay the rent for machinery or additional horsepower. Pilgrim owned no reaper in the earliest years of record and tried to give additional labor to the neighbor who cut his grain. Consistently, members of the work ring brought their teams to help run the horsepower of the threshing machine. During the late 1860's and early 1870's neighbors were using Pilgrim's mower and reaper. In late fall or winter the neighbors balanced out the labor accounts with small cash payments to the members who had given more labor than they had received. Aside from the work ring, Croft Pilgrim hired no farm labor during the span of his diaries with the exception of skilled workmen whom he retained for various projects of farm improvement—masons, carpenters, and tile layers. At intervals, a hired girl did assist Mrs. Pilgrim in her task of caring for six sons and a daughter.

As his family of six sons matured, Pilgrim's dependence on the neighbors diminished somewhat, and the work ring of the early 1880's had a membership of only five in comparison to the seven of the early sixties. We cannot overemphasize the importance of this growing family in Croft Pilgrim's business success. As they reached their teens, his sons entered increasingly into the work of the farm and provided a reliable supply of labor. The eldest boys, Charles Morey and John Henry, began to work for other farmers for several months at a time when they were in their mid-teens, and their employers paid the wages to Croft Pilgrim. Some 15 per cent of Pilgrim's receipts in 1873 came from the sale of labor in some form, and the largest item by far in this total was the money received in payment for the labor of Charles Morey and John Henry, then 17 and 16 years of age.

Croft Pilgrim was able to exchange labor directly for cash in another way as well. In an age when gross cash receipts were small by twentieth century standards, a few dollars derived from political office or jury duty was of considerable importance. Croft Pilgrim frequently served on the county juries, and as local roadmaster in 1873 he bargained with some of his neighbors to work out their road tax, thus deriving an additional income of some $30.

Pilgrim's terse diary entries reflected the changes in agricultural technology that were revolutionizing midwestern agriculture during the last half of the nineteenth century. He owned no reaper in 1862, but at least one member of the work ring did. Thereafter Croft Pilgrim acquired a succession of mowers, reapers, hay rakes, sulky plows, and John Deere iron-beam plows. By 1873 his sons no longer dropped corn before the flashing hoes of their father and a member of the work ring; Croft Pilgrim was using a borrowed horse-planter. During the next year he purchased both corn-planter and cultivator. In 1878 a Grinnell merchant brought a check-rower attachment to the farm for trial; it did not work satisfactorily, Pilgrim recorded. Through the 1860's and 1870's he watched his teams and those of his neighbors monotonously circling the central gearing of the horsepower during threshing. In 1882 he noted that his thresher was using a steam engine.

Pilgrim's farm improvements also revealed the changing technology of the times. Board and hedge were his earliest fencing materials, and trimming hedge was a task that occupied several days of his time between the seeding of the small grains and corn-planting during the early 1870's. After he moved to Iowa, he noted large expenditures for fence posts and wire, and one entry recorded a payment for labor expended in placing barbs on old wire. During the mid-1870's he engaged a ditching-and-tiling outfit to lay 202 rods of tile on his property. Technically speaking, the results were evidently excellent. He bought several carloads of tile shortly after establishing himself near Grinnell.

Pilgrim's earliest venture in tiling disrupted the harmony of the neighborhood. No sooner was the drain completed than his neighbor Tom Mellor dammed the outlet, claiming that the tiling system was flooding his fields. Thus in 1876 began a long-drawn-out litigation, which started in the court of the local justice of the peace and moved ultimately into the district court. After a series of decisions and appeals, the case still stood on the docket at Toulon, the county seat, in 1882, and by this time had cost Croft Pilgrim several hundred dollars. Despite the location of his land, Mellor was not, incidentally, a member of Pilgrim's work or visiting circle—an indication that the nineteenth century rural neighborhood was not the pool of togetherness that some rural sociologists have imagined. To compound the unpleasantness of the warfare, a former member of Pilgrim's labor ring and ally in local politics joined Mellor's camp and instituted a companion action.

The young Pilgrims did not grow up in an age of homespun. During the 1860's and 1870's Susan Pilgrim did make many of the work clothes for her family from hickory shirting, denim, and the like, but the members of the family purchased suits and shoes and occasional overalls in the nearby trade centers. Although Pilgrim slaughtered hogs and cattle for home use, he frequently bought beef from a local butcher during the summer. The family did most of its trading at the nearby station and post office of Bradford; they also patronized the stores of Buda in Bureau County, and specific needs or errands took them to Neponset, Lombardville, and to the county seat, Toulon.

During their residence in Illinois, the Pilgrims did business consistently with five merchants—a harness maker, a blacksmith, an agricultural-implement salesman, a cobbler, and the proprietor of a coal bank. To Brewer, Davis, and Company at Bradford, Croft Pilgrim sold his grain, and from them he purchased his lumber and some general merchandise. Household supplies for the Pilgrim family came, for the most part, from the store of Pilgrim's brother William, a general merchant of Bradford. All of the general merchants were willing, on occasion, to take butter and eggs on account, and with all of them, Pilgrim kept small running accounts that he settled every few months. After moving to Iowa, he developed a similar trading pattern among the merchants of Grinnell.

In some years Croft Pilgrim kept a day-by-day record of expenditures and receipts. Table 25 shows statements of his farm business during

TABLE 25   Croft Pilgrim's Farm Business

Receipts

	1873	1877	1882
Butter & eggs	$ 93.00	$ 5.55	$ 4.20
Grain	244.04	525.20	1,936.81
Potatoes	.....	6.00	.....
Stock	780.06	1,508.35	1,202.45
Labor	214.85	76.74	.....
Miscellaneous	88.58	17.25	30.60
	$1,420.53	$2,139.09	$3,174.06

Farm Expenditures

	1873	1877	1882
Equipment, Improvements and supplies	$114.59	$125.75	$ 618.19
Seed and crop expense	15.50	2.50	55.35
Stock	154.00	73.70	331.88
Labor	21.15	23.35	36.70
Threshing and shelling	21.44	30.78	37.94
Legal services	30.16	38.56	17.23
Taxes	....	16.35	98.97
	$356.84	$310.99	$1,196.26

Household Expenses

	1873	1877	1882
Provisions and supplies	$334.96	$205.45	$ 520.22
Apparel	82.13	109.92	217.44
Labor	7.00	14.00	128.01
Education	2.55	60.55	8.00
Gifts	6.00	....	60.00
Miscellaneous	5.27	....	2.35
	437.91	389.92	936.02
Travel	20.45	84.07	23.65
	$458.36	$473.99	$ 959.67

the years 1873, 1877, and 1882 based on the memoranda in his diary. Unfortunately, he was not entirely consistent in recording his business transactions. On occasion, he evidently entered the same expenditure twice. Other entries were so terse that they are difficult to categorize. The family used a few items, notably salt, in both house and barn; these were counted among the household expenses. The costs of travel posed a similar problem. On occasion, Pilgrim or members of his family traveled on business, sometimes on pleasure, and, probably most often, they mixed both motives, merging farm and household expenses. Pilgrim did not record his tax bill in 1873; that of 1877 was probably incomplete. Nor was it possible to learn the value of improvements made in the various years, nor changes in the inventory of stock, grain, and feed. Granted such limitations, however, Table 25 does shed considerable light on Pilgrim's farm business during the 1870's and early 1880's.

Croft Pilgrim's receipts in 1873 show a diversified farm business in which he had at his disposal more labor than he could use effectively in his own operations. Subsequently, as he increased the size of his farm, he was able to utilize the labor of his growing family of sons at home. As he enlarged his grain and hog enterprises, the income from barnyard poultry and milk cows became of little importance. Hogs, corn, and oats were the dominant enterprises by the mid-1870's at least.

The statements of expenses in Table 25 speak largely for themselves. The rather large outlays on farm account in 1882 reflect extensive improvements that he was making on the new farm in Iowa, including, evidently, some remodeling of the house. After deducting farm expenditures from gross receipts, the net sum left assignable to depreciation account, to labor, and to capital was 75, 81, and 61 per cent. (Since some of Pilgrim's expenditures for improvements might properly be considered additions to capital rather than farm-business expenses, the calculations are crude.) After the deduction of household expenses, Croft Pilgrim still had 42, 63 and 32 per cent of the total receipts left at his disposal. Assuming that missing expenditures like the taxes of 1873 might reduce the figures by 5 or 10 per cent, the showing was still a handsome one. The Pilgrim family obviously had no pressing need for the several hundred dollars that Mrs. Pilgrim inherited from her mother's estate in 1873.

The accumulation of money brings pleasantly vexatious decisions about its management. Croft Pilgrim could no doubt have channeled much of his money into farm improvements. Unquestionably, he did improve his holdings. Diary entries show him buying lumber, bricks, fencing materials, and drainage tile. We cannot know, of course, the degree to which these expenditures simply represented repairs in contrast to new improvements. Pilgrim's major long-run decision in the management of his profits has already become obvious. He bought more land. In the interims between purchases and payments, he loaned a good deal of money—usually in sums of several hundred dollars. Some of these loans the Stark County farmer made to Brewer and Davis, a local mercantile firm; others were to William Pilgrim, his merchant brother; still others went to surrounding farmers. Most of these loans were for periods of only a few months, and in many cases the interest rate was not clearly revealed in the diary entries. Some of Pilgrim's farmer-borrowers, however, paid 10 per cent. Pilgrim did make smaller loans in amounts of $5.00 to $50.00. Usually the borrowers in such cases were members of Pilgrim's work ring, and the transactions were short-term accommodation loans. Occasionally, Pilgrim himself might borrow a few dollars from one of the group if momentarily pressed for funds.

His diaries show Croft Pilgrim to have been a hard-working, punctilious man, slightly litigious, perhaps, who regarded farming as a business and not simply as a way of life. Whether by luck or sound planning, few disasters happened on his farm. Occasionally, he found it necessary to replant corn, or the team ran away. Major crop failures or losses of stock did not occur. He was relatively well informed. He attended the agricultural fairs of his region regularly and in 1876 visited the Centennial Exhibition in Philadelphia. Apparently, however, he did not subscribe to an agricultural periodical. He was a man who was careful of his expenditures, although, judging from the nature of the occasional purchase not penurious. The uses of credit he well understood, and, Granger though he was, he was not afraid to put his knowledge to the test.

Croft Pilgrim did not allow himself to become intoxicated by the new technology of agriculture. He experimented with machines owned by his neighbors before he himself purchased implements of the same type, and he frequently obtained them on trial. He was no pioneer in laying tile, but he did so as soon as the advantages of doing so became established.

The combination of enterprises on the Pilgrim farm—cash grain and hogs—was not the only one that Croft Pilgrim could have made. He could instead have fed cattle or concentrated still more on the production of cash grain, for instance. But his combination of swine and grain balanced his business without demanding the capital investment that feeder cattle involved. Even when he was raising considerable amounts of wheat in 1862, he was growing more oats than was usual in central Illinois at the time, and his cropping decisions foreshadowed the growing importance of this crop in the 1870's.

In part, Croft Pilgrim benefited from the general increase in land values underway in Illinois after 1860; he had paid far less than the $10,500 for which his Illinois holdings were tentatively sold in 1877. If the deed register tells the whole story, the 85 acres in Stark County increased in value from $376 in 1861 to $4,500 in 1881. Some of his success was attributable to the happy combination of genes that made him the father of six healthy boys. He held to the patriarchal tradition that the labor of the sons belonged to the father until they had reached their majority. On the other hand, he recognized an obligation to help them acquire their own farms when they reached an appropriate age.

His diary entries make Croft Pilgrim's success appear absurdly easy —even inevitable. But we know that many Illinois and Iowa farmers found that success was neither easy nor inevitable during these same years. Perhaps the road to affluence did not seem easy to Pilgrim either. While he was making the decisions that spelled success, he was supporting the creed of the Granger and the Greenbacker. Anomalous though this may appear, it was by no means unusual. Commercially-oriented farmers with larger businesses than average provided much of the Grange and Greenback leadership in Iowa and Illinois. The fertile but relatively low-priced lands of Iowa might draw such a man irresistibly.

·   ·   ·

We have seen the midwestern farmer breaking the prairie, harvesting his crops, tending his livestock, and amassing capital. I have emphasized those farming activities and problems that must usually have held his attention. But the prairie farmer's world had wide boundaries by the 1840's at least. Never a landlocked Crusoe, he owed much thereafter to the expansion of both the domestic and foreign markets for his products and to the developments in transportation, processing techniques, and marketing methods that allowed him to enter those markets on a competitive basis. Local market, frontier post, forty-niner, southern plantation, industrial America, famine-racked Ireland, British mill town, and continental city—the prairie farmer supplied them all in varying degree. . . .

There is a time-hallowed tradition that the years between 1866 and 1896 were years of almost unalloyed agricultural depression in the United States. There is certainly evidence to support such a position. The prices of agricultural commodities fell during this period, as did prices in general, and it is generally agreed that primary producers are particularly hard hit in periods of declining prices. Both in the 1870's and the 1890's there were bursts of protest from the farmers of mid-America. On the other hand one need only read a few of the biographical sections in the many histories of prairie counties that were published during the last quarter of the nineteenth century to realize that a great many farmers in Illinois and Iowa prospered exceedingly in the years after the Civil War. On the pages of these county "mug books" are spread the success stories of countless farmers who started with little and who in the 1880's or 1890's were able to report broad holdings of valuable land.

Certainly it is true that there began a period of almost unrivaled prosperity for midwestern farmers in the late 1890's and that this continued until the end of the first world war. In only one year between 1900 and 1920 were there as many as five mortgage foreclosures in Story County, Iowa. During the twenty years, 1880–99, the number of foreclosures reached thirteen in one year but was above ten in only three; these figures were far below the level of foreclosures during the previous thirty years in the county. In the years 1865, 1876, and 1877 there were twenty-five farm mortgages foreclosed in Story County. During 1871 the number was twenty-six, and in 1879, the nineteenth-century high, thirty-eight. In three widely scattered Iowa townships the percentage of real estate mortgages that went to foreclosure proceedings between 1852 and 1896 was 3.2. But of the mortgages filed between 1870 and 1874 inclusive and between 1875 and 1879 inclusive, the average number going to court was 5.2 per cent in both cases. By contrast the failure rate on mortgages filed in the years 1885–89 and 1890–96 was 1.7 and 1.8 per cent. Somewhat less precise evidence reveals a similar picture in Illinois. Clearly the 1870's were the years of greatest tribulation for prairie farmers. Midwestern farm protest in the late 1880's and early 1890's emanated from the plains states rather than from the prairies. Here farmers were already entering the golden age of midwestern agriculture. Even in the 1870's, there was no disaster on the prairies comparable to the crisis that occurred in portions of the plains states in the Populist era.

Undoubtedly declining prices did press hard upon prairie farmers during the thirty years after the Civil War. But at the same time horse-power technology was allowing them to increase their productivity greatly. Farmers who exploited machinery effectively could and did prosper. It is clear, too, that the man who studied his markets and was alert to relative changes in the prices of farm products could outstrip his neighbor. The index of Iowa wheat prices, for instance, declined relatively far more between 1866 and 1896 than did the indexes of oats, corn, hogs, or beef. On the other hand the index of beef prices showed considerable stability throughout most of the post Civil War period despite the bitter complaints of many Illinois feeders after 1885. Almost invariably, too, during these years the relationship between corn and hog prices made it almost always profitable to feed hogs. One hundred pounds of pork was worth less than 10 bushels of corn in only three years between 1861 and 1900 in Iowa.

Evidently also, there were subregional differences in farm income in the prairie states. In a recent study, Frank T. Bachmura discovered that the gross returns for each member of the agricultural labor force in nine subdivisions of Iowa differed substantially in state and federal census years from 1869 to 1930. His findings also suggest that returns per agri-

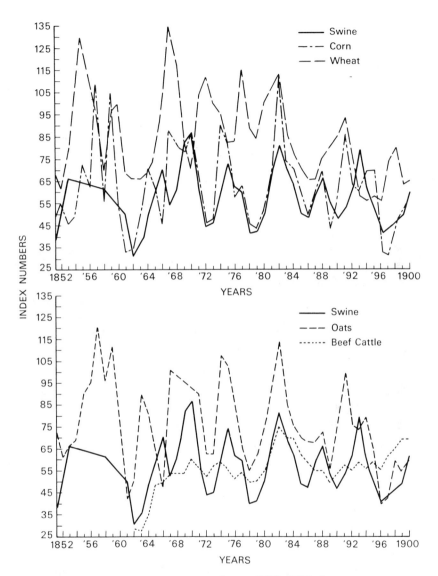

FIGURE 1   *Iowa price indexes, 1851–1900 (currency prices adjusted to gold values, 1862–78)*

cultural worker were usually low in frontier regions. In 1869 and 1875 gross returns per agricultural worker in the twelve counties of northwestern Iowa were the lowest in the state. By 1910 this district led all others.

The more progressive farmers of the prairie triangle evidently entered the 1880's aware that their best future lay in increasing the size of their farm units to take advantage of the new technology. They had learned, too, that profit lay in judicious combinations of corn, hogs, and cattle while not discarding the small grains, particularly oats, nor ignoring tame grasses and clovers—a necessity as the prairie grass commons disappeared. Corn rootworm and smut convinced farmers who cast their lots unreservedly with the corn crop that some rotation paid. They found now, too, that tiling rewarded the investment. The farmers of the Illinois black-earth counties took up this task seriously in the 1880's, although there had, of course, been much ditch drainage earlier. The farmers of the wet prairies in Iowa followed suit in a few years time. Cheap labor and falling interest rates helped speed the tasks of adjustment. The usual rate on farm mortgages in 1878 in central Illinois and much of Iowa was 10 per cent; it had fallen to 6 per cent by 1896.

If owner-operators were apparently solving their problems with considerable success during the 1880's and 1890's, the same was hardly true of the tenants or farm laborers who aspired to ownership. During the last half of the nineteenth century, the increased productivity of agricultural labor benefited the farm-operator considerably more than it did the laborer. At the same time the land equivalent of the monthly agricultural wage fell drastically. Land obtained for $1.25 per acre in central Illinois or eastern Iowa in the 1830's or 1840's now commanded prices of $40 to $60 and, in many cases, even more. The cost of drainage alone could add from $5 to $20 to the farmer's investment in his acres. The cost of necessary machinery had also increased during the same period, but in the face of rising land values it became proportionately less important in the total investment of the owner-operator. The value of land and buildings was 76 per cent of the total investment in land, machinery, and livestock for the "average farm" of 1850 in Illinois; the percentage was 89 in 1900. Tenancy rates, therefore, edged upward in Illinois and Iowa during the last years of the nineteenth century. We should remember, however, that no agricultural area in the national history of this country has been able to absorb all of its would-be farmers.

On the prairies of Illinois and Iowa—as in adjacent states—a mobile energetic population made the Corn Belt. Spurred by technological achievements and expanding markets, commercial farmers built one of the most prosperous agricultural economies the world had ever seen in this land, where each year the rains, the summer heat, and productive soils produced the broad-leafed fields of dark green. Here work often brought

TABLE 29   Average Farm Business

	Acres	Total Invest-ment	Value Land & Bldgs.	Per Cent of Total	Value Mach. & Imple-ments	Per Cent of Total	Value Live-stock	Per Cent of Total
			Iowa					
1850	185	$1453.54	$1125.13	77	$ 79.22	6	$ 249.19	17
1860	165	2477.07	2010.75	81	89.33	4	376.93	15
1870	134	4266.48	3376.52	79	176.36	4	713.60	17
1880	134	3892.69	3061.38	79	158.46	4	672.85	17
1890	151	5451.53	4247.49	78	181.59	3	1022.45	19
1900	151	9496.62	8023.48	84	253.52	3	1219.61	13
			Illinois					
1850	158	$1666.64	$1261.00	76	$ 87.97	5	$ 317.67	19
1860	146	3503.47	2873.04	82	121.08	3	509.35	15
1870	128	5447.83	4538.91	83	170.49	3	738.43	14
1880	124	4597.50	3947.72	86	131.93	3	517.85	11
1890	127	6139.90	5247.07	86	143.16	3	749.67	12
1900	124	8491.54	7587.76	89	170.27	2	733.51	9

success; work plus good luck often brought great success. In the biographical sketches of the county histories there are implicit the values that the Corn Belt farmers cherished in the fading years of the nineteenth century. It was good to have pioneered here, to have been an "old settler," and made virgin prairie "productive" by stocking it with fine animals and raising bountiful crops. He had lived a good life who started with little and added to his acres so that in middle or old age he could start his sons on farms or rent to others. These, of course, were the values of the successful and only part of the reality of farm life in the prairie peninsula. More farm-makers got a head start in the race for success than admitted it in their biographies. There were two sides to tenancy; many farm boys could not win the prize of unencumbered ownership. Some owners failed miserably. Land was often a lucrative speculation no less than a factor of production. But in sum the achievements had been striking. By the 1890's the work of the pioneers was done; their successors were moving forward into the golden age of middle-western agriculture.

10

Cuba, the Philippines, and Manifest Destiny

RICHARD HOFSTADTER

No historian has proved more gifted than Richard Hofstadter in applying the insights of social psychology to the study of American history. Accordingly, he has proposed plausible psychological explanations for the origins of the radical right, the Progressive movement, and American imperialism in 1898. In explaining why America declared war on Spain and why it acquired the Philippines, Hofstadter rejects both economic motives and the newspaper circulation war as prime factors. Instead he finds the explanation in the "psychic crisis of the 1890's."

The taking of the Philippine Islands from Spain in 1899 marked a major historical departure for the American people, a breach in their traditions and a shock to their established values. To be sure, from their national beginnings they had constantly engaged in expansion, but almost entirely into contiguous territory. Now they were extending themselves to distant extra-hemispheric colonies. They were abandoning a strategy of defense hitherto limited to the continent and its appurtenances, in favor of a major strategic commitment in the Far East. Thus far their expansion had been confined to the spread of a relatively homogeneous population into territories planned from the beginning to develop self-government; now control was to be imposed by force on millions of ethnic aliens. The

From Richard Hofstadter, *The Paranoid Style in American Politics and Other Essays* (New York: Alfred A. Knopf, 1965), pp. 147–50, 152–53, 158–61, 174–87. © 1952 by Richard Hofstadter. Reprinted by permission of Alfred A. Knopf, Inc.

acquisition of the islands, therefore, was understood by contemporaries on both sides of the debate, as it is readily understood today, to be a turning point in our history.

To discuss the debate in isolation from other events, however, would be to deprive it of its full significance. America's entrance into the Philippine Islands was a by-product of the Spanish-American War. The Philippine crisis is inseparable from the war crisis, and the war crisis itself is inseparable from a larger constellation that might be called "the psychic crisis of the 1890's."

Central in the background of the psychic crisis was the great depression that broke in 1893 and was still very acute when the agitation over the war in Cuba began. Severe depression, by itself, does not always generate an emotional crisis as intense as that of the nineties. In the 1870's the country had been swept by a depression of comparable acuteness and duration which, however, did not give rise to all the phenomena that appeared in the 1890's or to very many of them with comparable intensity and impact. It is often said that the 1890's, unlike the 1870's, form a "watershed" in American history. The difference between the emotional and intellectual impact of these two depressions can be measured, I believe, not by the difference in severity, but rather by reference to a number of singular events that in the 1890's converged with the depression to heighten its impact upon the public mind.

First in importance was the Populist movement, the free-silver agitation, the heated campaign of 1896. For the first time in our history a depression had created a protest movement strong enough to capture a major party and raise the specter, however unreal, of drastic social convulsion. Second was the maturation and bureaucratization of American business, the completion of its essential industrial plant, and the development of trusts on a scale sufficient to stir the anxiety that the old order of competitive opportunities was approaching an eclipse. Third, and of immense symbolic importance, was the apparent filling up of the continent and the disappearance of the frontier line. We now know how much land had not yet been taken up and how great were the remaining possibilities for internal expansion both in business and on the land; but to the mind of the 1890's it seemed that the resource that had engaged the energies of the people for three centuries had been used up. The frightening possibility suggested itself that a serious juncture in the nation's history had come. As Frederick Jackson Turner expressed it in his famous paper of 1893: "Now, four centuries from the discovery of America, at the end of one hundred years of life under the Constitution, the frontier has gone, and with its going has closed the first period of American history."

To middle-class citizens who had been brought up to think in terms of the nineteenth-century order, the outlook seemed grim. Farmers in the staple-growing region had gone mad over silver and Bryan; workers were stirring in bloody struggles like the Homestead and Pullman strikes; the supply of new land seemed at an end; the trust threatened the spirit of business enterprise; civic corruption was at a high point in the large cities; great waves of seemingly unassimilable immigrants arrived yearly and settled in hideous slums. To many historically conscious writers, the nation appeared overripe, like an empire ready for collapse through a stroke from outside or through internal upheaval. Acute as the situation was for all those who lived by the symbols of national power—for the governing and thinking classes—it was especially poignant for young people, who would have to make their careers in the dark world that seemed to be emerging.

The symptomatology of the crisis would record several tendencies in popular thought and behavior that had previously existed only in pale and tenuous form. These symptoms were manifest in two quite different moods. The key to one of them was an intensification of protest and humanitarian reform. Populism, utopianism, the rise of the Christian Social gospel, the growing intellectual interest in socialism, the social settlement movement that appealed so strongly to the college generation of the nineties, the quickening of protest and social criticism in the realistic novel— all these are expressions of this mood. The other mood was one of national self-assertion, aggression, expansion. The motif of the first was social sympathy; of the second, national power. During the 1890's far more patriotic groups were founded than in any other decade of our history; the naval theories of Captain Mahan were gaining in influence; naval construction was booming; there was an immense quickening of the American cult of Napoleon and a vogue of the virile and martial writings of Rudyard Kipling; young Theodore Roosevelt became the exemplar of the vigorous, masterful, out-of-doors man; the revival of European imperialism stirred speculation over what America's place would be in the world of renewed colonial rivalries, and in some stirred a demand to get into the imperial race to avoid the risk of being overwhelmed by other powers. But most significant was the rising tide of jingoism, a matter of constant comment among observers of American life during the decade. . . .

.   .   .

Three primary incidents fired American jingoism between the spring of 1891 and the close of 1895. First came Secretary of State Blaine's tart and provocative reply to the Italian minister's protest over the lynching of eleven Italians in New Orleans. Then there was friction with Chile over a riot in Valparaíso in which two American sailors were killed and several injured by a Chilean mob. In 1895 occurred the more famous Venezuela boundary dispute with Britain. Discussion of these incidents would take us too far afield, but note that they all had these characteristics in common: in none of them was national security or the natural interest vitally and immediately involved; in all three American diplomacy was extraordinarily and disproportionately aggressive; in all three the possibility of war was contemplated; and in each case the response of the American public and press was enthusiastically nationalist and almost unanimous.

It is hard to read the history of these events without concluding that politicians were persistently using jingoism to restore their prestige, mend their party fences, and divert the public mind from grave internal discontents. It hardly seems an accident that jingoism and populism rose together. Documentary evidence for the political exploitation of foreign crises is not overwhelmingly abundant, in part because such a motive is not necessarily conscious and where it is conscious it is not always confessed or recorded. The persistence of jingoism in every administration from Harrison's to Theodore Roosevelt's, however, is too suggestive to be ignored. During the nineties the press of each party was fond of accusing the other of exploiting foreign conflict. Blaine was not above twisting the British lion's tail for political purposes; and it is hardly likely that he would have exempted Italy from the same treatment. Harrison, on the eve of the Chile affair, for the acuteness of which he was primarily responsible, was being urged by prominent Republican politicians who had the coming presidential campaign in mind to pursue a more aggressive foreign policy because it would "have the . . . effect of diverting attention from stagnant political discussions." And although some Democratic papers charged that he was planning to run for re-election during hostilities so that he could use the "don't swap horses in the middle of the stream" appeal, many Democrats felt that it was politically necessary for them to back him against Chile so that, as one of their congressmen remarked, the Republicans could not "run away with all the capital there is to be made in an attempt to assert national self-respect." . . .

Historians often say that the war was brought on by sensational newspapers. The press, spurred by the rivalry between Pulitzer and Hearst, aroused sympathy with the Cubans and hatred of Spain and catered to the bellicosity of the public. No one seems to have asked: *Why was the public so fatally receptive to war propaganda?* I believe the answer must be sought in the causes of the jingoism that had raged for seven years before the war actually broke out. The events of the nineties had brought frustration and anxiety to civically conscious Americans. On one hand, as Mark Sullivan has commented, the American during this period was disposed "to see himself as an underdog in economic situations and controversies in his own country"; but the civic frustrations of the era created also a restless aggressiveness, a desire to be assured that the power and vitality of the nation were not waning. The capacity for sympathy and the need for power existed side by side. That highly typical American, William Allen White, recalls in his *Autobiography* how during the nineties he was "bound to my idols—Whitman, the great democrat, and Kipling, the imperialist." In varying degrees the democrat and the imperialist existed in the hearts of White's countrymen—the democrat disposed to free Cuba; the imperialist, to vent his spleen on Spain.

I suspect that the readiness of the public to overreact to the Cuban situation can be understood in part through the displacement of feelings of sympathy or social protest generated in domestic affairs; these impulses found a safe and satisfactory discharge in foreign conflict. Spain was portrayed in the press as waging a heartless and inhuman war; the Cubans were portrayed as noble victims of Spanish tyranny, their situation as analogous to that of Americans in 1776. When one examines the sectional and political elements that were most enthusiastic about policies that led to war, one finds them not primarily among the wealthy eastern big-business Republicans who gave McKinley his strongest support and read the dignified conservative newspapers, but in the Bryan sections of the country, in the Democratic party, among western Republicans, and among the readers of the yellow journals. A great many businessmen were known to fear the effects of a war on the prosperity that was just returning, and some thought that a war might strengthen the free-silver movement. During the controversy significant charges were hurled back and forth: conservative peace advocates claimed that many jingoists were hoping for a costly war over Cuba that could be made the occasion of a return to free silver; in reply, the inflammatory press often fell into the pattern of Populist rhetoric, declaiming, for example, about "the eminently respectable porcine citizens who—for dollars in the money-grubbing sty, support 'conservative' newspapers and consider the starvation of . . . inoffensive men, women and children, and the murder of 250 American sailors . . . of less importance than a fall of two points in a price of stocks." As Margaret Leech has remarked, peace "had become a symbol of obedience to avarice." In the case of some of the war enthusiasts it is not clear whether they favored action more because they bled for the sufferings of the Cubans or because they hated the materialism and the flaccid pacifism of the *haute bourgeoisie*. Theodore Roosevelt, who was not in the habit of brooding over the wrongs done to the underdog in the United States, expressed some of this when he cried at Mark Hanna: "We will have this war for the freedom of Cuba in spite of the timidity of the commercial interests."

Although imputations of base motives were made by both sides, it is also significant that the current of sympathy and agitation ran strong where a disconnected constituency, chagrined at Bryan's defeat, was most numerous. An opportunity to discharge hatred of "Wall Street interests" that were coolly indifferent to the fate of both Cuban *insurrectos* and staple farmers may have been more important than the more rationalized and abstract linkage between war and free silver. The primary significance of this war in the psychic economy of the 1890's was that it served as an outlet for expressing aggressive impulses while presenting itself, quite truthfully, as an idealistic and humanitarian crusade. It had the advantage of expressing in one issue both the hostilities and the generous moral passions of the public. The American public on the whole showed little interest in such material gains as might accrue from an intervention in Cuba. It never dreamed that the war would lead to the taking of the Philippines, of whose existence it was hardly aware. Starting a war for a high-minded and altruistic purpose and then transmuting it into a war for annexation was unimaginable. That would be, as McKinley put it in a phrase that later came back to haunt him, "criminal aggression."

.   .   .

In the arguments for annexation two essential moral and psychological themes appeared over and over again. These themes were expressed in the words of Duty and Destiny. According to the first, to reject annexation of the Philippines would be to fail of fulfilling a solemn obligation. According to the second, annexation of the Philippines in particular and expansion generally were inevitable and irresistible.

The people had entered the war for what they felt to be purely altruistic and humanitarian reasons—the relief and liberation of the Cubans. The idea that territorial gains should arise out of this pure-hearted war of liberation, and the fact that before long the Americans stood in the same relation to the Filipinos as the Spaniards had stood to the Cubans, was most uncomfortable. This situation raised moral questions that the anti-imperialists did not neglect to express and exploit. The imperialists were accused of breaking our national word, of violating the pledge made by McKinley himself that by our moral code forcible annexation would be "criminal aggression." They were also accused of violating the solemn injunctions of the Founding Fathers, particularly the principles of the Declaration of Independence. The rhetoric of Duty was a reassuring answer to this attempt to stir feelings of guilt.

The quick victories won by American arms strengthened the psychological position of the imperialists. The feeling that one may be guilty of wrongdoing can be heightened when the questionable act is followed by adversity. Conversely, it may be minimized by the successful execution of a venture. Misfortune is construed as Providential punishment; but success, as in the Calvinist scheme, is taken as an outward sign of an inward state of grace. One of the most conspicuous things about the war was the remarkable successes achieved by American arms, of which the most astonishing was Dewey's destruction, without losing a single American life, of the entire Spanish Eastern Fleet in Manila Bay. Victories of this sort could readily be interpreted as Providential signs, tokens of divine approval. It was widely reported in the United States that this was Dewey's own interpretation. "If I were a religious man, and hope I am," he said, "I should say that the hand of God was in it." This was precisely the sort of reassurance that was needed. "The magnificent fleets of Spain," declared a writer in a Baptist periodical, referring to Spain's senile and decrepit navy, "have gone down as marvelously, I had almost said, as miraculously, as the walls of Jericho went down." The victory, said an editor of the *Christian and Missionary Alliance,* "read almost like the stories of the ancient battles of the Lord in the times of Joshua, David, and Jehosophat."

Furthermore, what might have seemed a sin became transformed into a positive obligation, a duty. The feeling was: *Providence has been so indulgent to us, by giving us so richly of success, that we would be sinful if we did not accept the responsibility it has asked us to assume.* The Protestant clergy, as guardians of the national conscience, did not hesitate to make lavish use of such arguments. "To give to the world the life more abundant both for here and hereafter," reasoned a writer in the *Baptist Missionary Review,* "is the duty of the American people by virtue of the call of God. This call is very plain. The hand of God in history has ever been plain." "If God has brought us to the parting of the ways," insisted a writer in the *Churchman,* "we cannot hold back without rejecting divine leadership." The rhetoric of secular leaders was hardly less inspired. "We will not renounce our part in the mission of our race, trustees under God, of the civilization of the world," said Senator Albert J. Beveridge. "God has not been preparing the English-speaking and Teutonic peoples for a thousand years for nothing but vain and idle self-contemplation and self-admiration. No! He has made us the master organizers of the world to establish system where chaos reigns. He has made us adepts in government that we may administer government among savages and senile peoples."

The theme of Destiny was a corollary of the theme of Duty. Repeatedly it was declared that expansion was the result of a "cosmic tendency," that "destiny always arrives," that it was in the "inexorable logic of events," and so on. The doctrine that expansion was inevitable had of course long been familiar to Americans; we all know how often Manifest Destiny was invoked throughout the nineteenth century. Albert Weinberg has pointed out, however, that this expression took on a new meaning in the nineties. Previously destiny had meant primarily that American expansion, *when we willed it,* could not be resisted *by others* who might wish to stand in our way. During the nineties it came to mean that expansion "could not be resisted by Americans themselves, caught, willing or unwilling," in the coils of fate. A certain reluctance on our part was implied. This was not quite so much what we *wanted* to do; it was what we *had* to do. Our aggression was implicitly defined as compulsory—the product not of our own wills but of objective necessity (or the will of God).

"Duty," said President McKinley, "determines destiny." While Duty meant that we had a moral obligation, Destiny meant that we would certainly fulfill it, that the capacity to fulfill it was inherent in us. Ours had been a continuous history of expansion; it had always succeeded before, therefore it was certain to succeed in the future. Expansion was a national and "racial" inheritance, a deep and irresistible inner necessity. Here was a plausible traditionalist answer to the accusation of a grave breach of tradition.

It is not surprising that the public should have found some truth in this concept of inevitable destiny, for the acts that first involved their country with the fate of the Philippines were willed and carried out by others and were made objects of public discussion and decision only *after* the most important commitments had been made. The public will was not freely exercised upon the question, and for the citizens at large, who were in the presence of forces they could not understand or control, the rhetoric of Destiny may have been a way of softening and ennobling the *fait accompli* with which they were presented. But what of the men whose wills were really effective in the matter? If we examine their case, we find that the manufacturers of inevitability believed deeply in their own product. Indeed, while the extent to which the idea of Destiny was generally accepted is unknown, its wide prevalence among influential politicians, editors, and publicists is beyond argument. When Senator Lodge wrote to Theodore Roosevelt in 1898 that "the whole policy of annexation is growing rapidly under the irresistible pressure of events," when President McKinley remarked in private to his secretary, concerning the taking of Hawaii, "It is manifest destiny," when he declared in his private instructions to the peace commissioners that "the march of events rules and overrules human action"—what was involved was not an attempt to sell an idea to the public but a mode of communication in which the insiders felt thoroughly at home; perhaps a magical mode of thought by which they quieted their own uncertainties. It is easy to say, from the perspective of the twentieth century, that where contemporaries heard the voice of God we think we can discern the carnal larynx of Theodore Roosevelt. But if the insiders themselves imagined that they heard the voice of God, we must be careful of imputing hypocrisy. It is significant that the idea of Destiny was effective even among people who had very grave doubts about the desirability of remaining in the Philippines. Secretary of the Navy John D. Long, who was affectionately regarded by Theodore Roosevelt as an old fuddy-duddy on this score, confided to a friend in 1898 that he would really have preferred the United States to remain what it had been during the first half of the nineteenth century—"provincial," as he expressed it, and "dominated by the New England idea. But," he added, "I cannot shut my eyes to the march of events—a march which seems to be beyond human control."

It would be false to give the impression that only high moral and metaphysical concepts were employed in the imperialist argument. Talk about entry into the markets of Asia was heard often after Dewey's victory; but even those who talked about material gains showed a conspicuous and symptomatic inability to distinguish between interests, rights, and duties. Charles Denby, former minister to China and a member of McKinley's commission to study the Philippines, contributed to *The Forum* two interesting articles full of this confusion. The central business of diplomacy, confessed Denby, was to advance commerce. Our right to hold the Philippines was the right of conquerors. So far, Mr. Denby was all *Realpolitik*. But, he continued, he favored keeping the islands because he could not conceive any alternative to doing so except seizing territory in China, and he did not want to oppress further "the helpless Government and people of China"! Thus a rather odd scruple crept in; but Mr. Denby quickly explained that this was simply because China's strength and prosperity were in America's interest. "We are after markets," he went on sliding back into *Realpolitik* "and along with these markets"—sliding back into morality—"will go our beneficent institutions; and humanity will bless us." In a second article Mr. Denby shuttled back to "the cold, hard practical question. . . . Will the possession of these islands benefit us as a nation? If it will not, set them free tomorrow, and let their people, if they please, cut each other's throats." And yet, Mr. Denby made it clear, we did come as benefactors, bringing to our cut-throat friends "the choicest gifts—liberty and hope and happiness."

There was, besides the oscillatory rhetoric of Mr. Denby, a "let's be candid" school, whose views were expressed by the Washington *Post*: "All this talk about benevolent assimilation; all this hypocritical pretense of anxiety for the moral, social, and intellectual exaltation of the natives . . . deceives nobody, avails nothing. . . . We all know, down in our hearts, that these islands . . . are important to us only in the ratio of their practical possibilities, and by no other. . . . Why not be honest?"

There were others who found the primary benefit of our new imperial status in the social cohesion and military spirit that would result when the energies of the country were deflected from internal to external conflict. "Marse" Henry Watterson, the well-known editor of the Louisville *Courier-Journal*, told a New York reporter: "From a nation of shopkeepers we become a nation of warriors. We escape the menace and peril of socialism and agrarianism, as England has escaped them, by a policy of colonization and conquest. From a provincial huddle of petty sovereignties held together by a rope of sand we rise to the dignity and prowess of an imperial republic incomparably greater than Rome. It is true that we exchange domestic dangers for foreign dangers; but in every direction we multiply the opportunities of the people. We risk Caesarism, certainly; but even Caesarism is preferable to anarchism. We risk wars; but a man has but one time to die, and either in peace or war, he is not likely to die until his time comes. . . . In short, *anything is better than the pace we were going before these present forces were started into life.* Already the young manhood of the country is a goodly brand snatched from the burning, and given a perspective replete with noble deeds and elevating ideas."

Probably the most remarkable statement of the meaning of the war and the whole imperial adventure for American thinking was written by Walter Hines Page in the *Atlantic Monthly* not long after the battle of Manila. Page thought the American people would face graver problems after the war than they had experienced in the preceding years. "A change in our national policy may change our very character," he said, "and we are now playing with the great forces that may shape the future of the world—almost before we know it." Up to then, the nation had been going about the prosaic business of peace, a commercial nation absorbed in problems of finance and administration. Now it had come face to face with the sort of problems connected with the management of world empires, and its isolation was at an end. "Shall we be content with peaceful industry, or does there yet lurk in us the adventurous spirit of our Anglo-Saxon forefathers? And have we come to a time when, no more great enterprises awaiting us at home, we shall be tempted to seek them abroad?"

His own conviction was clear. The Americans had sprung from "a race that for a thousand years has done the adventurous and outdoor tasks of the world." Stemming from the English, themselves explorers, conquerors, and founders of states, the Americans had always been engaged with great practical enterprises—fighting Indians, clearing forests, building a new government, extending territory, developing wealth, settling the great issues connected with slavery and the Civil War. These had been "as great enterprises and as exciting, coming in rapid succession, as any race of men has ever had to engage it." The old outdoor spirit of the Anglo-Saxon had thus had wide scope in recent experience.

"But now a generation has come to manhood that has had no part in any great adventure." The chief tasks of domestic politics, like civil service and the reform of the currency and of municipal government, had not been exciting to the imagination, and our politics had been attractive only to petty brigands and second-rate men. In literature too we had fallen into decline. In fact, the three books which had found the most readers and most affected the masses were books of utopian social programs and fantastic philosophy—*Progress and Poverty, Looking Backward,* and *Coin's Financial School.* The proliferation of movements for petty social reforms, "societies for the prevention of minor vices and for the encouragement of minor virtues," denoted a lack of adventurous opportunities. It was quite possible that a life of quiet had grown irksome, that it was not "natural" to us. "Is it true that with a thousand years of adventure behind us we are unable to endure a life of occupations that do not feed the imagination?" Perhaps we were still the same old colonizing and fighting race of Anglo-Saxons at heart. "Before we knew the meaning of foreign possessions in a world ever growing more jealous, we have found ourselves the captors of islands in both great oceans; and from our home-staying policy of yesterday we are brought face to face with world-wide forces in Asia as well as in Europe, which seem to be working, by the opening of the Orient, for one of the greatest changes in human history. . . . And to nobody has the change come more unexpectedly than to ourselves. Has it come without our knowing the meaning of it?"

.   .   .

Since Julius W. Pratt published his *Expansionists of 1898* in 1936, it has been obvious that any interpretation of America's entry upon the paths of imperialism in the nineties in terms of rational economic motives would not fit the facts, and that a historian who approached the event with preconceptions no more supple than those, say, of Lenin's *Imperialism* would be helpless. This is not to say that markets and investments have no bearing; they do, but there are features of the situation that they do not explain at all. Insofar as the economic factor was important, it can be better studied by looking at the relation between the depression, the public mood, and the political system.

The alternative explanation has been the equally simple idea that the war was a newspapers' war. This notion, once again, has some point, but it certainly does not explain the war itself, much less its expansionist result. The New Deal period, when the political successes of F.D.R. were won in the face of overwhelming newspaper opposition, showed that the press is not powerful enough to impose upon the public mind a totally uncongenial view of public events. It must operate roughly within the framework of public predispositions. Moreover, not all the papers of the nineteen were yellow journals. We must inquire into the structure of journalistic power and also into the views of the owners and editors to find out what differentiated the sensational editors and publishers from those of the conservative press.

There is still another qualification that must be placed upon the role of the press: the press itself, whatever it can do with opinion, does not have the power to precipitate opinion into action. That is something that takes place within the *political* process, and we cannot tell that part of the story without examining the state of party rivalries, the origin and goals of the political elites, and indeed the entire political context. We must, then, supplement our story about the role of the newspapers with at least two other factors: the state of the public temper upon which the newspapers worked, and the manner in which party rivalries deflected domestic clashes into foreign aggression. Here a perennial problem of politics under the competitive two-party system became manifest again in the 1890's. When there is, for whatever reason, a strong current of jingoism running in the channels of public sentiment, party competition tends to speed it along. If the party in power is behaving circumspectly, the opposition tends to beat the drums. For example, in 1896, with Cleveland still in office, the Republican platform was much more exigent on the Cuba issue. When McKinley came into office and began to show reluctance to push toward intervention, the Democratic party became a center of interventionist pressure; this pressure was promptly supplemented by a large number of Republicans who, quite aside from their agreement on the issue, were concerned about its effect on the fate of their party.

When we examine the public temper, we find that the depression, together with such other events as the approaching completion of the settlement of the continent, the growth of trusts, and the intensification of internal social conflict, had brought to large numbers of people intense frustrations in their economic lives and their careers. To others they had brought anxiety that a period of stagnation in national wealth and power had set in. The restlessness of the discontented classes had been heightened by the defeat of Bryan in 1896. The anxieties about the nation's position had been increased among statesmen and publicists by the revival of world imperialism, in particular by the feeling that America was threatened by Germany, Russia, and Japan. The expansionist statesmen themselves were drawn largely from a restless upper-middle-class elite that had been fighting an unrewarding battle for conservative reform in domestic politics and looked with some eagerness toward a more spacious field of action.

Men often respond to frustration with acts of aggression, and allay their anxieties by threatening acts against others. It is revealing that the underdog forces in American society showed a considerably higher responsiveness to the idea of war with Spain than the groups that were satisfied with their economic or political positions. Our entry into the Philippines then aroused the interest of conservative groups that had been indifferent to the quixotism of freeing Cuba but were alert to the possibility of capturing new markets. Imperialism appealed to members of both the business and the political elites as an enlargement of the sphere of American power and profits; many of the underdogs also responded to this new note of national self-assertion. Others, however, looked upon our conduct in the Philippines as a betrayal of national principles. Anti-expansionists attempted to stir a sense of guilt and foreboding in the nation at large. But the circumstances of the period 1898–1900—the return of prosperity and the quick spectacular victories in war—made it difficult for them to impress this feeling upon the majority. The rhetoric of Duty and Destiny carried the day. The anti-expansionists had neither the numbers nor the morale of their opponents. The most conspicuous result of their lack of drive and confidence can be seen in the lamentable strategy of Bryan over the ratification of the treaty.

Clearly this attempt to see the war and expansion in the light of social history has led us onto the high and dangerous ground of social psychology and into the arena of conjecture. But simple rationalistic explanations of national behavior will also leave us dissatisfied. What I have attempted here is merely a preliminary sketch of a possible explanatory model. Further inquiry might make it seem more plausible at some points, more questionable at others.

This study has been narrowly focused on a single incident. Other expansionist crises in our own history would show important differences. I have not tried to compare American imperialism with that of other countries, or to decide how far our behavior is unique to our own country or similar to that which has been found elsewhere. In the history of other nations we can find many parallels to the role of the press and political parties in whipping up foreign crises, and to the role of the administration in committing the nation to a foreign policy before it could be made a matter of public discussion. The rhetoric and ideology of expansion also were not singular to us; duty, destiny, racism, and the other shibboleths were widespread.

I cannot refrain from adding to these notes on the methods of historical understanding another note on the tragicomic procedure of history itself. It may be of some value to us to be reminded how some of the more grandiose expectations of the nineties were realized. Cuba, to be sure, which might have been freed in peace, was freed in the war—insofar as the little country of Battista, Machado, and Castro can be considered free. The sensational newspapers that had boomed the war lost money on expensive extras, costly war-news coverage, and declining advertising. I do not know whether those silverites who wanted the war really expected that it would remonetize silver, but if they did they were rewarded with McKinley's renewed triumph and the Gold Standard Act of 1900. As for business, the gigantic markets of the East never materialized, and the precise value of the Philippines in getting at them is arguable. The islands themselves proved to be a mildly profitable colony that came to absorb a little over 1 per cent of all United States investments abroad. Yet within a generation the United States had committed itself to restoring independence to the Philippines. When this promise was enacted in 1934 many descendants of Aguinaldo's rebels were unenthusiastic about their new economic and strategic position. Finally, the exact estimation that is to be put on our strategic commitment in the Far East, which began with the Philippines, is still a matter of debate. We should, however, make note of the earlier opinion of one of our most brilliant and farsighted statesmen, who declared in 1907 that the Philippines were the Achilles' heel of our strategic position and should be given "nearly complete independence" at the "earliest possible moment." The author of these remarks was Theodore Roosevelt.

11

The Movement Toward Depoliticization: The "System of 1896" and the American Electorate

WALTER DEAN BURNHAM

While the third party system that grew out of the Civil War era was quite similar to the second party system, it differed markedly from the system of 1896 (the fourth party system). The election of 1896, Walter Dean Burnham has remarked, produced "the most enduringly sectional political alignment in American history," destroyed party competition, and transformed the more industrialized areas of the nation into bulwarks of Republicanism. Without conspiracy, violence, or formal disruption of the democratic-pluralist political structure, the new alignment "brought victory beyond expectation" to those who wished to insulate American elites and converted "a fairly democratic regime into a rather broadly based oligarchy." In the following selection, Burnham evaluates how changes instituted during and after "the great industrialist breakthrough of the 1890's" affected the voting universe.

Electoral politics in the last part of the nineteenth century was marked by a number of features which differentiate it sharply from the post-1920 variant. Most of these features were derived from the structure of politics which had been constructed during the second party system, in a largely rural political economy undergoing the first major push toward indus-

From Walter Dean Burnham, *Critical Elections and the Mainsprings of American Politics* (New York: W. W. Norton & Company, Inc., 1970), pp. 72–90. Reprinted with omissions by permission of the publisher. © 1970 by W. W. Norton & Company, Inc.

trialization and urbanization. They included such features as party-activist control of nominations and platforms through the convention; partisan printing and distribution of ballots or "tickets" to voters on—and some-times before—election day; large numbers of elective offices at all levels, and partisan patronage control of most appointive ones; and an extremely full mobilization of the potential electorate which was closely related to the intensity and rigidity of party competition.

The political style of this period has been described in a recent paper by Richard Jensen as "militarist." The images were those of armies drawn up for combat, and financial and communications "sinews of war" were provided by an elaborate, well-staffed, and strongly motivated organizational structure. In the field of communications, a partisan popu-lar press was dominant—a phenomenon very much evident in Norwegian party politics at present but which has become extinct here since the turn of the century. The "drilling" of voters in this period by their party captains was intense, and presupposed both highly stable partisan com-mitments in the mass electorate and a parallel cultural pattern of intense participation extending quite beyond even the very large turnout per-centages of the era. It is estimated, for instance, that 750,000 persons from all over the country visited McKinley's home during the "Front Porch" campaign of 1896, a figure which amounts to about 5 per cent of the total vote and 13 per cent of the Republican vote in November! Nor were such monster outpourings as the Sound Money parade in New York in that year less remarkable indicators of the extent of mass effort.

It is worth noting to what a large extent the then existing structure of voting behavior—under the rules of the game at the time, of course—shaped the strategic considerations of partisan elites. Little was to be gained by attempting ot convert a large "floating" or independent vote, for the good reason that almost none existed. In this period there was no popular cultural support for the "independent" voter as the man who evaluated candidates and issues on the merits and arrived at an informed decision. On the contrary, such people tended to be scorned as "traitors," "turncoats," or corrupt sellers of their votes. Thus rational party strategy and campaign tactics were overwhelmingly oriented to the "drill" and to the mobilization of the maximum possible number of known party followers at the polls. In such a context the purchase of votes also became a rational strategy. If the Republicans in part "bought" the election of 1888 by paying a five-dollar gold piece to each of some thousands of purchased and imported voters in Indiana, this was possible short of bank-ruptcy because rather narrow limits were fixed by the thoroughly mobi-lized and closely balanced "committed" electorate. What party leader would make the attempt today in a jurisdiction as large and volatile as a state?

The transition from this state of affairs was, in large measure, what the political side of progressive-era reform was all about. Not only the foreign observer Ostrogorski, but many of the "best men" associated with progressivism and deeply imbued with traditional old-stock American middle-class values (individualism, anticorruptionism, nativism, and anti-urbanism) came to regard the ascendancy of party organizations and the rigidity of mass voting behavior as the enemy to be attacked. Much of the agitation for such reforms as direct election of senators, the direct primary, the initiative, and women's suffrage was couched in a doubtless sincere democratic-egalitarian rhetoric. Some was not, as for example in the justifications used for deliberate malapportionment in the New York constitutional convention of 1894 or for the various measures employed to eliminate Negro voting in the South between 1890 and 1904. But most if not all of these fundamental changes in the "rules of the game" were in effect devices of political stabilization and control, with strongly conservative latent consequences if not overt justifications, and with an overwhelming antipartisan bias.

The reform of American electoral politics which took place in and after the 1890's can be subdivided into several generally complementary parts.

1. THE EROSION OF FUNCTIONS PERFORMED BY POLITICAL PARTIES

The first of these reforms was the introduction of the Australian ballot, begun on a statewide basis with Massachusetts in 1889 and largely completed by the end of the 1890's. This reform—which was supposed to purify elections of corruption and intimidation but of course did not in a number of notoriously machine-controlled jurisdictions—stripped from the parties a major organizational function: the printing and distribution of ballots. It was also associated in a number of states with the adoption of an office-block ballot form, which made voting a straight ticket much more complicated and confusing than it had been.

The second reform was the adoption of the direct-primary system, concentrated in the years 1903–13 and adopted by all but a few states by the 1920's. The literature dealing with the consequences of primaries —particularly when they become substitutes for general-election competition in one-party states—is by now voluminous and needs no further exposition here. Clearly a tremendous impetus for the adoption of this organization-undermining reform was the post-1896 conversion of most parts of the United States into one-party bailiwicks, with the consequent erosion of significant choice at the general election. There seems little question that, on the whole, adoption of the direct primary served by an interactive process to reinforce one-partyism by stripping the minority party of its sole remaining resource, monopoly of opposition.

The progressive era also witnessed a major assault led largely by the "best people" in local elite and middle-class positions against the evils of the urban machine. As Samuel P. Hays points out, these reforms, imbued with the image of the successful business corporation as applied to political affairs, were also and necessarily directed against the polyglot of local interests which had become deeply rooted in a largely immigrant-oriented community milieu. Successful implementation of such reforms as at-large elections of city council members, nonpartisan local elections, and the city-manager movement of the 1920's led not only to the erosion of party where they were carried out but also to heavy curtailment of the leverage previously exercised in the political arena by the class-ethnic infrastructure and its representatives.

Although legislation had little if any direct part in it, the disappearance of the old partisan-oriented press and the rise of a modern mass journalism which conspicuously prided itself on being far above mere partisan politics constituted a major sea change of the period. While the partisan press was not the only means by which a political organization could communicate with its following, it had been of immense importance in "spreading the word" and in contributing to the massive mobilizations characteristic of the third system. Its disappearance signaled not only the partial demise of a critically important partisan communication function but a basic cultural change in the mass public, which in turn required the development of entirely new party and candidate strategies for winning elections.

2. MANIPULATIONS OF VOTING QUALIFICATIONS AND REQUIREMENTS

A prominent aspect of the period was the rapid spread of women's suffrage, culminating in the Nineteenth Amendment (1920). Wyoming had adopted this reform in territorial elections as early as 1869, but the movement did not resume until Colorado's enfranchisement of 1893. The conventional view of this movement, until recently, was to accept it on face value as a democratic, egalitarian reform and so, of course, it was in the obvious sense. But a recent study by Alan Grimes has emphasized other facets: a strongly moralist and nativist flavor and a concentration of support for the reform among middle-class Protestants who were often deeply antagonistic to the corrupting influences of the polyglot metropolis.

It is, of course, highly unlikely that many reformers perceived clearly that women's suffrage would in the short run dilute the political power of the immigrants because of widespread cultural traditions among the latter that discouraged female participation in politics. Such was, however, the demonstrable effect, particularly before the 1928 election. Significantly, the movement spread first from west to east: from a colonial area of the country with relatively few "newer immigrants," a relative scarcity of women, strong moralist subcultural traditions, and a post-1900 stronghold of a political progressivism which had exceptionally pronounced antipartisan overtones.

Without much question, the most notable and fateful manipulation of the electorate occurred in the eleven ex-Confederate states once it had become clear after the failure of the Force Bill of 1891 and the partial repeal of Reconstruction statutes in 1894 that the federal government was no longer seriously interested in the conduct of southern elections. The precise timing of this movement can be pinpointed; it began in Florida and Mississippi in 1890, proceeded through the South Carolina convention of 1895, the North Carolina "coup d'état" of 1898, and the Alabama and Virginia disfranchisements of 1901–2, and was completed in Texas in 1904. The literature of the devices by which southern electorates were reduced to small fractions of their former size is voluminous and well known, as are the devices themselves: the poll tax, the excessively long residence requirement, the discriminatory literacy test, and, of course, a whole host of extralegal control measures.

A very recent treatment of this movement for one (not necessarily typical) southern state may, however, be mentioned here: Raymond H. Pulley's Old Virginia Restored. Drawing on insights from such revisionist historians as Robert Wiebe and Samuel P. Hays, Pulley makes an impressive case for the interpretation of disfranchisement and the solidification of one-party supremacy in Virginia as part of a progressive impulse toward control and management of a dangerously volatile colonial electorate. In this case, as he argues, the image was, of course, one of restoration of an hypostasized "Old Virginia" dominated by an elite filled with noblesse oblige and far removed from the corruption and turmoil of fully democratic politics. In view of the spectacularly radical proclivities of its white rural electorate as revealed in the traumatic Readjuster episode of the 1880's, its economically colonial status after the Civil War, and its ever-present "Negro problem"—progressivism and "good government" could only come about in Virginia through the substantial liquidation of political democracy. It might be useful here to indicate precisely how effective this set of controls came to be by examining turnout and party competition in Virginia presidential and gubernatorial elections since 1869 (Table 1).

TABLE 1   Party Voting and Turnout in Virginia, 1869–1969

Gubernatorial Elections			Presidential Elections		
	% Voting of Potential			% Voting of Potential	
Year	Electorate	% Dem.	Year	Electorate	% Dem.
1869	84.8	54.3			
1873	74.9	56.4	1872	66.2	49.5
1877	34.1	100.0	1876	77.6	59.6
1881	63.2	47.2	1880	64.1 45.5 +	15.1
1885	81.9	52.8	1884	81.7	51.1
1889	76.8	57.5	1888	83.2	50.3
1893	54.7	61.2	1892	75.3	59.2
1897	40.3	65.9	1896	71.0	53.4
1901	44.5	58.9	1900	59.6	55.8
1905	27.0	64.6	1904	27.7	62.6
1909	22.0	63.7	1908	27.4	61.2
1913	13.4	100.0	1912	25.7	66.7 *
1917	15.6	72.0	1916	27.1	67.6
1921	17.5	66.3	1920	19.4	61.8
1925	11.7	74.1	1924	18.1	62.5 *
1929	21.0	63.0	1928	24.0	46.0
1933	12.1	75.3	1932	22.1	69.5
1937	9.8	84.0	1936	23.0	70.5
1941	7.6	82.0	1940	22.1	68.3
1945	9.5	68.2	1944	22.3	62.5
1949	13.3	72.0	1948	21.6	48.2 *
1953	19.7	55.3	1952	29.9	43.5
1957	23.3	63.4	1956	31.8	40.9
1961	16.8	63.9	1960	33.3	47.2
1965	22.8	48.3 *	1964	42.7	53.7
1969	35.0	46.2	1968	52.9	32.7 *

* Democratic precentage of three-party vote; otherwise, of two-party vote.

This may seem an extreme example of the effectiveness of massed electorate-control measures during—indeed, well after—the fourth national voting system; if so, it was frequently paralleled elsewhere in this period, particularly in the South. If Pulley is correct in his view that the elite impulse to convert democracy into oligarchy was not only specifically Virginian but specifically progressive as well, the case becomes more interesting still. For it may well be argued that Virginia, in dismantling political parties and erecting high legal and customary barriers to political participation at the mass base after 1890, only carried to a local extreme an impulse which profoundly influenced American politics as a whole during those years.

Finally, one finds the development of personal-registration requirements in nearly all states during this period. This change in the rules of the game requires somewhat more extensive discussion, not least because of its role in a dynamic interaction process that is not yet well understood. One may begin by noting that the drive toward registration grew out of the same interrelated complex of impulses toward control and management which we have already discussed. The original impetus to the adoption of personal-registration requirements clearly grew out of that old-stock nativist and corporate-minded hostility to the political machine, the polyglot city, and the immigrant which was so important a component of the progressive mentality. Here too there were flagrant abuses which had developed in the "militarist" politics of the nineteenth century as they were modified by industrial-urban development. In large anonymous metropolitan hives the old practice of personally recognizing qualified voters at the polls, which had been effective (and still is) in rural areas and small towns, became an obvious vehicle of political corruption.

Compulsory registration was first required for residents of cities above a certain size, and was only later, if ever, extended to the whole population of a state; this is still the procedure in a number of states, including Ohio and Missouri. In some cases the urge to control the possibly dangerous or subversive potential of mass urban electorates was clearly expressed: thus—verbally—in the 1894 decision to malapportion to protect the "true Americans" of upstate New York from the immigrant masses of New York City, and—statutorily—in the requirement, applicable to New York City alone for many years, that registration not only be personal but periodic.

Stanley Kelley and his associates are surely right in their argument that the imposition of a personal-registration requirement serves to depress voter participation by differentially increasing costs of access. In the present era, for example, the differential in turnout between registration and nonregistration territory in Missouri and Ohio ranges between 10 and 15 per cent. Nor is there any doubt that the differential costs of registration (as well as other variables) are duly revealed in any class-stratification analysis of voter participation. To take one example where fairly detailed contemporary voting and other data are available, one may examine participation and partisan voting in the 1960 election in Baltimore (Table 2).

This heavily class-oriented skewing of participation is a characteristic feature of contemporary American electoral politics. The extremely high turnout figures which are typical in the last quarter of the nineteenth century make it very doubtful that such bias existed in this country prior

TABLE 2   Class, Party, and Turnout: The Case of Baltimore, 1960

% Professional-Managerial of Adult Males by Racial Composition, 1960	Number of Political Tracts Analyzed	Mean Turnout	Mean % Democratic of 2-Party Presidential Vote
White (0–49.9% Nonwhite)			
40% and Over	8	70.8	43.9%
20–39.9%	18	62.1	55.0
10–19.9%	14	52.6	61.9
0– 9.9%	14	52.1	71.2
Black (50% + Nonwhite)			
10% and Over	7	51.9	72.3
0– 9.9%	23	41.0	75.1
City as a Whole	84	54.0	63.9

to 1900 on anything like the scale it does now. Nor, granting the incentives of machine politics toward the maximum possible mobilization of party supporters during the "militarist" era, should this be greatly surprising. Moreover, as is well known, this class differential in participation is far less visible in most other present-day Western democracies, particularly in those with multiparty systems and thorough social organization of the class infrastructure.

To take an extreme case on this side, electoral participation in Sweden is both very high and quite invariant along class lines. Thus, for example, the 1960 Swedish elections to the lower chamber of the Riksdag revealed a turnout of 88 per cent among working-class males, with a national cross-class participation rate of 87.6 per cent, and 91.2 per cent among female workers, with a national cross-class participation rate among married women of 91.1 per cent. One might anticipate this in a small country with very limited problems of ethnicity, a dominant class structuring of electoral politics, and a well-organized social infrastructure, but it should be noted that it has a system of electoral law—shared in one form or another with practically all other developed democratic polities—in which the responsibility for compiling electoral registers and keeping them up to date falls on the state, not on the individual.

This, of course, is precisely the point. Kelley's analysis must be regarded as only a beginning in exploring the problems of turnout in the United States. There are several important questions to be asked regarding this singular American electoral rule. Why is it that we have statutes requiring *personal* registration? Why has this device been so widely adopted as to permit few deviations, except of detail, from one state statute to another? Why has it received so little attention, on the whole, from reform-minded political scientists and others interested in democratizing the base of our electoral politics? Finally, what might be the implications of its confinement to urban areas, which was originally very widespread and is still frequently encountered? Merely to ask such questions is to suggest, and rather strongly, that the American peculiarity of personal registration ought not to be received by analysts as a given. It is a phenomenon which has deeply involved electorate-control decisions, even if the involvement has often been implicit and the decisions unconscious because the values on which they were based are so universally shared in the political culture.

In addition, there is the problem of attempting to identify the extent to which the adoption of personal-registration requirements actually affected the steep post-1900 decline in voter participation. The evidence, of course, has to be inferential or circumstantial rather than direct, but it is cumulatively very impressive: while the introduction of personal registration clearly played some role, the decline in turnout which occurred after 1896 and *before* the date of women's suffrage was not only widespread but cut across registration-territory boundaries. Of course, it was much steeper in some areas than in others, especially in the South, where the costs of voting were deliberately made so high by those in charge of local politics that probably half of the white electorate was effectively disfranchised along with almost all the Negroes.

But among the thirty-four nonsouthern states participating in both the 1896 and 1916 elections, only eight showed some increases in participation; twenty-six showed more or less severe declines. Five of these states with increases (Nebraska, Nevada, North Dakota, Utah, and Wyoming) are in the trans-Mississippi west, where the general effect of the 1896 realignment was to make politics more competitive than it had been previously; the other three include two in New England (Maine and Rhode Island), where local factors seem to have been involved, and Delaware, where competitive politics survived the realignments of the 1890's. On the other hand, most of the larger industrial states lost 15 to 20 per cent of their presidential electorates during this period, despite the partisan upheavals of 1912 and the closeness of the 1916 election. It is extremely unclear that the introduction of personal registration at the beginning of the fourth electoral era had more than a very marginal contributing effect to this outcome, particularly in such states as Ohio, Indiana, and Kansas, where it was applicable only in cities of varying minimum sizes. The movement was systemic, and seems to be clearly related to the disappearance of effective interparty competition throughout much of the country.

This can be confirmed by a somewhat closer examination. Between 1906 and 1937 a set of registration statutes was enacted by the Pennsylvania legislature which required personal registration in cities, but not in rural areas or small towns. In this respect the "rules of the game" were similar to those adopted at about the same time and still in existence in Missouri and some other states. But unlike Pennsylvania, in Missouri, a border state, the net effect of the realignments of the 1890's was to make the parties more competitive than they had been before 1894 or than they were to be after 1930. Assuming a rough similarity of classes of people covered by personal registration requirements (although not, of course, the relative proportion of each state's electorate so covered), one would anticipate finding considerable differences in turnout regression lines plotted over time. Such differences are very clearly marked, and are indicated in Table 3.

TABLE 3   Contrasts in Participation, 1874–1968: The Cases of Missouri and Pennsylvania

Period	$Y_c =$	Net % Change (on regression line)	Dropoff at Beginning	Dropoff at End
Missouri				
1876–1916 (President)	$78.81 + 0.10X$	$+1.3$	14.7	17.1
1874–1918 (No major office)	$67.56 - 0.11X$	-1.8		
1920–1968 (President)	$69.27 - 0.10X$	-1.9	28.0	37.4
1922–1966 (No major office)	$50.52 - 0.73X$	-8.0		
Pennsylvania				
1876–1916 (President)	$90.36 - 2.26X$	-25.6	15.2	20.8
1875–1918 (Governor)	$79.23 - 2.28X$	-32.6		
1920–1968 (President)	$50.20 + 1.56X$	$+36.2$	27.7	13.5
1922–1966 (Governor)	$35.29 + 2.14X$	$+62.9$		

The decline in Pennsylvania's turnout along a regression line extending from the 1870's to World War I was precipitate, both in presidential and off-year elections. For Missouri, on the other hand, almost no secular trend is visible in this period. Similarly for the 1920–68 period: Pennsylvania's turnout shows a heavy increase in presidential years and an even more substantial one in off-year gubernatorial contests, revealing a tendency for electoral slack or dropoff in this state to undergo severe secular decline after the onset of the New Deal realignment. Missouri, on the other hand, continues to show very slight secular trend in presidential elections during this period.

What is impressive here is the considerable opening up of electoral slack in off-year elections after 1920, which may be said to have an obvious institutional explanation: in Missouri the major contests affecting state politics are decided in presidential years, in Pennsylvania they are not. Even so, however, one highly visible office—that of U.S. Senator—has come up for election in Missouri in two of every three off-year elections since 1914. Moreover, of course, the same institutional differences between these states can be traced back to the 1870's, while the behavioral differences cannot.

Interesting as these findings are, however, and suggestive as they may be of the quite different impacts of the New Deal realignment on a state with a very highly developed socioeconomic system, on the one hand, and a border state with many nineteenth-century survivals, on the other, one major point concerning registration requirements and turnout seems clear. The differences are overwhelmingly systemic, not rules-related. This is obviously the case for the 1876–1916 period, when the rules were largely the same. Even for the contemporary period, it may be worth noting that in 1960 Pennsylvania had statewide personal reg.s-tration while Missouri had such requirements in an urban-metropolitan minority of its counties which cast 59 per cent of the total statewide vote. Despite this, their turnout rates were virtually identical.

A more detailed examination of turnout within Pennsylvania reveals something of the enormous magnitudes of both the post-1900 decline in the size of the active voting universe and that of the post-1924 increase. Some quantitative estimate of the possible effect of personal registration as an intervening variable can also be made. Prior to 1937, more than half the state's counties, lacking cities of at least the third class within their borders, had no mandatory personal-registration requirements. Indeed, one of the more interesting fruits of the 1935–38 "little New Deal" in Pennsylvania was the complete revamping of the state's election laws, including the extension of personal-registration requirements to all jurisdictions in the state. Because of this convenient division of the state between 1906 and 1937 into registration and nonregistration territory, it becomes possible to construct a straightforward statistical test of both the 1900–16 slump and the 1920–36 recovery (Table 4).

The suspicion that far more powerful forces were at work to depress Pennsylvania turnout after 1900 than the introduction of personal registration alone is at once raised by noting that every county in the state shared in this depression. Similarly, all sixty-seven counties in the state, whether or not they contained registration territory, showed positive

TABLE 4   The Effects of Registration Requirements in Pennsylvania Turnout, 1900–1936, by Registration Categories

Year or Period	Mean Turnout Registration Areas	Mean Turnout Nonregistration Areas	t	Significance p
1900	77.8	80.9	1.850	.05 > p > .025
1916	63.0	68.5	3.359	.005 > p > .0005
Mean Shift, 1900–1916	−14.4	−12.4	1.451	.10 > p > .05
1920	41.5	47.1	4.470	p > .0005
1936	66.3	75.7	6.372	p > .0005
Mean Shift, 1920–1936	+24.9	+28.5	2.608	.025 > p > .01

slopes on the 1920–36 regression lines. If one applies a standard test to the two categories of counties, this evaluation of the difference of means suggests the plausibility of the hypothesis that registration eventually affected turnout, but there are significant ambiguities even here.

Employing the more exacting standards of a one-tailed test—since one can assume in advance that turnout is likely to be higher where there were no registration requirements than where such requirements existed—it is clear enough that the null hypothesis must be rejected for 1916, 1920, and 1938—that is, for the three points in time after adoption of the 1906 legislation. Assuming a .025 standard for rejection, one can also presume that registration, or something associated with it in the same clusters of counties, involved a differential effect in the 1920–36 upward shift in turnout. But the *downward* shift along the 1900–16 regression line is a different story. Here it is rather unreasonable to reject the null hypothesis; the difference in the rate of turnout decline between the two groups of counties in this critical period may have been due to some phenomenon having nothing to do with the introduction or effects of personal registration.

The problem becomes more obscure still. Assuming that personal registration was the variable actually measured in Table 4—and the evidence is circumstantially very impressive, barring analysis on a level which is still prohibitively minute at this stage—there was a systematic tendency *both before 1906 and after 1937* for Pennsylvania turnout to be correlated inversely with urbanization. The data in selected years is shown in Table 5.

Thus, while it seems evident that factors associated with both urban-

TABLE 5   Urbanization and Turnout: Pennsylvania, 1900–1960

Year	Mean Turnout (All Counties)	r (% Turnout, % Urban, Nearest Census)	r^2
1900	79.6	—.398	.159
1916	66.5	—.484	.234
1936	75.5	—.562	.316
1940	66.7	—.370	.137
1960	70.8	—.266	.071

ization and personal registration were significantly related to differences in turnout, more work than has been done here would be required to disentangle the persistent tendency toward higher turnout in rural areas—all of which were non-registration territory between 1906 and 1937—from differential effects due to registration alone.

What seems to be the most likely explanation of these phenomena is that the introduction of personal registration almost certainly counted for something, and in the direction Kelley's analysis indicates. But putting first things first, one concludes that the systemic forces at work during these periods were far broader in their scope and far heavier in their impact than any single change in the rules of the game or, in all probability, of all such changes put together. Indeed, these forces were the context in which the rules changes occurred, and the subsequent effects of the latter have been heavily influenced by the demands placed on electoral politics at given points in time by those elements of the potential electorate which were then mobilized. They were, in the main, devices by which a large and possibly dangerous mass electorate could be brought to heel and subjected to management and control within the political system appropriate to "capitalist democracy." But they were not the ultimate causes or origins of the conditions which made possible such a remarkable solution to the problem of adjusting mass politics to the exigencies of industrialism.

12

Social Tensions and the Origins of Progressivism

DAVID P. THELEN

Since its publication in 1955, Richard Hofstadter's The Age of Reform: From Bryan to F.D.R. has been the most important book on progressivism. Hofstadter described Progressive leaders as young, well-educated, urban business and professional men who inherited both social position and moderate wealth. He argued that with their roots in and ideas from an older rural America, these men were born to lead, but failed to have their talents properly appreciated by industrial tycoons and political bosses. Frustrated by their loss of status, Hofstadter concluded, these men turned to reform. Using roll-call and collective-biographical data on the Wisconsin legislature from 1897 to 1903 and taking into account recent sociological and psychological theory, David P. Thelen examines Hofstadter's thesis and other hypotheses relating to tensions.

Recent historians have explained the origins of the Progressive movement in several ways. They have represented progressivism, in turn, as a continuation of the western and southern farmers' revolt, as a desperate attempt by the urban gentry to regain status from the new robber barons, as a thrust from the depths of slum life, and as a campaign by businessmen to prevent workers from securing political power. Behind such seemingly conflicting theories, however, rests a single assumption about the origins of progressivism: the class and status conflicts of the late-nine-

From Journal of American History 56 (1969):323–41. Footnotes omitted. Reprinted with permission of the author and The Journal of American History.

teenth century formed the driving forces that made men become reformers. Whether viewed by the historian as a farmer, worker, urban
elitist, or businessman, the progressive was motivated primarily by his
social position; and each scholar has painted a compelling picture of the
insecurities and tensions felt by the group that he placed in the vanguard
of progressivism. Pressures and threats from other social groups drove
men to espouse reform. In these class and status conflicts can be found the
roots of progressivism.

How adequately does this focus on social tensions and insecurities
explain the origins of progressivism? Since some of these scholars have
invoked concepts from social science to support their rejection of earlier
approaches, the validity and application of some of the sociological and
psychological assumptions which make up the conceptual framework for
the idea that social tensions impelled the progressive require analysis. Is
the focus on social classes relevant to the rise of political movements like
progressivism? Is it useful to rely upon a narrow, untestable and unproved
conception of motivation when other approaches are available? How
much of a concrete situation does an abstract model explain?

First, theories borrowed from one discipline are not designed to encompass the data of another. In questioning the application of models
from physiology and physics to psychology, the noted personality theorist
George A. Kelly explained: "We are skeptical about the value of copying
ready-made theories which were designed for other foci of convenience";
and he urged his fellow psychologists to resist the temptation of "poking
about in the neighbors' back yards for methodological windfalls." Just
as physiology and physics encompass only part of the psychologist's realm,
so psychology, sociology, and political science are concerned with only
part of the historian's realm.

Those historians who have borrowed the idea that social stratification explains the rise of political movements like progressivism illustrate
the dangers inherent in borrowing theories from other fields. Most sociologists and political scientists now doubt the relevance of social stratification to the emergence of political movements. Reinhard Bendix, for
example, maintained that "the study of social stratification, whether or not
it is adumbrated by psychological analysis, is not the proper approach
to an understanding of the role of cumulative political experience." In
their pleas for more pluralistic approaches to political power, such political scientists as Nelson W. Polsby and Robert A. Dahl have found that
social stratification is largely irrelevant to the exercise of political power.
So severe were these criticisms of the assumption that social class determined political power that one sociologist, reviewing the literature of the
field in 1964, concluded that "the problem has simply been dropped."

But an even greater problem with placing emphasis on social tensions is that it is ahistorical. Even sociologists like Seymour M. Lipset and Bendix have complained about the "increasingly ahistorical" drift of the focus of this field. After analyzing the major models of social change, another sociologist concluded that the fundamental error of these models was their failure to incorporate the dimension of time. Few scholars would deny that social tensions exist at all times and in all societies. For at least twenty years before 1900, various business groups had tried to take political power away from workers and bosses. But to focus on the social class motivation of businessmen is to obscure the basic historical problem of why progressivism emerged *when* it did. Conflicts between businessmen and workers were hardly unique to the years around 1900. The emphasis on social tensions obscures chronology. When sociologists are disturbed about this problem, historians should be wary indeed.

The assumption that progressivism derived from social tensions is at least as vulnerable to attack by psychologists. If the kinds of questions historians generally ask about the origins of political and social movements are reduced to the psychological level, then the theories of class and status motivation would seem to be premised on very debatable assumptions about individual motivation. Most historians would want to know the conditions that existed before a change occurred, why the change happened, and what were the results of that change.

The first problem—the conditions before a change occurred—reduces in psychological terms to the way an individual perceives himself, his self-image. Psychologists have approached this question in many ways, but a theory of change which assumes that social tensions were the basic cause implicitly accepts only one of these approaches. It assumes that an individual defines himself primarily in terms of his particular social role, that his behavior is motivated mainly by his class and status role perceptions. Only about one out of every three psychologists, however, would accept this premise to any real extent. Even some sociologists and anthropologists, who have traditionally seen individual behavior as primarily determined by culture, have retreated from that position and now see a more symmetrical interaction in which personality also influences culture. An overwhelming majority of psychologists have rejected role theory as an adequate explanation for the way an individual who enlists in a reform movement forms his self-image.

The second problem—why the change happened—reduces in psychological terms to the mechanism by which an individual feels impelled to join a political movement like progressivism. Here again those scholars who emphasize social tensions have implicitly chosen only one of several alternatives offered by psychologists. They assume that the threat from some other social group frustrated the would-be progressive who, in turn, reacted aggressively against that threat. Very few psychologists, however, would claim that social tensions are the main source of frustration. Furthermore, individuals are generally capable of reacting to new roles without experiencing any major frustrations. The different ways in which Theodore Roosevelt and Calvin Coolidge, for example, remade the role of the presidency to fit their own personalities suggest how flexible roles can be without deeply frustrating an individual. Furthermore, different members of the same social class will perceive social challenges in different ways; many will experience no frustration at all.

Even if historians concede that social stresses can frustrate an individual, does it follow that he will react aggressively toward the source of that frustration? The frustration-produces-aggression model is one of the most debated propositions in psychology. Extreme critics have called it "nonsensical." Others have shown that frustration more often produces anxiety, submission, dependence, or avoidance than aggression. Even presumably simpleminded creatures like rats and pigeons do not necessarily react aggressively when they are frustrated. If some psychologists have shown that aggression is only one possible result of frustration, others have shown that frustration is only one possible source of aggression. Indeed, prior to 1939 most psychologists accepted Sigmund Freud's *Beyond the Pleasure Principle,* which contended that aggression derived from the Death Wish. Others have found the source of aggression in neither frustration nor the Death Wish. The assumption that social tensions will frustrate an individual and drive him to react aggressively has been riddled by the artillery of a great many psychologists. For historians to continue to assume that men react primarily to social threats is to ignore an impressive body of psychological literature.

The third problem—what were the results of that change—reduces in psychological terms to the way an individual outwardly expresses the internal change. If an individual felt angry following threats from another social group, how would he express that anger? The idea that he will sublimate his aggressive propensities into cries for political reform is one which is endorsed by many Freudians who follow *Civilization and Its Discontents.* But even some psychoanalysts claim that Freud never adequately explained sublimation. Other personality theorists have asserted that "everyone recognizes . . . that at present we have no theory which really explains the dynamics" of sublimation. Many psychologists have seen sublimation as only one possible way of expressing aggressive proclivities. Political reform is only one of hundreds of directions an individual can channel hostile impulses. But most personality theorists are so unimpressed by the concept of sublimation that they simply ignore it in their own theories.

By assuming that social tensions produced progressivism, historians have approached the basic questions about social and political movements from a very narrow psychological viewpoint. Even more important, the psychological underpinnings of this assumption are either disproved, disputed, ignored, or "untestable" by modern psychologists.

Moreover, the whole psychological framework which includes these theories has recently come under attack. Both behaviorists and psychoanalysts had previously assumed that individuals were motivated by "a state of tenseness that leads us to seek equilibrium, rest, adjustment, satisfaction, or homeostasis. From this point of view, personality is nothing more than our habitual modes of reducing tension." Men became reformers to relieve tensions, perhaps impelled by class and status anxieties. Now, however, many psychologists contend that personality theorists too long overemphasized the irrational components in motivation. As early as 1953 Gordon Allport reported that the trend in motivational theory was away from the tension reduction approach and toward an emphasis on the rational and healthy side of individuals. By stressing the rationality of free choice, these psychologists have argued that a commitment to reform, for example, may in fact be the ultimate expression of a mature personality and reflect a man who is capable of getting outside of his self-preoccupation. Indeed, Erich Fromm has said that the revolutionary leader might well be the only "sane person in an insane world." The decision to embrace progressivism may simply represent a conscious choice between alternative programs, not an attempt to reduce tensions which grew out of a man's efforts to maintain his social position.

There is another problem in borrowing models: the more inclusive the model, the farther it is removed from the reality it is attempting to explain. The data must be squeezed and distorted to make them conform to the model. Many social scientists themselves have revolted against the top-heavy and abstract models which have prevailed in their fields. One student of social stratification, for example, concluded from a review of 333 studies that his field suffered from "the disease of overconceptualization." Similarly, many psychologists have rejected the abstract personality constructs used to explain motivation because they are too far removed from the reality of individual people. Arguing for a focus on the "life style" of each person, Allport has attacked theories which emphasize "the abstract motivation of an impersonal and therefore non-existent mind-in-general," preferring "the concrete, viable motives of each and every mind-in-particular." In a like vein, Kelly has argued that most psychological constructs ignore an individual's "private domain, within which his behavior aligns itself within its own lawful system." These abstract constructs can only account for the individual as "an inert object wafted about in a public domain by external forces, or as a solitary datum sitting on its own continuum." Allport even charged that psychologists who build universal models to explain human motivation are seeking a "scientific will of the wisp"; the "'irreducible unlearned motives' of men" they are seeking cannot be found because they do not exist.

This is not a critique of any particular psychological theory or approach to behavior. Rather it is a plea to be aware of the dangers in building a conceptual approach to such a problem as progressivism upon so many rickety psychological foundations. Historians should recognize that psychologists are not that different; they are at least as divided in their interpretations as we are. For historians to accept the assumptions that underlie the idea that social tensions produced progressivism would be similar to a psychologist borrowing Frederick Jackson Turner's frontier hypothesis for his research. Many of us would complain that there are other explanations for the development of American history; and a great many psychologists, in effect, are shuddering at the weak psychological underpinnings of the assumption that their social backgrounds made men become reformers.

The real test for the soundness of any approach is not theoretical, of course, but empirical. In this case the inadequacy of the sociological and psychological ideas which inform the assumption that social tensions produced progressivism becomes obvious after an examination of the types of men who became progressives and conservatives. If social tensions were relevant to the rise of progressivism, then clearly the class and status experiences of progressives should have differed in some fundamental way from those of the conservatives.

How different, in fact, were the social origins of progressives and conservatives? Following George E. Mowry's publication in 1951 of *The California Progressives,* several scholars examined the external social class attributes of progressive leaders and concluded that the reformers were drawn from the young urban gentry. But because they neglected to sample a comparable group of conservatives, these studies failed to prove their contention that class and status experiences impelled the progressives. Subsequent profiles of both progressive and conservative leaders in the election of 1912 and the legislative sessions of 1911 in Washington and 1905 in Missouri showed that both groups came from nearly the same social background. Objective measures of their social origins failed to predict the programs and ideologies of political leaders.

Scholars may not accept this finding because they question whether the 1912 campaign reflected political ideologies so much as the personalities of leaders and the desire for office. The studies of legislatures in Washington and Missouri might be questioned because in a single session such extraneous pressures as the personality of a powerful governor or the use of bribes might have interfered with a legislator's expression of his natural preferences. Furthermore, neither Washington nor Missouri was ever noted as a banner progressive state. Perhaps the issues in these states were not as hotly contested—and hence did not reveal as sharp social tensions—as in the more radical states.

The following profile of Wisconsin legislators was designed to avoid some of the possible objections to the other studies. Since contemporaries and historians alike have agreed on the pivotal position of Wisconsin, it is an ideal state to test whether social tensions were important in the development of progressivism. This sample begins with the 1897 session because it was then, for the first time, that the Progressive Republicans identified in their speeches, platforms, and votes the issues which divided them from the stalwarts, and concludes with the 1903 session, when many of their programs were enacted. The index for "progressivism" was based on votes growing out of the campaigns for a more equitable distribution of the tax burden, for regulation of quasi-public corporations, and for purification of the electoral and legislative processes. These were the issues which gave the thrust and tone to Wisconsin progressivism and served as the dividing lines between the old guard and the insurgents.

During these four sessions there were 286 roll calls on these issues. A "progressive" legislator was defined as one who voted for more than 75 percent of the progressive measures; a "moderate" favored between 50 and 75 percent of the progressive measures; and a "conservative" opposed more than half of the progressive measures. Of the 360 Republican legislators included in this profile, 40 percent were progressives, 38 percent were moderates, and 22 percent were conservatives.

If social conflicts were important to the emergence of progressivism, the variable which would be most likely to reveal that fact would be the occupations of legislators. Convincing generalizations from the following chart would need to be based upon large statistical differences, since the relatively small sample is divided so many ways. Occupation clearly made little difference in a legislator's vote on progressive measures.

TABLE I

	Farmer Percent	Merchant Percent	Professional Percent	Manufacturer Percent	Financier Percent	Worker Percent
Progressives	20	27	26	13	9	5
Moderates	22	24	29	6	13	6
Conservatives	12	27	32	16	10	3

The extent of a man's education helps to locate his social position. In Wisconsin neither progressives (22 percent), moderates (24 percent), nor conservatives (27 percent) were dominated by college graduates. At a time and place where college degrees were rare, perhaps a better measure of educational aspirations would be the proportion of men who sought any kind of formal schooling—high school, business college, night school—beyond the level of the common school. Here again, however, the differences in achievement between progressives (58 percent), moderates (60 percent), and conservatives (66 percent) are insignificant.

The place of a man's birth also indicates his social background. But the nativity of Wisconsin's legislators failed to differentiate progressives from conservatives (see Table II).

If the Wisconsin sample corresponds roughly to those of other states in the occupations, education, and nativity of political leaders, it differs

TABLE II

	Midwest Percent	East and New England Percent	Canada Percent	Europe Percent
Progressives	47	29	6	18
Moderates	61	24	2	13
Conservatives	49	30	5	16

from them in two other respects. Students of the 1912 election found the progressives to be considerably younger than the conservatives in both age and political experience, a fact which led them to see progressivism as a revolt of the young, would-be politicians. In Wisconsin, however, progressives and conservatives both had an average age of forty-eight, and the moderates averaged forty-six. The median ages of progressives (49), moderates (45), and conservatives (47) likewise fail to suggest the existence of any generational conflict between progressives and conservatives.

Nor were Wisconsin's progressives the most politically immature of the rival factions. While service in the legislature is only one measure of political experience, it does reveal the effectiveness of politicians in winning renomination from their local organizations. Although Wisconsin's conservatives had the longest tenure in the legislature, they contrasted not so much with the progressives as with the moderates. Table III indicates the number of previous sessions attended by legislators.

TABLE III

	None Percent	One Percent	Two or more Percent
Progressives	52	28	20
Moderates	62	27	11
Conservatives	35	37	28

The social origins of Wisconsin legislators between 1897 and 1903 clearly suggest that no particular manner of man became a progressive. Such variables as occupation, education, nativity, age, and previous legislative experience fail to differentiate the average progressive from the average conservative. The theories that progressivism was motivated by status or class tensions felt by the urban gentry, the businessmen, the workers, the farmers, or the incipient politicians are challenged in Wisconsin by the fact that members of these groups were as likely to become conservatives as progressives. And the Wisconsin profile parallels other studies. To the extent that social class allegiance can be measured by such attributes as occupation, nativity, education, and age, social tensions were apparently irrelevant to the formation of progressivism since the "typical" progressive and conservative came from the same social background.

Collective statistical profiles can, however, obscure more than they reveal. The five more prominent early Wisconsin progressive leaders, the men who forged the issues which Robert M. La Follette subsequently adopted, were most noteworthy for their different social origins. The man contemporaries hailed as the "father of Wisconsin progressivism" was Albert R. Hall, a small dairy farmer in the western part of the state. Nephew of national Grange head Oliver Kelley, Hall was basically an agrarian radical who developed the reputation of a fearless enemy of the railroads and other large corporations. No less important was John A. Butler, the lengthened shadow of the powerful Milwaukee Municipal League. A sharper contrast to Hall could scarcely be found than this independently wealthy and highly educated Brahmin who seemed to spend more time in his villa than he did in his Milwaukee law office. Milwaukee also contributed Julius E. Roehr, organized labor's leading champion in the legislature. Born in New York City—the son of German immigrants—this hardworking lawyer and dissident Republican politician would have been extremely uncomfortable with the smells of either Hall's farm or Butler's villa. James H. Stout, the most respected of the early progressives in the legislature, was born and raised in Iowa and educated at the University of Chicago. A fabulously wealthy lumber baron, Stout used his company town of Menomonie to pioneer in vocational education and in welfare benefits for his workers. The orator of these early legislative progressives was James J. McGillivray, a self-made Canadian-born architect and manufacturer who lived in Black River Falls and authored the state's antitrust acts. It would seem almost pointless to hunt for a common social "type" in these early progressives. A Brahmin man of leisure and self-made manufacturer, an agrarian radical who knew no workers and a lawyer who never lived outside a large city and was the workers' champion, young men and old men, Yankees and immigrants, these were the leaders who made common cause in Wisconsin and developed the progressive program.

The widely scattered backgrounds of the most prominent early leaders and the remarkable collective similarity between the average progressive and conservative confirm the weaknesses in the sociological and psychological framework for the assumption that progressivism was rooted in social tensions. The widespread emphasis on social tensions is unsound sociologically because it draws upon only a narrow spectrum of personality theory, and those models upon which it does draw are either unproved or unprovable. The statistical profiles from Wisconsin and elsewhere reveal empirically that the origins of progressivism cannot be found by studying the social backgrounds and tensions of progressive leaders. Remembering Kelly's injunction to avoid "poking about in the neighbors' back yards for methodological windfalls," historians must develop alternative approaches which encompass not only the realm of sociology and psychology but also that of history.

Such an alternative approach should at least restore chronology, a major casualty in the repeated emphasis on men's class and status feelings, to a more prominent position. At this point it is possible to offer a tentative explanation for the origins of progressivism when that movement is placed in the context of the chronological evolution of both industrialism and reform.

When the Progressive era is put against the backdrop of the growth of industrialism in America, the remarkable fact about that period is its relative freedom from social tensions. If conflicts between city and farm, worker and boss, younger and older generations, native-born and immigrant are more or less natural results of industrialization, then the years between the late 1890s and the early 1910s stand as a period of social peace when contrasted with either the Gilded Age or the 1920s, when those conflicts were raw and ragged. Not competition but cooperation between different social groups—ministers, businessmen, workers, farmers, social workers, doctors, and politicians—was what distinguished progressivism from such earlier reform movements as Mugwumpery, Populism, the labor movement, and civil service reform. To the extent that men and groups were motivated by tensions deriving from their class and status perceptions, they would have been unable to cooperate with men from different backgrounds. In focusing on the broadly based progressive thrust, the real question is not what drove groups apart, but what drove them together? To answer this question, progressivism must be located in the development of reform in the late-nineteenth century.

The roots of progressivism reach far back into the Gilded Age. Dozens of groups and individuals in the 1880s envisioned some change that would improve society. Reformers came forward to demand civil service reform, the eight hour day, scientific agriculture, woman suffrage, enforcement of vice laws, factory inspection, nonpartisan local elections, trust-busting, wildlife conservation, tax reform, abolition of child labor, businesslike local government, regulation of railway rates, less patronizing local charity, and hundreds of other causes which would subsequently be identified with progressivism. Younger social scientists, particularly economists, were not only beginning to lambast the formalism and conservatism in their fields and to advocate the ideas which would undergird progressivism but they were also seeking to force governments to accept their ideas. Richard T. Ely's work on the Maryland Tax Commission in the mid-1880s, for example, pioneered in the application of the new economics to government and generated many of the programs which future reformers and politicians would soon adopt.

But this fertility of reform in the Gilded Age did not conceal the basic fact that individuals and groups remained fragmented. There was no common program which could rally all groups, and the general prosperity tended to reassure people that industrialism might cure its own ills. As late as 1892 one editor, reflecting this optimistic frame of mind, could state that "the rich are growing richer, some of them, and the poor are growing richer, all of them." Men and groups seeking major changes, whether elitists or Populists, were generally stereotyped as cranks who were blind to the vast blessings and bright future of industrialism. Circumscribed by such problems and attitudes reformers were understandably fragmented in the Gilded Age.

The catastrophic depression of 1893–1897 radically altered this pattern of reform. It vividly dramatized the failures of industrialism. The widening chasm between the rich and the poor, which a few observers had earlier called a natural result of industrialism, could no longer be ignored. As several tattered bands of men known as Coxey's Army tramped from town to town in 1894, they drew attention to the plight of the millions of unemployed and vividly portrayed the striking contrasts between the way of life of the poor and the "conspicuous consumption" of the rich. Furthermore, as Thorstein Veblen observed, they showed that large numbers of Americans no longer cherished the old gospel of self-help, the very basis for mobility in a democratic society. As desperation mounted, businessmen and politicians tried the traditional ways of reversing the business cycle, but by 1895 they realized that the time-honored formulas of the tariff and the currency simply could not dispel the dark pall that hung over the land. Worse still, President Grover Cleveland seemed utterly incapable of comprehending, let alone relieving, the national crisis.

The collapse of prosperity and the failure of national partisan politicians to alleviate the crisis by the traditional methods generated an atmosphere of restless and profound questioning which few could escape. "On every corner stands a man whose fortune in these dull times has made him an ugly critic of everything and everybody," wrote one editor. A state university president warned his graduates in 1894 that "you will see everywhere in the country symptoms of social and political discontent. You will observe that these disquietudes do not result from the questions that arise in the ordinary course of political discussion . . . but that they spring out of questions that are connected with the very foundations of society and have to do with some of the most elemental principles of human liberty and modern civilization." Was the American dream of economic democracy and mobility impossible in an industrial society? Would the poor overthrow an unresponsive political and economic system? Such questions urgently demanded answers, and it was no longer either wise or safe to summarily dismiss as a crank anyone who had an answer. "The time is at hand," cried one editor, "when some of the great problems which the Nineteenth century civilization has encountered are crying for a solution. . . . Never before in the history of the world were people so willing to accept true teaching on any of these subjects and give to them a just and practical trial." A man's social origins were now less important than his proposals, and many men began to cooperate with people from different backgrounds to devise and implement solutions.

This depression-inspired search for answers sprouted hundreds of discussion groups at which men met, regardless of background, to propose remedies. These groups gave men the habit of ignoring previously firm class lines in the face of the national crisis. When Victor Berger urged the Milwaukee Liberal Club to adopt socialism as the answer, for example, his audience included wealthy bankers, merchants, and lawyers. In the same city, at the Church and Labor Social Union, banker John Johnston urged a "new society" where "class privileges will be abolished because all will belong to the human family," and the discussion was joined by Populists and Socialists as well as clergymen and conservative editors. In this context, too, all types of people sought the wisdom of the men who had made a career of studying the social and economic breakdown. No one was surprised when unions, Granges, women's clubs, and other groups wanted University of Wisconsin economists like Ely to address them. Maybe they had an answer. The social unrest accompanying the depression weakened class and status allegiances.

The direct political effects of the depression also broke down the previous rigidity and fragmentation of reform. The depression created a clear sense of priorities among the many causes which Gilded Age reformers had advocated. It generated broadly based new issues which all classes could unite behind. One such program was the urgent necessity for tax reform. When the depression struck, individuals and corporations were forced to devise ways of economizing as property values, sales, and revenues declined precipitously. Caught between higher taxes to cover the rising costs of local government and their own diminishing revenues, many wealthy individuals and corporations began to hide their personal assets from the assessors, to lobby tax relief through local governments, and even to refuse to pay any taxes. The progressive program was forged and received widespread popular support as a response to these economies. Citizens who lacked the economic or political resources to dodge their taxes mounted such a crusade against these tax dodgers that former President Benjamin Harrison warned the wealthiest leaders that unless they stopped concealing their true wealth from the tax assessors they could expect a revolution led by enraged taxpayers. The programs for tax reform—including inheritance, income, and ad valorem corporation taxes—varied from place to place, but the important fact was that most citizens had developed specific programs for tax reform and had now agreed that certain individuals and corporations had evaded a primary responsibility of citizenship.

A second major area which proved capable of uniting men of different backgrounds was "corporate arrogance." Facing declining revenues, many corporations adopted economies which ranged from raising fares and rates to lobbying all manner of relief measures through city and state governments. Even more important, perhaps, they could not afford necessary improvements which elementary considerations of safety and health had led local governments to demand that they adopt. Corporate arrogance was no longer a doctrinaire cry of reformers. Now it was an unprotected railway crossing where children were killed as they came home from school or the refusal of an impoverished water company to make improvements needed to provide the healthful water which could stop the epidemics of typhoid fever. Such incidents made the corporation look like a killer. These specific threats united all classes: anyone's child might be careless at a railroad crossing, and typhoid fever was no respecter of social origins.

From such new, direct, and immediate threats progressivism developed its thrust. The more corporations used their political influence to resist making the small improvements, the more communities developed increasingly radical economic programs like municipal ownership or consumer-owned utilities and fought to overthrow the machines that gave immunity to the corporations. Political reforms like the initiative, direct primary, and home rule became increasingly important in the early stages of progressivism because, as William Allen White said, men had first to get the gun before they could hit anything with it. But it was the failure of the political system to respond to the new and immediate threats of the depression that convinced people that more desperate programs were needed.

Perhaps there are, after all, times and places where issues cut across class lines. These are the times and places where men identify less with their occupational roles as producers and more with their roles as consumers—of death-dealing water, unsafe railway crossings, polluted air, high streetcar rates, corrupt politicians—which serve to unite them across social barriers. There are also universal emotions—anger and fear—which possess all men regardless of their backgrounds. The importance of the depression of the 1890s was that it aroused those universal emotions, posed dramatic and desperate enough threats to lead men of all types to agree that tax dodging and corporate arrogance had to be ended and thereby served to unite many previously fragmented reformers and to enlist the support of the majority that had earlier been either silent or enthusiastic only about partisan issues like the tariff or symbols like Abraham Lincoln. The conversion of the National Municipal League showed how issues were becoming more important than backgrounds. Originally composed of elitists who favored such Mugwumpish concerns as civil service reform, the League by 1898 had become so desperate with the domination over political machines by utility companies that it devoted its energies to municipal ownership and to political devices which promised "more trust in the people, more democracy" than its earlier elitism had permitted. The attitude of moral indignation, such an obvious feature of the early stages of progressivism, was not rooted in social tensions but in the universal emotion of anger.

Whether this emphasis on the results of the depression—unrest, new threats and new issues, and cooperation among social groups—has widespread relevance or validity remains to be seen, but it does help to explain the roots of progressivism in Wisconsin. The most important factor in producing the intensity of Wisconsin progressivism was the cooperation between previously discrete and fragmented social groups both in forging popular issues and getting reforms adopted. And the most important factor in defining the popular issues was the arrogance of certain corporations. In Milwaukee the traction and electricity monopoly between 1894 and 1896 alone, for reasons ranging from extreme overcapitalization to confidence in its political powers, raised both its lighting and streetcar fares, refused to arbitrate with its striking employees, enjoined the city from enforcing ordinances lowering its fares, and used its political power —the company's chief manager was the state's leading Republican boss— to cut its tax bill in half, kill an ordinance which would have prevented it from polluting the air, and thwart generally popular attempts at regulation. Each time the monopoly refused to obey an order, lobbied special favors from the city or state, or prostituted the Republican party to the company, the progressive coalition grew. By the end of the depression, the coalition drew together both ends of the economic spectrum—the Merchants and Manufacturers Association and the Chamber of Commerce as well as several labor unions and the Federated Trades Council. Politically it included the county Republican Club, the Democratic Jefferson Club, and the Socialists and Populists. The Mugwumpish and upper-class Municipal League was joined by German social clubs like the Turn-vereine. So defiant was the company—so desperate were the people—that the traction managers became the state's most hated men by 1899; and humorist-politician George Peck observed that Wisconsin's parents "frighten children when they are bad, by telling them that if they don't look out," the traction magnates "will get them." Four hundred miles away, in Superior, the story was remarkably similar. Angered by the repeated refusals of that city's water company to provide the city with healthful enough water to prevent the typhoid fever epidemics that killed dozens of people each year, and blaming the company's political power within both parties for the failure of regulation, labor unions and Populists cooperated with business and professional men and with dissident politicians to try to secure pure water and to overthrow the politicians owned by the company. In Superior, political debate had indeed narrowed, as an editor observed, to a fight of "the people against corporate insolence." The water company, like the traction monopoly at Milwaukee, stood isolated and alone, the enemy of men from all backgrounds. In Wisconsin, at least, the community's groups continued to perform their special functions; and, by the end of the depression, they were all agreed that corporate arrogance had to be abolished. Their desperation made them willing to speak, lobby, and work together.

If, as the Wisconsin experience suggests, cooperation was the underpinning of progressivism, historians should focus on reformers not as victims of social tensions, but as reformers. At any given time and place, hundreds of men and groups are seeking supporters for their plans to change society and government. The basic problem for the reformer is to win mass support for his program. In Wisconsin a reformer's effectiveness depended on how well he manipulated acts of corporate and individual arrogance that infuriated everyone in order to demonstrate the plausibility of his program. Desperate events had made tax dodging, corporate defiance and control of politics the main political issues and had allowed this program to swallow the older reformers at the same time that they created a much broader constituency for reform. The question then becomes: Why did some succeed while others failed? North Dakota never developed a full-blown progressive movement because that state's progressives never demonstrated the plausibility of their programs. Wisconsin's early progressives did succeed in drawing together such diverse groups as unions, businessmen, Populists, and dissident politicians because they adapted their program and rhetoric to the menacing events which angered everyone. Reformers operate in their hometowns and not in some contrived social background which could as easily apply to New York or Keokuk, and it is in their hometowns that they should be studied. Historians should determine why they succeeded or failed to rally the support of their communities to their programs, for the most significant criterion for any reformer is, in the end, his effectiveness.

When the progressive characteristically spoke of reform as a fight of "the people" or the "public interest" against the "selfish interests," he was speaking quite literally of his political coalition because the important fact about progressivism, at least in Wisconsin, was the degree of cooperation between previously discrete social groups now united under the banner of the "public interest." When the progressive politician denounced the arrogance of quasi-public corporations and tax-dodgers, he knew that experiences and events had made his attacks popular with voters from all backgrounds. Both conceptually and empirically it would seem safer and more productive to view reformers first as reformers and only secondarily as men who were trying to relieve class and status anxieties. The basic riddle in progressivism is not what drove groups apart, but what made them seek common cause.

13

Women Reformers and
American Culture, 1870–1930

JILL CONWAY

During the Progressive era women made enormous strides toward their goal of equal rights. Not only did they win the vote, but they also provided leadership and expert direction to a variety of social reform movements. Although impressive, these advances are misleading. From the 1870s to the 1930s there was little change in the stereotype of the female temperament. Jill Conway documents the effect that steretoype had on women reformers and on the feminist movement.

The history of American feminism has an Alice in Wonderland quality. The story of the achievement of legal and institutional liberties for women in America must be accompanied by an account of their loss of psychological autonomy and social segregation. The historian of American feminism must write a double narrative in which something more than the reversals of Looking-Glass Land must be advanced. The historian must relate the outward story of a successful agitation to some causal analysis of why this agitation first for legal rights, then for access to higher education, then for the franchise and for liberation from a traditional Christian view of marriage had so little influence on actual behavior. For there is no escaping the fact that in the very decade of the twenties when the franchise was secured and when a liberal view of marriage ties had finally

---

From *Journal of Social History* 5 (1971–72):164–75. Footnotes omitted. Reprinted by permission of the editor.

gained acceptance the vast majority of American women began to find social activism unattractive and to return to an ethic of domesticity as romantic and suffocating as any code of the high Victorian era. In fact the stereotype of femininity which became dominant in the popular culture of the thirties differed little from the stereotype of the Victorian lady except that the twentieth-century American woman had physical appetites which dictated that she could only know fulfillment by experiencing maternity and joyfully adapting to the exclusively feminine world of suburbia.

To some historians and social analysts this paradox has seemed so puzzling that nothing short of a plot theory of history can explain this sudden alteration in what appeared to be the direction of social change. Betty Friedan, for instance, feels that the triumph of domesticity can only be accounted for by the recognition by capitalists that women could best serve the economy of abundance as passive consumers. Yet her diagnosis does not take into account the fact that before the thirties women made the role of consumer an important one for social criticism through the organization of the National Consumers' League, a body which pioneered in legal and political campaigns in favor of state and federal welfare legislation. As the history of the League ably demonstrated between 1899, the year of its foundation, and the beginning of the New Deal welfare programs, consumers need not be passive victims of the capitalist system.

More recently historians of feminism have seen an underlying continuity behind the appearance of change in the social position of American women. Both Aileen Kraditor and William O'Neill have concluded that the remarkable stability of the bourgeois family in the twentieth century was the social fact which led to the frustration of all aspirations for change in the role and status of women. Thus the reformers who made divorce and birth control acceptable in the early decades of the twentieth century put emphasis on the need to strengthen the family in a secular society. Both divorce and limitation of family size finally won popular acceptance when they were advocated as reforms which would allow the bourgeois family the flexibility necessary to survive the pressures of an upwardly mobile urban society rather than as reforms which would permit real changes in sexual behavior. In the light of the evidence of historical demography we see the logic working for this kind of reform to preserve the family. Demographic study indicates that the duration of marriage unions was actually lengthening in the twentieth century as compared with earlier centuries such as the seventeenth, customarily regarded as a period of family stability. In fact, increased life expectancy in the twentieth century meant that fewer marriage partnerships were terminated after a short period by death; consequently, the sanctioning of divorce became a social necessity. There is thus no contradiction between the development of liberal attitudes toward the dissolution of marriage and the renewed stress on the value of maternity and domesticity for women. Divorce and birth control, both reforms which could have been advocated in terms opposed to female domesticity, actually won acceptance as measures to preserve the family and along with it female domesticity.

While historians are correct in emphasizing these underlying continuities in the history of American feminism between the Civil War and the 1930s, it is misleading to do so without drawing attention to the fact that women activists of the period represented a real change in feminine behavior. The failure of feminists to understand the significance of the intense social activism of women reformers during these years indicates that new ways of behaving do not necessarily evoke any new view of the female temperament. Though women of the stature of Jane Addams and Lillian Wald were actually wielding national power and influencing the decisions of the White House, neither they nor any of their contemporaries thought about adjusting the image of the female to this position of command. This failure to see women's activism for what it was, a real departure from women's traditional domesticity, indicates the controlling power of the stereotype of the female temperament which continued unaltered from the 1870s to the 1930s. Acquiescence in this control was indeed the major weakness in the ideology of feminism for the stereotype of the female personality was an essentially conservative one although women reformers coupled it with social innovation and occasionally with trenchant social criticism.

We see the controlling power of the stereotype of the female temperament most clearly in the thought of Jane Addams and Lillian Wald. Both women were aggressive public campaigners who relished a good political fight and who hungered after power. Yet they claimed to be reformers in the name of specialized feminine perceptions of social injustice. These specialized perceptions came from women's innate passivity and from women's ability to empathize with the weak and dependent. Like all reformers with a program for action, Jane Addams and Lillian Wald believed they had found a social group who would bring a new, just social order into being, but theirs was a group defined by sex rather than by class. Lacking a clear class consciousness, they expected a sex group to be agents of social change because of the unique qualities with which they believed the feminine temperament was endowed. Because of these qualities women were capable of direct, intuitive awareness of social injustice exactly in the style of the abolitionists who had been fired for the antislavery crusade through direct intuitive perception of social sin. Just what it was in the psyche of a Jane Addams or a Lillian Wald which would permit empathy with the weak and dependent remains shrouded in mystery for the most assiduous biographer. Both women gave evidence from an early age of the capacity to create and dominate large organizations, and they moved naturally into a position of leadership in any area of reform which they took up whether it be settlement work, child welfare legislation or the international peace movement.

Even though Jane Addams and Lillian Wald could not recognize their drive to power, their adoption of feminine intuition as a style of reform by which to come to grips with the problems of industrial cities is a puzzling choice. One expects tough-minded economic analysis from critics of industrial society. However, middle-class women reformers of their generation needed to find a basis for criticizing an exploitive economic system in which women of their class played no active part. It was for this reason that they were obliged to make such claims for the intuitive social power of the female temperament. They were encouraged in these claims by the dominant biological view of social evolution which did place great emphasis upon the evolutionary significance of biologically determined male and female temperaments. However, to base one's social criticism upon the idea that feminine intuition could both diagnose and direct social change was to tie one's identity as a social critic to acquiescence in the traditional stereotype of women. Further, to the extent that such women succeeded in gaining popular acceptance as reformers they were lending strength to the stereotype and helping to prepare the ground for the acceptance of another view of sexually specialized intellect, the neo-Freudian, romantic and conservative one, which began to gain acceptance in American culture in the twenties and the thirties.

In my study of American women who were both feminists and social critics in the post-Civil War era, two clearly distinct social types have emerged. The first is a borrowing from European culture, the type of the sage or prophetess who claimed access to hidden wisdom by virtue of feminine insights. The second is the type of the professional expert or the scientist, a social identity highly esteemed in American culture but sexually neutral. Jane Addams represents the best example of the Victorian sage to be found in American culture during her active public career from the 1890s to the 1930s. Florence Kelley, the organizer of the National Consumers' League and a kind of composite Sidney and Beatrice Webb for American industrial society, represents one of the best examples of the professional expert who took on the role of the social engineer. What is interesting about the two types is that the sage had great resonance for American popular culture and was celebrated in endless biographies, memoirs and eulogistic sketches. Women who took on that role became great public figures, culture heroines known in households throughout the nation. But the woman as expert did not captivate the popular imagination and did not become a model of feminine excellence beyond a small circle of highly educated women of a single generation. Julia Lathrop, who was the pioneer strategist of the mental health movement, the innovator responsible for the juvenile court movement and the head of the first Federal Child Welfare Bureau which became the model for many New Deal welfare agencies, simply did not excite the faintest ripple of public attention during a lifetime exactly contemporaneous with Jane Addams. Indeed this remarkable woman remained so anonymous despite a lifetime devoted to public service that Jane Addams wrote a biography of her so that she could serve as a model for future generations of American women. The biography was little read and could not serve its purpose because Jane Addams lost the substance of this consummate political strategist's life in describing the empathetic and unaggressive woman heroine which the stereotype of female excellence required. Similarly Florence Kelley's biographer, Josephine Goldmark, was unable to preserve for future generations any of the fiery personality of this powerhouse of a woman. The surface account of her lifetime devoted to the welfare of the industrial working class was accurately recorded. But the volcanic personality whose rages were so monumental that she could stamp out of a White House conference slamming the door in the face of Theodore Roosevelt is lost. Since women were supposed to be gentle, none of Mrs. Kelley's passion could come through the uncharacteristic calm imposed by her biographer. Thus the achievements of the experts were lost to subsequent generations and the significance of their actual behavior was completely misunderstood.

What survived for popular consumption was the woman reformer as sage and prophetess, the social type of which Jane Addams is the perfect exemplar. This survival led to an unfortunate association of critical perceptions of society with unquestioning acceptance of traditional views of the female psyche. It is the development of this type which we must understand if we want to comprehend how radical discontent could be expended in every social direction except the one which required questioning the stereotype of women.

The path to Jane Addam's identity as a sage lay through the experience of higher education and the recognition that she had access to learning of a scale and quality not available to preceding generations. The Addams family was involved in the abolition movement and important in local Republican politics and through these concerns became committed to equality with men in women's legal rights and educational opportunities. Daughters of the Addams family thus inherited a family tradition of reform without the corresponding obligation to business success which was imposed by such families on their sons. However, the standard curriculum for women's colleges like Rockford Seminary which Jane Addams attended entirely neglected the question of relevance for future vocational or intellectual purposes. Jane Addams was exposed at Rockford to the standard Victorian literary culture together with a high saturation of Protestant Christianity since the seminary's founder hoped to raise up a race of Christian women who could civilize the West.

The result of rigorous training in moral and aesthetic concerns was considerable disorientation when Jane Addams left college and began to try to define some social role in which her education could be put to use. Not only did her education fail to relate her in any significant way to the occupational structure of society, it had also trained her to be a moral agent in a society which expected middle-class women to be passive spectators and consumers. Two possible responses to this situation seem to have attracted the post-Civil War generation of college-educated women. The first was to withdraw to graduate study and acquire a re-spectable social role through professional training. Graduate school of-fered both escape from the family and the opportunity to enter a neutral social territory where the traditional rigidity of the American division of labor between men and women had not had time to establish itself. Those of an intellectual bent for graduate work seem to have found this adapta-tion a satisfactory one. It was the path to the social type of the woman expert. However, for those to whom graduate school was merely a strategy to escape from family discipline, only the second response was possible. Self-deception about an intellectual or professional career culminated in the standard Victorian ailment of emotional prostration. A minor illness took Jane Addams out of the Women's Medical College in Philadelphia in 1882 and kept her an invalid for over twelve months. Travel was of course the major therapy for such persistent nervous and emotional ail-ments, and it was while visiting London that Jane Addams began to develop the first signs of a nagging social conscience. In England the stereotypes of nativism could not inhibit perception of the sufferings of the London poor. The faces which stared back at the visitor to London's East End were not the faces of degenerate Irish or Poles, but English faces which could arouse the racially selective democratic feelings of young native Americans as no other sight could.

Travel next suggested the idea of expatriation and the refinement of a literary education through involvement in European aristocratic culture. For a woman who had been trained to see herself as an heir to the abolitionist tradition of moral fervor, however, there could be no more than temporary dabbling in the expatriate life. Once she had recognized her common human ties with the urban poor, it was only a matter of time before she put the two styles of life together by visiting an immigrant ghetto in Chicago and espousing the lot of the common man now seen as the logical object of reforming zeal which an earlier generation had directed toward the Negro.

The consequences of the life style which Jane Addams pioneered and other educated women emulated are well known. In New York and Chicago, women were the first founders of settlement houses. They also were preponderant among settlement residents in Philadelphia, Boston and Cleveland. The initial impulse for this kind of feminine migration to the slums was not identification with the working class, as in the European settlement movement, but the recognition that there was a social cure for the neurotic ills of privileged young women in America because their ailments were socially induced. As Jane Addams and Ellen Starr put it when they were looking for a house in an immigrant ward of Chicago in 1889: moving to the ghetto was ". . . more for the benefit of the people who do it than for the other class. . . . Nervous people do not crave rest but activity of a certain kind." By definition "nervous people" in need of releasing activity in American society were not men but women. Men were also discarded as irrelevant in the planning of Hull-House and other women's settlements because they were thought of as "less Christian" in spirit than women and motivated to action entirely by commercial rewards. It was thus as a consequence of an accurate perception of the problems of educated women in American society that middle-class women were brought into contact with the social problems of urban-industrial America. They were on location, settled and ready to become involved in urban problems just before the great depression of 1893–94 struck. Living in an urban slum that winter was the searing, unforgettable confrontation with social injustice which turned all of them into real critics of American society and obliterated their earlier concern with personal adjustment. But in forgetting the reasons for their presence in the urban slums women began to equate their recognition of social problems with special qualities of feminine insight. In *Democracy and Social Ethics* for instance, the work which was the most popular of Jane Addams' early writings on social problems, the culture of poverty is seen through the eyes of a middle-class woman visitor and the perception of the way American society exploited immigrants is made a feminine one. Exploiters are masculine and those who can see the true vision of a democratic society are women.

Quite apart from the process of social selection which took women reformers to the city there were good intellectual grounds for ascribing special qualities to the female intellect. These were to be found in the current interpretation of the significance of sex differences in the evolution of society. Jane Addams' papers show that she derived her views on this subject from three supposedly unimpeachable sources. She read Herbert Spencer's *Study of Sociology* of 1873 early in her career and accepted from it Spencer's view that the female psyche and mind were of special significance in the evolutionary process because of the innate feminine capacity to empathize with the weak. Once she had met Lester Ward at Hull-House in the decade of the 1890s, she accepted Ward's assumption that the female was the prototype of the human being and the most highly evolved of the two sexes. In 1900 she met the Scottish biologist and sociologist Patrick Geddes whose *The Evolution of Sex* of 1889 was the major work in English by a biologist of repute on the evolutionary significance of sex differences. Geddes believed that from the smallest single-celled organism to man sex differences were tied to differences in cell metabolism which made female organisms passive and nurturing and male organisms warlike and aggressive. After she met Geddes, she added a natural bent of pacifism to women's special capacity for social insight and played her role as sage with confidence that it conformed to everything current biology and sociology had to say about the place of women in society.

While she held to this traditional picture of women, however, Jane Addams had by 1900 arrived at some fundamental criticisms of American society. She recognized that political institutions which conformed to the classical theory of democracy were incapable of creating the kind of social equality which was central to the American democratic belief. She was convinced that traditional Puritan individualism was no guide to morality in an urban-industrial society. She saw that every social and political institution in America needed radical change if immigrants and workers were to participate in political decisions and receive the benefits of the Amercan industrial economy to the same degree that native Americans did. She thought the family should be modified so that its members could not settle into a private domesticity which made them blind to social suffering outside the family circle; church and charitable institutions needed to be pried loose from adherence to the old Puritan economic ethic and negative morality; business corporations and trade unions needed to be less concerned with productivity and material rewards and more aware of human values; political parties needed to be reformed so that they could become more responsive to the needs and concerns of the urban immigrant. The tendency to violence in American life which she saw as the heritage of the need to coerce a slave population in the South must be eradicated if the divisions in industrial society were not to lead to class warfare. As a diagnosis of American social ills, this was not unimpressive. It was free from the usual Progressive concern with institutionalizing middle-class values. It was future oriented, ready to accept radical change and optimistic about the potential of the American city to become a genuinely creative, pluralistic community.

One can say that important elements of radical discontent are present in this social criticism—an accurate diagnosis of the present and a creative, dynamizing view of the future. Contemporaries certainly thought so. In 1902 when Jane Addams published *Democracy and Social Ethics*, the work that contained the major themes of her social criticism up to 1900, her mail ranged from appreciative notes from John Dewey and William James calling it "one of the great books of our time" to emotional letters from college students who said they found reading the book a religious experience which liberated them to be moral beings for the first time.

What *Democracy and Social Ethics* lacked was a realistic perception of the social group who would be agents of desirable social change. To Jane Addams and women reformers of her generation, it seemed perfectly clear that women were the only people in America capable of bringing about a new order in which democracy would find social as well as political expression. As an organized force in politics, they would moralize and socialize a state which Jane Addams recognized was at present organized to protect and promote the interests of businessmen. Of even greater importance, women would be able to solve the problems of city government because the efficient management of urban affairs involved generalizing the skills of housekeeping which were exclusively feminine skills.

This celebration of women as makers of the future democratic society was a position from which there was no retreating as the suffrage agitation mounted. Indeed after 1900 the only modification of this feminist creed which Jane Addams made was to celebrate women's unique capacities for internationalism and the mediation of war. The woman as diplomat could settle the problems of world order as well as those of urban government. Such delusions are comic, but they are also very significant when entertained by minds with the range and scope for social analysis which Jane Addams certainly had.

They point to a predicament which was almost universal for middle-class American women of Jane Addams' generation. Intellectually they had to work within the tradition which saw women as civilizing and moralizing forces in society, a tradition given spurious scientific authority in evolutionary social thought. Yet within American society there was no naturally occurring social milieu in which these assumptions about the exclusive attributes of women could be seen for what they were. Women had to create the very institutions which were their vehicle for departure from middle-class feminine life, and in doing so they naturally duplicated existing assumptions about the sexes and their roles. Beatrice Webb remarked after visiting Hull-House that "the residents consist, in the main, of strong-minded energetic women, bustling about their various enterprises and professions, interspersed with earnest-faced self-subordinating and mild-mannered men who slide from room to room apologetically." Since Beatrice Webb knew this model well in herself and Sidney, it is highly probable that the perception was accurate. In settlement houses women could find endless opportunities for social action but no way out of the prevailing romantic stereotypes of men and women as social beings. As social workers struggling to solve the problems of the poor in American cities, women met mostly businessmen-philanthropists and clergymen with wide social concerns. The businessmen could be disregarded as tainted by acquisitiveness and the profits of commercial exploitation. The clergymen were representatives of a religious tradition which had failed to recognize the superior moral qualities of women. Such men could not be accepted as moral or intellectual equals no matter how readily they wrote checks or served on community charities for they were distrusted as agents of a society which subordinated women for economic or religious purposes. Yet without seeing men and women as moral equals, women reformers could find no way out of the traditional stereotype of the female temperament; and they could not see themselves as they really were, notably aggressive, hard-working, independent, pragmatic and rational in every good cause but that of feminism.

The consequence of this failure to question traditional views of femininity meant that the genuine changes in behavior and the impact of women's social criticism were short-lived. On the other hand, the national eminence of the woman reformer as sage merely strengthened sterile romanticism in popular attitudes to women. In this way a generation of women who lived as rebels against middle-class mores was finally imprisoned by them. We see the limitations imposed by this imprisonment in the absence of thought about or concern for sexual liberty in the lives of two women reformers of national eminence always in search of social issues to explore. For them rejection of Victorian bourgeois and economic values was never accompanied by questioning of Victorian sexual stereotypes.

Nothing is more pathetic than the shocked incomprehension of Jane Addams and Lillian Wald when faced with a popularized version of Freudian thought towards the close of their lives. Each in writing the concluding chapters of her memoirs towards the end of the decade of the twenties tried to grapple with the problem of explaining how their intuitive female sage could be distinguished from Freud's irrational woman whose destiny is shaped by her biological nature. They were powerless to deal with the assertion that their long careers as social reformers were merely evidence of failures in sexual adjustment because they had always accepted the romantic view of women as passive and irrational. This acceptance left them with no recourse when they were told their careers of activism represented deviance; for in terms of the stereotype of femininity which they had always accepted, they had been deviant. They had adopted a feminist ideology and a public identity which gave the widest possible currency to a modernized version of the romantic woman. They had acted very differently but had never understood the significance of the difference, much less reflected upon it until it was too late. Quite unwittingly they had helped to prepare a cultural climate ideally suited to the reception of Freudian ideas. Had they ever reflected on the significance of their behavior it is possible that with their superb talents for publicity and popular writing they could have dramatized some other model of feminine excellence beside the gentle, intuitive woman. Certainly they could have brought in question the negative image of the career women emerging in the mass media of the thirties. As it was they were silent, and the mass media were left free to begin the commercial exploitation of the romantic female without a murmur of dissent from two women who had used the identity of the romantic sage for far more elevated social purposes.

14

Woodrow Wilson's Neurological Illness

EDWIN A. WEINSTEIN

Of all presidents, Woodrow Wilson has received the greatest psychoanalytic and medical attention. He has been psychoanalyzed by Alexander L. and Juliette L. George (*Woodrow Wilson and Colonel House: A Personality Study*, 1956) and perhaps less satisfactorily by Sigmund Freud and William C. Bullitt (*Thomas Woodrow Wilson, Twenty-eighth President of the United States: A Psychological Study*, 1967). Edwin A. Weinstein, a neurologist, suggests that the key to many of Wilson's political actions and changes in personal behavior lay not in his childhood but rather in his neurological illness.

Woodrow Wilson had a long history of cerebral vascular disease, beginning when he was a professor at Princeton and culminating in September 1919, when he had a massive stroke which paralyzed the left side of his body and affected his vision and sensation on that side. His illness was also associated with alterations in behavior and personality, and there is a relationship between these changes and the events of Woodrow Wilson's later professional and political careers.

This study is limited by the paucity of medical records, by the state of medical knowledge in his time, and by the circumstances connected with the unique office of President of the United States. Following his major stroke, President Wilson was not hospitalized; case records were not

From *Journal of American History* 57 (1970):324–51. Footnotes omitted. Reprinted by permission of the author and *The Journal of American History*.

kept (or they may have been kept and subsequently destroyed); no technical procedures to define the exact location and extent of the brain lesion were carried out; and no tests to evaluate mental function were made. The medical data are restricted further by the nature of the relationship of the President's physicians to their patient, and some of the observations of other persons on the scene are biased for personal and political reasons. There is also the methodological problem of clinical versus historical evidence. The report of one observer may be credited more than that from a more qualified source if the event fits into some clinical syndrome or meets with medical expectations.

The demonstration on neurological grounds of impaired brain function does not necessarily mean that such impairment will contribute in a major way to political inefficiency. In a political system with checks and correctives an executive may respond to reduced capacity by accepting more help and delegating more responsibility. The behavioral sequelae of brain damage, also, may appear predominantly in the area of "private" activity rather than in the political sphere. Moreover, grossly irrational political behavior may occur in the presence of normal brain function. The changes in behavior associated with brain damage take a number of forms. They may involve not only a deficit in intellectual performance but also alterations in social, emotional, and "moral" behavior, which may exist relatively independently of defects in memory and thinking ability. The form is determined by a number of factors. The first is the type, location, extent, and rapidity of development of the brain lesion. The second is the premorbid personality, particularly as it influences the patient's attitude toward his disability and the way he adapts to and compensates for it. The third is the social milieu in which the person functions and the way others in the environment respond to and reinforce his behavior.

In the consideration that one is dealing with a complex interaction of many factors, three tentative criteria for the acceptance of impaired brain function as an etiological or causal agent in political behavior may be set up. First, the appearance of clinical evidence of brain damage should coincide with behavioral change. Second, the behavioral change should involve some impairment in performance. Third, it should be possible to classify actions in the political field into behavioral syndromes known to be associated with certain types of brain damage.

Woodrow Wilson's medical history may be divided conveniently into three stages. The first period, during which his ailments were largely psychosomatic, consisting of a nervous stomach and tension headaches, goes up to 1896 when the first definite manifestations of cerebral vascular disease occurred. The second phase extends to the fall of 1919 when he had his massive stroke resulting in the left hemiplegia (paralysis of the left face, arm, and leg). The third takes up the remainder of his presidential term when much of his ineffective political behavior can be explained on the basis of the changes in symbolic organization that occur after certain lesions of the right cerebral hemisphere.

A great deal has been written about Woodrow Wilson's personality from both the descriptive and psychodynamic points of view, and this account does not attempt to give a rounded picture. Rather, it provides a baseline along which later behavioral changes can be evaluated. A formulation of personality that has been useful in previous studies of the effects of brain damage concerns the behaviors and forms of language with which the person has habitually adapted to stress. The approach involves the way a person organizes his environment and relates to people so that new experiences can be symbolically represented and fitted into coherent patterns. These patterns of relatedness in the social environment include those based on family and gender roles; on religious, political, and social class orientation; on attitudes toward work and accomplishment, the physical self, health, and illness; and on general styles of language and communication. These values are a guide to an individual's perception of reality and furnish the context in which feelings, motives, and goals take on form and meaning. They also provide a means whereby dissonant information can be screened out, disbelieved, reclassified, or otherwise altered so that it fits into what are felt as stable, predictable systems.

The importance of Woodrow Wilson's close relationship with his family, especially his father, has been emphasized by him and his biographers. He grew up enjoying the complete loyalty, interest, devotion, and admiration of his parents, sisters, and younger brother. His mother was wholly approving and uncritical, and on the occasions when his father criticized or reproached him, he did so in the context of Christian love, duty, and morality. For example, when Joseph Wilson scolded his son for cutting classes at law school, he wrote that he did so only because love made him tell the truth. The family relationships were characterized by the absence of any overt expressions of anger, resentment, envy, or other negative feelings. Woodrow Wilson not only was a dutiful son but also took responsibility for and supported many relatives in his home. Each of his wives adored him, and his children found him enchanting. The strong identification with his family was linked with a certain reticence with outsiders until they had shown what he felt was their complete loyalty and devotion. It also led to his treating close friends—John Grier Hibben and Colonel Edward M. House—as family members and to the intense sorrow that resulted after the break with them.

Woodrow Wilson's concepts of masculine and feminine roles were also shaped by his family and regional background. His parents appeared quite opposite in personality. His father was handsome, forceful, talkative, outgoing, and a leader in the community. His mother, quiet and retiring, confined her interests to her family. He made a sharp dichotomy in his expectations of the behavior of men and women. Toward women he had a chivalrous and patronizing attitude, a view that doubtless contributed to his difficulties at Bryn Mawr where he encountered such "strong-minded women" as Carey Thomas and Lucy Salmon. Throughout his life, he cherished the companionship of loving and devoted women, a need that may have led to his early remarriage. He saw intellectual power, leadership, and logical thinking as masculine qualities, and with men he tended to be competitive and challenging, relishing the opportunity to "match minds."

He and his father had similar attitudes toward work and accomplishment. Their correspondence emphasizes application, success, and self-improvement. In his letters, Joseph Wilson constantly exhorted, encouraged, evaluated, and criticized his son and himself. Each man was firmly convinced that any goal could be reached provided one had enough faith and self-discipline. Achievement and failure, alike, were incentives for further effort. Thus, when Woodrow Wilson was a senior at Princeton, his father wrote, "That you are yourself dissatisfied with your own performance I am glad to know. For dissatisfaction with present achievement implies further progress. And *I* do not pronounce what you have written, perfect. It might be considerably improved—and you *will* improve upon it." While praising his son for some accomplishment, Joseph Wilson might point out how things could have been done even more efficiently and might warn him not to let success go to his head. The father motivated his son to aspire to perfection and gave him confidence in his capabilities, but, at times, he inculcated the feeling that, even at the peak of success, Woodrow Wilson had not fully realized his capacity. Even in the moments of his greatest triumphs, Woodrow Wilson was made cognizant of tasks which lay ahead.

An extremely methodical and efficient worker, he functioned deliberately and systematically without wasted time or motion. He dictated letters without hesitations, repetitions, or later corrections. He did not, as a rule, work long hours at Wesleyan or Princeton, and, prior to 1896, he seemed to have a good deal of time for conversation, quiet walks, bicycle rides, and tennis. For him, orderly work habits were a sign of an orderly mind. He told Irwin "Ike" Hoover, the White House usher, that "if a man knows his job, he does not have to work hard." Prior to the outbreak of the war, Woodrow Wilson completed his work as President in three or four hours a day. He had a remarkable ability to grasp and formulate the essentials of a problem with which he had had little or no previous experience. In preparing many of his speeches he would set down the main points and then fill in the illustrations and details, usually in extemporaneous fashion.

Woodrow Wilson's motivations to work and his confidence in his ability were a part of his religious belief. In the Calvinistic ethic of the Wilsons, God used men for His purposes; and in carrying them out, one could strive for goals and face crises with supreme confidence. This orientation sometimes led to overconfidence and rigidity, and to greater concern for success and victory than for the nature of the achievement itself. It also tended to make Woodrow Wilson feel anxious and guilty when not achieving. Work also served to overcome feelings of loneliness, depression, and grief. He worked to get over the "blues" when he was separated from Ellen L. Axson in his Johns Hopkins years, and after the death of his mother in 1888, he worked to deaden the pain of the loss.

An important facet of Woodrow Wilson's character was his conviction that one had the ability to control one's actions, feelings, and thoughts. This belief is expressed in his enormous powers of concentration, in his habitual self-discipline, and in his idea that one could, by force of will, put certain thoughts out of one's mind and make one's self feel or think in certain ways. While a professor at Princeton, he told a colleague, Bliss Perry, that when he could not think of a word that he wanted, he did not light up his pipe and walk across the room but would force himself to sit with his fingers on the typewriter keys and make the right word come to him. The quality is also seen in his mastery, prior to his brain illness, of his temper and impatience.

The separation of the controlling and observing self from the experiencing self is illustrated in his habit of self-scrutiny, expressed in his methodical and detailed recording of his thoughts and feelings and his habit of giving a reason for them. In his earlier years, particularly, he was apt to include in his letters a statement of his motive for writing. At Johns Hopkins he began a letter to his fiancée, "I feel justified in writing on this particular day because. . . ." He deplored his self-consciousness, comparing it unfavorably to smallpox. The dichotomy is indicated, also, in his statement of how, in a crisis, he felt guided by some intelligent power outside of himself, and is vividly described when, shortly after his inauguration as President, he wrote: "The old kink in me is still there. Everything is persistently *impersonal.* I am administering a great office,— no doubt the greatest in the world,—but I do not seem to be identified with it; it is not me, and I am not it. I am only a commissioner, in charge of its apparatus, living in its offices, and taking upon myself its functions. This impersonality of my life is a very odd thing, and perhaps robs it of intensity, as it certainly does of pride and self-consciousness (and, maybe, of enjoyment) but at least prevents me from becoming a fool, and thinking myself *It!*"

Woodrow Wilson had a rather ascetic attitude toward the material self. He felt that the body was the servant of the mind and totally disliked pomp and show. He never took more food on his plate than he could consume and, although neat in dress, did not pay attention to the style of his clothes until after he had entered the White House. He seemed indifferent to physical danger and showed no fear of assassination. He demonstrated his belief that the principle transcended the physical aspects of a situation when, wearing a high hat and a cutaway coat and mounted on a horse, he reviewed a regiment of the New Jersey National Guard.

All of these features of Woodrow Wilson's personality entered into his attitudes toward health and illness. His mother was frequently ill and was extremely apprehensive for the health and safety of her family. Her letters to him at college regularly expressed concern, and if he had not written for several days, she was apt to inquire if he had fallen ill. One letter reads: "I shall not be quite satisfied till I hear that you are *quite* rid of your cold. Please tell me particularly how it affects you now—and how it sickened you so seriously at first. Now dont [sic] forget to tell me all this, dear, please. . . ." She worried greatly that he might have to go to a doctor, possibly a not too irrational fear at the time. She avoided upsetting her son with news of her own ailments, about which he would learn later from his father. Her worries were in some degree a projection of her own fears for her health and a means of controlling and feeling close to her son. One senses in Woodrow Wilson's dutiful reporting of his symptoms the fulfilling of a filial obligation.

Joseph Wilson's concern for his son's health was expressed in the context of religious principles and moral exhortation. To feel well and be in good spirits depended on carrying out the laws of right living and having a good conscience before God. The maintenance of one's health was part of one's responsibility to God, and illness was seen as a kind of sin or enemy force to be overcome by the power of will and moral rectitude. Joseph Wilson was himself subject to spells of depression, and, noting the tendency in his son, advised him to throw himself into his daily studies and trust in God. When Woodrow Wilson confessed that he was depressed about the study of the law, his father replied that he could think of no reason for the blues to come to him except that he might fight and conquer them.

While Woodrow Wilson could use his symptoms as a way of gaining sympathy and affection, as shown in his letters to Ellen L. Axson during their courtship, his numerous ailments never interfered with what he considered his duty; and his response to threatened incapacity was to work harder. Prior to 1896, he rarely went to a doctor; and the few consultations recorded were mainly casual encounters and correspondence with medical friends and relatives. From Johns Hopkins in November 1883, he wrote that he had caught a cold and felt thickheaded, but "I am so seldom unwell that it fills me with impatience to be deprived of the full use and command of myself by sickness—which may be proof that discipline is needed; . . ." In apparently incongruous fashion, after complaining to Ellen L. Axson about headaches brought on by too much work and loneliness, he assured her that there was nothing wrong with him. Here, again, is the idea that the physical manifestations of illness are something apart from the responsible self.

The way in which complaints of illness and refusal to admit incapacity can be combined is illustrated in the circumstances of Woodrow Wilson's withdrawal from the University of Virginia Law School. Soon after he entered in the fall of 1879, his letters to his parents became filled with complaints of feelings of depression, dyspepsia, and a cold. Despite these reports of his suffering, he refused to accept the advice of his parents that he withdraw; and eventually left only when his father insisted that it was his duty not to endanger his life and his mother begged him not to sacrifice his health to stubborn pride. He departed suddenly without the usual amenities of leave-taking, suggesting that he had some feelings of guilt. On his return home, his recovery was instantaneous.

Woodrow Wilson's language was an important mode of shaping his social environment and adapting to stress. Someone said that he was born halfway between the Bible and the dictionary, and he was fond of telling how his own clear, precise speech was the result of his father's insistence that he be able to say exactly what he meant. Speaking, especially in public addresses, was a stimulating experience for him. He could establish an emotional bond with and sway his audiences by his use of figures of speech. He had the ability to represent complex political, economic, and social issues in homely illustrations and could make a moral issue of some mundane event. He depended on verbal content for his impact and did not use vocal effects or much gesture. Willam Bayard Hale, a one-time associate and, later, severe critic, made a valuable content analysis of Woodrow Wilson's linguistic style. Hale cites his predilection for adjectives and tropes and his repetition of favorite words like "counsel" and "process." He pokes fun at the affectations and romantic rhetoric of Woodrow Wilson's *George Washington*. Writing in 1919, when knowledge of the functions of symbols was limited, he claimed that Woodrow Wilson's fondness for images and figures of speech was the sign of an inferior mind and a substitute for rational thought. Actually, Woodrow Wilson used metaphorical speech because through it he could relate to people by reason of the way such language enlivens one's sense of reality and evokes a feeling of consensual experience. As Woodrow Wilson once told his fiancée, his speeches gave him a sense of power in dealing with men collectively that he did not feel with them individually. Henry W. Bragdon, a biographer of Woodrow Wilson's Princeton years, tells how during the stress of the Quadrangle Plan, Woodrow Wilson at a meeting with three close faculty friends in his study rose to address them.

The language of Woodrow Wilson's early biographical essays reinforced his sense of identity and served as an antidote to depression. He wrote his articles on William Gladstone and John Bright in March and April of 1880 when he was discontented with the study of law at the University of Virginia, feeling depressed and discouraged, and complaining of bad health. In the ornate figures of speech in which he admired the minds of these great men and in his praise of Bright for maintaining an "undeviating purpose and a will that knows no discouragement and no defeat," he was raising his own spirits.

Woodrow Wilson wrote *George Washington* in 1895–1896 when he was under a great financial strain and heavy pressures of work and time. Probably, his flowery style with its archaisms was a playful indulgence and a means of relaxation. He loved to play with language. As a child he was fascinated by symbols—by names, titles, ranks, and orders. His fondness for reciting poetry, limericks, and nonsense rhymes and doing parodies and comic imitations for his family is well known. The security-making aspects of these activities is emphasized by his repetition of certain passages of which he never tired. He had a large stock of jokes and anecdotes and liked puns. Some people, who had known him at Princeton, felt that he used these to cover up his self-consciousness. Certainly, he used humor to create rapport, disarm opponents, and dominate situations. He was apt to joke about his medical ailments, saying that he had worn out his pen hand, and referring to his digestive troubles as "disturbances in the equatorial regions" and "turmoil in Central America."

While most of Woodrow Wilson's biographers have stated that he had delicate health as a child, there is no firsthand evidence of any ailment in his early years. He complained of a cold during his freshman year at Davidson but completed the term before withdrawing from the college. At Princeton, he had occasional headaches, feelings of dizziness and dullness, gastro-intestinal disturbances, and colds. These symptoms were not frequent and did not cause him to miss classes, and their severity may have been exaggerated by biographers in view of his later record of illness. Dr. Hiram Woods, a Princeton classmate, did not recall that Woodrow Wilson had ever been ill in college. At the University of Virginia Law School, his dyspepsia and headaches were clearly psychosomatic manifestations of anxiety and depression brought on by conflicts over the study of the law, his failure to meet his own and his parents' expectations, and his inability or reluctance to express opposition more openly. These symptoms returned during his unhappy practice of law in Atlanta where they were ascribed to "biliousness." By this time his father had diagnosed their cause and advised him to conquer his real enemy, his *"mental* liver."

Woodrow Wilson entered Johns Hopkins for graduate study in the fall of 1883. There he complained of headaches, occasionally at first but more frequently in the spring of 1884. In February 1884, he saw his friend, Dr. Woods, who assured him they were harmless. Woodrow Wilson attributed his headaches to overwork, to uncertainty over his plans, and to his longing for Ellen L. Axson. At Bryn Mawr, his headaches continued along with bowel disturbances. His illnesses at Bryn Mawr could have been related to general unhappiness, to the stress of writing *The State,* and to the preparation of lectures for numerous courses. Disgusted with his "treacherous digestive organs," he went to a physician who *"laughed"* at him and prescribed some pills, but Woodrow Wilson did not take them and was soon relieved in "mind and bowel." His move to Wesleyan in 1888 was accompanied by a marked improvement in health, which he maintained during his early Princeton years.

Woodrow Wilson's gastrointestinal disturbances recurred in severe fashion in the winter of 1895–1896 when he was teaching post-graduate courses at Johns Hopkins. It was a period when he was under heavy pressure of work and finances. He treated his symptoms by siphoning out the contents of his stomach with a pump that had been recommended by Dr. Francis Delafield of New York. Also, on the advice of his friend, Dr. Charles Mitchell of Baltimore, he planned a vacation trip to England for the summer. The first clinical evidence of structural damage to his nervous system came in late May 1896, probably while he was spending a weekend in Princeton. He suddenly developed weakness and pain in his right arm and numbness in the fingers of his right hand. Over the summer, his condition improved; and in July he wrote from England that his only disability was slight numbness of the ends of his first and second fingers. However, his symptoms persisted after his return to Princeton and it was not until March 1897, that he was able to write consistently with his right hand. Subsequent attacks of weakness and paresthesia (abnormal sensation) in the right upper extremity, necessitating the use of a special, large penholder and a rubber signature stamp, were to recur intermittently in transient fashion throughout his career at Princeton.

His response to the events of 1896 was typical of the way he reacted to incapacity. According to Ray Stannard Baker, Woodrow Wilson expressed neither worry nor complaint and was so reticent about letting some of his friends know that they felt aggrieved because of his seeming neglect of them. To some friends, he wrote apologizing for not using his right hand. His family, in contrast, was alarmed; Joseph Wilson exclaimed: "I am afraid Woodrow is going to die." There is no record that

Woodrow Wilson consulted a doctor prior to his return from England. In characteristic fashion, he learned to write extremely well with his left hand and, later, to hit a golf ball left-handed. In his letters to his wife from abroad, he complained more of his clumsy *left* hand and his hemorrhoids, as if these were his major concerns. (He habitually complained more about his relatively minor psychosomatic ills than he did about serious organic symptoms, which he tended to deny.) The condition was diagnosed as "neuritis," and he himself called it "writer's cramp."

The nature of his ailment becomes clear in the light of the catastrophic events of 1906. On May 28, he awoke completely blind in his left eye. He was taken by his close friend Hibben to Philadelphia to consult the famous ophthalmologist, Dr. George de Schweinitz. De Schweinitz found that the blindness had been caused by the bursting of a blood vessel in the eye and that this was a manifestation of a more general disease of the arteries, probably high blood pressure, and told Woodrow Wilson that he must give up active work. In a letter to her cousins, Ellen Axson Wilson describes the condition as "incurable" and due to "premature old age," and notes that it is the same disease that killed his father. Woodrow Wilson was also seen by an internist, Dr. Alfred Stengel, who found a moderate degree of arterial tension that did not suggest a progressive course, and he felt confident that a rest of three months would restore the patient.

The sequence of episodes of paresthesia in one hand and blindness in the opposite eye is characteristic of occlusive disease of the internal carotid artery, the major supplier of blood to the brain. This vessel gives off a branch, the ophthalmic artery, whose continuation, the central retinal artery, goes to the homolateral retina, and continues on to supply the cerebral hemisphere. Interference with circulation to the hemisphere gives impairment of motion and sensation on the opposite, contralateral side of the body. Thus, the combination of symptoms indicates that there was blocking of the left internal carotid artery. There is no medical evidence for the diagnosis of neuritis because the findings point so clearly to involvement of the brain rather than the peripheral nerves.

The exact way in which occlusive and stenotic disease—a narrowing of the internal carotid artery—produces symptoms is not clearly understood, but it is likely that the paresthesias in the right hand and blindness in the left eye result when clots from the larger vessel block the smaller branches. The clinical course is variable, but tends to be episodic with frequent remissions. The age of onset is between thirty and sixty. The overall duration may be very long with periods of up to twenty-five years reportedly elapsing from initial manifestations to final incapacity. Transient, brief episodes lasting from thirty minutes to several hours, especially involving the hand, are common. These either abate spontaneously or terminate in an enduring hemiplegia (paralysis of a side of the body). The attacks of blindness do not occur at the same time as the other neurological disturbances, and, in contrast to the transitory nature of the paresthesias and weakness, the blindness is enduring. Some of Woodrow Wilson's vision returned, but he had impaired sight in his left eye for the rest of his life. He had another attack involving his right hand in 1908, but no further episodes of paresthesia occurred during his terms as governor and President.

Wilson probably was seen in 1906 by the neurologist Dr. Francis X. Dercum of Philadelphia, who also attended him after his massive stroke of 1919. Dercum's files were destroyed under the terms of his will, but de Schweinitz continued to examine Wilson at approximately yearly intervals. His records have also been discarded, but Dr. Edward S. Gifford, Jr., of Philadelphia, who took over the practice from de Schweinitz's associate, observed: "Woodrow Wilson suffered from a very high blood pressure and his fundi (retinas) showed hypertensive vascular changes with advanced atherosclerosis (thickening of vessel walls), angiospasticity (spasm of retinal vessels), retinal hemorrhages and exudates." These observations were made while Wilson was President.

Eleanor Wilson vividly recalled her father's return from the examination by Dr. de Schweinitz. While the family was engulfed in panic and despair, he was outwardly calm and even gay. Dr. Cary T. Grayson, Woodrow Wilson's physician during his presidency, later told Baker that Woodrow Wilson was extremely despondent. Whatever his feelings, Woodrow Wilson continued in his routine duties as president of Princeton. His letters during his three-month vacation abroad were optimistic despite the minimal improvement in vision. "I am puzzled what to report about myself," he wrote his sister, "I have never felt as if there were anything the matter with me, you know, except for my eye and I can only guess I am improving from the unmistakable increase in energy that comes to me from week to week." He consulted an ophthalmologist, Dr. George A. Berry, and an internist, Dr. F. D. Boyd, in Edinburgh. He cites their opinion that he is fit for work and that a man of his temperament should not stay away from work for too long. It is likely that the Scottish physicians' knowledge of Woodrow Wilson's temperament came from Woodrow Wilson himself. (Boyd was ten years younger than Woodrow Wilson and Berry his approximate age.)

According to Stockton Axson, a subtle change took place in Wilson after 1896. He relaxed less and appeared more intense and all business. He became more impatient of theoretical discussion and more demanding of facts. He no longer would take long bicycle rides on which he would sit by the roadside and chat. It is not likely that the relatively slight degree of brain damage was directly involved in these changes in behavior.

One does not know whether Wilson suspected that he had sustained a stroke, but he must have experienced a great deal of anxiety over an ailment which, unlike his previous ones, did not yield to rest and relaxation of tension, and which recurred in unpredictable fashion.

From 1906, the behavioral changes were more marked. He became irritable and impulsive, more openly aggressive and less tolerant of criticism and opposition. In the Quadrangle Plan and graduate school controversies he was inconsistent in his statements and actions. This behavior is commonly associated with cerebral vascular disease and in the early stages may be the only clinical manifestation. However, the symptoms are not specific for brain damage and may occur in other situations of stress unassociated with structural brain pathology. While the coincidence with clear evidence of brain damage makes it likely that the latter was a causal factor, it does not, in itself, explain the behavior. Another person similarly afflicted might have responded in a different way. Other factors were his personality and the responses of others to the way he adapted to the stress of his disability.

With the dismal prognosis that he received in 1906, he must have felt that he did not have long to live and that his mental faculties might deteriorate as his father's had. In characteristic fashion, he sought his salvation in work. In April 1907, he said he had originally thought that the Quadrangle Plan would take twenty years, but that now it seemed immediately obtainable. He methodically reorganized his life in the interests of conserving his strength. He obtained a full-time secretary, played golf faithfully, and went on regular vacations to Bermuda. He took naps and learned to fall asleep at will. He reduced his personal contacts and tended to meet members of the Princeton community only on official business. This lack of informal communication proved a serious handicap as, prior to presenting his plan for the abolition of the eating clubs in June 1907, he had mentioned the idea only to three of his intimate friends on the faculty and had ignored the alumni.

The content of the language in which Woodrow Wilson put forth his proposals can be interpreted from the standpoint of his adaptation to stress. He could have made a good case if he had fought the issue of the eating clubs on the basis of social snobbery. Yet, over and over again he asserted that the aim was not social but intellectual and academic. He reiterated that he stood for the attainment of the full intellectual life of the University. Here he may have been symbolically representing and compensating for what he felt was a danger to his own intellectual capacity and morale. One notes his emphasis on "restoration," on "revitalization," and on the "life of the mind." In July 1907, he wrote, "the fight is on, and I regard it, not as a fight for development, but as a fight for the restoration of Princeton. My heart is in it more than it has been in anything else because it is a scheme for salvation." In his December 1906 supplementary report to the Princeton trustees he charged that the club system had disintegrated undergraduate morale. These remarks, however, were interpreted by his adversaries not as self-referential representations but as distortions of fact.

On the whole, Woodrow Wilson made a good clinical recovery which, in retrospect, is not surprising in view of the episodic nature of his illness. At the time, however, his improvement ran counter to the medical knowledge, as evidenced by the later prediction of Dr. S. Weir Mitchell, the eminent neurologist, that Woodrow Wilson would not live through his presidential term of office. The President's recovery also, in a person of his beliefs, may have given him the conviction that God had preserved him and destined him for some great purpose. When he entered the White House in 1913, Woodrow Wilson looked extremely well. Grayson stated that "careful examination and all the medical tests revealed that there was no organic disease," a statement of doubtful validity in view of de Schweinitz's report on the condition of Woodrow Wilson's eye grounds.

In the spring of 1915, Woodrow Wilson experienced several days of severe, blinding headaches; and he saw de Schweinitz in August of that year. The headaches persisted intermittently, and he continued to consult de Schweinitz semi-annually. Over this period he had frequent "colds," the nature of which is not stated. From about early 1916, he began to show signs of increased tension in the form of irritability and intolerance of opposition. Edmund W. Starling, the Secret Service agent assigned to protect the President, says that Woodrow Wilson first showed signs of strain in December 1917, with outbursts of anger in relatively trivial situations. In view of the great stress to which the President was subject during the war, it is impossible to judge to what degree impaired vascular supply to the brain was a factor in his behavior.

The relationship of Wilson to his physician, Grayson, is of great significance. Grayson was a young navy doctor, who had served in the White House in the William Howard Taft administration. Woodrow Wilson took a liking to him when he did a prompt first aid job on Woodrow Wilson's sister when she fell at a White House reception. Grayson was highly personable and the President was probably wary of doctors in their professional roles after the virtual death sentence passed on him in 1906. He needed a doctor with whom he could have a warm relationship, who was thoroughly devoted to him and whom he could treat as a member of his family. Grayson carried out these roles admirably, much as House did in the political sphere. Grayson gave the President emotional support and supervised his routine of diet and regular exercise.

Grayson's close relationship with the Wilson family, however, created difficulties in his functioning as a physician because his emotional identification contributed to his overlooking or denying the seriousness of illnesses. During the progressively downhill course of Ellen Axson Wilson's fatal sickness (she died in 1914 of tuberculosis of the kidneys), the President and Grayson continued to give out optimistic forecasts. When Stockton Axson saw his sister at the William G. McAdoo wedding, at which Grayson was best man, Stockton Axson was shocked to see how feeble she had become. When he expressed his apprehension, he was reassured by Woodrow Wilson that she was getting well and that Grayson had expressed full expectation of her recovery. Shortly before the end, the facts were given to the President by a friend and former family physician, Dr. E. P. Davis.

It is generally agreed that Woodrow Wilson's first great political mistake was the issuing of an appeal to the people, in October 1918, to show their confidence in his leadership by electing a Democratic Congress. The action itself was, of course, not indicative of any impairment of brain function, but what was disturbing was the language, which Seward W. Livermore describes as "splenetic in temper and petulant in tone." Even Edith Wilson called it undignified. Although the President changed the wording, he insisted on issuing the statement, which contained bitter references to the Republicans, such as the charge that "the return of a Republican majority to either House of Congress would be interpreted on the other side of the water as a repudiation of my leadership." In a similar incident, Richard Hooker, the editor of the Springfield *Republican*, a paper friendly to the administration, urged Wilson to select Taft and another Republican on the peace delegation. Hooker states, "his reply, while personally gracious in the extreme . . . disturbed me at the time by the severity of its condemnation of Taft and made me feel that Wilson's judgment owing to increasing irritation was not as good as it had been." According to Arthur S. Link, the deciding factor in the Democratic defeat of 1918 was not Woodrow Wilson's offense to the supporters of a bipartisan foreign policy, but the resentment of midwestern wheat farmers over a price ceiling while southern cotton was uncontrolled. The President, however, blamed the defeat on the insufficient loyalty to him of Democratic congressmen. As if to compensate further for any feeling of not maintaining his leadership, he told the American experts traveling with him to Paris that the French and British leaders did not represent their people.

On April 3, 1919, at the Paris Peace Conference, Woodrow Wilson was taken sick suddenly with high fever, cough, vomiting, diarrhea, and insomnia. Because of the suddenness and the gastro-intestinal symptoms, Grayson first suspected that the President had been poisoned and then made a diagnosis of influenza. Despite his condition, Woodrow Wilson, in characteristic fashion, insisted on working; and business was conducted from his bedside for several days. According to William C. Bullitt, the President, on April 4, had bloody urine and twitching of the left leg and the left side of his face. Ike Hoover states that the President developed markedly irrational behavior. While still in bed, he issued an order forbidding members of the American delegation to use automobiles for recreation, in exact contrary fashion to his previous solicitous suggestions that they take as much diversion motoring as possible. After getting back on his feet, Woodrow Wilson expressed the idea that all the French servants were spies, who spoke perfect English and overheard everything that was said. According to Ike Hoover's account, Woodrow Wilson also claimed that he was personally responsible for the furniture in the palace and became disturbed because some of it had been removed.

These reports pose problems of clinical diagnosis and in the evaluation of the evidence. Bullitt was not present in Woodrow Wilson's bedroom, and his book contains so many inaccuracies and so much anti-Wilson prejudice that he hardly qualifies as a competent witness. However, during the preceding month, the President's left facial muscles had been observed by others as twitching involuntarily, and, in the fall of 1919, he did go on to a full-fledged paralysis of his left side. The President did have an enlarged prostate gland, and urinary obstruction was a serious complication after the September 1919 stroke. The veracity of Ike Hoover's account has been disputed by Thomas A. Bailey, who calls him "not-too-reliable" because Ike Hoover knew nothing of Woodrow Wilson's pre-conference ill health. Yet, Wilson would hardly complain in front of the White House domestic staff. Moreover, Ike Hoover admired Woodrow Wilson's intellect and his considerate attitude toward the staff, and can be considered an impartial witness.

The best reason for accepting Ike Hoover's account of the President's irrational behavior is that the symbolic themes of his delusions and preoccupations were those which Woodrow Wilson had habitually used to express his thoughts and feelings and to adapt to stress. Automobiles were a favorite figure of speech. (Woodrow Wilson, incidentally, was the first President to ride to his inaugural in an automobile.) In 1906, he had predicted ominously that the automobile would spread socialism in the United States because it gave people the picture of the arrogance of great wealth. In his speeches, Woodrow Wilson liked to use the metaphor to express his ideas about the abuses of trusts, saying that he objected not to automobiles but to people taking joy rides in them. Along with golf, motoring was his favorite relaxation and recreation. In the White House, motoring was a daily activity with each trip numbered and no deviation permitted from a set route. To emphasize his convictions about special privileges before the law, he had insisted that no member of his family or staff exceed the speed limit. The theme was to recur in disturbed behavior when, after his stroke, he was permitted to take automobile rides. When his car was passed by another vehicle, the President would demand that the offending motorists be arrested and tried for speeding. If one considers Woodrow Wilson's habitual passion for motoring and his previous generosity with the staff, his strange action in forbidding the use of cars suggests that he was projecting some sense of guilt and was symbolically punishing himself.

The delusion that all the French servants were spies who spoke perfect English is a highly condensed symbolic representation of his problems with the French, which were acute at the time. In a delusion, one represents his problems in symbols that explain and impart a particularly vivid feeling to the experience by reason of the way the language is an expression of personal identity. "Perfect English" was a favorite idiom and a mainstay of his identity system. The idea that everything he said was overheard by the French suggests that he was symbolizing his defeat by Georges Clemenceau on the Saar and other matters of French security.

In view of Woodrow Wilson's history and his subsequent massive stroke six months later, the most likely cause of his illness in Paris was a cerebral vascular occlusion (blood clot in the brain). A less feasible diagnosis is a virus inflammation of the brain, associated with influenza. The episode is an example of what Dr. Walter Alvarez has called "little strokes," as differentiated from "big strokes" associated with gross paralyses and aphasia (loss of speech).

There is also some scattered evidence of other neurological sequelae. Bernard Baruch describes the President coming in to ask Grayson to look at his eye while Baruch and the doctor were conversing. After joining them for a time, the President left and Grayson told Baruch, "He didn't have anything the matter with his eye. He just wanted to come up and be with us." Knowing Grayson's attitude, the remark may have been made to remove any suspicion of Baruch's that the President was ailing. Edith Benham, Edith Bolling Wilson's social secretary, states that in Paris the President avoided walking. This would be a marked change, as walking had long been a favorite diversion. That some motor weakness or incoordination may have been present is suggested by Starling's recollection of how on shipboard returning to America the President stumbled repeatedly over an iron ring set in the deck.

Various observers comment on the change in the President after the April episode. Starling says that he tired more easily and never did regain his old grasp. Herbert Hoover states that prior to the acute illness, Woodrow Wilson was incisive, quick to grasp essentials, unhesitating in his conclusions, and willing to listen to advice. Afterward, he groped for ideas and his mind constantly strove for precedents and previous decisions even in minor matters. In later years, David Lloyd George told Harold Nicholson that he thought Woodrow Wilson had sustained some sort of a stroke and that after April 1 he had fallen increasingly under the influence of Clemenceau. There was a striking change in the President's sleep and work habits. Although feeling tired, he slept poorly in contrast to his usual ability to put himself to sleep regardless of the stress. According to Grayson, Woodrow Wilson deliberately neglected his health by working all hours of the day and night, and even on Sunday. His tour of the western states in September was taken against the advice of his physician.

The episode of April 2 to 5 suggests that he sustained a lesion in the right cerebral hemisphere extending to include deeper structures in the limbic-reticular system. With the history of lesions of the left side of the brain, indicated by the attacks of right-sided paresthesia and left monocular blindness from 1896 to 1908, he now had evidence of bilateral damage, a condition affecting emotional and social behavior more severely than a unilateral lesion. With such involvement, there occur changes in the patient's perception and classification of his environment, so that his designation and recall of issues, events, and people tend to become *metaphorical* representations of his own problems and feelings. This appears in selective fashion so that one may forget and falsify events connected with one's personal problems without showing an overall deficit in memory or thinking. One may recall an incident accurately in one context but not in another where it is being used as the vehicle for the representation of some aspect of illness or incapacity. These patterns of language occur in some degree in any situation of stress but they are more marked and persistent with structural brain damage. Also, the person becomes less aware of the self-referential aspects.

The President's use of ostensibly referential language to represent aspects of his illness symbolically can be seen in the record of the meeting of the American delegation on June 3. General Tasker Howard Bliss stated his opposition to a French military occupation of Germany. In answer, the President proposed that the matter be taken up by a small group who would meet to exchange views without the usual roundabout expressions of international intercourse, "to learn each others' minds, real minds. . . ." In this statement he may have been resolving concern about his own mind. At the same session, he dismissed the fears of the British and some of his American colleagues that the terms of the treaty in respect to Germany's eastern frontier, reparations, period of occupation, and admission to the League were so harsh that the Germans would not sign the treaty. The President said: "It makes me a little tired for people to come and say now that they are afraid the Germans won't sign, and their fear is based on things that they insisted upon at the time of the writing of the treaty; that makes me very sick. And that is the thing that happened. These people that over-rode our judgment and wrote things into the treaty that are now the stumbling blocks, are falling over themselves to remove these stumbling blocks. . . ." He then specifically cited the British: "They are all unani-mous . . . in their funk. Now that makes me very tired. They ought to have been rational to begin with and then they would not have needed to have funked at the end. . . ." One might wonder less at the vehemence of this tirade when it is considered that he may have been referring also to his sickness, fatigue, and stumbling gait.

The President's most direct symbolic representation of his illness came up in a discussion of reparations. Thomas W. Lamont had said that the difficulties would be cleared up if the President, Lloyd George, and Clemenceau would instruct their technical experts to arrive at a definite sum in twenty-four hours. The President replied: "We in-structed them once to find a definite sum. And then we got Klotz on the brain." (Louis L. Klotz was the French minister of finance.)

The choice of metaphor in which the patient represents his prob-lems depends on the nature of the problems and the concepts in which he has habitually classified his environment and related to people. For Woodrow Wilson, the significant concepts were those of God, Christian morality and duty, democracy and the people. These were the categories to which experiences were assimilated and given meaning and unity. Under the conditions of altered brain function, he continued to use the same organizing principles and the same "problem solving" lan-guage. However, the symbols were now more highly condensed, and the categories contained many more diverse and otherwise unconnected referents. With increasing impairment of brain function, the meaning of events depended less on the actual situation in which they occurred and more on the way they fitted into Wilson's personal identity system. Whereas formerly Woodrow Wilson had used language to shape his environment and control the behavior of others, now his own behavior was to come increasingly under the control of his language.

Much of the controversy over the treaty had to do with changes in the language. Most Democrats saw the alterations in wording that moderate reservations would have required as inconsequential if the treaty could only be ratified, particularly when it was evident that it would not pass the Senate in its original form. For Woodrow Wilson, however, the words had a different order of significance because they were such highly condensed symbols of intense personal experience. This preoccupation with language contributed to the unfavorable result of his meeting with the Senate Foreign Relations Committee in August 1919. The President was asked whether the United States would be obligated to go to war to punish an aggressor should a commercial boycott fail. He replied that while there was no legal obligation, there was a moral one. He agreed that each country would determine for itself what was aggression, but he rejected the suggestion that it be explicitly stated that Congress use its own judgment, insisting that a moral obligation was superior to a legal one and in itself carried the force of truth and righteousness. He maintained that if the United States lived up to its moral obligation, then its judgment would of necessity be right. While a person might escape legal technicalities, he could not escape his own conscience.

This kind of language produced the Republican charge that the President had been evasive, although the Democrats considered his performance eloquent and high-minded. Woodrow Wilson was probably using the word "moral" in an idiosyncratic, personalized context. He had asked for a declaration of war only after a period of great reluctance and had sought justification for the war on moral grounds. His insistence on the specific language appears to have been his defense against feelings of guilt and inadequacy, especially after the compromises that he had been forced to make at Paris. When he said that moral obligations were superior to legal ones and that one could not escape one's conscience, he may well have meant his own conscience and the feeling that, while he was legally justified in declaring war, he had not absolved himself of the moral guilt.

At this meeting the President also denied having had knowledge of the secret treaties prior to going to Europe. These were the arrangements to divide up the territory of the defeated Central Powers that the Allies had made among themselves, and they proved to be the greatest obstacle in the way of the President's aim of a just peace. Despite his denial, the treaties were known to him, and the provision in the Fourteen Points about open covenants was deliberately designed to offset the effect of Soviet revelations about the treaties after the Bolshevik Revolution. For a long time the President had probably wished to deny their existence and consequently acted as though they did not exist. However, it was only under the conditions of altered brain function that he could deny them in the form of a selective amnesia. This explanation is more plausible than the charge that the President was deliberately lying or had become grossly incompetent. Bailey points out that during the questioning the President freely and accurately gave intimate details of subjects that were no less important. In his monograph, Alvarez comments that after a "little stroke" a patient may remember quickly and easily a hundred thousand scientific facts and the meaning of thousands of words in languages not his own, but may forget the name of an old friend whom he wants to introduce to someone. Possibly the same type of amnesia had occurred at the Princeton trustees' meeting of January 13, 1910, when Woodrow Wilson denied that he had read Dean Andrew F. West's graduate school brochure, which he had not only read but also for which he had written a laudatory preface.

On the ill-fated western tour in September 1919, the President had definite signs of cardiac decompensation and brain involvement. He experienced nocturnal episodes of coughing which forced him to sleep in a sitting position, and he complained of severe headaches and double vision. In his last speech at Pueblo on September 25, he stumbled when getting on to the platform, and, uncharacteristically, allowed Starling to assist him. His voice was weak, he mumbled, and there were long pauses as if he were having difficulty in following a train of thought. In the early morning of the next day, September 26, Joseph Tumulty, the President's secretary, found him dressed and sitting in a chair. His whole left side was paralyzed, and he had difficulty in articulating. He pleaded with Tumulty not to cut the trip short as the President's friends and Senator Lodge would say that he was a quitter, and the treaty would be lost. He went on to tell Tumulty that he would be all right if the trip could be postponed for twenty-four hours. By the time the party reached Washington, some power in the left limbs had returned, and the President was able to walk from the train. He felt better over the next few days, but Grayson was alarmed enough to make appointments for de Schweinitz and Dercum to see the President. On the evening of October 1, he appeared cheerful and played some billiards, but early the next morning Edith Bolling Wilson found him unable to use his left arm and complaining of loss of feeling in it. When she returned from calling Grayson, she found him unconscious on the floor. The hemiplegia proved to be permanent. On November 17, he was able to sit up in a specially braced wheel chair, for the first time; but Woodrow Wilson never recovered any power in his left arm and was able to walk only a short distance with support. Weakness of the left face and jaw persisted. In addition, he probably had sensory loss on his left side and absent vision in the left visual field of both eyes. Superimposed on the visual loss sustained in 1906, the probable hemianopia must have caused almost complete blindness in the left eye and made it extremely difficult for the President to read. He was not aphasic, but after speaking for a time his voice would become weak and indistinct. The illness was complicated by a threat of uremia from a urinary obstruction, which became acute on October 17, but which relieved itself spontaneously.

Following his stroke, the outstanding feature of the President's behavior was his denial of his incapacity. Denial of illness, or anosognosia, literally lack of knowledge of disease, is a common sequel of the type of brain injury received by Wilson. In this condition, the patient denies or appears unaware of such deficits as paralysis or blindness. While recognizing a limb as paralyzed, he may regard it as not a part of his body, attributing its ownership to another person, or referring to it as an inanimate object, often in humorous fashion. Patients commonly talk of their incapacities in the "third person," as if they were occurring in someone else, as in saying that another person is weak or incompetent. When denial is well established, patients are bland and serene or mildly paranoid, as in cases where the patient attributes his paralysis to a faulty injection or mistreatment by the doctors and nurses. Improvement in brain function is often accompanied by weakening of the denial with outbursts of irritability and the appearance of depression. To casual observers, anosognosic patients may appear quite normal and even bright and witty. When not on the subject of their disabilities, they are quite rational; and tests of intelligence may show no deficit. The syndrome of anosognosia, given the necessary conditions of brain dysfunction, is most marked in persons, who, like Woodrow Wilson, have habitually perceived the physical manifestations and consequences of illness in the context of principles and values, and as separate from the real self, who are highly work and efficiency oriented, and who have been accustomed to the overcoming of physical indispositions by force of will and character.

The President did not deny that his left side was paralyzed, but neither he nor Edith Bolling Wilson was aware, or would admit, that the paralysis was a symptom of brain damage. He referred to himself as "lame" and refused to accept the fact that he could not carry on his office. Three days after his stroke, he attempted to dictate to his stenographer, but was dissuaded by his wife on the grounds that it was Sunday. On October 7, he dictated a diplomatic note and communicated his displeasure that a cabinet meeting had been held in his absence. For the President to admit that the meeting was held properly would have meant the admission that he was too ill to attend. Immediately after recovering from his near-fatal urinary obstruction he began to work, sending letters and signing bills. During November he received a few visitors, but he carried on only in a very limited way. Messages were screened by Edith Bolling Wilson and Grayson, and the President was seen for only occasional, brief periods by Tumulty, cabinet members, and Democratic leaders. Usually, Edith Bolling Wilson received them in her sitting room and repeated to them what the President had told her should be done about a particular problem. Memoranda were either not acknowledged or were answered in a short note, in Edith Bolling Wilson's handwriting, quoting the President. Cabinet members did what they could on their own or waited on the President. A factor in Woodrow Wilson's isolation is that he may have felt ashamed of his incapacity. Visitors noted, for example, that he would cover himself in such a way as to conceal the paralyzed side. He did not resign his office, and he was to seek a third nomination.

In January 1920, the President drafted a remarkable proposal suggesting that his Republican opponents, who he listed by name, resign and seek reelection on the issue of the League. If a majority were returned, then he, with his vice-president, would resign after appointing a Republican as secretary of state, who, according to the order of succession, would assume the presidency. To assume that Republicans would resign was, of course, unrealistic, and the President was persuaded to pigeonhole his proposals. Yet, in his denial system the gesture was highly meaningful. He was coping with the issue of resignation by representing it in the "third person plural," by talking about the resignation of other people. Also, he was indicating that he might resign not because he was disabled but because he was carrying out the will of the people.

The attitudes of other persons toward the illness were determined by their relationships to the President in personal, professional, and political contexts. Edith Bolling Wilson indignantly rejected the idea that her husband was disabled or had sustained brain damage, regarding these facts as scurrilous rumors. She states that Dercum advised that the President remain in office because he would lose his greatest incentive to get well should he resign and quotes Dercum as pointing out that Louis Pasteur had recovered from the same condition and had gone on to do some of his most brilliant work.

Grayson similarly expressed a great deal of denial of the seriousness of the President's condition. When he met with the cabinet on October 6, he refused to tell the members anything beyond that Woodrow Wilson was suffering from "a nervous breakdown, indigestion and a depleted condition," adding the warning that any excitement might kill him. Later, Grayson told Secretary of the Navy Josephus Daniels that he did not want the truth disclosed and it was not until February 10, 1920, that any reference to Woodrow Wilson's hemiplegia appeared in the press. At that time, Dr. Hugh Young, the urologist who had been called in when the President developed his urinary obstruction, said that there had been some impairment of function in the left limbs but that now the President was organically sound and that only the inclement weather prevented him from leaving the White House. Young maintained that the vigor and lucidity of the President's mental processes had not been affected in the slightest degree.

Grayson was in conflict over his professional, personal, and family roles. When Stockton Axson asked him if the President had had a stroke, the doctor replied that he did not know. Possibly Grayson was mindful of Ellen Axson Wilson's request to him, on her deathbed, that he "take good care of my husband." Grayson also could not bring himself to tell the President that he could not adequately perform the duties of his office, and his behavior, like that of Edith Bolling Wilson, strongly reinforced Wilson's denial. When, on March 25, Woodrow Wilson brought up the third term issue with Grayson, the doctor stated that "for medical reasons, I preferred not to volunteer any advice. I did not want to tell him that it would be impossible for him to take part in such a campaign, as I was fearful that it might have a depressing effect upon him." In a conversation of April 13, he asked his doctor's advice about resignation in view of the time it would take for him to recover his health and strength. Grayson replied by assuring the President how well he was keeping in touch with and conducting the affairs of the government. He then persuaded the President to call his first cabinet meeting, which was held the next day. In June, however, evidently without Woodrow Wilson's knowledge, Grayson asked Senator Carter Glass of Virginia to convince the President not to seek a third term.

In recalling the cabinet meeting of April 14, Secretary of Agriculture David F. Houston commented on his surprise at hearing his and the others' names announced as they entered, a procedure evidently necessitated by the President's poor vision. Woodrow Wilson appeared bright and cheerful and began the session by telling a joke about the Chicago aldermen who got their heads together to form a solid surface. Then there was a silence as the President did not follow up the initiative. When the critical railroad situation was brought up, he seemed to have difficulty at first in fixing his mind on the topic. Grayson looked in several times as if to warn against tiring the President, and at the end of an hour Edith Bolling Wilson suggested that the members leave.

According to Stockton Axson, the President alternated between states of abject depression and periods of a week or so when he would be in good spirits and would dictate. He had uncontrolled outbursts of emotion and temper, often without apparent reason, directed even at his wife and Grayson. This behavior suggests some improvement in brain function because it meant that his denial was not being maintained as completely. It coincided with an increase in initiative expressed in the abrupt dismissal of Secretary of State Robert Lansing in February 1920 and the issuance of optimistic reports of his condition to the press as a part of the campaign for renomination. Lansing's dismissal can be interpreted as a symbolic gesture of presidential authority, which Woodrow Wilson accused Lansing of usurping.

While the President was incapable of sustained work, he could, at times, appear to be bright and witty, as in his famous encounter with Senator Albert B. Fall of New Mexico who, with Senator Gilbert M. Hitchcock of Nebraska, had been delegated by the Senate Foreign Relations Committee ostensibly to discuss the Mexican situation but actually to report on the clarity of the President's mind. When Fall unctuously observed: "Well, Mr. President, we have all been praying for you," the President responded with, "Which way, Senator?" Much of his humor symbolized his physical disabilities—his inability to walk and to make speeches. He called his cane his "third leg" and recited the following limerick:

> There was a young girl from Missouri,
> Who took her case to the jury
> She said, "Car Ninety-three
> Ran over my knee,"
> But the jury said "We're from Missouri."

One of his favorite stories was about a Scotsman, who let his wife fall out of an airplane to win a wager dependent on his not speaking. His sardonic references to the League and jokes about its death in cabinet meetings seem to be defenses against feelings of failure and despair.

To some degree, his anosognosia shielded him from the impact of political misfortune. When Houston tried to prepare him for the shock of Warren G. Harding's almost certain victory, Houston was assured that the people would not elect Harding. When Stockton Axson brought up the subject, the President smiled indulgently and said, "You pessimist! You don't know the American people. They always rise to a moral occasion. Harding will be deluged." Stockton Axson stated, "Up to the last day I could make no impression on him. The day after the election I was so nervous about him that I called up the White House early and was told he was all right. As soon as I knew I could see him, I went over. He was as serene as in the moments of his own preceding victories (and the matter can't be stated stronger than that). His first words, after greetings, were (and I remember them verbatim), 'I have not lost faith in the American people. They have merely been temporarily deceived. They will realize their error in a little while.' ." With great insight, Stockton Axson wondered if Wilson's attitude might not be a symptom of his illness.

This account of Woodrow Wilson's neurological illnesses may help to explain some of his political actions and should be of value to students of his personality. While it is quite true that the character traits formed in his childhood were important determinants of his political career, attempts to interpret his defeats as predestined or as stemming inevitably from insatiable ambition or unconscious self-destructive drives are unwarranted oversimplifications. If one has all the variables, then there is some value in an interpretation of political events based on the tenets of a particular psychological theory, as in Alexander and Juliette George's application of Harold Lasswell's hypothesis that a drive to power is a compensation for self-esteem damaged in childhood. However, neither the Georges' study nor the more recent one by Sigmund Freud and Bullitt take into account the factor of brain damage. If one were to judge Woodrow Wilson's potentialities for political success on the basis of his personality make-up, the major emphasis should be his behavior prior to 1906.

AFL's Concept of Big Business: A Quantitative Study of Attitudes Toward the Large Corporation, 1894–1931

LOUIS GALAMBOS

Organized labor in the late nineteenth and early twentieth centuries was neither totally hostile to nor completely tolerant of the large corporation. A content analysis of labor publications by Louis Galambos reveals not only labor's fluctuating hostility toward big business but also why its attitude changed.

In the latter part of the nineteenth century American society encountered a series of complex problems. Rapid industrialization, immigration, and urbanization created what Robert H. Wiebe has described as a "distended society," a nation pervaded by a sense of "crisis" and a "search for order." One of the focal points of discontent was the large corporation. Because of its power, its wealth, its new elite, and its all too frequent displays of antisocial behavior, big business became one of the major negative symbols of American reform. The social relations of the large corporation were all the more important because it was big business which first adopted the bureaucratic values and authority structure

From *Journal of American History* 57 (1971):847–63. Footnotes omitted. Reprinted by permission of the author and *The Journal of American History*.

which ultimately provided most Americans—including reformers—with the means of imposing a new type of order on their society. The image of big business which was held by various other elements in society is thus highly important to the historian.

American labor's attitude toward the large corporation is especially interesting because union relations with big business were often strained during the years of changing economic conditions and social values in the first three decades of the twentieth century. The emphasis here is upon the American Federation of Labor, and the major source of information is labor journals, in particular, AFL's official publication, the *American Federationist*. This is supplemented with material from the *National Labor Tribune* (1898–1915), a Pittsburgh publication directed primarily to workers in the iron, steel, and coal industries; and *Solidarity* (1910–1930), a radical paper issued by the Industrial Workers of the World (IWW). Ideally, one would not use official publications for this type of study, since these journals were tied to an organization's structure of authority and to the controlling faction within that structure. In labor history, however, this seems to present an insurmountable problem. For the organized workers, one must depend upon the available sources, which are generally those provided by their unions. In this essay the images appearing in the labor journals are accepted as proxies for union attitudes.

The opinions of big business in the labor papers were assessed by content analysis. In an effort to develop a quantitative profile of a journal's image of big business, the following procedure was used. When a journal was being studied, the entire issue (excepting only advertisements, fiction, and poems or jokes) was read; information was taken on all items (any separate article, letter to the editor, or editorial) which mentioned big business. All such items were counted as equal, regardless of length, and no attempt was made to measure the intensity of feeling, other than to indicate that the item was favorable, unfavorable, neutral, or ambivalent about big business. The image was broken down into its constituent elements, so that one could determine which aspects of big business (for example, price policy) received the most attention; these separate characteristics were each scored as favorable, unfavorable, neutral, or ambivalent. Finally, all of the data was combined and averaged by years, so as to yield a result which could be called the composite image projected by one journal in any one year.

The time period covered—1894–1931—is bound on each end by a major organizational and ideological struggle within the labor movement. By 1894, the battle between AFL and the Knights of Labor was virtually over. The Knights of Labor was a dying union, and the central ideology of the labor movement was the pragmatic, craft-oriented, apolitical philosophy of AFL. In the 1930s a similar change took place; this time it was AFL which gave way. It was unable to prevent the rise of the Congress of Industrial Organizations, a new type of union with a more radical ideology. Between these two periods, organized labor's ideology was relatively stable, but the union image of big business nonetheless experienced several important changes.

In the 1890s the concept of big business projected by the *American Federationist* was extremely hostile to the large corporation. From 1894 to 1899, over 80 percent of the items which discussed large firms portrayed their subject in an unfavorable light (see Table I). Only 8 percent

TABLE I Percentage of Unfavorable Items in *American Federationist*, 1894–1931

Year	Percent	Year	Percent	Year	Percent
1894	82	1907	42	1920	55
1895	92	1908	57	1921	50
1896	84	1909	57	1922	48
1897	86	1910	49	1923	57
1898	78	1911	46	1924	75
1899	76	1912	50	1925	59
1900	44	1913	56	1926	62
1901	55	1914	72	1927	50
1902	79	1915	50	1928	65
1903	48	1916	30	1929	50
1904	75	1917	39	1930	59
1905	77	1918	21	1931	61
1906	80	1919	11		

were basically favorable (see Table II). According to Selig Perlman and Philip Taft:

> the American Federation of Labor broke away from the middle class and farmer reformers on the "trust" issue. It declared unequivocally that the "trusts" were an inevitable economic development before which the law was completely helpless, but that its power could be controlled to society's advantage under an industrial government in which it would be checked by the power of the fully "recognized" trade union.

This was, no doubt, AFL's explicit policy. It was certainly Samuel Gompers' position. This policy seems, however, to have existed alongside a viewpoint which included far more enmity toward big business than Perlman and Taft indicate. The data indicate that there was tension between the union's concept of the large corporation and its policy toward

TABLE II   Percentage of Favorable Items in *American Federationist,* 1894–1931

Year	Percent	Year	Percent	Year	Percent
1894	9	1907	33	1920	25
1895	0	1908	13	1921	18
1896	8	1909	13	1922	42
1897	14	1910	27	1923	25
1898	11	1911	15	1924	11
1899	6	1912	11	1925	23
1900	12	1913	13	1926	23
1901	15	1914	16	1927	27
1902	6	1915	7	1928	22
1903	14	1916	44	1929	12
1904	10	1917	26	1930	10
1905	0	1918	27	1931	21
1906	10	1919	12		

this new institution. The inevitability of trust formation was not a subject which aroused much discussion in the *American Federationist;* and, indeed, the union's hostility toward the trusts was strikingly similar to the attitudes expressed in farm journals during the nineties.

Farm and labor journals presented a negative image of big business during these years, and both groups were primarily interested in business' economic activities. In the *American Federationist* (1894–1899) from 83 to 100 percent of the items mentioned the economic behavior of big business. While political aspects of the large firm were much less important, they still received a fair amount of attention; from 11 to 42 percent of the articles touched upon this subject. The social implications of the giant firm—for example, its impact upon the rank order of status or upon community values—ran a poor third. Such matters were rarely discussed. In this regard, too, the farm and labor papers advanced similar viewpoints.

A closer examination of these two images, however, discloses that farmers and laborers were concerned about different problems. Farmers had an overwhelming interest in price policies—in the general level of prices and in price discrimination. These were relatively unimportant subjects to AFL and to the *National Labor Tribune.*

In the Federation's eyes the major economic issues were labor relations and wage-hour policies. It found opportunities to criticize big business when the Northern Pacific Railroad cut wages (but not the salaries of its receivers), when Andrew Carnegie used "the arbitrary power of discharge from employment . . . ," when men requesting a wage increase were locked out of their shops, and when laborers were "penned behind Pullman's . . . silent walls." The *American Federationist* also discussed political facts of big business and emphasized the special forms of political aid which business received, particularly the injunctions which were issued to thwart union efforts. Other aspects of the corporation received substantial attention from year-to-year, but these three factors dominated AFL's attention. This remained true long after 1900. From 1900 to 1920, labor relations was the salient aspect of big business, as seen in the *American Federationist*. It was mentioned in 40 to 85 percent of the articles. Wage and hour policies continued to hold down second or third place for most of this period. In this sense, the content of the union's view of the large corporation remained relatively stable for two decades.

In another sense, however, the Federation's image changed dramatically during these years. A number of the statistical series reflect a basic shift in attitudes in the years around 1907. From 1900 to 1906, the degree of hostility toward big business fluctuated sharply, but returned each time to a high level (see Table I). After 1906, however, the percentage of items reflecting an unfavorable attitude dropped substantially; this particular series remained fairly stable for seven years (1907–1913), and then declined again during World War I. By 1919 only 11 percent of the items in the *American Federationist* were unfriendly to big business.

As the Federation became less worried about the trust question, its image of the large corporation became less specific and more diffuse. For the years 1894–1905, the degree of specificity was high; from 1906 to 1915, it was somewhat lower; it dropped to its lowest level during the years 1916–1920. The correlation between specificity and the percentage of items which were unfavorable is obvious. When the union was upset with big business, it had in mind grievances involving specific companies; neutral and favorable attitudes were more likely to be expressed in abstracts. This dimension of the union's image changed and the change took place at approximately the same time that the level of hostility began to decline.

Even the vocabulary of antitrust shifted in the early years of the twentieth century. In the period from 1894 to 1903, the journal's discussions of big business were frequently expressed in manifestly pejorative terms. Large firms were "trusts," "monopolies," or "syndicates." They were the domain of "robber barons" and "kings." AFL's language was never as vigorous as that of the agrarian journals; the farmers found "hogs," "dogs" and "serpents" in the world of business. But the union did occasionally find an opportunity to call on stronger symbols such as the "octopus" or the "outlaw." Carnegie was cynically labeled the " 'triumphant Democrat' of Homestead" and compared with the medieval baron: "Brutal the baron undeniably was; but he was no sneaking hypocrite vaunting his superior civilization while oozing from every pore the foulest and purulent corruption." In 1903, three quarters of the nouns (other than proper names) used to refer to big business could be classified as obviously pejorative. From 1904 on, however, the percentage of pejorative terms declined, reaching zero in 1912 (see Table III). Neutral words

TABLE III   Percentage of Pejoratives Used in *American Federationist*, 1894–1920

Year	Percent	Year	Percent	Year	Percent
1894	45	1903	75	1912	0
1895	32	1904	64	1913	3
1896	38	1905	50	1914	26
1897	73	1906	40	1915	67
1898	22	1907	25	1916	28
1899	37	1908	20	1917	7
1900	48	1909	25	1918	0
1901	68	1910	25	1919	50
1902	40	1911	11	1920	9

such as "firm," "company," or "business" replaced the denigrating terms. In particular years of labor unrest—1915 and 1919—the use of pejorative words increased, but the secular trend was clearly toward a more neutral terminology. While the level of unfavorable items in the *National Labor Tribune* remained fairly stable, the percentage of pejorative terms experienced a sharp decline during these same years. By 1912–1915, hardly any pejorative nouns were used. It seems fairly clear that labor's public language, as well as its fundamental attitude toward the large corporation, was undergoing a significant transformation.

A change also took place in the way AFL distributed its attention among the several industries associated with big business. The *American Federationist* gave substantial consideration to only four industries in the years 1894–1900: railroads (mentioned forty-eight times); food manufacturing (twenty); primary metal manufacturing (eighteen); and tobacco manufacturing (thirteen). Eight industries could be included in the list for 1901–1905: railroads (fifty-five); foods (thirty-seven); tobacco (twenty-eight); primary metals (eleven); stone-clay-glass manufacturing (eight); and three others (tied with six appearances). During the next five-year period, railroads again held first place, but there was an important change in the amount of attention devoted to other industries. No longer did the second, third, and fourth industries receive the consideration they had been given in previous years. The same pattern is evident during the years 1911–1915 and 1916–1920. If references to railroads are excluded, the data indicate that the union image of big business was "flattening out" during the years 1906–1920. Fewer industries received the concentrated attention of AFL. The journal mentioned only three industries—railroads, transportation equipment, and primary metals— more than once a year during the war period.

All of these series indicate that the union image of big business changed significantly during the first decade of the twentieth century. Between 1907 and 1919, neutral, and in some cases favorable, attitudes replaced unfavorable concepts (see Tables I, II, and IV). The vocabu-

TABLE IV   Percentage of Neutral-Ambivalent Items in American Federationist, 1894– 1931

Year	Percent	Year	Percent	Year	Percent
1894	9	1907	25	1920	20
1895	8	1908	30	1921	32
1896	8	1909	30	1922	10
1897	0	1910	24	1923	18
1898	11	1911	39	1924	14
1899	18	1912	39	1925	18
1900	44	1913	31	1926	15
1901	30	1914	12	1927	23
1902	15	1915	43	1928	13
1903	38	1916	26	1929	38
1904	15	1917	35	1930	31
1905	23	1918	52	1931	18
1906	10	1919	77		

lary of antitrust became more placid. Gradually, the union found fewer industries and fewer specific companies which seemed to demand substantial attention. By 1919, obviously, a significant process of accommodation had taken place between AFL and the nation's largest industrial firms.

Statistical data and the available secondary studies indicate some of the factors—other than the personal style of editors—which appear to account for these changes. Most important were the economic performance of big business and the economic and organizational context within which the unions and firms operated. Social and political characteristics of giant enterprise continued to be substantially less important to AFL than business' economic functions. During the years 1900–1919, from 85 to 100 percent of the items touched upon some economic activity of big business. Hardly any items considered the firm's influence on values or status relationships (that is, on the general category labeled social aspects). Although a number (from 0 to 33 percent, depending on the year) of the articles included some consideration of the large corporation's involvement in politics, the trends evident here cannot be explained by these data: almost all of the references to political behavior were unfavorable and they remained essentially negative throughout most of this period. By contrast, important changes took place in the Federation's evaluation of big business' economic role.

One element which obviously demands consideration was the changing strength of AFL, as indicated by union membership. During approximately the same years in which the combination movement in industry reached its peak, AFL unions were gathering in hundreds of thousands of new supporters. In 1897, total AFL membership was estimated at 272,100; by 1904, affiliated unions included 1,681,800 workers. It is possible to relate the decline in hostility toward big business to this increased membership, on the grounds that AFL now felt more secure and was naturally less worried about the large corporation. It is important to note, however, that the union's growth rate slowed after 1904; and the changes in attitude took place after that date. This indicates that the increase in membership and organizational power could be a necessary but probably not a sufficient cause. It seems likely that this increased strength was an underlying precondition, an element essential to the shift in attitude which took place in the next few years. Before the process of accommodation could begin, however, big business had to legitimate itself in certain special regards.

The large firm's policies on wages and hours were especially important. During the 1890's, the union concept of these policies was extremely unfavorable, but its attitude began to shift around 1900. Increasingly, the union found opportunities to comment favorably on the wage and hour policies of the large corporation. This was especially true around 1907. During and after the panic, the union looked with greater interest and more favor at the big corporation's position on wages and hours. From 1907 through 1912, half or more of the references to wage-hour matters were either favorable, neutral, or ambivalent; at the low point, in 1910, only 17 percent of the remarks were unfavorable. When the business cycle turned down, large enterprises seemed to AFL to be slower to cut wages than were smaller businesses. Subsequent studies of wages in the railroad and communications industries confirm the union viewpoint. Average earnings of the workers in these industries were relatively stable under conditions of depression. This was particularly important because these two industries received more attention from the Federation than any others during the period 1906–1910.

The union was also interested in the manufacturing of electrical machinery. This was a technologically progressive industry which compiled a good record on the hourly earnings of its employees. Less progressive and less concentrated industries—for example, those in textile production—were more vulnerable to cyclical fluctuations; they generally experienced a slower growth rate over the long run. Later, AFL would begin to worry about some of the less favorable characteristics of the modern industries, but at this time the greater stability offered by the large corporation in these sectors of the economy appealed to the union.

A similar, although less dramatic, change took place in AFL's attitude toward big business' labor relations. This was the most important topic discussed in the *American Federationist* during these years. From 1907 to 1913, it appeared in from 42 to 75 percent of the items scored. Through 1906 most of these references were unfavorable: the Federation protested when giant firms refused to bargain with the unions or dealt unfairly with their employees as individuals. After 1906, the percentage of unfavorable references began to decline; from 1909 to 1913, it was 50 percent or below each year. The low point was reached in 1910, when only 29 percent of such remarks could be considered negative. When business resistance to union demands caused strikes and when large firms opposed unionization, AFL was still quick to criticize. U. S. Steel's "war of extermination" against the union (1910) was important to AFL. But after 1906, the Federation found more and more instances in which large employers were complying with union demands, compromising after disagreements arose, accepting the fact of unionization, and even negotiating in good faith.

The contrast between large and small businesses was probably heightened for AFL by the development of two prominent organizations which advocated extreme positions on organized labor's role in the industrial economy. The National Association of Manufacturers (NAM) enjoyed a substantial increase in strength and effectiveness after 1903, when it began to crusade against organized labor. NAM soon became the nation's leading spokesman for anti-union principles. It was the voice of primarily small- and middle-sized businesses. In opposition to NAM stood the National Civic Federation, which spoke the language of compromise: "the leaders of the Civic Federation were convinced that modern industry needed organized labor if serious social tensions were to be averted." The National Civic Federation was primarily supported by businessmen associated with large corporations. These two organizations helped to polarize and shape attitudes toward the unions, and, indirectly, toward business itself. In a complex, urban society, ideas had to be filtered through strong organizations before they could achieve a high degree of visibility. Thus, the institutionalization of these two contrasting positions on organized labor contributed to the development of a more favorable attitude toward big business on the part of AFL (whose president was active in the National Civic Federation). NAM and the National Civic Federation were carrot and stick, coaxing and driving the union toward accommodation with the large corporation.

Another factor contributing to this new attitude was a shift in AFL's general cultural environment—a change in values which is partially reflected in the data on pejorative and non-pejorative words in the *American Federationist* (see Table III). An important change in the language of antitrust took place in the years following 1903, and a similar pattern can be found in the *National Labor Tribune*. The same sort of change occurred in a midwestern agrarian journal, although in this instance the downward trend in the use of pejorative terms began after 1912. The fact that the same pattern appeared in these different journals during approximately the same years suggests the existence of a general cultural phenomenon. The basic way of talking and thinking about large-scale organizations was changing as a more subtle, bureaucratic culture began to take shape. In the new, bureaucratic society, affective words and ideas gave way before more neutral modes of orientation. This change in the values of the general society probably had the effect of dampening AFL's hostility toward the large corporation.

After World War I began, the union had even more reason to favor the giant firm. Wartime conditions promoted unionization, raised wages, and boosted employment opportunities. After America entered the war, government support of the unions, particularly in the railroad industry, lent further strength to AFL. Patriotism and the demands for wartime harmony doubtless had a similar effect, although the evidence indicates that these factors were less important than income and bargaining power. By 1916–1917, only one-third of the items mentioning big business' general relations to labor cast this subject in an unfavorable light. By 1919, the figure was down to 9 percent. A similar change took place in the union view of the large firm's wage and hour policies. There was, moreover, a new emphasis upon the impact that big business had upon the individual's economic opportunities. Large corporations were providing more jobs, and the importance of this was not lost upon AFL. By 1919, the percentage of unfavorable attitudes toward big business had reached an all-time low in the *American Federationist* (see Table I).

In the following years this trend was suddenly reversed. As a number of labor historians have shown, the end of the war and the subsequent period of economic readjustment created a major crisis for organized labor. Wages declined and a series of unsuccessful strikes, against the background of a nation fearful of the rise of Bolshevism abroad, set the stage for an employer offensive. This anti-union campaign, labeled the American Plan, was unusually successful in breaking down union organization and engendering a political and intellectual environment opposed to union activity.

AFL became more hostile to big business. There was no contrast between a friendly National Civic Federation and NAM; all too often, big business seemed to be leading the American Plan campaign. The violent steel strike of 1919–1920 also focused attention on the large corporation. The data from the *American Federationist* reflects the impact of this new situation. The percentage of unfavorable opinions increased from 11 in 1919, to 55 in 1920. In 1924 the percentage of unfavorable opinions reached a peak (75 percent) and then leveled off at around 60 percent (see Table I). As the union's antipathy increased, the *American Federationist* found more and more large companies which deserved attention. The image of big business became increasingly specific in the early twenties.

The customary explanations of labor's attitude following the war are convincing, but the quantitative data suggest some elements which deserve more consideration than they have received. Before World War I, a substantial number of the leading industries which AFL identified with big business were those which could be classified as older and technologically less progressive; a number of these were engaged in processing the products of field and forest—products of the older, agrarian-commercial economy. In relation to these industries AFL's members could feel a good measure of security because of their confidence in the continued importance of skilled labor as an economic and social institution, and a correlated measure of assurance that their conservative, craft-oriented unions would continue to be relevant to their market situation. The same could be said of industries in the public utility category, although in this case, the government helped to protect the skilled laborer and his union. After the war, part of this security was lost. During the years 1921–1925, AFL grew increasingly concerned about a new array of industries. These industries ranked in order of the frequency of references to them in the *American Federationist* were: railroads; primary metals; transportation equipment; and petroleum. In the years 1926–1931, the leaders, similarly ranked, were: railroads; transportation equipment; and petroleum, which was tied with communications and with electricity-gas-sanitary services. The Federation's attention was shifting to the modern, mass-production industries, to those industries in which the skilled worker was extremely vulnerable. These were the industries that were best able to do without skilled labor. These were the industries in which firms had met with the greatest success in rooting out existing craft unions or in preventing labor organizations from establishing a foothold. In the automobile industry, for example, the unions were virtually powerless.

The insecurity that labor felt vis-à-vis these industries was reflected in the emphasis the journal now gave to the impact of big business upon the individual's job opportunities. For years, the *American Federationist* had concentrated primarily on the large firm's labor relations and its wage and hour policies. In 1921 and 1922, however, the leading aspect of big business, so far as AFL was concerned, was its influence on the individual's economic opportunities. In subsequent years this remained one of the leading facets of the union image of big business. The Federation had at last come to recognize the problems faced by skilled labor and the craft unions in the modern, mass-production economy. But AFL was unable to solve these problems. This conclusion is indicated both by its declining membership and by the high level of animosity that the *American Federationist* continued to feel toward the large corporations which were prime carriers of the new industrial system.

The union's hostility did not, however, approach the level it had reached in the 1890s. The union was no longer very concerned about the large firm's political activities. During the 1890s one of the important aspects of the large corporation had been its frequent dependence upon political support. Big business and the injunction were, for a time, practically synonymous to AFL. This was no longer true after World War I. Political characteristics received relatively little attention, and no single political activity bulked large in the union's image. Since AFL regarded virtually all political involvement by the big corporation with disfavor, the declining interest in the corporation's political functions partially accounted for the lower percentage of unfavorable opinions.

Another reason for the difference was probably a time-related process of increasing familiarity with a new institution, combined with the long run effects of the previous phases of accommodation. One might expect powerful organizations such as big business to attract a great deal of animosity when they first develop. In varying degree, these initial grievances would involve a combination of realistic and unrealistic appraisals of what, exactly, the new institution would do. AFL had some very realistic concerns about a type of organization which was introducing a new mode of authority and exercising control over matters vital to the skilled craftsman. Some of the union's fears were, however, unrealistic. Once these attitudes had begun to change, a form of social inertia seems to have influenced opinions, making it difficult for persons ever to become as upset as they had been at first. With a pragmatic, interest-oriented union such as AFL one would expect subsequent waves of hostility to reach lower peaks, simply on the basis of the lasting effects of the intervening process of accommodation, as well as greater familiarity with the subject at hand. This appears to have been the case with the *American Federationist*, just as it was with the farm journals.

Another factor dampening the second wave of animosity toward the corporation was the new cultural environment which has already been identified with the shifting vocabulary of antitrust. In the years before 1919, the percentage of pejorative terms declined, as did the percentage of unfavorable items. When the level of unfavorable opinions went up after 1919, however, the percentage of pejorative terms remained relatively low. The new pattern of language and the related bureaucratic culture continued to be an important part of the union's environment in the twenties. This too had the effect of keeping the level of hostility below the high points reached in the nineties.

If the Federation had been guided by socialist ideology, the results would no doubt have been different. Marxism provided *Solidarity* with a relatively inflexible orientation to big business. During World War I, IWW's hostility toward the trusts appears to have declined slightly (see Table V). But by 1917, *Solidarity* was back to normal, lashing out at the

TABLE V   Percentage of Unfavorable Items in *Solidarity*, 1910–1930

Year	Percent	Year	Percent	Year	Percent
1910	90	1917	91	1924	81
1911	50	1918	no data	1925	75
1912	100	1919	87	1926	88
1913	100	1920	80	1927	82
1914	73	1921	80	1928	94
1915	75	1922	78	1929	89
1916	79	1923	84	1930	57

great capitalistic combines which Marx had clearly labeled as the most formidable enemy of the proletariat. *Solidarity* was insulated by its ideology from the type of cultural change which influenced the *American Federationist;* the series on pejorative words in *Solidarity* reflects this difference. By contrast, the AFL's apolitical, pragmatic ideology left the union relatively vulnerable to changes in its cultural environment, changes which in this instance made for accommodation between AFL and the giant firm.

By 1932 AFL's image of big business had passed through at least three distinct phases, but the long run, secular trend was toward a lower degree of hostility. Several major factors helped to shape these attitudes during the years 1894–1931. Most important was the actual performance of big business, as seen by the union, performance on wages, hours, employment, and labor relations. The Federation's interests were precise and relatively narrow. Almost by itself, good performance in these areas could legitimate the power that the giant firm held. AFL was no more opposed to bigness than it was to the basic capitalistic system. By 1919 labor seemed to accept big business, but after the war, it found new cause for concern. The union at last clearly recognized how important the modern mass-production industries were and how weak skilled labor and AFL's organizations were in this part of the economy. On the eve of the New Deal, the union's intellectual baggage included this complex and unresolved problem.

16

Symbols of the Jazz Age:
The New Negro and
Harlem Discovered

GILBERT OSOFSKY

Myths reveal more about those who create and espouse them than about their subjects. A striking myth developed in the 1920s was that of the exotic, sensuous, creative New Negro who inhabited the erotic utopia of Harlem. Gilbert Osofsky evaluates the meaning of this myth for an important group of black writers as well as for the white intellectuals who created these new symbols.

American society has anticipated the arrival of a "New Negro" for at least seventy-five years. In the white South of the 1890s, for example, it was common to contrast the former slaves with the first Negro generation born in freedom—to the detriment of the latter. "The good old Negroes," said a southern farmer at the turn of the century, "are a first-rate class of labor. The younger ones [are] discontented and want to be roaming." At about the same time Booker T. Washington surveyed America's racial scene and, contrary to the view of white Southerners, found it good. He related tales of Negro achievement and success since the Civil War which encouraged him to believe that the

From *American Quarterly* 17 (1965):229–38. Footnotes omitted. Reprinted by permission of the author and *American Quarterly*. Copyright, 1965, Trustees of the University of Pennsylvania.

"Negro of to-day is in every phase of life far advanced over the Negro of thirty years ago." Washington hoped all Negroes would strive to achieve "the new life" and, accordingly, called his book *A New Negro for a New Century.* The racial crisis that followed the two world wars of the present century revived the concept. William Pickens, Negro educator and NAACP official, discovered a "New Negro" militancy and racial consciousness in 1916, and others have used the phrase to describe the Negro protest movements of the 1950s and 1960s.

Amid the confusions that have hovered around the meaning of the term "New Negro" is one solid fact: the phrase entered the main stream of American thought in the 1920s, in the Jazz Age. A "New Negro," and his supposed place of residence, Harlem, were discovered by the white world then. Despite the romance and pride traditionally associated with the "Harlem Renaissance," the portrayal of the Negro that developed in the 1920s was *primarily* a product of broader changes in American society. It would be difficult to find a better example of the confusions, distortions, half-truths and quarter-truths that are the foundations of racial and ethnic stereotypes than the white world's image of the "New Negro" and Harlem in the 1920s.

The 1920s, as is well known, was a remarkable age in American intellectual history. A cultural rebellion of the first order erupted from beneath the complacency and conservatism that were dominant characteristics of American society and politics then. It was the time when writers, artists, scholars, aesthetes, and bohemians became aware of the standardization of life that resulted from mass production and large-scale, efficient industrialization—the "Machine Civilization," that "profound national impulse [that] drives the hundred millions steadily toward uniformity." These intellectuals declared war on tenets of American thought and faith that had remained sacrosanct for three hundred years. As a by-product of their attack on traditional American middle-class values, which were constantly called "Puritanical," literary rebels and others discovered the Negro, America's "outcast," and created a semi-mythical dreamland which they came to idealize—"storied Harlem."

In some part, this growing national awareness was caused by significant changes within Negro society. There seemed to be a new militancy in the Negro world after World War I—reflected in Harlem's well-known Silent Parade to protest the East St. Louis race riots, in the racial program and consciousness of Marcus Garvey, in A. Philip Randolph's struggling movement to found the Brotherhood of Sleeping Car Porters and Maids, in the numerous little leftist groups active in the Negro ghettos, in the national campaign to promote federal anti-lynching legislation. Yet American society never really took these movements seriously in the 1920s—Garvey was considered a comical figure; an anti-lynching law was never enacted; riots continued; Randolph's union made little headway until the Great Depression; the leftists were ignored or considered crackpots.

The 1920s also saw the rise of a noteworthy group of Negro writers and scholars, and America gave *them* considerable recognition. Some of the novels, plays, books and articles of Countee Cullen, James Weldon Johnson, George S. Schuyler, Claude McKay, Wallace Thurman, Zora Neale Hurston, Jessie Fauset, Rudolph Fisher, Jean Toomer, Charles S. Johnson, E. Franklin Frazier, and others were good enough in their own right to justify public acclaim. The poetry of Langston Hughes continues to be widely read. Harlem was the center of this "New Negro Renaissance" and, like an "ebony flute," it lured Negro writers to it: "Harlem was like a great magnet for the Negro intellectual, pulling him from everywhere," wrote Langston Hughes. Claude McKay came to Harlem from Jamaica, after two years at an agricultural college in Kansas; Jean Toomer was from an Alabama plantation; Langston Hughes arrived in 1921 after a sojourn in Mexico. "I can never put on paper the thrill of the underground ride to Harlem," Hughes recalled. "I went up the steps and out into the bright September sunlight. Harlem! I stood there, dropped my bags, took a deep breath and felt happy again." Wherever they wandered in the 1920s, and many went to Paris or Africa for a time, the Negro literati always returned *Home to Harlem* (to use the title of a McKay novel). Little theater, art and political discussion groups flourished in the community. Negro literary and political magazines made their appearance: *Fire, The Messenger, Voice of the Negro, The Negro Champion, Harlem.* The 135th Street library became Harlem's cultural center. "The Schomburg Collection," remembered George S. Schuyler, "used to be a great gathering place for all the people of the Renaissance." In the 1920s one could hear lectures there by such prominent people as Franz Boas, W. E. B. DuBois, Carl Van Doren, James Weldon Johnson, Carter G. Woodson, Kelly Miller, Melville J. Herskovits, R. R. Moton, and Arthur A. Schomburg. Harlem became what contemporaries called the "Mecca of the New Negro."

Some observers, Negro and white, looked to this outburst of literary and artistic expression as a significant step in the direction of a more general acceptance of Negroes by American society. Alain Locke, gifted writer and Howard University professor, argued that social equality would result from the recognition of the "New Negro" as an "artist class." ". . . it seems that the interest in the cultural expression of Negro life . . . heralds an almost revolutionary revaluation of the Negro," he wrote in 1927. It was "an augury of a new democracy in American culture." Heywood Broun, well-known journalist and critic, addressed the New York Urban League at a Harlem church. He believed "a supremely great Negro artist, [an artist] who could catch the imagination of the world, would do more than any other agency to remove the disabilities against which the Negro race now labors. . . . This great artist may come at any time," Broun concluded, and he asked his audience to remain silent for ten seconds to imagine the coming of the savior-genius. This same theme of a broad cultural acceptance evolving from the recognition of the "New Negro" as "a creator" dominates the writings of James Weldon Johnson in the 1920s. Johnson and others somehow believed that American racism was a process that could be reasoned with; a phenomenon that would crumble when whites recognized Negroes had extraordinary and unique artistic talents. "I am coming to believe," Johnson wrote his close friend Carl Van Vechten, "that nothing can go farther to destroy race prejudice than the recognition of the Negro as a creator and contributor to American civilization." "Harlemites thought the millennium had come," remembered Langston Hughes. "They thought the race problem had at last been solved through Art. . . ."

There was an element of realism in the romantic hopes of Johnson, Broun, and Locke. For white Americans to grant that the Negro was capable of making *any* contribution to American culture was in itself a new idea—"that the Negro is a creator as well as creature . . . a giver as well as . . . receiver." A new and more liberal vision of democracy developed among social scientists in the 1920s. Scholars like Robert E. Park, Herbert A. Miller, Franz Boas, Melville J. Herskovits, Charles S. Johnson, Bruno Lasker, E. Franklin Frazier, and Horace M. Kallen attacked traditional American attitudes toward assimilation and "Americanization." A more vital and beautiful democracy would arise, they argued, by permitting ethnic groups to maintain their individuality, rather than conceiving them swallowed up (or melted down) in the one dominant American culture. Each group, given freedom of expression and development, would then make valuable contributions to American society. Diversity, cultural pluralism, should be fostered and encouraged, not stifled, they wrote.

A spate of articles and books published in the 1920s seriously analyzed and attempted to understand the Negro's place in the nation. The dozens of volumes about Negroes written by pseudo-scientists and racists at the turn of the century were now replaced by works which attempted to cut through racial stereotypes ("generalized theories about racial qualities") and tried to find some viable program for "interracial cooperation." "The American Negro can no longer be dismissed as an unimportant element in the population of the United States," concluded one man. Bruno Lasker's *And Who Is My Neighbor?* and *All Colors* were among the earliest serious studies of American interracial attitudes. *The Annals* of the American Academy of Political and Social Science printed a thick volume of studies on Negroes by the nation's leading social scientists. *The World Tomorrow*, a fascinating Christian Pacifist journal, devoted two full issues to similar articles in the 1920s. Most of the major periodicals of the decade contained large numbers of serious and important studies of Negro life. The artistic and human value of Negro spirituals, folk songs, folk legends and music was first recognized in the 1920s (many considered them America's most important contribution to world culture); Darius Milhaud, after listening to Negro music in Lenox Avenue cafes, composed pieces which made use of jazz rhythms and instruments; *In Abraham's Bosom*, one of Paul Green's many plays of southern Negro life, won the Pulitzer Prize in 1926; Eugene O'Neill and Robert E. Sherwood constructed plays and novels around Negro characters and themes. As important as this new recognition was, however, it was a minor trend in American thought. The generation that advocated cultural pluralism was also the generation that saw the revival of the Ku Klux Klan, and permanently restricted foreign immigration to the United States.

Had intellectuals like Johnson and Locke looked more critically at the stereotype of the "New Negro" that developed in the writings of most white commentators of the 1920s, they would have had further cause to question the extent of interracial understanding that existed then. White literary rebels created a "vogue in things Negro," "an enthusiasm for negro life and art" that bordered on being a cult. They saw Negroes not as people but as symbols of everything America was not. The concept of the existence of a "New Negro" and the publicity given to it in the 1920s was primarily the result of this new awareness and interest in Negro society by what one writer called the "New White Man." The generation that discovered "newness" all around itself—New Humanism, New Thought, New Woman, New Psychology, New Masses, New Poetry, New Criticism, and so on—also found a "New Negro"; and the concept became a cultural weapon: "Another Bombshell Fired into the Heart of Bourgeois Culture." "Negro stock is going up," wrote novelist Rudolph Fisher, "and everybody's buying."

In the literature of the 1920s Negroes were conceived as "expressive" ("a singing race") in a society burdened with "unnatural inhibitions"; their lives were "primitive" and "exotic" (these two words appear repeatedly) in a "dull," "weary" and "monotonous" age; they could laugh and love freely in a "land flowing with Socony and Bryan and pristine Rotary purity." Negroes were presented as people who lived an "entire lifetime of laughs and thrills, [of] excitement and fun"—they had an "innate gayety of soul." "Ecstasy," wrote Joseph Wood Krutch in *The Nation*, "seems . . . to be his natural state." The stereotype of the Negro that had existed in American society in the nineteenth century was largely untouched by the new interest in Negro life. It was continued, for example, in such "all-talking melodramas" as "Lucky Sambo," "Hearts in Dixie," and "Hallelujah," and in the new radio hit "Amos and Andy." In the 1920s, however, the ludicrous image of Negro as "darkey" became a subordinate theme, eclipsed by the conception of the Negro as sensuous and rhythmic African. Negroes were still thought to be alienated from traditional American virtues and values, as they had been since colonial times, but this was now considered a great asset. "To Americans," wrote a perceptive contemporary in 1929, "the Negro is not a human being but a concept."

This was the background against which white America and the world came to know the "New Negro" and Harlem: "with our eyes focused on the Harlem scene we may dramatically glimpse the New Negro." A large Negro community had gathered in Harlem prior to World War I but, aside from small numbers of dedicated social workers, American society seemed willing to overlook its existence. In the 1920s, however, Harlem was made a national symbol—a symbol of the Jazz Age. It was seen as the antithesis of Main Street, Zenith, and Gopher Prairie. Whatever seemed thrilling, bizzare or sensuous about Harlem life was made a part of the community's image; whatever was tragic about it, ignored.

Harlem of the Twenties was presented as a "great playground," America's answer to Paris. The institution that best describes this aspect of Harlem's image was the white slumming party: "it became quite a rage . . . to go to night clubs in Harlem," recalled Carl Van Vechten. Cabarets were filled nightly with handsomely dressed white slummers who danced the Charleston, Turkey, or Black Bottom, listened to jazz or watched risqué revues. Some night spots, like the Cotton Club (which had "the hottest show in town"), and Connie's Inn (which competed for the honor), catered exclusively to whites. They were, wrote a journalist, dives "where white people from downtown could be entertained by colored girls." If one was looking "to go on a moral vacation," or wished to soften "the asperities of a Puritan conscience," Harlem's cabarets promised to do the job. The following is an advertisement, written especially for "white consumption," and distributed by a man who supplied "Slumming Hostesses" to "inquisitive Nordics" (each card was said to have a suggestive picture on it):

> Here in the world's greatest city it would both amuse and also interest you to see the real inside of the New Negro Race of Harlem. You have

heard it discussed, but there are very few who really know. . . . I am in a position to carry you through Harlem as you would go slumming through Chinatown. My guides are honest and have been instructed to give the best service. . . . Your season is not completed with thrills until you have visited Harlem.

"White people," editorialized a Negro journal, "are taking a morbid interest in the night life of [Harlem]."

And the interest continued to grow throughout the decade. Carl Van Vechten's novel of Harlem life, *Nigger Heaven* (1925), sold 100,000 copies "almost immediately," and brought its author a substantial fortune. It was translated into French, Swedish, Russian and Japanese. Van Vechten's book contained some interesting commentaries on the structure and problems of Negro society (the role of the middle class; "passing"; prejudice; color consciousness) but its plot was contrived, sensational, and melodramatic; replete with orgies, drugs, and seduction; a hodgepodge of *True Confessions* and the front pages of a tabloid. Its characters were unbelievable as people. "The squalor of Negro life, the vice of Negro life," wrote Van Vechten, "offer a wealth of novel, exotic, picturesque materials to the artist." *Nigger Heaven* was "recognized in every quarter . . . as *the* portrayal of contemporary life in Harlem," said its publisher (and it undoubtedly was). The white world looked curiously at the success of Marcus Garvey (whose movement basically reflected a profound Negro desire for racial pride and respect in a society that denied it), and concluded that Negroes "have parades almost every day." White intellectuals and bohemians knew Harlem only through the cabarets, or the famous parties in the salon of the "joy-goddess of Harlem"—A'Lelia Walker's "Dark Tower": "dedicated to the aesthetes, young writers, sculptors, painters—a rendezvous where they may feel at home." Bessie Smith, the great blues singer, toured America with her "Harlem Frolic" company. Josephine Baker ("Josephine of the Jazz Age") wowed them in Harlem as a young chorus girl, and went on to international acclaim in Europe. "From a world of stone with metal decoys/Drab stone streets and drab stone masses/New York's mold for the great middleclasses, Africa passes/With syncopated talking the Congo arouses."

White audiences, like gluttons at a feast, vicariously tasted the "high yallers," "tantalizin tans" and "hot chocolates" that strutted around in the Blackbird Revues, or in such plays as *Lulu Belle* (1926) and *Harlem* (1928)—and made them top box-office successes. (*Black Boy* and *Deep River*, dramas which emphasized a more serious side of Negro life, were failures.) "Ten years ago," wrote one Negro reviewer of *Lulu Belle*, "this play would have been unprofitable. Twenty years ago it would have caused a riot." The following is a handbill distributed to advertise the play *Harlem* ("A Thrilling Play of the Black Belt"):

> Harlem! . . . The City that Never Sleeps! . . . A Strange, Exotic Island in the Heart of New York; . . . Rent Parties! . . . Number Runners! . . . Chippies! . . . Jazz Love! . . . Primitive Passion!

"How soon this common theme shall reach the nauseating state," remarked a caustic critic, "is not easy to tell."

The Great Depression brought an abrupt end to the dream of a "New Negro" and the image of Harlem as erotic utopia. A nation sobered by bread lines no longer searched for a paradise inhabited by people who danced and loved and laughed for an "entire lifetime." Connie's Inn and other places of white entertainment closed down. Leading figures of the Renaissance: Wallace Thurman, Richard B. Harrison, A'Lelia Walker, Charles S. Gilpin, Florence Mills, Arthur A. Schomburg, died in the late 1920s or 1930s. Most of the Negro literati, though not all, stopped writing or, if they continued to do so, found a less responsive American audience for their works. All the Negro literary magazines folded.

And, as the exotic vision of the 1920s passed, a new image of the Negro and Harlem emerged—a Harlem already known to stolid census-takers, city health officers and social workers. "The rosy enthusiasms and hopes of 1925," wrote Alain Locke ten years later, "were . . . cruelly deceptive mirage[s]." The ghetto was revealed in the 1930s as "a nasty, sorbid corner into which black folk are herded"—"*a Harlem that the social worker knew all along but had not been able to dramatize. . . . There is no cure or saving magic in poetry and art for . . . precarious marginal employment, high mortality rates, civic neglect,*" concluded Locke. It was this Harlem, the neighborhood not visible "from the raucous interior of a smoke-filled, jazz-drunken cabaret," the Harlem hidden by the "bright surface . . . of . . . night clubs, cabaret tours and . . . arty magazines," that was devastated by the depression; and has remained a community with an inordinate share of sorrow and deprivation ever since. "The depression brought everybody down a peg or two," wrote Langston Hughes. "And the Negroes had but few pegs to fall." The myth-world of the 1920s had ended.

17

Freudianism and Child-Rearing
in the Twenties

GEOFFREY H. STEERE

The 1920s are renowned for a revolution of manners and morals. If Americans did not discover sex in that decade, they at least talked more freely about it, citing as their ultimate authority Dr. Sigmund Freud. Historians have judged that during that decade Freud's influence on American society extended far beyond the cocktail party chitchat of intellectuals. Given Freud's emphasis on childhood, Geoffrey H. Steere reasons that the depth and breadth of Freud's impact on middle-class Americans in the 1920s can be measured by a systematic analysis of that decade's child-rearing manuals.

The impact of Sigmund Freud on the life of 20th century America is commonly assumed; and Freudianism, at least in distorted forms, has been associated with the 1920s especially. If claims for Freud's importance in the 1920s are justified, they should be validated by contemporary writing about child-rearing practices. Child-rearing processes, dependent as they are on the total social system, can be taken as sensitive indicators of large-scale change in thought and behavior. Since Freud's ideas emphasized the importance of childhood experience in forming adult personality, one would expect his ideas to have influenced the thinking of opinion leaders on child-rearing.

From *American Quarterly* 20 (1968):759–65. Footnotes omitted. Reprinted by permission from the author and *American Quarterly*. Copyright, 1968, Trustees of the University of Pennsylvania.

Testimony to the general influence of Freud is not hard to find. For example, Alfred Kazin, well-known student of America, says that "no other system of thought in modern times, except the great religions, has been adopted by so many people as a systematic interpretation of individual behavior. Consequently, to those who have no other belief, Freudianism sometimes serves as a philosophy of life." And Kazin further states that "the greatest and most beautiful effect of Freudianism is the increasing awareness of childhood as the most important single influence on personal development." Viewing Freud's significance at this level of generalization, one well might anticipate an affirmative answer to Benjamin Nelson's question, "Will the Twentieth Century go down in history as the *Freudian Century?*

Moving to a lower level of generalization limited to discussion of the extent of Freudian impact on the 1920s in particular and child-rearing specifically, commentators would seem to support the expectation aroused by Kazin. Thomas C. Cochran writes of the "dramatic" and "exciting" quality of the theories of Freud for the educated urban middle class, and says "the popularity of his ideas in the United States in the 1920s fitted the social trends arising from urban industrialism as well as from [a] whole complex of experimental attitudes." He further refers to "the general acceptance [in medicine and the social sciences] of the view of mental processes generated by Freud's theories" in the 1920s. Sociologist John Sirjamaki, writing of the improvement in child status following the interest by the social sciences in child study after 1910 and through the 1930s, says "the greatest individual influence during this time came from Freud." Celia B. Stendler says that "the twenties had . . . seen widespread acceptance of Freudian theory and many extreme applications of it to the training of children." And history textbooks, if they discuss Freud's influence in the 1920s, often make two points: that American intellectuals eagerly discussed psychoanalytic ideas and that Freudianism was popularly distorted to mean that sexual expression should exceed conventional limits to avoid the danger of neurotic repression.

Yet despite such testimony, I found very little Freudianism in the child-rearing manuals from the 1920s. Indeed, of these manuals, forty-two in all, only one appeared to be written avowedly and systematically according to Freudian theory, while in the remaining books Freudianism seemed to be present only in scattered, occasional references, or altogether absent. Therefore I decided to re-examine my data, with the *express* purpose of determining its Freudian content.

Delineating Freudianism in child-rearing texts is not easy. The ambiguity arises from the difficulty in deciding what statements in any given book can clearly be distinguished as Freudian, rather than, say, Darwinian, Jamesian or Watsonian.

To help try to distinguish Freudianism in the material collected according to the categories already mentioned, another set of categories was used, drawn from the table of contents in Calvin S. Hall's *A Primer of Freudian Psychology*. From among the Hall categories, explicit references appeared in the child-rearing literature to only the following three categories: Development of the Sexual Instinct, Defense Mechanisms of the Ego, and Unconscious.

The number of books which provided even one reference to Freudian-associated terms and concepts was sixteen. Only three texts provided data in all three Freudian categories. In the other texts the psychoanalytic references were either infrequent or non-existent.

The following passages reproduce most of the material which probably is Freudian influenced. The unconscious was mentioned in six books, as exemplified in the following quotations. One author speaks of "the theory of the unconscious, with its complete and satisfying explanation upon natural grounds of so many of the things that we have long been accustomed to look upon as mysterious. . . ." and later mentions "our unconscious self." Another writer talks of behavior both consciously and unconsciously imitated. Readers are told in one text that a form of aggressive behavior may "represent an unconscious protest against the thwarting of some fundamental desire. . . ." And elsewhere reference is made to "a real unconscious wish to control" behavior. A less brief statement about the unconscious says that "present-day psychologists are as much interested in what functions in the subconscious as in the conscious part of the mind, because they believe that the former gives color to all one's feelings and guides one in one's actions and, at least to some extent, determines what one will think about."

References to the ego and its defense mechanisms occur in nine books and are similarly brief and scattered. Several authors mention the phenomena of inhibition and repression. "Inhibitions and repressions of natural instincts and desire are hurtful to the child's development," says one author; and [Mary] Chadwick warns that "we can more quickly inhibit healthy development, which prevents one stage from passing over into the next, than we may encourage it to do so." Elsewhere readers were told that "you cannot get rid of an impulse through repression." Advice using the concepts of sublimation and suppression runs typically as follows: "These primitive instincts [e.g., sex, flight, fear] are neither good nor bad in themselves; they are 'natural.' Rightly used, they make for happiness; uncontrolled and perverted they are ugly and the cause of intense misery. Character depends to a large extent on their control and sublimation"; "Most emotions that the child gives vent to are instinctive and natural and cannot be successfully suppressed. They can, however, be redirected into channels that are helpful and useful in the building of character." These references to ego defense mechanisms, with their emphasis on the power of instinctive forces, strongly suggest a Freudian influence in the few places they appear.

The presence in the literature of one further category—in its Freudian context—Development of the Sexual Instinct, occurs in six books. Again, the references are few and center on discussion of pregenital stages of sexual development (that is, the oral, anal and phallic stages). "The whole *oral libido* . . . ," says Chadwick, "which we may call, roughly, interest in food and the mouth zone generally, will become repressed, [if there is an] early trauma of deprivation, and an unconscious hatred of the mother, or depriving agent, will take its place. . . ." Referring to the anal stage, another writer says that "[elimination] is another habit that psychologists have a great deal to say about. For they believe that according to the way in which the child is taught to control these functions will his attitude toward sex be governed in later years." There would seem to be references to the phallic stage in the passage where one writer states that "the child reacts positively to emotional stimulation from the mother, to caresses, to appeals for demonstrations of affection. Such mutual approaches have both their value and their dangers. They are dangerous if they force a premature development of the sex impulses. . . ." Writing in a similar vein, another author warns that "as a result of such punishment [i.e., spanking on the buttocks] many children develop actual 'erotic zones' and experience actual pleasurable sexual sensations. . . ." In addition two books discussed the Freudian concept of the Oedipus complex: Chadwick devotes an entire chapter to "Both Sides of the Oedipus Conflict," and [Frank Howard] Richardson explains the Oedipal drama in the family constellation when he says: "whether we like to believe it or not, there is undoubtedly a very definite element of jealousy, usually quite unrecognized by any of the actors, operative in the reaction of father and son toward the object of their common affection, the wife and mother. . . ." And finally, there appears in Chadwick an analysis of another phenomenon delineated by Freud, i.e., penis envy, wherein girls suffer disappointment and envy at discovering that boys proudly possess what girls do not. "This double-sided pride and envy," says Chadwick, "which may each contribute to the other, is largely responsible for the conscious and unconscious feelings of hostility between the two sexes." Most of these passages on sex probably reflect a Freudian influence. It is surprising, however, that more material of this nature doesn't appear in the literature, since the initial impact of Freud in the 1920s has been thought to have stressed sexual repression as a primary cause of neurosis.

Why is there so little in child-rearing manuals of the 1920s that can be securely attributed to Freud? One might assume that there was hostility to Freud from opinion leaders on child-rearing who, with some members of press and pulpit, might have abhorred Freud's speaking of sex and other taboo topics. But the manuals show little hostility to Freud on any grounds. Only one manual takes a wholesale stand in opposition to Freudianism, and in only one other book is there criticism of contemporary child-rearing theory which is also clearly criticism of Freudianism. This occurs when an author states that "many later investigators are inclined to disagree with certain of the outworkings of Freud's theories, especially with the extreme emphasis he places upon sexual experiences as the almost exclusive source of complexes. . . ." A more likely explanation for the scarcity of Freudianism is that there were theories and schools of child care successfully competing with Freudianism in the 1920s. Psychologist Gardner Murphy points out that:

> A genuine psychology of personality . . . still innocent of Freudian coloration, was taking shape in the early years of this century. And by 1920 there was a full-fledged American personality psychology, dominated by concepts from Pavlov and Bechterev, and especially J. B. Watson. Watson did, indeed, borrow a very considerable chunk from Freud in his discussion of dreams and of symbolic behavior; but there was likewise a very substantial personality psychology standing on objectivist or behaviorist legs.

Orville G. Brim, authority on child-rearing education, agrees with Murphy's assessment of the importance of non-Freudian ideas in his opinion that child care in the 1920s was dominated, not by emphasis on love, support and an intelligent permissiveness associated with Freud and others, but by "the strict, routinized care of the child" advocated in Emmett Holt's book, *The Care and Feeding of Children,* originally published in 1894, which Brim feels was substantially more important to parents in the 1920s than Watson's writings. Historian Thomas C. Cochran refers to behaviorism in the 1920s as attractive for many middle-class parents because its ideas were "easier to understand than Freud's and more concerned with normal psychology." And Gardner Murphy would seem to support assumptions about Freud's limited impact on parents by estimating an equally small Freudian influence on child psychologists. Using what he calls "a crude scale [running from 0 (none) to 6 (very great)] which may . . . give some first approximation of a guess as to the impact of Freud on the various specialized divisions of modern psychology," Murphy rates Freud's impact on child and adolescent psychology at "2 (limited)," concluding that these remained among the areas of psychology relatively unaffected by Freudianism. These diverse comments from social scientists in disciplines concerned with child socialization, testifying to the greater importance in the 1920s of non-Freudian ideas, supports the evidence derived from systematic examination of the child-rearing manuals.

From what has been written by historians and others, it would be hard to deny that Freud's ideas were influential during the 1920s, especially in the thinking of artists, writers, intellectuals and advanced minds in the urban centers. But if educated middle-class people were touched by Freud—through literature, art, some aspects of medicine and the social sciences, or the tabloids—it would seem that they were seldom so touched through the medium of child-rearing manuals. Middle-class Americans in the 1920s, as they prepared to rear their children and perpetuate their society, were offered advice coming from many sides, but not significantly from Sigmund Freud.

18

Country Music During the Depression: Survival and Expansion

BILL C. MALONE

Not all folklorists accept hillbilly music as a "valid facet of folk culture." Those who do accept it are interested more in its anthropological than in its artistic value. Hillbilly songs are living documents reflecting the social and historical climate of their origin. The documentary value of hillbilly music has attracted a growing group of folklorists and social historians. In this music they have found what is probably the most vivid expression of the cataclysmic impact of the Great Depression on humble people.

The technological revolution that did so much to drive singers . . . from the entertainment business affected country music from its very beginnings and was, in fact, responsible for its dissemination throughout the United States. The very commercial process that introduced rural music to a receptive national audience has also incessantly absorbed that music. Country music, therefore, cannot be studied as a purely rural phenomenon. It must always be considered in relation to the dominant society that lies around it, the industrial-technological-urban society that has modified and transformed all American values.

To this point in this study most country music considered has been of the traditional, blues, or gospel variety, and has been that

From Bill C. Malone, *Country Music U.S.A.: A Fifty-Year History* (Austin: The University of Texas Press, 1968), pp. 131–43. Reprinted with omissions by permission. © 1968 by the American Folklore Society.

which evokes images of quaint pastoral life: the rural church, the placid mountain brook, the family fireside, and the hillside farm. The South itself has possessed more than just a rural tradition. As pervasive as the rural ethos has been, the South has agonizingly and slowly succumbed to the inroads made by the industrial revolution. A steady and never ending procession of forces—the railroads, the iron and coal interests, timber companies, textile mills, and oil operators—have gradually transformed the South, its inhabitants and the music which they have made.

Southern rural music, both before and after commercialization, has persistently chronicled the developing stages of industrialization, sometimes with disgust, often with amusement, and nearly always with fascination. Literally hundreds of songs have described the rural folk's open-eyed wonder and curiosity about the new gadgets and inventions that have revolutionized southern and American society. The first great economic phenomenon to break through the South's wall of isolation—the railroad—inspired a body of songs that comprise one of the single largest categories in country and folk music. Such songs as "Wreck on the Southern Old 97," "Casey Jones," "Waiting for a Train," and "Wabash Cannon Ball" have thrilled generations of American listeners. In more recent times the train songs have given way to songs about more modern means of communication, as is witnessed by the spate of truck-driving songs, such as "Six Days on the Road." In accepting and chronicling the story of innovations, however, the southern country folk have not lost their age-old tendency to moralize and to use the objects of this life to symbolize eternal truths. "Life's Railway to Heaven," "The Automobile of Life," "Life's Elevator," and scores of songs similar to them have all emphasized the ancient theme of the transcience of temporal life. The only difference between these and older songs is the depiction of modern transportation devices to symbolize the brief passage of man's life through earth's vale of tears.

This literary-musical device was effectively used by Dorsey Dixon in a song in which the automobile collision supplants the classic motif of the train tragedy: "Wreck on the Highway," recorded and made famous by Roy Acuff. Universally known by country- and folk-music fans, "Wreck on the Highway" reminds the listener that despite the accelerating changes of modern life, some things never change. The Grim Reaper still exacts his deadly toll, and even when life seems its gayest, the very vehicle that has contributed most to one's pleasure may also be the means through which this pleasure turns into tragedy.

Southerners have not viewed the industrial revolution as an unmixed blessing, and, though it is often overlooked by historians, a strain of radicalism—as evidenced by the Populist movement—has run through the fabric of southern history. Southern country music, therefore, has occasionally lent itself to a form of expression which has been of continuing interest to folklorists and social historians: protest music. The civil rights revolution of the sixties, with its use of stirring songs to dramatize and inspire the movement, serves as a modern reminder that the protest song has played a vital role in the unceasing efforts to reform and humanize American society. Through the study of folk music, the folklorist and social historian can gain a greater understanding of the attitudes and ideals of those stratums in American society which leave few if any written documents. The scholar may obtain his source of information directly from the lips of the informant, or perhaps more easily through the medium of a phonograph recording. Both folksongs and folk attitudes of the depression years of the thirties have evoked continuing response from scholars who have demonstrated an intellectual and social concern for the plight of suffering farmers and unemployed laborers. Few eras have elicited more responses of a protest nature, and no groups in American society had greater traditions of expressing their basic attitudes in song than did rural white and Negro southerners.

The question of protest music presents some interesting problems. It is obvious that the southern people were confronted by conditions that needed to be protested, but did they protest, and if so, how was their protest directed? Southern poor whites—tenant farmers, coal miners, textile workers—were beset with the problems of low prices, low wages, poor housing, and job insecurity. Despite the multitude of problems, and despite the persistence of the ballad tradition of expressing stories in song, the number of protest songs in country music, commercial and otherwise, is extremely low. Although individual items can be detailed, as a class of songs they comprise a small percentage of the total folk repertory. Of course, the number of social "comments" in recorded hillbilly music make up a tremendous percentage of the over-all total, but they certainly cannot all be construed as protest songs. Admittedly, however, since the recording companies are profit-minded business organizations, it would be generous indeed for them to allow a large quantity of protest songs to be placed on the market.

It should be made clear at the outset that in this discussion "protest" means "overt" protest—an utterance or outcry against social and economic grievances, or a call for action against them. The outcries of a poor farmer against the landlord or the credit system, or of a laborer against the lords of capital, have been few indeed. Instead, the southern rural white has more often directed his protests against other factors in society, usually individual personal misfortunes. The sorrows of this world, fatalistically explained as the fruits of individual error or as divine payments for past sins, are expressed through songs of self-pity or of yearning for solace through heavenly reward. But the system that produced these sorrows is seldom attacked.

Regardless of their relatively minor position in the field of folk music, protest and semi-protest songs became a fairly important part of southern rural music during the thirties. This type of song could be heard in both commercial and noncommercial country music. The most explosive areas in the South, and those where class hostility was most extreme, were the drought-ridden Southwest, the textile-mill region of the Carolinas, and the coal fields around Harlan, Kentucky. All three areas have been important ballad-producing regions, and each has contributed greatly to the formation of country music.

The unhappy region of Harlan County, Kentucky, particularly produced some of the most bitter class feeling and labor violence that the country has known. It has also produced some of the truest expressions of protest music and labor songs that are available in the American experience. In this region of eastern Kentucky singing and the tradition of ballad-making were deeply ingrained. The Kentucky mountain people, who provided the bulk of the work force, carried their stubbornly individualistic attitudes into the Kentucky coal fields. The stark misery and oppressive conditions of the coal mines made the mountaineers loyal union people, and their individualism made them among the most militant of American union members. In their organizational drives and on the picket lines, they sang melodies that expressed their discontent or the necessity for unity. Generally, their protest songs were set to traditional or sacred melodies.

The most productive and talented spokesman of the Kentucky coal miners was Aunt Molly Jackson, the wife of a union member. Along with her sister Sarah Ogan Gunning, she did much to popularize labor and protest music in New York and other areas outside Kentucky. Aunt Molly made only one commercial recording (Sarah Gunning has been recently recorded), but she was a favorite informant of the folklorists who gathered material for the Library of Congress. Her store of ballads and folksongs was almost limitless, and she generally set her labor lyrics to some older melody with which she was familiar. Aunt Molly took her songs from wherever she could get them—from traditional or commercial sources. An example of the traditional influence was her "Dreadful Memories"—the story of coal miners' children who had died because of malnutrition—which was modeled upon the popular southern gospel song, "Precious Memories." Aunt Molly Jackson, Sarah Ogan Gunning, and similar individuals, such as Woody Guthrie, are interesting examples of people who sprang from the folk and sang melodies that were partly influenced by commercial sources. They were border-line cases who borrowed their songs from a variety of sources and in their appeal went far beyond the limits of their native folk audiences. In fact, they were enthusiastically accepted by northern urban groups, and at least in the case of Guthrie they became more identified with the urban "folk" than with the rural.

Woodrow Wilson (Woody) Guthrie occupies an unusual position in American country and folk music. He began as a hillbilly singer with strong traditional roots and advanced to the position of America's most revered urban folksinger and writer. Born in Okemah, Oklahoma, in 1912, Woody learned a wide variety of traditional melodies from his parents. In 1929, his parents being in an impoverished condition, he went out on his own and traveled over much of the Southwest doing odd jobs. In Pampa, Texas, where he experienced the dust storms for the first time, he learned a few basic guitar chords from his uncle Jeff, one of the local deputy sheriffs. The two of them formed a hillbilly band and began entertaining at local functions in the Pampa area.

Woody Guthrie gained his earliest experience in the small towns of Oklahoma and Texas when those areas were experiencing the social flux of the twenties and thirties. The late twenties and early thirties saw the eruption of the southwestern oil boom, and, with its passage, the coming of the dust storms and the Great Depression. In this atmosphere of social upheaval Woody Guthrie developed the style and politics that made him the "darling" of urban folksong enthusiasts. Building upon a traditional repertory, Guthrie perfected his technique in the southwestern oil-town honky-tonks.

Guthrie was imbued with a strong sense of social consciousness, and the unfortunate decade of the thirties inflamed this feeling, as it did with many people, to outright rebelliousness. Guthrie moved to California and, in typical hillbilly fashion, obtained a job on Station KFVD in Los Angeles. California at that time was being deluged with victims of the depression and the southwestern dust bowl. Guthrie felt a strong emotional kinship with the homeless migratory workers, especially his fellow Okies, and he began to compose songs which expressed his sympathies with these people and his anger at the system which caused their misfortunes. Thus, Guthrie began to change from a simple singer of hillbilly songs to a full-fledged performer of protest music. By the end of the thirties he had accumulated an extensive aggregation of original compositions dealing with the dust storms. These ballands, usually set to traditional Oklahoma and Texas melodies, included "Dust Bowl Refugee," "Talking Dust Bowl Blues," and "I Ain't Got No Home in This World Anymore." The songs were performed with Guthrie's distinctive southwestern twang and his rhythmic, Carter Family-inspired guitar playing.

In 1938 Guthrie moved to New York where he gained the attention of folk-music enthusiasts in that area. He recorded for the National Archives, performed on New York radio stations, and recorded his "Dust Bowl Ballads" for Victor. With his sojourn in New York Guthrie all but severed his ties with the southern rural folk, and became instead the chief apostle of the urban folk movement. Guthrie immediately became associated with assorted intellectuals and folk-music devotees who wished to use the music as a propaganda vehicle for liberal programs. Guthrie, along with Aunt Molly Jackson and Negro folksinger Huddie Ledbetter, were readily accepted by New York intellectual groups. Guthrie seemed to be a living example of exactly the sort of person the liberals were fighting for, a flesh-and-blood proletarian from the poverty-stricken dust bowl who lent his support to liberal causes. And better yet, he sang protest songs. Here was a proletarian, of almost storybook proportions, who acted as a proletarian should act. Woody Guthrie became a popular and sought after performer before college groups, union organization meetings, and intellectual gatherings of one kind or another. Along with Pete Seeger, Lee Hays, and Millard Lampell, he organized in 1940, a folksinging group called the Almanac Singers, who sang labor and patriotic songs, such as "The Good Reuben James," during World War II. Before his tragic death from Huntington's chorea in 1967, Woody Guthrie had been most responsible for the course that the urban folk movement had assumed in the United States. Guthrie was the most quoted and, to many urban enthusiasts, the greatest folk poet the United States had produced.

Guthrie's relationship to commercial country music is seen in the influences that shaped his own particular style. Despite his urban orientation after 1938, Guthrie's vocal and instrumental styles were firmly within the southern hillbilly tradition. In fact, as Dick Reuss had indicated, Guthrie never used the word "folk" or "folksinger" to refer to himself before he made his move to New York. The Woody Guthrie of the pre-1938 period was a hillbilly singer who sang for hillbilly audiences. His guitar accompaniment was a modification of that of Maybelle Carter, and the lyrics of his songs, in many cases, were set to older melodies of commerical and noncommercial origin. His ballad "Tom Joad" (based on the John Steinbeck creation) was set to the melody of "John Hardy"; his popular "The Philadelphia Lawyer" was set to the melody of "The Jealous Lover"; and, evidencing further Carter Family influence, Guthrie used the melody of "The Wildwood Flower" in "The Reuben James" and that of "Little Darling, Pal of Mine" in "This Land Is Your Land." The list of Guthrie's melodic borrowings is much more extensive than this.

Some of Guthrie's compositions gained wide popularity among hillbilly enthusiasts. These include such numbers as "So Long, It's Been Good to Know You," "The Philadelphia Lawyer," and the very popular

"Oklahoma Hills," recorded by his cousin Jack Guthrie in the 1940's. Although Woody Guthrie acknowledged his debt to the Carter Family and freely borrowed from hillbilly sources, it is doubtful whether he identified himself with the hillbilly performers of the post-1938 period. After that date he became associated with the urban folk movement and never thereafter had anything but remote connections with hillbilly music. He began a series of recording ventures with Folkways, a company then catering only to a limited, sophisticated audience, and his concerts were given usually to Eastern college groups and sophisticates. Guthrie was well known, but not among the rural folk who had spawned both him and his music. The course of Guthrie's career was roughly equivalent to what was happening to folk music as a whole. "Folk" music was becoming the province of intellectuals and sophisticates and was becoming farther and farther removed from the "folk." In the following decades Woody Guthrie's disciples would create a public image of folk music that generally would have no room for hillbilly music.

Apart from Guthrie, hillbilly singers responded to the rigors of the depression with a variety of songs. Some of the singers joked about their predicaments; others made perceptive comments about the social scene; a few rejoiced at the changes wrought by the New Deal; and some engaged in self-pity and expressed longings for a land beyond the grave where no depressions would come. The southern United States was hard hit by the depression. In fact, the southern farmer had suffered throughout the 1920's while the remainder of the nation experienced a general prosperity. Whereas in preceding years the South had been generally characterized by a net loss of migration, the trend was reversed from 1930 to 1940 and the bulk of migrations tended to be internal. Southerners, in general, remained at home or moved into southern cities.

Despite the population stability of the greater part of the South, a substantial, and socially important, exodus occurred from the Southwest: the states of Oklahoma, Arkansas, and Texas. Dispossessed farmers of this region, made homeless by automation, dust storms, and the depression, trekked westward, lured by the fabled promises of California as a land of hope for the migrants and an area of material abundance. This concept, graphically described in John Steinbeck's *Grapes of Wrath*, was later pictured in humorous fashion in a hillbilly song that described jobs as being so abundant in California that all a man needed was a shovel—to pick up the gold.

California was not the Garden of Eden that the migrants expected. Jobs were scarce, wages were incredibly low, and California public opinion was bitterly hostile to the migrants. The Okies were resented because of their religious, speech, and cultural differences, and because of their poverty. The southwestern migrants carried with them to California their inherited store of beliefs, values, attitudes, and institutions. This included hillbilly music.

In the Farm Security Administration camps, where the majority of the migrants temporarily resided, the dwellers amused themselves at night by singing and playing the old songs which eased their minds or reminded them of their former homes. One observer remarked that in his meanderings through the camps he heard "fragments of tunes that a more prosperous America has forgotten in the process of growing up and getting rich." These songs ("Going Down the Road Feeling Bad" was said to be the most popular) included both the traditional songs and the newer ones produced by the commercial hillbillies. Songs popular among the Okies included "The Great Speckled Bird," "The Convict and the Rose," and "Carter Blues." The Okies' choice of songs was resented by many staid, respectable Californians who looked upon the music as one long wailing, nasal lament, but the dispossessed southern migrants made their songs a permanent part of California musical life. Southern California, in particular, remained a stronghold of hillbilly music. The California migration was representative of the process which in the forties spread hillbilly music all over the United States—the transplantation of a musical culture through population migration.

The surprising feature of commercial hillbilly protest songs was not necessarily their existence but the fact that the phonograph companies allowed them to be recorded. But it has been said that white southerners who suffered from the hard times demanded songs that spoke to them of their difficulties. The record companies, therefore, had no choice but to comply with the demand. Okeh released a record by Bill Cox, entitled "Franklin Roosevelt's Back Again," applauding Roosevelt's re-election in 1936. Because of FDR's great personal popularity the existence of partisan songs is not surprising. Cox, who has recently been rediscovered in West Virginia and re-recorded on Kanawha Records, had an acute, partisan Democratic way of viewing society. Although he wrote some of the great perennials of country music, such as "Sparkling Brown Eyes" and "Filipino Baby," his most interesting compositions of the thirties were those which dealt with social problems. His "NRA Blues," for example, extolled the efforts of one of the major New Deal agencies to alleviate unemployment and to improve working conditions. Some of the depression songs, like Slim Smith's "Breadline Blues," were partisanly political; others, like Roy Acuff's "Old Age Pension Check," poked good-natured fun at some of the social legislation of the time. The Acuff song related how "poor old grandma" would suddenly become like a frivolous sixteen-year-old when the social security payments started rolling in. Uncle Dave Macon, always a perceptive and witty critic of the social scene, recorded a few songs that at least bordered on the "protest" category. They were, however, more in the nature of commentaries than denunciations. They included such songs as "All I've Got's Gone" (Vocalion 14904), which described what had happened to the people who had lived beyond their means during the twenties, and "All in Down and Out Blues" (Bluebird 7350), which showed that for millions of Americans "Wall Street's propositions were not all roses."

One of the richest, but as yet incompletely documented, bodies of industrial and protest songs on hillbilly records are those from the textile-mill villages of the Carolina piedmont region. The existence of the textile factories—with their regimentation, long hours, low pay, and child labor—provide a grim refutation of the idea that the South has had no industrial tradition. The textile mills were brick-and-stone testimonials to those "New South" propagandists who sought to bring progress to the South by ending its economic colonial dependence on the North. They sought to "bring the factory to the field." The textile mills did bring progress to the South, and prosperity to some, but they also brought misery to many. Thousands of mountain- and hill-country people willingly left their farms to seek the promise of a better life, only to find that they had merely traded rural deprivation for an industrial poverty which robbed them even of their independence. Kept close to economic penury, depressed by a burdensome regimentation, and ostracized by middle-class southerners who called them "lintheads" and "factory trash," the textile operatives found solace in old-time religion, protection through the trade-union movement, and comfort in their age-old tradition of ballad-making.

The textile mills produced not only an important body of folksongs, they also spawned a high percentage of commercial country singers, such as David McCarn, Henry Whitter, Fiddlin' John Carson, Jimmie Tarlton, Kelly Harrell, and the Dixon Brothers, all of whom worked full or part time in the mills, and the Bolick Brothers (the Blue Sky Boys) whose parents had been mill operatives. While many of the textile songs of the period were performed by well-known entertainers such as the Dixon Brothers (of "Weave Room Blues" fame), some important songs were recorded by individuals who have a more obscure place in country-music history. Two important protest items, "The Marion Massacre" and "The North Carolina Textile Strike," were recorded on Paramount Records by Frank Welling and John McGhee under the name of the Martin Brothers. Another fine example of the unsung balladeer is the case of David Mc-Carn, who, after leaving the North Carolina mountains to gain employment in a textile mill, composed ballads and songs for the amusement of his fellow workers. Six of these songs were recorded for Victor, including

"Cotton Mill Colic" and the sardonic "Serves 'Em Fine," which poked fun at the mountaineers foolish enough to leave their placid homes for the material lure of the textile mills.

The textile songs and the other socially-conscious hillbilly songs of the thirties were continuations of the broadside tradition in that they commented on the social and political events of the time and were intended only for temporary circulation. But imprinted on phonograph records they become important social documents of the period. Commercial phonograph discs, produced by the folk, can provide useful commentaries on both their originators' social milieu and that of the nation.

Regardless of the particular style conveyed, social protest or otherwise, country music by the end of the thirties had gained a firm enough footing in American musical life to ensure its endurance. Although it had lost many of the characteristics it possessed in the twenties, country music had developed through an evolutionary process, and even its most sophisticated performers had emerged out of a folk past. Some country entertainers, such as the Blue Sky Boys, leaned heavily upon traditional material, while others, such as the Delmore Brothers, borrowed from many musical sources. Nevertheless, despite the persistence of tradition within country music, the music (and its performers) were becoming more sophisticated and complex. And while the musicians of the Southeast and deep South were perpetuating certain styles and modifying others, musical winds were blowing in from the Southwest—particularly from Texas—which would have far reaching and dynamic effects upon the future course of the music.

19

A Conservative Coalition
Forms in Congress, 1933–1939

JAMES T. PATTERSON

With Franklin D. Roosevelt's New Deal came a fifth ordering of the party system. The Depression, the administration's New Deal programs, and Roosevelt himself—a shrewd politician and a charismatic leader—transformed the Democrats from a minority to a majority party. To the traditional Democratic strength in the rural South and the urban North, the New Deal added labor, farmers, the unemployed, blacks, reformers, and intellectuals. Yet the smashing victory of the New Deal coalition in 1936 was as misleading as it was impressive. The New Deal was not as strong as it appeared. Some of its supporters—farmers for example—were not firm converts to the Democratic party, and others were not firm converts to the New Deal. In Congress, the latter frequently united with Republicans to oppose the New Deal. Through a careful study of key congressional roll-call votes, James T. Patterson traces the development of this powerful conservative coalition.

Few political developments in recent American history have been more significant than the creation of a conservative coalition in Congress. Formed by Republicans and conservative Democrats to combat the New Deal, this "unholy alliance" operated effectively as early as 1937, and by 1939 it was strong enough to block extensions of the administration's program. It has functioned with varying degrees of success since that time, harassing and alarming Presidents of both parties.

From *Journal of American History* 52 (1966):757–72. Footnotes omitted. Reprinted by permission of the author and *The Journal of American History*.

Certain aspects of the coalition are well known and open to little question. Undoubtedly, both houses of Congress were more cantankerous in President Franklin D. Roosevelt's second term than they had been in his first, and most of the uncooperative congressmen were conservative on key issues. They tended to favor balanced budgets, to oppose welfare programs, to be suspicious of organized labor, and to speak favorably of states rights and limited government.

But historians have seldom ventured beyond these generalizations. They have not identified the members of the coalition. They have not tried to generalize about them as a group. They have not probed into the questions of why or when the coalition began. Finally, they have not shown whether the coalition was consciously organized, well disciplined, or coherent on crucial roll calls. These matters deserve attention.

Actually, the conservative leaders were well known. In the House the focus of conservative strength was the Rules Committee, dominated after 1938 by Edward E. Cox, a fiery Georgian who was a ranking Democratic member, and by Howard W. Smith, a Jeffersonian Democrat from Virginia. These two men, with three other southern Democrats and four Republicans, composed a majority of the fourteen-man committee after 1936. Cox was friendly with Joseph W. Martin, Jr. of Massachusetts, the leading Republican member of the committee in 1937–1938 who became House minority leader in 1939. When controversial issues arose, Cox and Martin usually conferred. If they agreed—which was often—Martin instructed his Republican colleagues on the committee to vote with Cox and the southern Democrats. Martin said later that he and Cox were the "principal points of contact between the northern Republicans and the southern Democratic conservatives."

Conservative leadership in the Senate was more diverse. The official Republican leader was Charles L. McNary of Oregon. The popular McNary was neither an orator nor a conservative by nature; indeed, he had voted for most New Deal measures before 1937. Though McNary participated in GOP strategy conferences, the most aggressive Republican senator after 1936 was the moderately conservative Arthur H. Vandenberg of Michigan. Other well-known Republicans who usually voted against major administration proposals included Henry Cabot Lodge, Jr. of Massachusetts, Warren R. Austin of Vermont, and Hiram W. Johnson of California, who became one of the most vitriolic foes of the New Deal after 1936.

Democratic conservatives in the Senate were a varied group. On the extreme right was a cluster of irreconcilables who had voted against most New Deal programs since 1933. These included Carter Glass and Harry F. Byrd of Virginia and Josiah W. Bailey of North Carolina. Bailey was particularly pungent in his criticism of Roosevelt. The President, he wrote,

> figures on hard times and does not wish for recovery. He would perish like a rattlesnake in the sun under conditions of prosperity. Pardon the illustration. Mr. Roosevelt is not a rattlesnake. He rattles a great deal, but that is all I am willing to say. Perhaps you know the rattlesnake must stay in the swamp for the reason that he does not have any means of sweating or panting. His heat accumulates. Mr. Roosevelt belongs to that type of man who lives on hard times and discontent.

Other Democrats, equally irreconcilable, joined Bailey in 1935–1936. These included Edward R. Burke of Nebraska, Peter G. Gerry of Rhode Island, Walter F. George of Georgia, and Ellison D. ("Cotton Ed") Smith of South Carolina. Such powerful veterans as Byron ("Pat") Harrison of Mississippi and James F. Byrnes of South Carolina, early supporters of the New Deal, also voted consistently against New Deal spending, tax, and labor programs after 1937. Vice-President John N. Garner of Texas, an influential figure in both houses, was another Democrat who by 1937 was counselling Roosevelt to move in a conservative direction.

While these men were unquestionably the most prominent congressional conservatives, it is not easy to generalize about them as a group. In the main they were not simply old men who had outlived their times. True, some like "Cotton Ed" Smith and Glass undoubtedly had. "Perhaps I am a relic of constitutional government," Glass admitted in 1938. "I entertain what may be the misguided notion that the Constitution of the United States, as it existed in the time of Grover Cleveland, is the same Constitution that exists today. . . ." But others, such as Byrd, Martin, and Howard Smith, were relatively young men. The average age of the most conservative Democratic senators in 1937 was precisely that of the Senate as a whole, while the most conservative Democratic representatives in 1937 averaged fifty years of age, two years less than the entire House.

Furthermore, the conservatives were by no means all veterans whose congressional service preceded the New Deal. Glass, George, and some others fitted this category, but many more first served in 1933 or thereafter, and the percentage of veteran and "coat-tail" Democrats who opposed the New Deal on most crucial roll calls was very much the same. Moreover, the most senior Republicans after 1935 included the moderately progressive McNary, William E. Borah of Idaho, and Arthur Capper of Kansas, while newcomers Austin of Vermont and H. Styles Bridges of New Hampshire tended to be among the most consistent opponents of the New Deal. Democratic veterans included not only conservatives of the Glass variety but New Deal regulars Alben W. Barkley of Kentucky, Hugo L. Black of Alabama, and Robert F. Wagner of New York. As Arthur S. Link has pointed out, the Congresses of the 1920s contained many relics of the progressive era; some of these veteran congressmen became reliable supporters of the New Deal in the 1930s.

Similarly, it is not entirely accurate to say that conservative strength in Congress derived from chairmanships of key committees. In the House, committee chairmen John J. O'Connor of New York and Hatton W. Sumners of Texas occasionally blocked administration proposals. So did "Cotton Ed" Smith, Glass, and Harrison in the Senate. But these men were counterbalanced by such liberal chairmen as Senators Black, Wagner, and Elbert D. Thomas of Utah and Representatives Sam Rayburn of Texas, Adolph J. Sabath of Illinois, and Sol Bloom of New York. More often than not, committee chairmen cooperated with the administration.

Roosevelt's congressional troubles after 1936 stemmed not so much from uncooperative committee chairmen as from more widespread opposition to his programs. In the House, for example, his three most painful defeats on domestic legislation from 1937 through 1939 were the recommittal of the fair labor standards bill in 1937, the recommittal of executive reorganization in 1938, and the defeat of his lending program in 1939. All three came at the hands of the entire House. In the Senate he lost three successive battles for increased relief expenditures in 1939, and each time the reason was the adverse vote of the entire Senate. It is too easy—and too misleading—to blame the seniority rule for Roosevelt's congressional problems.

At first glance it would appear that the conservative bloc was composed of Republicans and southern Democrats, but such was not always the case. It is undeniable that Republicans, especially in the House, opposed the administration with remarkable solidarity after 1936, but the stance of southerners was less easy to determine. Occasionally, it seemed that Cox and Bailey were representative southern spokesmen. For instance, when the House recommitted the fair labor standards bill by a vote of 216–198 in December 1937, 81 of the 99 southern Democrats voted for recommittal, as opposed to but 51 of the remaining 230 Democrats in the House. And when the Senate in August 1937 adopted, 44–39, the so-called Byrd amendment aimed at damaging the Wagner housing bill, 10 of the 22 southern Democrats supported the amendment, while only 19 of the remaining 54 Senate Democrats were with the majority.

Two factors dispel much of this seeming clarity. First, voting alignments depended upon the issue. The labor bill, by proposing to destroy southern competitive wage advantages, upset southerners of all persuasions. Walter Lippmann, in fact, called the bill "sectional legislation disguised as humanitarian reform." On other crucial votes in the House, however, such as those which recommitted reorganization in 1938 and defeated the death sentence provision of the utility holding company bill in 1935, representatives from the South divided as did Democrats from other sections. Secondly, southerners were seldom united. As V. O. Key put it, "while individual southern Senators may frequently vote with the Republicans, a majority rarely does; and when it does, the group as a whole is badly split more than half the time." The New Deal Congress had their Glasses and Baileys, but they also had their Blacks and Rayburns. Except on race legislation, southern congressmen were never "solid."

Three things, nonetheless, were generally true of the congressional conservatives as a group. First of all, most of the vocal conservatives came from safe states or districts. The Glass-Byrd machine in Virginia, for instance, was able not only to keep veterans like Glass in the Senate but to send new conservatives to the House throughout the period. With all his power and prestige Roosevelt was too often unable to influence congressional nominations; the result was the nomination and election of many conservative Democrats during the New Deal years. In 1935 alone, new Senate Democrats included Rush D. Holt of West Virginia, Gerry of Rhode Island, and Burke of Nebraska, all of whom were soon to become staunch foes of the New Deal. That such men could be nominated in a year of unusually restive and liberal politics indicates both the limitations of presidential political power and the continuing strength of local political organizations.

Second, most of the effective Democratic conservatives, though not committee chairmen, were ranking or near-ranking members of important committees. Cox was the most strategically placed of these men, but there were several others. In the House they included Martin Dies, Jr. of Texas on the Rules Committee and Clifton A. Woodrum of Virginia on appropriations. In the Senate Bailey, George, William H. King of Utah, and many others comprised this group. Those conservative Democrats without responsibility, it seemed, often felt free to act as they pleased.

Thirdly, most conservative congressmen after 1936 were from rural districts or states. Too much should not be made of this fact: so, too, were many liberals. There were also many conservative Democrats from urbanized states, such as Senators Gerry of Rhode Island and Millard E. Tydings of Maryland. The nature of opposition to administration programs depended greatly upon the type of issue: New Deal farm bills, for example, often aroused considerable hostility among urban congressmen. Generally, however, rural congressmen voted against New Deal programs more consistently than did urban congressmen. The coalition was composed not so much of Republicans and southern Democrats as of Republicans and rural Democrats; urban southerners were often more favorably disposed to administration programs than their rural counterparts.

The existence of this urban-rural split upon many economic issues after 1936 was indisputable. Democratic votes in the House against administration measures in the 1937–1939 period were: investigation of sit-downs, 82 percent rural; recommit fair labor standards, 74 percent rural; investigate National Labor Relations Board, 77 percent rural; lending bill, 69 percent rural; and housing bill, 83 percent rural. Since the percentage of Democrats who represented rural districts was 54 in 1937 and 57 in 1939, it is clear that the Democratic opposition on these bills was heavily rural in character.

It is difficult to say that any given issue or year "created" the conservative group. Rather, different groups of inherently conservative men switched at different times from unhappy allegiance to the New Deal to open hostility. In most cases these men changed their positions because they discovered that they could oppose the administration without fear of electoral extinction. The state of the President's prestige, as much as the nature of his program, determined the kind of reception he received on Capitol Hill.

Roosevelt's great popularity before 1937 was undeniable. Even Republicans bowed before it. "There can be no doubt," wrote one Republican senator in 1933, "that at the moment the President has an extraordinary support throughout the country and is able to do with the Congress as he wills. I suppose prudence dictates that one should not attempt to swim against the tide." Thus, Republicans through 1936 split sharply on final votes on major pieces of legislation. Cautious men like Vandenberg supported part of the administration program; others, not so astute, lost in 1934 or 1936. Many congressmen of both parties were unhappy with the New Deal well before 1937, but few dared to publicize their discontent with adverse votes.

Nevertheless, Democratic disaffection in Congress grew ominously as early as 1935. In that year the House three times defeated the death sentence clause of the utility holding company bill, and in the Senate the "wealth tax" bill antagonized not only the Democratic irreconcilables but also moderates like Harrison and Byrnes. Roosevelt's success with his 1935 Congress was indeed remarkable, but it cost him some political capital. Even if he had not thrown Congress into turmoil in 1937 with his court reform plan, he probably would have had great difficulty with the many congressmen who had already chafed at his relentless leadership and who considered the reform era at an end.

The court reform plan, presented in February 1937, provided these fractious congressmen with the ideal occasion for open rebellion. While

Harrison and some other leaders remained outwardly loyal, the plan caused many formerly dependable Democrats to oppose the President openly. In addition, it united progressive and conservative Republicans, created intense personal rancor, and left all but the "100 percent New Dealers" suspicious of the President's motives. Above all, it emboldened congressmen who had not dared speak out before.

Other events after 1936 increased congressional courage. The wave of sit-down strikes in 1937 caused many to blame the New Deal for the growth of labor "radicalism." The recession of 1937–1938 convinced others that the New Deal had failed. The President's plan to reorganize the executive branch, a divisive issue in 1938, provided another occasion for successful coalition effort. And Roosevelt's unsuccessful attempt to purge his conservative opponents in 1938 encouraged disenchanted congressmen to become still more outspoken.

The election of 1938 solidified this trend. Republicans gained 80 seats in the House and 8 in the Senate, increasing their numbers to 169 and 23 respectively. Since unreliable Democrats already numbered some 40 in the House and 20 in the Senate, the administration faced a divided Congress before the session began. The President's achievements in 1939 were negligible; the domestic New Deal, for all intents and purposes, made no more striking gains.

These external events, however, were not the only causes of Roosevelt's difficulties, nor should the President receive all the blame for the change. Two other developments—the changing nature of the liberal coalition and improved economic conditions—also contributed materially to the growth of congressional conservatism after 1936.

Roosevelt's liberal coalition had changed dramatically from the largely southern-western alliance of 1932 to a congeries of politically conscious pressure groups. Composed of labor unions, underprivileged ethnic groups, Negroes, and relief recipients, this aggregation was essentially northern-urban in character. Enormously encouraged by the 1936 election, these groups pressed relentlessly for their objectives in ensuing sessions, often without Roosevelt's approval. The sit-downs, for instance, were not Roosevelt's idea, and he refused to take sides in the matter. Similarly, relief workers and Democratic mayors badgered the President for higher relief expenditures than he was willing to seek. The fair labor standards bill, criticized by conservative southerners, faced even more serious opposition from AFL spokesmen fearful of government interference with collective bargaining. The President did not press either for housing or antilynching legislation, but liberal congressmen insisted upon introducing them, and bitter struggles ensued. Except for the court plan, unquestionably a major presidential blunder, Roosevelt made few tactically serious errors after 1936. But the well organized elements of his predominantly northern-urban coalition were demanding more aid at the same time that many other congressmen, not so dependent upon these elements for political survival, were convinced of the need for retrenchment. And many rural congressmen, while friendly to much of the New Deal, believed these urban elements were preempting funds or favors which might otherwise have benefited rural areas. The result was a largely urban-rural split within the unwieldy coalition which was the Democratic party. No amount of presidential flattery could have prevented it.

It is also worth noting that the changed emphasis on the New Deal in 1935—such as it was—was not nearly so disturbing to many congressmen as the pressure generated by urban elements in 1937. Southerners, Harrison and Byrnes for instance, had in 1935 approved social security, banking reform, and moderate tax reform. And men like Cox, hostile to abuses by private utilities, had even found it possible to vote for the death sentence clause of the utility bill. But none of these men favored the more urban liberalism espoused by liberal congressmen in 1937–1939. Prior to 1936 the economic emergency, together with the administration's emphasis upon measures benefiting all areas of the nation, had temporarily obscured the urban-rural fissures so apparent in the Democratic party in the 1920s. But when the urban wing of the party, awakened and dominant, sought to gain beneficial legislation in 1937–1939, the split reappeared to plague the New Deal and subsequent liberal administrations.

Improved economic conditions were of great significance to this split, for if one examines executive-congressional relations in the twentieth century, he finds that congressmen were never so tractable as in the desperate years from 1933 through 1935. Without detracting from Roosevelt's able congressional leadership in these years, it is certain that the emergency provided ideal conditions for the success of his program in Congress. Practically every congressman, besieged for relief by his constituents, responded with alacrity to the President's activist leadership. By 1937 this sense of crisis had diminished. Thus many of the same moderate congressmen who had so gratefully supported the administration through 1935 became unreliable two and three years later. And the recession of 1937–1938, far from reviving this sense of crisis, served instead to suggest that Roosevelt was not the magician he had previously seemed to be. Indeed, to many hostile congressmen the period was the "Roosevelt recession." In a sense, the economic state of the nation was the President's greatest ally before 1936, his greatest adversary thereafter.

The sit-down strikes, the defeat of the court plan and the purge, and the recession gave considerable confidence to many inherently conservative congressmen who had already been uneasy or restive with the

New Deal in 1935–1936. The beginning of effective conservative opposition in Congress, accordingly, can be set in 1937. But the roots stemmed at least to 1935, and in retrospect it seems that the court plan merely hastened the development of an inevitable division among the disparate elements of the dominant Democratic party.

One major problem remains: how did the conservative bloc function as a group? Was it a well organized conspiracy, or was it simply a loose combination of the moment?

At a glance, the coalition appears to have been well organized. In the Senate fight against the court plan, Burton K. Wheeler of Montana led a bipartisan team against the President. Senators from both parties not only cooperated but met from time to time in private homes to plan joint strategy. And Republicans agreed to keep quiet lest their partisan charges antagonize moderate Democrats. As Vandenberg admitted later, there was a "bipartisan high command. . . . Only a coalition could succeed—a preponderantly Democratic coalition. This was frankly recognized. There was no secret about it. . . . Republicans voluntarily subordinated themselves and withdrew to the reserve lines. . . ."

Many of the senators who opposed the court plan remained at odds with the administration in the 1938 and 1939 sessions, and Wheeler led quite similar blocs against executive reorganization. And in the House, 1937 was the year when the conservative bloc in the Rules Committee first began to operate against the administration, refusing three times between August 1937 and May 1938 to report out the fair labor standards bill. Unquestionably, conservatives in both houses developed networks of personal communications across party lines in 1937 and 1938. On crucial roll call votes it was safe to predict that an all but unanimous group of Republicans in both houses would be joined by at least 20 Democrats in the Senate and from 40 to 110 in the House.

Such evidence, however, does not prove the existence of a coordinated group functioning as a team on all—or even most—issues. Wheeler, for example, was not so reactionary as liberals insisted, and he continued after 1937 to back many administration relief, labor, and farm bills. Conversely, Harrison and Byrnes remained loyal to the administration during both the court and reorganization battles, while stridently opposing the fair labor standards bill, increased spending for relief, and the undistributed profits tax. And foreign policy questions created completely different alignments.

That the type of issue determined the composition of the conservative bloc was especially clear in the 1939 session. In the Senate, conservative alliances defeated the administration in struggles over relief spending in January and temporarily over reorganization in March. The crucial votes were 47–46 and 45–44 respectively. On both occasions Republicans voted solidly against the administration; of the 23 in the Senate, 20 voted against relief and 22 against reorganization. Of the 69 Democrats, 26 opposed relief and 21 reorganization. But the bloc was not monolithic. Eleven of the 26 Democrats against the relief bill supported the President on reorganization; 7 Democrats who had backed the President on relief deserted him on reorganization. A conservative nucleus of 20 Republicans and 15 Democrats opposed the administration on both bills. The others shifted in and out at will. For partisan reasons Republicans were remarkably united, but conservative Democrats were seldom able to work together in either house.

Furthermore, even the predictable core of very conservative Democrats ordinarily voted with Republicans because there was a meeting of the minds, not because they had conferred secretly with them in advance of crucial votes. The fate which befell the one serious effort in the direction of long-range conservative planning revealed the insuperable problems involved in developing such bipartisan agreement. This effort occurred in the fall of 1937.

After the Supreme Court's "switch in time that saved nine" in the spring of 1937, Bailey realized that the Senate must replace the court as the bulwark of conservative strength in the country, and he became anxious to form a more cohesive bloc against the New Deal. "What we have to do," he wrote Byrd in September, "is to preserve, if we can, the Democratic Party against his [Roosevelt's] efforts to make it the Roosevelt Party. But above this we must place the preservation of Constitutional Representative Government. We must frame a policy and maintain it—and this must be done in the next Congress. We must ascertain on whom we may rely—get them together and make our battle, win or lose."

When Bailey and his fellow conservatives returned for a special session in November they determined to put their coalition into effect. On December 2 ten conservative Democrats and two Republicans feasted on quail in a Senate dining room and laid plans for the future. As Vandenberg, one of the participants, put it privately, the group "informally resolved upon attempting a coalition statement to the country." For the next ten days this group, led by Vandenberg, Bailey, and Gerry, worked diligently at consulting conservative colleagues and trying to draft a statement of principles. They sought to present Roosevelt with a show of bipartisan strength and to persuade him to adopt a program more conciliatory to business. But their plan was also "replete with the possibility of open coalition upon the floor of the Senate." Senators who subscribed to the principles enunciated in the statement—broad phrases covering tax, spending, and labor policy—were expected to vote accordingly when these issues arose in subsequent congressional sessions.

Bailey's effort failed dismally. To begin with, moderately conservative Democrats like Harrison and Byrnes refused to participate. As southerners they did not relish formal associations with Republicans, nor did they wish to antagonize the President for no good purpose. Others naturally preferred to maintain their freedom of action in the future. And still others feared that such a challenge would drive Roosevelt, then pursuing an uncertain course in dealing with the recession, into the hands of the spenders. Before Bailey and his cohorts had time to circulate the finished document, McNary secured a copy and gave it to the press, which published it without delay on December 16. The surprised conservatives fumed silently. "Premature publicity—*thanks to treachery*—ended the episode," Vandenberg noted in his scrapbook. "The next time we want to plan a patriotically dramatic contribution to the welfare of the country, we shall let no one in who is not *tried and true*." Bailey added that the "premature publicity was brought about wholly because this man [McNary] and some of his associates took a partisan view that the declaration of principles would help the Democratic cause and hurt the Republican cause." As both men realized, McNary's action ended the frail hopes for a resounding, well-timed demonstration of conservative strength.

McNary's thinking was indeed partly partisan. At that time he was conferring with Alfred M. Landon, Frank Knox, Republican leaders in the Capitol. Encouraged by Roosevelt's declining prestige, these men believed that Republicans could survive without seeking coalitions with conservative Democrats. The idea of a bipartisan statement of conservatism seemed to them considerably less attractive than it did to Vandenberg. Yet McNary's chief motivation was ideological; like other progressive Republicans, he frankly disagreed with the views of the conservatives involved. If Republicans associated with men like Bailey, he believed, they would give the GOP an even more reactionary coloring than it already wore. McNary's "treachery" was evidence both of the power of partisanship and of the divisions within his party.

Neither Bailey nor his fellow conservatives again pressed seriously for the plan. Republicans became increasingly partisan, driving Democrats of all persuasions into uneasy unity for the coming campaign. Despite the attempted purges which followed, both Republicans and Democrats in the ensuing primaries acted along partisan rather than conservative-liberal lines, and the flimsy chances for bipartisan conservative cooperation in the Senate faded quickly. Conservatives continued to vote together in 1938 and 1939 if there was a meeting of the minds; otherwise, as Bailey had feared, they voted apart. As a newsman close to the scene explained at the close of the 1939 session,

> in both houses, when a pro- and anti-New Deal issue is squarely presented, a shifting population of conservative Democrats can be counted upon to join the Republicans to vote against the President. The arrange-

ment is not formal. There is nothing calculated about it, except the Republican strategy originated . . . by McNary of refraining from arousing the Democrats' partisan feelings by inflammatory oratory.

A conservative bipartisan bloc was often able by 1939 to block major legislative extensions of the New Deal. But it was not united, and it followed no blueprint. Conservative congressmen, representing widely differing states and districts, faced widely differing political exigencies. They refused to be chained to a "conspiracy." More important, most congressmen were first of all partisans. For all but a few the party organizations of their constituencies were the chief facts of their political careers, and few of these organizations, in 1937 or at any time, wished bipartisanship to operate for long.

20

A Demographic Profile
of the Mexican Immigration
to the United States, 1910–1950

JOSE HERNANDEZ ALVAREZ

The word *immigration* brings to mind steamships, Ellis Island, tenement houses in eastern and midwestern cities, hard labor in mines, mills, and factories, and the nostalgia of the somewhat remote late nineteenth and twentieth centuries. Immigration should also suggest Mexican origins, decrepit buses, inadequate housing in the Southwest, hard labor on farms and railroads, all part of the brutal present or not so distant past. Through census data, José Hernández Alvarez has studied the largely neglected population movement that started in the 1920s and has provided precise information about Mexican migrants to the United States.

During the first half of the present century, about one million Mexicans were involved in a singular instance of large scale entry into the United States. Arriving just before the influx of foreigners abated sharply, they provide an example of recent immigration. In contrast to the experience of other groups entering one or more generations before, Mexican settlement occurred during the drastic changes caused by rapid economic growth and depression. by two world wars and the nation's reorganization for modern living. Nor did the newcomers from the South follow

From *Journal of Inter-American Studies* 8 (1966):471–75, 484–96. These excerpts are reprinted by permission of the publisher, Sage Publications, Inc.

the traditional pattern of residence and occupation. Instead of locating in the densely urban and industrial Northeast of the United States, they flowed into rural areas in the Southwest, working in agriculture, railroad construction and related activities. Except for Canadian immigrants, the Mexicans were the only major immigrant group having relatively easy access to the home country by an overland route. Lastly, their distinctively Latin American culture had added novelty to history of immigration to the United States.

These unique features combine to provide an interesting and valuable opportunity for a demographic case study of issues such as geographic distribution, urbanization, language, education and occupational mobility. Moreover, the availability of census materials for decennial intervals from 1910 to 1950 facilitates longitudinal comparisons. It also aids in research concerning the evolution of the immigrant family structure. The Mexican group offers the advantage of having two clearly distinguishable generations during the period just mentioned. This situation permits the application of the developmental theory of family life to the entire population, thereby rendering the discovery of changes more meaningful. An approach of this kind appears to be in keeping with the general perspective of the following analysis. Our objective is to present a concise overview of as many demographic characteristics as possible, providing a single picture of the Mexican immigrant population which could serve as a point of departure for more detailed research.

GEOGRAPHIC DISPERSAL AND CONCENTRATION

In 1910 about two hundred thousand persons born in Mexico were living in the United States, mainly concentrated in the territories of Arizona and New Mexico. During the next twenty years the Mexican immigrant group increased by at least three times. By 1930, close to a million and a half persons were enumerated as born in Mexico or of Mexican parentage. At that time slightly less than 90 per cent were living in the states of Arizona, California, Colorado, New Mexico and Texas. This proportion remained approximately the same up to 1950. Clearly, the primary concentration of persons of Mexican descent has been and continues to be located in the states closest to the Mexican border. In the present article, for purposes of convenience, we have chosen to call this five-state area "the Southwest."

Notable variations occurred in the spatial distribution of Mexicans within the Southwest during the period under investigation. In general, the Mexican population of California and Colorado increased at least twice as rapidly as that of Texas and New Mexico. From 1920 to 1930, the average annual increase in California was 20.4 per cent and in Colorado 30.2 per cent. Meanwhile the average rate of increase in Texas was 7.6 yearly and a similar percentage was recorded in New Mexico. In Arizona, only a slight increase took place during the same decade. These differences are largely due to the current of internal migration among Mexicans already living in the states of Arizona, New Mexico and Texas. This movement reached westward to the Pacific Ocean and northward to the Rocky Mountain area.

From 1910 to 1950, geographic dispersal also occurred in a direction extending northeastward to Michigan. The balance of Mexicans living outside the Southwest settled along this line of migration. Although this group never comprised more than 10 per cent of the national total, their rates of increase were considerably higher than those in California and Colorado. The sudden appearance of Mexican immigrants in Illinois, Indiana, Kansas and Michigan principally represented a response to the availability of employment. About 50 per cent of the Midwest settlers found jobs in manufacturing industries which were expanding rapidly in Chicago, Detroit and Gary. Similarly, opportunities in sugar beet farming and railroad construction, repair and maintenance attracted Mexicans to the rural areas of the states mentioned.

At first glance, one might expect a process of replacement in the fan of settlement. According to this hypothesis, earlier immigrants would tend to move away from traditional areas of concentration. Their experience and knowledge of the receiving nation would provide an aid and incentive for pioneering new settlements. Meanwhile, the vacancies in employment and housing left by this group would await later newcomers.

The data provided by the 1930 Census appear to disprove this conjecture. In the *Reports on Population*, replies to the question concerning year of immigration were divided into chronological groups. This procedure permits an analysis of the rates of immigrants arriving in a given period of time according to their place of residence in 1930 (Table I). Among persons immigrating from 1925 to 1930 a considerably higher rate settled in the Midwest than among those who entered before 1910. Within the Southwest the rates for Arizona, New Mexico and Texas generally decline from 1911 to 1930, while successively higher rates appear in California and Colorado. About a third of the latest arrivals were residents of California, the largest proportion claimed by any state. This stands in striking contrast to the group entering the United States before 1900, 65 per cent of whom were living in Texas in 1930.

Several suggestions could be made in order to explain the tendency of earlier immigrants to remain in Arizona, New Mexico and Texas while late arrivals went through and beyond these states. In general, economic opportunities outside traditional centers of concentration did not develop until the 1920's. Persons who entered the United States during this decade may have been faced with a saturation of opportunities in the original areas of settlement. They were younger and may have been attracted by the possibility of living elsewhere. These factors seem to be associated with the recruitment of Mexican laborers in cities such as San Antonio and El Paso for work outside Texas. The migration "tunnel" seems to have been reinforced by the diffusion of knowledge in Mexico concerning job opportunities in the Midwest and in California and Colorado. One of the primary vehicles of this communication was the labor contractor who traveled through Mexico seeking workers.

Recruitment of Mexican workers was almost exclusively for jobs which would relegate them to life in rural areas: agriculture, mining and railroad work. On the basis of the pattern of settlement just described one might infer that later immigrants became residents of rural areas, whereas the vast majority of those entering the United States at the turn of the century were urban dwellers. According to the statistics presented in Table I, both of these assumptions seem incorrect.

TABLE 1   Rates of Immigration in Given Periods of Time for the Foreign-Born Mexican Population, by Residence in Selected States, 1930 (States for which figures are presented are those having a foreign-born Mexican population of 5,000 or more in 1930.)

	Mexican 1900 or Earlier	Foreign-Born: 1901– 1910	1911– 1914	Rate Arriving in 1915– 1919	1920– 1924	1925– 1930	Total 1930
United States	100.0	100.0	100.0	100.0	100.0	100.0	100.0
Urban	52.3	56.8	59.8	58.5	57.2	60.1	57.6
Rural	47.7	43.2	40.2	41.5	42.8	39.9	42.5
Arizona	9.3	7.4	6.3	8.0	8.1	7.6	7.8
California	18.3	30.9	25.7	33.4	35.4	32.2	31.0
Colorado	0.9	1.8	1.9	2.7	2.3	1.4	2.1
New Mexico	3.9	2.9	2.7	2.6	2.6	1.5	2.6
Texas	64.5	49.3	55.1	41.2	36.1	30.4	42.6
Illinois	0.4	1.3	1.5	2.7	3.8	7.1	3.3
Indiana	0.1	0.4	0.5	0.7	1.6	3.0	1.2
Kansas	0.2	1.3	1.3	2.1	1.7	2.4	1.8
Michigan	0.3	0.6	0.9	1.1	1.9	3.2	1.5
All other States	2.1	4.1	4.0	5.4	6.7	10.3	6.1

For purposes of analysis, the category of time "unknown" has been eliminated. Due to the rounding of decimals, rates do not total 100.0 in every case.

At one extreme, the least urban were persons immigrating before 1900, while the highest proportion of city residents occurred among the latest newcomers, those who arrived from 1925 to 1930. It must be noted, however, that the difference is not great; a range of only 7.8 per cent appears among the various time intervals according to urban or rural residence in 1930. As a consistent pattern, slightly more Mexicans settled in urban areas and the urban immigrant population contained a slightly greater proportion of recent arrivals than the rural counterpart.

During the era of economic depression, from 1930 to 1940, decreases in the number of persons of Mexican birth or descent were recorded throughout the United States. The demand for immigrant labor had virtually ceased and at the beginning of this decade the entry of Mexicans diminished sharply. As hard times continued, a substantial return migration occurred, receiving an added impulse as a result of mechanical innovations in agricultural industries. This reverse movement seems to have ended after 1940; however, large-scale immigration to the United States has never been renewed. Hence, Mexicans who were residents of the United States in 1950 were largely those comprising the core that remained during the depression years and their children.

Perhaps the most important change in the geographic distribution of Mexicans in the United States from 1930 to 1950 was rapid and substantial urbanization. As indicated in Table I, immigrants arriving from 1900 to 1930 increasingly settled in urban areas; by 1930, 57.5 per cent of the national total were living in cities. This trend continued and became strong during World War II and the early postwar years. As a result, in 1950 more than 70 per cent of the Mexican immigrant population and their children were classified as urban dwellers. Thus, as the nationality group under study consolidated its establishment in the United States, surviving a reverse migration and producing a second generation, it also shifted away from a rural way of life.

. . . THE MEXICAN FAMILY LIFE CYCLE

.   .   .

In general, most Mexican immigrant families were formed from 1920 to 1940. The childbirth which accompanied this formation led to the emergence of the second generation, native born persons who were becoming adults and leaving the family of orientation by 1950. This implies that the majority of the immigrants' children were reared during the economic depression of the 1930's and the second World War. As a result, both generations experienced exceedingly trying times during the development of the family life cycle. Added to the historical events just mentioned, many Mexican families were displaced during their period of childrearing and ultimately relocated in large metropolitan areas such as Los Angeles. Thus, a change from rural to urban living accompanied the process of assimilation and integration to the society of the host country.

Certain segments of the Mexican immigrant population seem to have had a slightly different experience. Family formation and development took place later in the Midwest and, to some extent, in California and urban places in general. In this instance, many adolescents appeared among the second generation in 1950, indicating a continuation of child-rearing during the 1940's. Most Mexican immigrants appear to have married other Mexican immigrants. However, in rural areas throughout the United States and the urban Midwest many families were formed with a mother from another nationality group. Thus, several types of families could be distinguished; for example, the Mexican immigrant family with average development (the Southwest in general); the immigrant family with late development (urban California) and the mixed immigrant-other family with still later development (the Midwest).

LANGUAGE AND EDUCATION

In 1930, 55 per cent of the Mexican immigrant population could not speak English. Compared with rates among other nationality groups, this percentage was extraordinarily high. However, a comparison of this nature must be qualified by noting that almost all the other immigrant groups arrived before the Mexican immigrant had begun. Had a tabulation been made two or three decades before, probably data similar to the Mexican statistics of 1930 would have been gathered among Poles, Italians and Russians. Even in 1930, local concentrations of other immigrants had relatively high rates of inability to speak English. Twenty per cent of the foreign-born Italian population of Rhode Island could not speak English. Slightly lower measures were recorded among French-Canadians in Maine, the Polish in the Midwest, the Finns in Michigan and Minnesota and the Japanese living in the far west.

The language data compiled in 1930 reveal important geographic variations among Mexican immigrants. The highest rates of inability to speak English (between 57.6 and 66.2 per cent) correspond to long-established settlements: Arizona, New Mexico and Texas. This is not surprising, in view of the frequent use of Spanish in many communities located in these states. The same measure was lower in California and Colorado; in the Midwest rates varied from 43.8 to 49.5 per cent. Probably, immigrants who ventured forth to new areas found that knowledge of English was an important asset and the inability to communicate with the larger society a great liability. Secondly, higher rates of intermarriage with other nationality groups outside the Southwest may have contributed to a lowering of the proportion of persons unable to speak English.

Apart from the issue of regional variations, perhaps the most important implication of high rates of inability to speak English for Mexican family life is the fact that they coincided with an economic depression. While members of the second generation were being reared in the 1930's, their parents probably had extraordinary difficulties finding and keeping employment. Inability to speak English undoubtedly increased this hardship. Given these circumstances, we can assume that the language barrier represented a major impelling force for returning to Mexico. This would seem to be particularly true of late immigrants, many of whom may not have been established by the onset of hard times.

According to the 1940 Census, relatively few Mexican immigrants raised their children with English as the prevailing language at home. This implies that, in contrast to the experience of other nationality groups, the mother language largely remained the medium of expression between generations. Therefore we could expect a different set of sociological consequences affecting the parent-child relationship as a result of the use of the host country's language. Unfortunately, data concerning bilingualism are not available; these statistics might qualify and illuminate the issue of language. The Census definition, "the principal language spoken in the home of the person in his earliest childhood" does not preclude the possibility of learning English, nor the total loss of the nationality tongue.

In addition to the difficulty concerning bilingualism, estimates of variations in the use of English as a mother tongue according to sex, urban-rural residence, regions, divisions and states are liable to a large degree of error: no population base by nationality was given for the detailed analysis of mother languages in the 1940 Census. Hence, we do not know how many persons born in Mexico or of Mexican parentage were included in the total whose mother tongue was Spanish in a given location. Within these limitations, we find that 718,980 native-born persons of native parentage were enumerated as having had Spanish as a mother tongue. Approximately 55 per cent were living in rural areas, and 88 per cent were concentrated in the South and West. The coincidence of urban-rural and regional characteristics seems to indicate that a large measure of this group consisted of third generation Mexican-Americans and persons of Mexican descent in succeeding generations. Hence, there is some statistical basis for assuming that the use of Spanish as a means of communication is not limited to the second generation.

More impressionistic evidence, such as the continuing use of Spanish in public services (radio broadcasting stations, newspapers and the like) seems to indicate that the mother language has remained an important, if not the primary medium of expression within the Mexican community. It is also likely that failure to speak English effectively has had serious implications for the education of the Mexican nationality group outside those areas where an adequate bilingual school system is available. In order to evaluate the significance of this relation, it seems important to review the scholastic achievement data for the close of the period under study.

According to the 1950 Census, about half of the foreign-born Mexican male population of the United States, fourteen years of age or older had not reached the fourth grade of elementary school. The median years of school completed varied considerably by region, urban-rural residence and age. The lowest medians correspond to immigrants forty-five years of age and older, living in rural farm areas. By way of contrast, among younger immigrants in Los Angeles, more than half had completed eight years of elementary school, the number generally considered the equivalent of a primary education in the United States.

Age differentials were not so sharply defined in the second generation and their scholastic achievement was clearly greater than that of the first. However, a considerable difference appears between city and farm and between West and South. In urban areas throughout the United States about half of the native-born had at least an elementary school education. By way of contrast, in the rural areas of the South (principally Texas), 22 per cent of the second generation had never attended school. While much lower than its rural counterpart, the measure of 10 per cent with no schooling in Southern cities is notably higher than the measure of 3 per cent in the urban areas of the West. Hence, although as a group the second generation had surpassed the first in scholastic achievement, important segments remained at low educational levels.

At mid-century the immigrants' children who were reaching adulthood and forming families encountered a highly competitive labor market and a rapid upgrading of educational requirements for employment. Whereas their parents may have been able to earn a living with an elementary schooling, it now became important to obtain a high-school degree and, if possible, a college or university education. The educational attainment of the second generation was clearly an advance over the record for Mexican immigrants and compared favorably with that of ethnic groups with Spanish surname (Table V). However, compared with the total United States population and the second generation of other nationality groups, the Mexican-Americans scored exceedingly low. Thus, a crucial element in the complex of social and economic

TABLE V   United States Population by Educational Attainment: Selected Percent Distributions for Persons 25 Years Old and Over, 1950

U. S. Population, Educational Attainment
Persons 25 Years Old and Over, 1950

Male, Percent	Total U.S. Population	Native-Born of Foreign or Mixed Parentage		Persons with Spanish Surname
		Mexican	Other	
Reaching 4th Yr.				
High School	17.6	8.9	20.4	7.2
1–3 Yr. College	6.8	2.7	7.2	2.2
4th Yr. College	7.1	1.3	8.1	1.4
Female, Percent				
Reaching 4th Yr.				
High School	22.5	9.5	25.8	8.4
1–3 Yr. College	7.5	1.6	6.9	1.8
4th Yr. College	5.0	0.9	4.6	1.1

handicaps which beset them in the competition for employment was an unfavorable level of training. The fact that the second generation of other nationality groups scored higher than the national total seems to provide evidence that the retention of Spanish as the only or predominant language among Mexicans seriously affected their educational as well as their economic life chances.

OCCUPATIONAL AND ECONOMIC SITUATION

In order to clarify the implications of the disadvantage just described it seems important to review briefly some of the economic and employment data available for the period under investigation. The census taken in 1930 provided data in regard to the occupational distribution of the entire Mexican ethnic group, including the third and succeeding generations (Table VI). These statistics indicate that most male workers of Mexican birth or ancestry were employed in the same occupations which had been an influential factor in the pattern and chronology of settlement of the first generation. Throughout the United States, agriculture, manufacturing and transportation (principally railroad work) were the leading types of employment. Mining, trade and domestic service proved to be residual classifications, while very few Mexicans were employed in public services and as clerical and professional personnel.

TABLE VI   United States Population of Mexican Birth or Descent: Gainfully Employed
Males, 10 Years of Age and Over, Percent Distribution by Occupation, for
the United States and Selected States: 1930

U. S. Mexican Population: Gainfully Employed Males
10 Years of Age and Over: 1930

Percent in All	Total	Ariz.	Calif.	Colo.	N. Mex.	Texas	Mid-west *
Occupations	100.0	100.0	100.0	100.0	100.0	100.0	100.0
Agriculture	40.5	28.8	37.0	54.5	49.0	50.9	2.1
(owners-tenants)	8.6	2.3	1.0	5.6	13.5	15.7	0.0
(laborers)	31.7	26.4	35.7	48.8	35.1	35.0	2.0
Forestry/Fishing	0.4	1.0	0.3	0.4	0.9	0.4	0.0
Mining	3.9	19.5	1.5	11.6	16.3	1.2	0.8
Manufacturing	26.0	24.1	31.1	14.3	13.3	21.4	53.7
(Building)	7.5	5.8	10.4	4.0	4.6	8.0	2.4
(Iron-Steel)	3.8	1.6	2.3	3.5	0.2	0.6	29.7
Transportation	16.3	13.2	16.8	14.8	12.4	11.0	35.6
(Railroad)	11.3	8.4	10.4	12.7	8.7	5.6	33.4
Trade	5.7	6.2	5.4	1.5	3.0	7.3	2.9
Public Service	0.9	1.6	0.8	0.4	0.8	1.1	0.4
Professional	1.2	1.3	1.6	0.5	1.1	1.1	0.8
Domestic	4.2	3.2	4.6	1.8	2.8	4.7	3.2
Clerical	0.9	1.1	0.9	0.2	0.4	0.9	0.7

* Midwest includes Illinois, Indiana, Kansas and Michigan.
Due to the rounding of decimals, rates do not total 100.0 in every case. Only the principal
subcategories are presented in parentheses; hence, they do not include the entire composition of
major occupational headings in the percent distribution.

While the pattern just described generally applies to the Southwest,
individual states show important variations. In Colorado, New Mexico
and Texas, about half or more of the Mexicans were engaged in farming, a proportion higher than that in the United States as a whole.
The balance of workers in Colorado also had typically rural jobs; approximately one quarter were employed in mining and railroad work.
By way of contrast, in Texas and New Mexico non-agricultural workers
tended to be working in characteristically urban occupations, such as
manufacturing and trade. Moreover, the proportion of farm owners
and tenants was significantly higher. These differences appear to be a
consequence of the relative length of establishment. In New Mexico,
Texas as well as Arizona the early newcomers and their children had
succeeded in obtaining property and in the peripheral services demanded
by the Mexican *colonia* itself, enterprises such as barber shops, grocery
stores and so forth.

The employment situation in California, a more recent settlement, differed strikingly from that of Colorado. There, many Mexicans were engaged in manufacturing, a typically urban occupation, and in construction. As a unit, these classification overshadowed agriculture and mining. California also had the highest percentage of transportation workers not employed in railroad jobs. Thus, the original area of Mexican settlement contained a mixture of many rural workers and an assortment of urban occupations. In areas characterized by late immigration, there were extremes: Colorado, with a very large proportion of farmers and miners, California with numerous urban workers.

In the Midwestern states (Illinois, Indiana, Kansas and Michigan) there were scarcely any farmers. Here, more than half of the employed labor force were engaged in manufacturing, with approximately 30 per cent working in iron and steel industries. Railroad construction, repair and maintenance constituted the only other major occupational category, taking up the balance of workers, except for a scattering of individuals in domestic service and trade. The social implications of this economic situation have been summarized as follows:

> Here the colony is strikingly similar to that of the typical "foreign settlement . . . Mexicans in Chicago and Detroit work with members of other nationality groups in highly mechanized industries. . . . The boundaries of the *colonia* are not sharply defined and, in some cases, have already disappeared.

It will be recalled that this area of settlement was also characterized by late immigration, a large proportion of urban residents, intermarriage with other nationality groups and the most extensive adoption of the English language. Although only one-tenth of the United States total, the Mexican community in the Midwest provides an interesting subject for further research. A unique phenomenon within the Mexican population of the United States, it also constitutes the only group which developed in an environment similar to that of the large majority of immigrants in the United States.

The consensus of writers on the subject of Mexican immigrants in the Southwest is that their occupations in 1930 were not highly paid. Unfortunately, the 1930 census did not provide information in regard to income in the two reports concerning the foreign stock; hence, it is difficult to gauge the economic standing of the Southwest communities accurately. In the census taken ten years later, statistics were gathered concerning the value and tenure of housing. In lieu of information about occupations and income, these data provide a secondary index of the economic situation at the close of the depression years.

In 1940, about two-thirds of the population of Mexican immigrants and their children were living in rented housing (Table VII). More

TABLE VII   United States Population of Mexican Stock According to Nativity and Parentage: Percent Distribution by Tenure, Value or Rent of Housing, for the United States and Los Angeles: 1940

U. S. Population of Mexican Stock, 1940 *

	United States			Los Angeles		
	Foreign-Born	Native-Born	Nativity Ratio	Foreign-Born	Native-Born	Nativity Ratio
Percent by Type of Housing						
Total	100.0	100.0	—	100.0	100.0	—
Rented	63.7	65.7	209.8	73.5	75.3	164.1
Owner-Occupied	29.4	31.2	215.6	20.8	20.7	159.0
No information	6.9	3.1	—	5.7	4.0	—
Percent by Monthly Rent						
Total	100.0	100.0	—	100.0	100.0	—
Less than $10.	57.0	61.2	224.4	6.7	5.8	143.0
$10. to $19.	30.1	28.7	199.5	53.4	55.3	170.2
$20. to $29.	9.5	7.8	173.1	29.6	32.0	177.6
$30. to $49.	2.8	1.9	140.0	9.2	6.1	108.5
$50. and over	0.5	0.3	147.3	1.0	0.5	103.8
Percent by Value of Owned House						
Total	100.0	100.0	—	100.0	100.0	—
Under $1,000.	67.4	69.9	223.7	14.5	20.8	226.4
$1,000–$1,999.	17.6	16.8	206.3	33.1	33.9	163.3
$2,000–$2,999.	7.6	6.7	190.6	24.8	22.7	145.6
$3,000–$4,999.	4.9	4.3	189.4	20.4	17.8	139.2
$5,000 and over	2.4	2.2	196.7	7.2	4.7	84.6

* Figures presented are for persons related to head of household renting or owning housing. Unrelated individuals were included in the group not reporting tenure and excluded from the rent and value tabulations. Persons not reporting rent or value of owned house were excluded from the respective percent distribution. The category, "native-born" includes only the native-born of foreign or mixed parentage, i.e., the second generation.
Due to the rounding of decimals, rates do not total 100.0 in every case.

than half of this segment paid less than ten dollars monthly rent. Assuming these figures as a point of departure, it is clear that the depression had kept or relegated the majority of Mexicans to life in some of the nation's poorest dwellings. The 1940 Census information for housing in the United States as a whole indicates that only a quarter of all tenant-occupied dwellings were renting for less than ten dollars; in urban and rural-nonfarm areas this measure was even smaller (17.4 per cent). Similarly, in the renting group of the Mexican population only 13 per cent spent twenty dollars a month or more for housing. By way of contrast, about half of the United States dwellings were rented for at least twenty dollars.

A similar situation appears in regard to the 30 per cent of the Mexican population who were living in owner-occupied housing. In this instance, about 70 per cent were living in structures valued at less than $1,000. Meanwhile, in the United States, more than 70 per cent of owner-occupied dwelling had values greater than $1,000, with approximately half of the homes in urban and rural-nonfarm areas valued at more than $3,000. Thus, whether owning or renting, the Mexicans appear to have had a fairly low economic standing. Perhaps the most comparable group was that of the Negroes in urban and rural-nonfarm areas of the South. About 70 per cent of the dwellings with tenants from this group were classified as renting for less than ten dollars monthly. Even in this instance, Negro rentals in metropolitan districts were substantially higher than the figure just given.

Within the Mexican nationality group generational and geographic variations appear in the data concerning housing in 1940. In general, succeedingly higher rent categories were associated with lower ratios of native to foreign born. This may imply that the second generation was experiencing greater economic hardships. Since many of the immigrants' children were beginning their own family cycle, this explanation is plausible. The same tendency in the statistics may also indicate differential birth rates among socio-economic classes of Mexican immigrants. Perhaps lower-class households were characterized by larger families. In view of the relatively young age of the second generation in certain areas of the United States, differentials in fertility seem equally plausible. These conjectures seem to merit more intensive research of a sociological nature; they bear a close relationship to the development of the Mexican family life cycle as well as to the problems which Mexicans have encountered in the United States.

Unfortunately, the 1940 Census reports provide only limited information for housing among Mexicans at regional and state levels. The data available for the city of Los Angeles follow the national configuration with two exceptions (Table VII). A higher percentage of the population, both native and foreign-born, lived in rented housing. The scale of monthly rents was one step higher than the national measures and a wider distribution prevailed in the values of owner-occupied dwellings. These findings indicate that the national statistics were probably lowered by the value of property in rural areas. They also seem to show

that Mexicans living in metropolitan districts had a slightly higher
social and economic standing than those living in other areas.

It will be recalled that during the decade, 1940 to 1950, many Mexicans moved to the urban centers of the United States. The occupational
data which were gathered after this migration clearly demonstrate the
effects of thé change. In 1950, slightly more than 67 per cent of employed males of both generations were living in cities. The types of
employment held by these workers as well as by rural dwellers have
been summarized in Table VIII. In urban areas, the employed labor

TABLE VIII   Occupational and Income Statistics for the United States Population of
Mexican Stock, by Nativity and Selected Age Categories, According to
Urban-rural Residence: 1950

U. S. Population of Mexican Stock, 1950

	Foreign-Born		Native-Born	
	Age 25 to 44	45 & over	14 to 24	25 to 44
Urban:				
Percent Distribution by				
Employed Males	100.0	100.0	100.0	100.0
Professionals	3.9	2.1	1.4	2.8
Managers	1.6	1.9	0.3	1.2
Clerical, Sales	6.7	5.4	11.3	8.9
Craftsmen, Foremen	17.6	16.2	10.8	19.6
Operatives	24.4	17.3	29.0	28.3
Service Workers	7.2	8.2	8.5	6.6
Laborers	21.5	30.0	23.2	22.6
Other & No Information	17.1	18.9	15.4	9.9
Median Personal Income:	$1,824	$1,451	$915	$1,784
Rural:				
Percent Distribution by				
Employed Males	100.0	100.0	100.0	100.0
Farmers, Farm Managers	4.6	14.1	2.0	10.0
Laborers:				
Farm, unpaid	0.3	0.6	12.9	1.3
Farm, paid	69.7	49.3	30.3	40.7
Except Farm & Mine	9.1	15.2	10.1	15.9
Other & No Information	16.1	20.7	44.6	32.1
Median Personal Income:				
Farm	$ 868	$ 946	$502	$1,066
Nonfarm	$1,157	$1,152	$708	$1,327

Due to the rounding of decimals, rates do not total 100.0 in every case.

force was characteristically scattered among the seven major divisions of urban work. The largest concentrations were at the semi-skilled levels. However, a substantial percentage, about a quarter of each nativity and age group, was composed of white-collar workers, craftsmen and professionals. By way of contrast, the rural labor force was still largely concentrated in the category of farm laborers. Even in this instance, many Mexicans were employed in jobs other than farm labor. Thus, a significant shift had occurred away from marginal employment and toward the consolidation of the nationality group in the United States social and economic life.

Important variations appear by nativity and age. In urban areas, the second generation shows a greater tendency toward clerical, sales and kindred occupations. There are also larger concentrations of native-born persons in the "operative" category. In rural areas, proportionately more immigrants were employed as farm laborers, whereas their children were more frequently engaged in occupations other than agriculture. A significant percentage of the native-born from ages 14 to 25 were working as unpaid family farm workers.

These occupational trends are reflected in the data concerning income. The newly emerging second generation and older immigrants earned considerably less than persons 25 to 44 years of age in both generations. Perhaps underemployment and marginal occupational activities account for this difference. In urban areas, the middle-aged native-born group received slightly less income than the same group in the first generation.

It should be noted, however, that even in the case of urban immigrants from ages 25 to 44, whose median income was higher than other age and nativity groups, the amount received was not great, compared with the earnings of the general population. At mid-century, more than half of the Mexican nationality group in the United States were earning less than $2,000 yearly. In some areas and age categories, annual income was considerably less. Clearly, consolidation had not involved extraordinary economic gains for the Mexican population as a whole.

SUMMARY AND CONCLUSIONS

In the present article, an endeavor has been made to present a concise overview of the demographic data available for Mexican immigrants to the United States during the first half of the present century. Within this context, several population patterns appear:

1. During the period of heaviest immigration (1910–1930), a geographic dispersal took place in the form of a fan of settlement, radiating

about the original center of migration. This movement was disproportionately westward, to California, where employment was available for non-skilled and semi-skilled workers on produce farms and in large cities such as Los Angeles. However, an important line of settlement extended Northeastward, primarily associated with railroad construction and urban industry. Although a primary factor in the early stages of the immigration was labor recruitment for agricultural enterprises, its influence seems to have diminished as the movement developed. Proportionately more late arrivals settled in urban areas than earlier immigrants. Later immigrants also had a greater tendency to venture forth beyond the Southwest. These trends are reflected in the regional differences which appear in the ratio of native to foreign-born. At the close of large-scale immigration in 1930, this measure was highest in urban areas and in new settlements outside of Texas, New Mexico and Arizona.

2. From 1930 on, Mexicans of both generations became involved in an extensive process of urbanization; by 1950 only 30 per cent remained living in rural areas. Proportionately more native-born persons migrated and their migration coincided with the development of the second generation in urban areas. As a result, the urban Mexican population in the early 1940's was characterized by a large number of second generation persons reaching adolescence and early adulthood. Another consequence was the emergence of the third generation beginning about 1950, the date which marks the virtual conclusion of the immigrant family life cycle and the start of the period of consolidation. Some urban centers, notably Chicago, were out of phase with the general urban pattern. In these areas, which were characterized by late immigration, the emergence of the second generation was a post-World War II phenomenon. Meanwhile, in rural areas, the pattern of generational change took place earlier and was marked by the loss of second generation persons by way of migration to cities.

3. These regional variations in the Mexican family life cycle must be considered in relation to differences in the male-female ratio. In general males exceeded females in the immigrant population; this disproportion was greater in rural areas, indicating a greater probability of a mixed generational or nationality marriage. A pattern similar to the general trend in rural areas appears in urban areas outside the Southwest, particularly in the Midwest. In this instance, intermarriage with other nationality groups seems to have been more common.

4. Large differences do not appear among generations in regard to the use of English as the primary language of communication. It would seem as if the language barrier was an important factor in the return migration of Mexicans which took place during the years of economic depression (1930–1940). Deficiencies in the use of English have also been genuine handicaps in the education of the Mexican community. Despite these difficulties the second generation clearly surpassed the

first in educational achievement. They did not, however, reach a favorable level for competition with others of their own age.

5. At the close of the era of large-scale immigration in 1930, the majority of Mexican workers in the Southwest were engaged in agriculture. By way of contrast, most Mexicans in the Central States were employed in manufacturing and urban industries. By 1950, substantial changes were evident, particularly in the Southwest, where an intensive process of urbanization had taken place. At mid-century, Mexicans were engaged in a large variety of occupations; about a quarter of the urban workers were craftsmen, professionals and white-collar workers. However, the largest concentrations were at the semi-skilled and non-skilled levels. Both housing and income data seem to indicate that this consolidation of the Mexican community into the United States population has not been attended by significant economic gains. Perhaps one of the most important factors in this limited development has been a comparatively low level of educational attainment.

21

Testing Capabilities:
The House of Commons
and the Senate

BRUCE M. RUSSETT

In his novel sociological approach to British-American relations, Bruce M. Russett virtually ignores policy pronouncements, official notes, personal correspondence, diplomatic conferences, and secret meetings. Rather, he enumerates a variety of links between the two nations from the 1890s to the 1950s in an effort to determine whether they grew closer or drifted apart. Russett has discovered that economic and personal ties in the cabinet and legislature of both countries declined; that trade in merchandise and services, tourist and student exchange, and scholarly attention weakened; that migration fell off, as did mail, telephone, and telegraph communications; and that average citizens became less friendly toward the other nation. This decline in "capabilities" was offset only in part by the fact that newspaper interest in the other country increased; that the exchange of magazines and films either grew or remained constant; that trade restrictions and investment rivalry declined; and that elite approval, as reflected in the Times of London and the New York Times, increased. If there is a connection between such links and actions of political leaders, the British-American alliance is a weakening chain. In this selection, Russett deals with this crucial point.

From Bruce M. Russett, Community and Contention: Britain and America in the Twentieth Century (Cambridge: The M.I.T. Press, 1963), pp. 144–61. Reprinted with omissions by permission of the publisher. © 1963 by the Massachusetts Institute of Technology.

One serious gap remains to be filled—we must show that the decline in capabilities is relevant to the making of political decisions. . . . We [have] assumed, sometimes on the basis of ambiguous evidence from other studies, that the various links under consideration did tend to make individuals responsive to the other nation's needs. There was no evidence, however, that in the specific case of Britain and America these ties made an important difference. Particularly in this case, where so many channels of mass communication exist, the presence or absence of a direct personal tie might not, to any significant degree, affect the likelihood that a particular decision-maker will be responsive. If not, it would be hard to prove that a decline in many gross links, such as the proportion of the two economies engaged in Anglo-American trade, would seriously affect actual responsiveness. We shall fill this gap by examining the personal backgrounds of individual members of the House of Commons and the Senate, and by comparing their votes or public statements on policy matters.

TIES AND RESPONSIVENESS: COMMONS

For the House of Commons, I chose to analyze public statements on policy rather than voting patterns. A member of Parliament virtually *never* votes against his party; and almost all votes, certainly all votes on issues even remotely associated with foreign affairs, are ones on which the party takes a stand. If he does defy the whips, he risks expulsion from the Parliamentary party, abandonment by his constituency organization, and defeat in the next general election. A single lapse may be overlooked, but repeated violations of discipline will almost certainly end his political career. Even "crossing the floor" to the other party offers little hope—no member has done so, and been returned at the next election, since 1945. This is not to imply that British parties are dictatorial and can march M.P.'s into their lobbies at will. There may be much pushing and hauling before a policy is settled, and the leadership must always beware of antagonizing the rank-and-file too seriously. But once policy is set and made a matter of public record, the M.P. who attacks it does so at his great peril. Thus, an examination of voting records would tell us little about a Member's true feelings.

Although an M.P. seldom votes against his leaders, he may abstain from voting somewhat more freely. Abstention is a recognized way of showing disagreement and is less likely to be punished by the leadership unless done repeatedly. Unfortunately, the recording of abstentions (or better, absences) at divisions shows no significant pattern. Abstention can show those who are really interested how one feels on a matter

—constituents, interest groups, or fellow Members can note one's abstention, and the leaders against whom one wants to protest will surely notice it. But even on an important measure there usually are many involuntary absences due to illness and business or personal demands for Members' presence elsewhere. One who merely reads the report of a division several years after the event, without knowing the reasons for a particular M.P.'s failure to be recorded, can rarely discern a significant pattern.

But it is not unusual for a Member, even though he may vote as directed in the end, to criticize a policy during debate, to ask a hostile question during question time, or to oppose the policy in a speech to his constituents or another group. He feels particularly free to do so during the period before an official party position has been adopted. For example, the Labour party directed its members to abstain on ratification of the 1954 London and Paris agreements to rearm a sovereign West Germany. Yet by the time the vote was taken, almost half the Labour M.P.'s had expressed an opinion either in Parliament, in letters to newspapers, or in outside speeches reported by a London or major provincial paper. In addition to providing information on Members' real feelings about matters which come up for division in the House, this kind of analysis also gives their views on a great number of issues that are never made a matter of record vote.

Much of this material, and practically all of it for the earlier years analyzed, came from the Parliamentary debates themselves. For 1938 and 1954 this could be supplemented by reports of debates at the annual party conferences, and by party publications which cull from newspapers and private speeches relevant statements—particularly those which might embarrass the opposition. These include the Tory *Hints for Speakers* and the *Liberal Magazine*. For 1954 there was also a superb collection of clippings at the Conservative and Unionist Central Office in London, containing a complete file of all reports of statements by M.P.'s in the London press, the most important country papers, and periodicals like the *New Statesman*. Though the files for a few deceased M.P.'s had been disposed of, there were still, in 1960, clippings on over 90 per cent of the 1954 members of the Commons. Because these supplementary sources were not available for 1890, and only in part for 1938, the following tables record far more expressions of opinion in 1954 than in the two earlier years combined.

The following types of issues or statements were considered as involved in Anglo-American relations.

1. Explicit criticism or approval of the other government or nation. (Criticism of individuals was not included unless it appeared that

the speaker meant it to apply to the government itself or to all or most members of the other nationality. Thus, criticism of President Eisenhower would probably be recorded as an attack on the United States, but remarks about Senator McCarthy might not be.)

2. A call for weaker or stronger ties with the other country.
3. Policies intended to increase mutual capabilities for responsiveness (whether by the creation of common institutions or by such means as eliminating restrictions on travel).
4. Ratification of a treaty signed by both governments.
5. A direct economic interest of the other country (tariffs or foreign aid).
6. Restrictions on the freedom of the government to conclude international agreements (the Bricker Amendment).
7. An expressed desire by the other government.

The various kinds of ties an M.P. might have with America were identified and classified. . . . There were economic ties of several sorts: "strong" personal ties of birth, education, marriage, or residence; and "weak" personal ties of travel, war service, and honors. In addition, I obtained data on membership in the Pilgrims of Great Britain in 1938 and 1954 and in the English-Speaking Union in 1954. These associations have the specific aim of promoting closer Anglo-American relations. I also had some supplementary sources on travel to America by Members of Parliament in 1954. Publicity material provided by the party headquarters frequently mentioned Members' travel experiences. In addition, I learned from several individuals about particular M.P.'s who had visited in the United States before 1954. Thus, quite a few . . . M.P.'s will be listed in the following tables as having personal ties to America. . . . Even so, there must have been a number with ties that could not be identified. The class of M.P.'s without ties means, in the following tables, merely those with no known links. Nevertheless, we shall see that there is a significant difference between the responsiveness of M.P.'s who we know have ties and those for whom there is no such evidence.

The information on attitudes is analyzed in two ways. First, every M.P. is classified either as responsive, unresponsive, or neutral—"neutral" meaning here that no policy statement on any of these issues was recorded. Second, it was useful to record the number of statements on separate issues made by each M.P. Thus, if a Member is recorded as responsive on one issue and unresponsive on two others, he is treated as, on balance, unresponsive, and a one is entered in the appropriate cell on the *left*-hand side of Table 1. But on the *right*-hand side of the table we list individual statements on issues, so a one is recorded under

TABLE 1   Percentage of M.P.'s With and Without American Ties Who Were Responsive,
Unresponsive, and Neutral, and of Responsive and Unresponsive Statements

1890

M.P.'s	Res.	Neut.	Unres.	Statements by M.P.'s	Res.	Unres.
U.S. Ties (N = 24)	8	88	4	U.S. Ties (N = 4)	50	50
No U.S. Ties (N = 118)	0	96	4	No U.S. Ties (N = 5)	0	100

1938

M.P.'s	Res.	Neut.	Unres.	Statements by M.P.'s	Res.	Unres.
U.S. Ties (N = 31)	16	81	3	U.S. Ties (N = 8)	88	12
No U.S. Ties (N = 101)	8	88	4	No U.S. Ties (N = 19)	79	21

1954

M.P.'s	Res.	Neut.	Unres.	Statements by M.P.'s	Res.	Unres.
U.S. Ties (N = 40)	20	60	20	U.S. Ties (N = 56)	48	52
No U.S. Ties (N = 89)	16	52	33	No U.S. Ties (N = 125)	26	74

All Years Combined

M.P.'s	Res.	Neut.	Unres.	Statements by M.P.'s	Res.	Unres.
U.S. Ties (N = 95)	16	74	10	U.S. Ties (N = 68)	53	47
No U.S. Ties (N = 308)	7	81	12	No U.S. Ties (N = 149)	32	68

"responsive" and a two under "unresponsive." The totals will not always add up to 100 per cent because figures have been rounded.

In every subsection of Table 1 the same pattern holds. M.P.'s with ties of any sort to the United States are more likely to speak up on matters affecting Anglo-American relations than are M.P.'s without ties. And when they speak, they are more likely to be responsive. This is true whether each particular M.P. is characterized as responsive or unresponsive, or whether the statements are examined individually. In many of the subsections of Table 1 there are not enough cases for the results to be statistically significant even at the .10 level, but they are so in the three with the greatest number of cases. For M.P.'s, the relationship between ties and responsiveness is significant at the .02 level in the table for all years combined. And for statements, the relationship is significant at well above the .01 level both for 1954 and for all years combined.

For 1954, there are enough cases to control for party affiliation. (See Table 2.) The results are the same. For individual M.P.'s, the

TABLE 2   Percentage of M.P.'s With and Without American Ties Who Were Responsive, Unresponsive, and Neutral, and of Responsive and Unresponsive Statements, With Party Affiliation Controlled, 1954 *

M.P.'s	Res.	Neut.	Unres.	Statements by M.P.'s	Res.	Unres.
Conservative (N = 64)	(16)	(67)	(17)	Conservative (N = 44)	(50)	(50)
U.S. Ties (N = 26)	19	65	16	U.S. Ties (N = 20)	70	30
No U.S. Ties (N = 38)	13	68	19	No U.S. Ties (N = 24)	33	67
Labour (N = 62)	(18)	(40)	(42)	Labour (N = 132)	(26)	(74)
U.S. Ties (N = 14)	21	50	29	U.S. Ties (N = 36)	36	64
No U.S. Ties (N = 48)	17	37	46	No U.S. Ties (N = 96)	22	78

* Three M.P.'s—two Liberals and one Irish Nationalist—are not included.

association of ties and responsiveness is as hypothesized, but not to a statistically significant degree. For the analysis by statements, however, the association is significant at the .01 level. The uniformity of direction identified in the two sections of the table and the high significance often found form as persuasive a proof as could be expected with these data.

Note that the association between party and responsiveness is also quite strong, since Conservatives are much more likely to be responsive than are Labourites. In the "M.P.'s" section of the table the relationship is significant at the .02 level; in the "Statements" part it is significant at .001, an extremely high level. The relationship between party and responsiveness, in fact, is stronger on both sides of the table than is that between ties to the United States and responsiveness. A Labour M.P. *with* a tie to America is less likely to indicate responsiveness than is a Conservative M.P. *without* an identifiable tie. We can only speculate on the reasons. *Part* of the explanation undoubtedly is that Conservatives tend to get most of their ideas from other Conservatives, and the same is true of Labourites. Since almost twice as many Conservatives as Labourites have known ties with America, their views probably carry a heavier "weight" in the informal opinion-forming processes of their party. Similarly, the greater "weight" of men with ties in the Conservative party must give them a better chance of invoking party discipline in their favor. Although discipline is not enforced nearly so stringently in speeches as in voting, it is nevertheless a factor. But possibly the most important element lies in bonds with America of which we have no knowledge. It seems very probable that Conservatives, having on the whole more money, are more likely to have traveled to the United States than Labourites; and having more business connections, they are more likely to have an economic link with the United States that was not caught in the rather wide-meshed net used to find M.P.'s with commercial ties.

TIES AND RESPONSIVENESS: THE SENATE

One of the principal flaws in this kind of analysis is its implicit assumption that all topics on which an opinion might be expressed are of equal importance, both to the speaker and to the other government in question. Thus an M.P. might criticize the United States for its shipping subsidies, aid to Franco Spain, and lack of civil liberties, but support the American-backed program of German rearmament. Quite possibly, the United States government would value the support on German rearmament highly enough to offset the other criticisms, and in an important sense the M.P. would be more "pro-American" than another Member whose attitudes on all four issues were the opposite. Thus there might be a serious fallacy in simply counting the number of issues on which the Member supported or criticized American policy. Yet in practice there is no thoroughly satisfactory way of weighting the issues. No two observers could agree whether a statement on German rearmament was worth two statements on other policies, or worth four pronouncements, and so on, down a list of twenty additional issues.

In the particular case, this handicap was not too serious. For the three years under study, nearly three quarters of the M.P.'s expressing opinions did so uniformly—they were either always responsive to the United States, or always unresponsive, thus substantially eliminating the weighting difficulty. Still, a more systematic method of solving this problem would be desirable, and it is offered by Guttman scale analysis. The essential principle of scale analysis is this:

> The items can be arranged in an order so that an individual who agrees with, or responds to any particular item also responds positively to all items of lower rank order. The rank order of items is the scale of items; the scale of persons is very similar, people being arranged in order according to the highest rank order of items checked, which is equivalent to the number of positive responses in a perfect scale.

The classic illustration is a group of questions regarding height. If you ask a man if he is over six feet tall and he responds affirmatively, you know that he will also answer yes to questions asking if he is over five feet ten inches in height, or over five feet eight.

By finding that the issues in Anglo-American relations could be scaled, we would sidestep the "weight problem." That is, we might find that with regard to responsiveness to the United States, the four issues—Spain, civil liberties, subsidies, and German rearmament—ranked in that order. A man who opposed American aid to Spain would be unresponsive on all other issues. Similarly, if he defended the state of American civil liberties but criticized American shipping subsidies, he would also support assistance to Spain but oppose arming the Germans. We have not solved the weight problem in the sense of saying which issue is more "important," but we have avoided the necessity of worrying about it. We do not have to decide whether support on German rearmament is "worth" opposition on the other three matters, for such a situation will never occur. The procedure gives us a method of ordering M.P.'s from most responsive to least responsive in a meaningful and consistent way.

The result is that we can describe the pattern of responses as "unidimensional" in scale-analysis terms. The items in the scale measure related attitudes on a particular topic. We cannot be sure what basic feelings are responsible for the statements made by the various M.P.'s, but we can be reasonably sure that all the particular measures were regarded as aspects of one general policy by the Members. A man who is normally highly responsive will not have been unresponsive on one issue because of extraneous factors.

The discussion in the last two paragraphs is of course an oversimplification. Hardly ever is unidimensionality so perfect that there are no variations within the scale, no "errors" where a man is responsive when we should expect him to be unresponsive. Other factors do operate to some extent, but the amount of variation must be very limited if we still are to treat the list of issues as forming a scale. By convention, the response of no more than one man in ten may be in "error" on any item, and the total number of "errors" for all items may not exceed 10 per cent of the number of items times the number of men. Thus the effect of extraneous variables is kept to a minimum.

It must be emphasized that the creation of a scale does not eliminate the need for sound judgment by the researcher. One might indeed be measuring a single dimension, but it need not be the dimension which one is really trying to measure. In deciding what issues to try to put into the scale, and in interpreting the meaning of that scale when completed, one must know what the issues signified and have a set of independent criteria for picking them out. In this case I used the criteria specified earlier for issues involved in Anglo-American relations. No issues which did not meet the original criteria were proposed, and it was essential that at least most of those items which did meet the criteria be capable of incorporation into the scale.

This procedure makes it possible to rank legislators from most responsive to least responsive. The data are too incomplete to apply this method to the study of M.P.'s attitudes—most Members do not express themselves on any given issue—but I have been able to apply it to voting in the United States Senate. In most of the analysis below, it will be necessary to simplify the results, merely classifying lawmakers into three groups—responsive, moderate, and unresponsive—of as nearly equal size as possible. But the reader should remember that the information was made available through a complete ordering.

Like any other quantitative tool which imposes a certain amount of simplification on a complex reality, this procedure has its faults. It cannot tell us whether a legislator holds a particular opinion firmly or with little intensity. His action may stem from deep conviction or strong interest-group pressure, or he may simply be "logrolling" for support on issues of more importance to him. Perhaps an influential legislator determines the votes of a number of "satellites" on an issue.

These refinements can be made only with such other approaches as interviewing and analysis of debates and public statements. But if these two methods are used in tandem, it is possible to get the benefits of both while avoiding most of the pitfalls which either alone sets. The analysis of public statements is peculiarly suited to the House of Commons, where roll-call votes are relatively rare and a Member seldom votes against his party. On the other hand, the examination of voting patterns is peculiarly suited to the Senate, where the opposite conditions prevail. If, using the two techniques, one in each body, we find that similar variables have

TABLE 3   Percentage of Senators with and without British Ties Who Were Responsive, Moderate, and Unresponsive

	1890		
Senators	Responsive	Moderate	Unresponsive
U.K. Ties (N = 49)	37	33	31
No U.K. Ties (N = 35)	9	46	46
	1954		
Senators	Responsive	Moderate	Unresponsive
U.K. Ties (N = 23)	48	22	30
No U.K. Ties (N = 73)	27	33	40
	Both Years Combined		
Senators	Responsive	Moderate	Unresponsive
U.K. Ties (N = 72)	40	29	31
No U.K. Ties (N = 108)	21	37	42

similar effects on lawmakers' attitudes, we shall have very strong evidence of the validity of the relationships so identified.

Just as with M.P.'s, we find a consistent relationship between the possession of personal or economic ties and responsiveness. For 1890 the relationship is significant at the .01 level; for 1954 and for the two years combined it is significant at the .10 level. A similar pattern emerges when we control for party affiliation. Since the conditions of partisanship were quite different in the two years, we shall give no totals for both combined.

TABLE 4 Percentage of Senators with and without British Ties Who Were Responsive, Moderate, and Unresponsive, with Party Affiliation Controlled *

Senators	1890		
	Responsive	Moderate	Unresponsive
Democratic (N = 37)	(57)	(43)	(0)
U.K. Ties (N = 27)	67	33	0
No U.K. Ties (N = 10)	30	70	0
Republican (N = 47)	(0)	(34)	(66)
U.K. Ties (N = 22)	0	32	68
No U.K. Ties (N = 25)	0	36	64

Senators	1954		
	Responsive	Moderate	Unresponsive
Democratic (N = 48)	(40)	(25)	(35)
U.K. Ties (N = 15)	40	20	40
No U.K. Ties (N = 33)	39	27	33
Republican (N = 47)	(23)	(36)	(40)
U.K. Ties (N = 8)	63	25	13
No U.K. Ties (N = 39)	15	38	46

* The year 1954 excludes one Independent.

In two of the cases in Table 4 the control for party affiliation emphasizes the importance of personal and economic bonds. For Democrats in 1890 and Republicans in 1954, the relationship is marked and highly significant (.01 level). For Republicans in 1890 and Democrats in 1954, however, there is no such relationship. But as we shall show, the latter finding is due to the fact that in 1954 constituency ties were entirely without effect in promoting responsiveness. If only direct ties, economic and personal, are considered, those 1954 Democrats who have them prove highly responsive.

As is evident from the most cursory examination of these tables, party affiliation was an important variable. Particularly in 1890 party discipline (or perhaps like-mindedness, we cannot tell which) was extremely powerful in foreign affairs. We cannot be sure why, but an explanation would undoubtedly include many of the same factors as were offered regarding the difference in responsiveness between the Conservative and Labour parties. This sheds light on the political situation of the late nineteenth century when the Democratic party was often accused of being pro-British, despite its dependence on the votes of Irish Americans. Here is evidence that the Democrats were, in an important sense, much more "pro-British" than their opponents. On every issue affecting Anglo-American relations a majority of Democrats was ranged on the responsive side against a majority of Republicans. Exactly 62 per cent of the Senators never voted against the party on these issues—21 Democrats and 31 Republicans. The "moderate" section includes *all* who ever voted against their party.

We can use this information to illustrate the influence of ties in another way. In 24 instances a Democrat voted against his party in an unresponsive manner; in 31 cases a Republican went against his party in order to be responsive. If we distinguish between those Senators with and without ties and make a ratio of the number of votes against party over the number of Senators in each class, we have the figures given in Table 5. Note that the existence of a tie with Britain has a

TABLE 5   Votes Cast against Party per Senator, Senators with and without Ties to Britain, 1890

Senators	Ratio of Responsive Votes	Ratio of Unresponsive Votes
Ties to U.K.	0.73	0.33
No Ties to U.K.	0.60	1.50

greater effect in moderating opposition to British wishes (column 2) than as a positive force in promoting responsiveness (column 1).

KINDS OF TIES

I also wished to know whether two or more links per lawmaker would be more effective than a single tie. Table 6 gives data for the House of Commons. In the left-hand side of the table we see that Members with two ties were actually *less* likely to be responsive than those with only a

TABLE 6   Percentage of M.P.'s with and without American Ties Who Were Responsive, Unresponsive, and Neutral, and of Responsive and Unresponsive Statements, with Number of Ties Controlled, All Years Combined

M.P.'s	Res.	Neut.	Unres.	Statements by M.P.'s	Res.	Unres.
Two or More Ties (N = 28)	21	61	18	Two or More Ties (N = 28)	36	32
One U.S. Tie (N = 67)	13	79	7	One U.S. Tie (N = 40)	55	45
No U.S. Ties (N = 308)	7	81	12	No U.S. Ties (N = 149)	68	64

single tie. On the other hand, Members with two or more links tended to speak out somewhat more often, whatever the content of their remarks. In the right-hand half of the table there is a slight tendency, significant at the .10 level, for responsiveness to be more frequent where there is more than one tie.

Examination of the Senate was also inconclusive on this point. Although in 1954 only two Senators had more than one discernible bond with the British, and both of them were highly responsive, the cases were obviously too few to give any satisfactory indication. For 1890, however, the results were just the opposite of what one would expect. Though not to a statistically significant degree, Senators with two or more ties tended to be *less* responsive than those with only one. On this evidence, then, we must conclude that the existence of any link at all is far more important than the reinforcement of that link by one or two additional ones.

In addition, it seemed necessary to see whether the kind of tie made any difference, whether either economic or personal ties were more significant than the other. Table 7 lists separately all M.P.'s with economic ties, all with no economic but "strong" personal ties, those with only "weak" personal ties, those whose only connection with the United States is through the English-Speaking Union or the Pilgrims, and finally those with no known link at all.

TABLE 7   Percentage of M.P.'s with and without American Ties Who Were Responsive, Unresponsive, and Neutral, and of Responsive and Unresponsive Statements, with Type of Tie Controlled, All Years Combined

M.P.'s	Res.	Neut.	Unres.	Statements by M.P.'s	Res.	Unres.
Economic Ties (N = 53)	11	83	6	Economic Ties (N = 22)	73	27
"Strong" Ties (N = 15)	20	60	20	"Strong" Ties (N = 27)	48	52
"Weak" Ties (N = 19)	21	63	16	"Weak" Ties (N = 19)	63	37
ESU-Pilgrim (N = 8)	25	63	13	ESU-Pilgrim (N = 10)	50	50
No U.S. Ties (N = 308)	7	81	12	No U.S. Ties (N = 149)	32	68

The association of responsiveness with economic ties is evident on both sides of the table, and is significant at the .01 level in each case. Among those with various kinds of personal ties to the United States, it makes little difference whether the bonds are "weak," "strong," or merely those of membership in an organization like the Pilgrims. Possibly some differences would show up in a larger sample, though they are not evident here. But there is a *slight* difference, significant (at the .10 level) only in the right-hand half of the table, between all those with just personal ties and those with commercial bonds. Possibly economic self-interest plays a part. More likely, however, the difference is due to the fact that the ties of commerce are current ones: the legislator has a continuing channel of information and opinion from the United States. Most personal ties, on the other hand, lie in the individual's past, and it may have been many years since he talked to many Americans. Since most of the American policies in question, such as German rearmament and China policy, were of relatively recent vintage, it is not surprising that men with past but not current contacts with the United States should fail to perceive American wishes or their justification.

Notice that men with personal ties to America of any kind are more likely to speak up on matters affecting Anglo-American relations. Only 62 per cent of those with personal ties said nothing, whereas 81 per cent of those with no ties are unrecorded. They are even somewhat more likely to record unresponsiveness than are those without ties (17 per cent to 12 per cent). Perhaps this is because men who have been abroad or have personal contacts with foreigners naturally have more interest in foreign affairs (whether contacts cause interest, or vice versa, or whether it is a mutually reinforcing process is not relevant here). But it may also be that the experiences of these men have in some instances made them "anti-American." Clearly, it is a danger to be considered. If a wider experience of foreign contact in a population is likely, in general, to increase responsiveness, it may also result in a certain concomitant increase in the level of hostility as well.

We cannot reproduce the analysis of Table 7 for the Senate, because in the two years under study a total of only five Senators had personal ties of any nature without also having economic ties to the United Kingdom, and this is too few to produce interesting results. But it is possible to compare the effect of all kinds of direct ties, personal or economic, with that of constituency ties. Table 8 lists all Senators with constituency economic ties, those with only direct bonds, and those with none at all.

Although the number of Senators who have only direct ties to Britain is too small for us to talk of statistical significance, the figures are interesting nevertheless. They suggest that whereas constituency ties were once powerful forces in producing responsiveness, they are no longer very important. In fact, in 1954 Senators with no links at all were more

TABLE 8   Percentage of Senators with Constituency Economic Ties, Direct Ties Only, and No British Ties Who Were Responsive, Moderate, and Unresponsive

Senators	1890		
	Responsive	Moderate	Unresponsive
Constituency Ties (N = 46)	39	30	30
Direct Ties Only (N = 3)	0	67	33
No U.K. Ties (N = 35)	9	46	46

Senators	1954		
	Responsive	Moderate	Unresponsive
Constituency Ties (N = 12)	25	25	50
Direct Ties Only (N = 11)	73	18	9
No U.K. Ties (N = 73)	27	33	40

likely to be responsive than were those whose links passed through their constituencies. This apparent shift is not surprising when one examines the changes in America's economic structure since the turn of the century. In 1954 no state derived more than 12 per cent of its income from a commodity important in Anglo-American trade. But in 1890, seven states gained more than 12 per cent of their income from cotton: Texas (55 per cent), Mississippi (46 per cent), South Carolina (41 per cent), Arkansas (33 per cent), Alabama (32 per cent), Georgia (31 per cent), and Louisiana (19 per cent). Wheat contributed at least that much to three other states: North Dakota (55 per cent), South Dakota (29 per cent), and Minnesota (17 per cent). No wonder, then, that the economic nature of his constituency made so much less difference in the way a Senator voted in 1954 than it did in 1890. Anglo-American commerce has diminished greatly both as a power base and as a means of communicating to legislators who are not themselves directly tied in with it. Possibly also the British government's deliberate discrimination, for balance-of-payments reasons, against imports from the Dollar Area alienated some Senators from states producing goods whose export to Britain continued, but in limited quantities. In any case, the above figures provide dramatic evidence of the South's diminished "internationalism," which many writers have noted.

The conclusion that the effectiveness of constituency ties in promoting responsiveness is directly proportional to the weight of the economic interest in the constituency rests on scanty evidence, but it can be buttressed with another set of data. For 1954 and 1890, I ranked the states involved in Anglo-American trade according to the amount of income derived from goods important in that trade, and then ranked their Senators by degree of responsiveness. For 1954 (when no state derived more than 12 per cent of its income from such products), the correlation between the two rank orders was only .14, and not statistically significant. But for 1890, the same procedure produced a correlation of .34 (significant at the .05 level) for Democratic Senators and the astonishingly high correlation of .86 (significant at the .001 level) for Republican Senators. With this evidence, it is hard to imagine how the precipitous decline in Anglo-American commerce over the past seventy years could fail to work to the detriment of continued responsiveness from American policy-makers.

. . . Higher education in the United States, and particularly legal training, was probably important in instilling a favorable attitude toward Britain and a readiness to meet her needs. The lawyer's training might be particularly important in this respect, since such a high proportion of the American political elite was ‵originally prepared for the bar. Table 9 divides Senators according to the amount and kind of education they obtained.

TABLE 9   Percentage of Senators with Legal Training, Other Higher Education, and No Higher Education Who Were Responsive, Moderate, and Unresponsive, 1890 and 1954 Combined

Senators	Responsive	Moderate	Unresponsive
Legal Education (N = 133)	32	37	32
Other Higher Education (N = 24)	29	25	46
No Higher Education (N = 23)	13	26	61

Whether or not the legislator has had legal training does seem to make a difference, for lawyers were significantly (.01 level) more responsive than were Senators who had no higher education at all. But we cannot be certain whether it is the law training or merely university education in general that makes the difference. The latter group of Senators fell between the other two classes, less responsive than one but more so than the other. In neither direction was the difference statistically significant. An additional caution must be noted. Quite possibly it is not education that is relevant at all, but simply a third variable which tends to be associated with substantial schooling. We should expect an individual with a higher education to be exposed to more kinds of international communications than a man who never went beyond secondary school. There is no way we can, with these data, control for these other, less visible kinds of communication; the possibility is merely offered as an extra reason for treating this finding with restraint.

At this point let us consider two possible criticisms of the above findings. One is that we have the chain of causality wrong—people who already look favorably on another country are then willing to develop ties with it, not the reverse, though the association shows up equally in the analysis. With regard to bonds of education, travel, business, and particularly membership in Anglo-American organizations, this objection obviously carries some weight, but with many other ties self-selection is not a factor. A man has no influence over where he is born and is unlikely to have much more regarding where he does military service in wartime. Many of the business firms in question—Lloyds, Macmillan, Simmons— have international ties that long antedated the Members' or Senators' association with them. Nor are they companies whose bond with the other country would be a major factor in attracting the legislator.

Another potential objection concerns the degree to which these findings can be generalized. Although these influences may be important for ordinary legislators, they may not be effective on such others as members of the executive, who must take a wider view and who are subject to immensely more varied pressures. Especially in Britain fifty or more years ago, Cabinet members were likely to be rather wealthy landowners, and perhaps were less affected by narrow economic concerns. Joseph Chamberlain in the 1890's, for example, heartily championed an Anglo-American *rapprochement,* but he may well have had no strong economic interests in the United States. He wanted friendship with America to counterbalance the new threat of German power. The point, however, is that other men also feared Germany's might, but were not necessarily led to embrace the republic across the seas. But Chamberlain did, and it is perhaps no coincidence that he had an American-born wife. There is no attempt to argue cause in this particular case—he may have married an American because he already liked Americans generically; his marriage may have only reinforced an initial liking for Americans; or it may in fact have been no more than a coincidence. Yet since the association of links with responsiveness is so notable for M.P.'s and Senators, it may affect Cabinet members similarly. This seems particularly plausible because we are *not* arguing that one becomes responsive in any simple, direct way to one's economic stake in another country's welfare, but rather that the existence of an economic or personal link opens a man to messages he would otherwise never hear.

SOURCES OF FRICTION

Finally, we shall reiterate our earlier conclusions about the extent and severity of Anglo-American economic rivalry. I identified all those M.P.'s who were attached to firms with subsidiaries or investments in countries where British holdings were less than 75 per cent of the Anglo-American total—that is, countries where . . . America and Britain were in competition, or where the United States was dominant. Of the 132 members of the 1938 House sampled, 15, or 11.4 per cent, were attached to such companies. In 1954 the proportion had fallen to 12 of 129, or 9.3 per cent. Though not statistically significant, this change is in the hypothesized direction, suggesting that fewer legislators were subject to this kind of Anglo-American friction in the 1950's than before the war. In addition, there is evidence that the irritation was never very serious anyway: . . . M.P.'s attached to such firms were no more likely to be unresponsive than were Members with no ties to America at all. (Of 27 M.P.'s whose companies had holdings where America was dominant or the two countries competed, only two were unresponsive.)

We cannot repeat this analysis for Congress, since in 1954 there were only three Senators with links to firms that might be engaged in investment rivalry, and each of these also had direct economic bonds with Great Britain. But in its place we can examine the effect of British postwar quantitative restrictions on imports. Of the 96 Senators, 31 were tied to firms which produced goods that could be imported from the Dollar Area only by the procurement of specific, individual licenses. The British government generally tried to limit the importation of these goods, and where possible discriminated in favor of soft-currency suppliers. Here again the mode of identification is a crude one, for most imports from America, excluding agricultural and mineral raw materials (but including food, cotton, and copper), were subject to quantitative restrictions. With some products the limitations were applied rigorously, and in other cases licenses were granted freely to all applicants; there is no way of knowing in any detail what the pattern was. Yet even this measure produces the interesting results shown in Table 10.

TABLE 10   Percentage of Senators with and Without Ties to Firms Producing Goods Whose Importance into Britain Was Restricted—Responsive, Moderate, and Unresponsive, 1954

	Responsive	Moderate	Unresponsive
Restricted (N = 31)	23	19	58
No Restrictions (N = 65)	37	35	28

Senators associated with firms whose exports to Britain are limited are much less likely (significant at the .01 level) to be responsive than are legislators without such ties. The substantial removal of these restrictions since 1958 should reduce what really was an important irritant.

To summarize, we have found that:

1. Legislators with economic or personal ties to the other country are more likely to be responsive to the needs of that country than are legislators lacking those ties.
2. This holds true when party affiliation is controlled, though party is itself an important variable.
3. It makes little difference whether a legislator has a number of ties to the other country, or only one.
4. There is some evidence, though not enough to be conclusive, that economic ties are more likely to be effective than personal ones.
5. The importance of a constituency tie is directly proportional to the weight of the economic interest in the constituency.
6. Senators with education in the law are more likely to be responsive than Senators without higher education.
7. Anglo-American investment rivalry does not seem to diminish responsiveness among M.P.'s.
8. British trade discrimination did seem to reduce responsiveness among Senators.

The 1950's: McCarthyism

SEYMOUR MARTIN LIPSET and EARL RAAB

Though McCarthyism was the most striking political development in the 1950s, its sources and antecedents are not clear. Support for Senator Joseph McCarthy has been linked with that of populism, progressivism, and Father Charles E. Coughlin. Farmers, self-employed businessmen, and manual workers tended to support McCarthyism, but whether they supported it because they were ardent Republicans, because of their status anxieties, because of their religious and ethnic backgrounds, because they were hostile to communism, or because they had authoritarian personalities has been debated. Using survey research data, Seymour Martin Lipset and Earl Raab, political sociologists, evaluate who supported McCarthyism.

McCarthyism was not a political movement. It never had members, organized chapters, offered candidates, or formulated a platform. It was a tendency of the times, which McCarthy epitomized, to which he lent his name, but of which in a way he was finally an instrument rather than creator. He was, it is true, a particularly suitable and capable instrument.

As a Catholic, McCarthy was able to embody the traditional anti-Communism and the growing conservatism of that population, without the disability of Father Coughlin's collar. And as a Wisconsinite who followed a La Follette to the Senate, he was able to embrace the agrarian, isolationist, and ethnic sentiments of the Midwest. In fact, the states which were the backbone of agrarian radicalism before the New Deal

From Seymour Martin Lipset and Earl Raab, *The Politics of Unreason: Right-Wing Extremism in America, 1790–1970* (New York: Harper & Row, Publishers, 1970), pp. 220–35. Reprinted with omissions by permission of the publisher. © 1970 by Anti-Defamation League of B'nai B'rith.

gave McCarthy most of his support. A direct line has often been drawn between the La Follette Progressive populist tradition and McCarthy. This line has been given different implications, however. There is little question but that McCarthy drew on the same anti-interventionist sentiment that La Follette had invoked. There is also a certain similarity between their tactics.

> Both Wisconsin Senators conveyed a similar image of embattled insurgency. . . . McCarthy adopted the stance of continual attack that characterized the elder La Follette. McCarthy was a "fighter" for the people's interests, and the condemnation of respectable society only served to strengthen the image of McCarthy as "Battling Joe" just as it had worked for "Fighting Bob."

But there is more implied in the comparison than tactics. In stating that "McCarthy is the heir of La Follette," [Edward A.] Shils asks:

> What was populism if not the distrust of the effete East and its agents in the urban Middle West? Was not populism the forerunner of "grass roots" democracy? Did it not seek to subject the government to the people's will, to tumble the mighty from their high seats, to turn legislators into registrants of the people's will? Was it not suspicious of the upper classes of the East? . . . Did not populism allege to protect the people and their government from conspiracies, from cells of conspirators, who, contrary to the people's will and through the complacency or collusion of their rulers, were enabled to gain control of society?

Whether McCarthy personally "owed" these proclivities to the La Follette tradition is somewhat immaterial. McCarthyism did not, although the tendency prospered as a result of the consonance. Conspiracy theories in America have always leaned heavily on the concept of direct democracy, as an antidote to the secret elite who allegedly were contravening the people's will. One of the intrinsic links between conspiracy theory and monism is the anticonstitutional bias of direct democracy. This is one of the rationales for by-passing the rules, as McCarthy and McCarthyism often did. When McCarthy's censure was being formally considered by the Senate, Herman Welker said "the ninety-six senators are not the judges. The 150,000,000 Americans are the judges of the trial of McCarthy."

Likewise, conspiracy theories, by their nature, are anti-intellectual and invariably focus on some overeducated secret elite. In this case, the most singular link with midwestern populism was the identification of that elite with the eastern Brahmins. Even that identification coincided with the predispositions of other supporting populations: the Irish Catholics, the small businessmen, the new Texas millionaires.

As a matter of fact, McCarthy's was as abstract and "clean" an approach to conspiracy theory as any in American history and may have partly fallen of its own weight as a result. Since the first vague image of the Illuminati conspiracy in the eighteenth century, which also fell of its own weight, the effective conspiracy theories in America have involved two dimensions: a mysterious cabal and some less mysterious, more visible target group associated with the cabal. The offending Catholic immigrants in tandem with papist plots served this purpose; so did alien Jewish merchants in tandem with the Elders of Zion. Even nonethnic "eastern Bankers" could serve some purpose of group visibility for the agrarian mind. McCarthy invoked none of these. His traitors were pure: leaders who had sold out to a foreign power on an individual basis. There was the standard anti-intellectual, antielite appeal of denigrating the Ivy League character of many of the alleged conspirators—but finally there was no cogent group identity.

On first reading, McCarthy's plot theory seemed to be stated as vehemently and as explicitly as it had ever been stated. Our deplorable situation he ascribed to "an infamy so black and a conspiracy so immense as to dwarf any previous such venture in the history of man." He seemed to accuse the President, General Marshall, many State Department officials and government leaders of being part of the plot; but after the fierce rhetoric, he invariably ended up accusing them of being failures rather than plotters. "We were not [ever before] misled and enfeebled by abstractions such as collective security and by the tortured twisted reasoning of men of little minds and less morals who for the first time in the history of this nation argue that we should not vigorously fight back when attacked."

Of course, the Senator's stock in trade and his most effective tactic was promising to "name names." In his 1950 Wheeling, West Virginia, speech which abruptly launched his anti-Communist career he said, "I have here in my hand a list. . . ." He held many such lists in his hand during his public career. Not many names were ever actually revealed. But in any case they were only, finally, names of individuals who had presumably sold out to the foreign enemy.

For McCarthyism, the enemy was an ideology, Communism. True, there was a headquarters in Moscow, but the ideology was the enemy. When General MacArthur said in 1951 that the threat to America was not from the outside but "from the insidious forces working from within which have already so drastically altered the character of our free institutions, . . ." the altered institutions themselves were his target, the "insidious forces" remaining abstract. When Senator William Jenner said that the "collectivist machine" operating in the White House, the State Department, and elsewhere "emanated from some control tower we cannot see," he illustrated the ambiguity of this approach to conspiracy. If the Kremlin was the control tower, the threat was, in one sense, external rather than internal and not really a conspiracy, but a kind of dirty war. But if the threat was that the American people were being seduced by collectivism and internationalism, thus permitting the traitors to more easily deliver us, the prime danger was in fact an ideology and not a band of conspiratorial handmaidens.

It was in this sense that McCarthy's enemy, and that of many of his cohorts, was Communism itself rather than any singular group of conspirators. McCarthy's approach to politics, in the monistic mode, was apolitical; that is, highly moralistic. But his moralism was in tune with the universalist religious framework of America and indeed with the new moral tempo of America. McCarthy was cited by friends as being "a good Catholic, but not the kiss-the-book light-the-candle Catholic."

Richard Rovere noted that "where other politicians would seek to conceal a weakness for liquor or wenching or gambling, McCarthy tended to exploit, even to exaggerate, these wayward tastes. He was glad to have everyone believe that he was a drinker of heroic attainments, a passionate lover of horseflesh, a Clausewitz of the poker table, and a man to whom everything presentable in skirts was catnip." But he could accuse President Eisenhower of dealing with "the apostles of hell," of planning to make "territorial concessions to Red China."

One biographer quotes McCarthy as saying in a home-town speech: "There are two fundamental truths of religion: there is a God who is eternal, and each and every one of you has a soul which is immortal." McCarthy then indicated that his anti-Communist crusade was not just political, and the biographer comments: "The implication was clear: the campaign was religious. God and Joe, with the voters' help, would emerge victorious."

McCarthy himself stated it clearly: "The great difference between our western Christian world and the atheistic communist world is not political . . . it is moral." The thrust was to establish anti-Communism as the religion of America, with Communism as the antireligion. It cut across sectarian lines and blended with the secularized faith of America, although the fundamentalists could relate to it with their own more particularistic language.

Communism was being used as the broad general reference by which to identify the body of bad intentions and bad character in the world. It was not really that Communism was evil because it was atheistic, but rather that it was deemed "atheistic" because it was evil. The heart of the American religion was, simply, opposition to evil as it cohered in Communism, just as the heart of bedrock fundamentalism was opposition to evil as it cohered in Satan. Americanism was the set of values which embodied such an American religion.

In this sense, McCarthyist anti-Communism represented the ultimate movement to abstract and anomic nativism. The group identity was one of moral superiority. This had always been a characteristic of nativism, often as a kind of "cultural baggage" to strong and specific ethnic and regional ties. The appeal to ethnic and regional ties was still a subsurface nativist presence in many aspects of McCarthyism, but in general its nativism was more diffuse. On the other side of the nativist coin, it was not aliens but alien ideas which needed exorcising. Coughlin had moved toward such an abstract nativism; but in fusing his nativism with conspiracy theory, he had located a specific body of people as nativist backlash targets. In McCarthyism the same moral fervor and absolutism were present. The equating of Communism with anti-God was not new. But the relative absence of a singular cohesive body of plotters and fellow travelers was new to conspiracy theory.

Indeed, McCarthyism was more conspiracy style than conspiracy theory, more technique than theory of any kind. The technique, which bears his name, consisted of seeming to charge people with treason, without actually doing so. This involved "guilt by association," a phrase which resounded through the early 1950's in America; or innuendo, or the waving of undisclosed "lists." It spoke of conspiracy, but all it spelled out was treason and ideological defection. McCarthyism never succeeded in corporealizing the American conspiracy.

[Neil J.] Smelser's step-by-step analysis of the development of a political movement suggests that without the designation of a specific cause for the social strain in question, there is no movement, only hysteria. He defines a hysterical belief as "a belief empowering an ambiguous element in the environment with a generalized power to threaten or destroy." He cites certain institutionalized hysterical beliefs as superstitions, fears of witchcraft, demons, spirits, and the like. A corporealized conspiracy can provide specific cause. But McCarthy's Communism as an internal threat remained generalized, and McCarthyism remained more a hysteria than a political movement.

As a hysteria, however, it was potent; and even with a "faulted" conspiracy theory, it unlocked the monistic impulses of America. Partly, McCarthy and his associates were able to do this because there *were* traitors, there *were* spies, there *were* some significantly placed Communist cells in America. One of McCarthy's most severe journalistic critics affirmed that "a number, even if a relatively small number, of the shots called by McCarthy in his changing lists . . . of alleged loyalty, security and 'morals' risks were later proved to be on the target." Some individuals in the clear service of a foreign power were exposed. The slavish devotion to Soviet foreign policy on the part of a few influential people was established. These people were security threats and it can be presumed that they created a great deal of mischief. But the accumulation of all their activities could not explain the plight of America, internally or on the world scene.

At that point, the hysteria took over. Throughout the country, there was a witch hunt, not so much for conspirators as for ideological defectors. The basic monistic formula was applied: Communism was evil, and those who trafficked in such evil were illegitimate and to be excluded from the market place of ideas—and even from the market place of jobs. Since ideological defection, as distinct from membership in any specific group, was a matter of varying judgment, it was pluralism which was under attack. In Washington, McCarthy conducted a lengthy and public investigation of the personnel of the Voice of America, which resulted in the discovery of no Communists, but the discharge or resignation of some thirty employees. "Black lists" of suspect personnel were established for the information of industry's hiring offices. Libraries around the country were under pressure, to which they did or did not give in, to remove arbitrarily suspect books and magazines from their shelves. For example, on one list of books, which the city manager of San Antonio said in 1953 should be burned, were "Einstein's *Theory of Relativity,* Thomas Mann's *Joseph in Egypt* and *The Magic Mountain,* . . . Norbert Weiner's *Cybernetics;* also various anthologies of poetry and folk songs, also books on sculpture, the mentally ill, alcoholics, child care, architecture and mystery novels."

It was this kind of monistic attack which McCarthy symbolized and activated in America. Who supported him?

SOCIAL BASE

A number of quantitative analyses of the sources of McCarthy's support indicate that it came disproportionately from Catholics, New Englanders, Republicans, the less educated, the lower class, manual workers, farmers, older people, and the Irish. Nelson Polsby, who in 1960 summarized the findings of many of these studies, suggests that the evidence from these surveys and from an examination of the results of different election campaigns in which McCarthy or McCarthyism were issues indicates that most of McCarthy's support can be attributed to his identification as a Republican fighting Democrats. In other words, the vast bulk of his backing came from regular Republicans, while the large majority of Democrats opposed him.

Undoubtedly Polsby is correct in stressing the linkage between party identification and attitude toward McCarthy. Some earlier evidence making the same point was reported in a study of the 1954 election by the University of Michigan's Survey Research Center, which showed the positive relationship between degrees of party commitment and attitude toward McCarthy (Table 19).

TABLE 19   Relationship of Party Identification to Attitude Toward McCarthy, October 1954

Attitude toward McCarthy	Party Commitment						
	Strong Demo- crat	Weak Demo- crat	Inde- pendent Demo- crat	Inde- pend- ent	Inde- pendent Repub- lican	Weak Repub- lican	Strong Repub- lican
Pro-McCarthy	10%	9%	8%	12%	12%	12%	25%
Neutral	37	44	42	54	50	47	43
Anti-McCarthy	50	40	41	21	32	33	27
Other responses	3	7	9	13	6	8	5
	100%	100%	100%	100%	100%	100%	100%
Excess of Antis over Pros	40%	31%	33%	9%	20%	21%	2%
Number	(248)	(288)	(97)	(82)	(68)	(159)	(146)

Source: Angus Campbell and Homer C. Cooper, Group Differences in Attitudes and Votes (Ann Arbor: Survey Research Center, University of Michigan, 1956), p. 92.
    Based on replies to question: "If you knew that Senator McCarthy was supporting a candidate for Congress, would you be more likely to vote for that candidate, or less likely to vote for that candidate, or wouldn't it make any difference to you?"

The association between McCarthy support and Republicanism does not tell us, of course, how many former Democrats and Independents may have joined Republican ranks prior to 1954, because their social situation or personal values made them sympathetic to McCarthy's version of radical right ideology. As has been noted, a considerable section of Coughlin's 1938 backing came from individuals who had supported Roosevelt in 1936, but had later rejected him. There is no reliable means of demonstrating the extent to which McCarthy contributed to a move away from the Democrats, but the available evidence is at least compatible with the hypothesis that he was to some extent influential. A 1954 study made available for secondary analysis by the International Research Associates (INRA) inquired as to the respondents' votes in 1948 and 1952. A comparison of the relationship between 1948 voting, attitude toward McCarthy, and 1952 Presidential vote indicates that over half of those who voted for Truman in 1948 and subsequently favored McCarthy voted for Eisenhower in 1952, while two-thirds of the anti-McCarthy

Truman voters favored Stevenson (Table 20). A similar relationship between supporting McCarthy and shifting away from the Democrats is suggested in a study supplied to us for further analysis by the Roper public opinion organization.

TABLE 20   Relationship Between 1948 Presidential Vote and Attitude Toward McCarthy, 1952 (INRA)

| | 1948 Vote | | | |
| | Truman | | Dewey | |
1952 Vote	Pro-McCarthy	Anti-McCarthy	Pro-McCarthy	Anti-McCarthy
Eisenhower	53%	31%	99%	95%
Stevenson	47	69	1	5
Number	(506)	(1,381)	(583)	(732)

A more detailed analysis of the sources of McCarthy's support conducted along the lines of the analysis of Coughlin's backing, however, belies the suggestion that party affiliation had more bearing on approval or disapproval of McCarthy than other explanatory variables. The 1952 Roper study and the 1954 INRA survey both suggest that the most important attribute associated with opinion of McCarthy was education, while a 1954 national study conducted by the University of Michigan's Survey Research Center indicated that religious affiliation was of greater significance than party. Table 21 shows the relationship between education, party identification, and attitude toward McCarthy.

TABLE 21   Support for McCarthy by Education and Party Preference, 1954 (INRA) (Percent Difference between Approvers and Disapprovers)

| | | Party Identification | |
Education	Democrat	Independent	Republican
Graduate school	—59	—44	—28
College	—44	—24	—19
Vocational	—41	—20	—19
High school	—27	— 8	— 5
Grammar school	—18	— 8	+ 6

Note: Cell entries refer to percentage differences between approval and disapproval of McCarthy. For example, among grammar-school Republicans, 24 percent were pro-McCarthy and 18 percent were anti-McCarthy; among Democrats with graduate education, 8 percent were pro-McCarthy, and 67 percent anti-McCarthy.

The relationship between less education and support of McCarthy is consistent with what is known about the effect of education on political attitudes in general: higher education often makes for greater tolerance, greater regard for due process, and increased tolerance of ambiguity.

The findings from the surveys with respect to occupation are what might be anticipated, given the preceding results. Nonmanual occupations that require the highest education—that is, professional and executive or managerial positions—were the most anti-McCarthy (Table 22).

TABLE 22   Relationship Between Occupation and Attitudes Toward McCarthy (Percent Difference between Approvers and Disapprovers)

INRA 1954 [a]			Roper 1952 [b]		
	Percent	Number		Percent	Number
Professional	−35	(731)	Professional and		
Executive and managerial	−24	(511)	Executive	−17	(219)
White collar	−19	(1,144)	Small business	− 0	(123)
Industry and business	−14	(583)	Clerical and sales	−11	(387)
Supervisor and foreman	−16	(405)	Factory labor	− 3	(317)
Skilled	−14	(2,323)	Nonfactory labor	− 6	(235)
Unskilled	−14	(1,019)	Services	− 4	(178)
Personal service	−10	(677)	Farm owner/manager	− 6	(184)
Farmers	−21	(824)	Gallup—December 1954 [c]		
Retired	− 3	(709)			
Students	−34	(59)	Professional	−44	(163)
			Executive	−24	(154)
Michigan 1954 [c]			Clerical and sales	−23	(188)
Professional and business	−40	(246)	Skilled	−10	(237)
Clerical and sales	−44	(102)	Unskilled	8	(286)
Skilled	−30	(337)	Labor	7	(68)
Unskilled	−16	(144)	Service	−10	(103)
Farmers	−17	(104)	Farm owner	− 9	(165)

Note: Cell entries represent difference between approval and disapproval of McCarthy. The more negative the entry, the greater the predominance of anti-McCarthy sentiment.

[a] Occupation of respondent recorded as of chief wage earner if respondent is a housewife.

[b] Occupation of respondent recorded, housewives omitted from table.

[c] Occupation of head of household recorded.

Independent businessmen were the most favorable to McCarthy among middle-class or nonmanual occupations. Workers (including those engaged in personal service) were more favorable to McCarthy than were those in the middle-class occupations, with the exception of independent businessmen.

Farmers were also a pro-McCarthy group, according to three of the four surveys we reanalyzed and the many studies summarized by Polsby. When viewed in occupational categories, McCarthy's main opponents were to be found among professional, managerial, and clerical personnel, while his support was disproportionately located among self-employed businessmen, farmers, and manual workers.

In the INRA survey, it was possible to examine the attitudes of two groups not in the labor force: students and retired persons. Students were overwhelmingly opposed to McCarthy, while retired persons were among the groups least antagonistic to the Senator. These findings presumably reflect the combined influences of age and education. The attitudes of the retired may have been colored by several factors associated with age, such as particular sensitivity to the rise of Communism and the decline of American prestige, greater political conservatism, and greater rigidity. Moreover, retired persons probably felt most acutely the effects of status deprivation because of both their decline in social importance and their disadvantageous economic position in a period of moderate inflation.

Thus far, the analysis suggests that McCarthy's support was in many ways similar to Father Coughlin's. Both men derived strength from the lower classes and the rural population. They differed only in the relatively greater appeal of the Senator to self-employed businessmen. These results would suggest that the differences in the ideologies of the two men are not paralleled by differences in the character of their support. However, when socioeconmoic status rather than occupation is taken as an indicator of class, differing patterns of support emerge for the Senator and for Coughlin. The Coughlin analysis indicated a high correlation between socioeconomic status (a measure of the style of life of the respondent, largely reflecting income) and approval of the priest. Those of low status were much more likely to approve of him than those of high status. When the corresponding comparison is made for McCarthy, we find a much smaller, almost insignificant, association. Lower-status persons were slightly less likely to support McCarthy than the more privileged ones. This result is initially quite surprising, since both education and occupation, themselves highly correlated with socioeconomic status, were, as we have seen, related to attitudes toward McCarthy. The solution to this apparent puzzle lies in the finding that when either education or occupation is held constant—that is, when we compare those high or low on socioeconomic status within the same educational or occupational categories—the data show that *the higher the socioeconomic-status level, the greater the proportion of McCarthy supporters*. This finding holds true particularly among Republicans; in general, the socioeconomic-status level had little effect on attitude toward McCarthy among Democrats of a given occupational or educational level. Thus, while lower educational and occupational status were associated with support for the Wisconsin Senator, within either category *higher* socioeconomic status made for greater receptivity to his message among Republicans. Perhaps the higher-income people in lower occupational or educational strata were precisely those who were most drawn to an ideology that attacked as pro-Communist both liberal lower-class-based politics and moderate, conservative old upper-class-elitist groups.

It has been suggested that McCarthy's strength reflected the frustrations inherent in status discrepancies. In periods of full employment and widespread economic opportunity, some who rise economically do not secure the social status commensurate with their new economic position. Conversely, others, whose financial position has not improved at a corresponding rate (or has worsened), find their social status relatively higher than their economic position. Such status incongruities were presumed to have created sharp resentments about general social developments, which predisposed individuals to welcome McCarthy's attack on the elite and on the New Deal. Efforts to test these hypotheses with the data available for the most part proved unfruitful.

One study, however, did find some empirical support for these assumptions. Robert Sokol attempted to see whether the subjective perception of status discrepancy ("felt status inconsistency") was related to McCarthyism. The analysis indicated that conscious concern with status inconsistency and McCarthyism were related: "The more strain, the greater will be the tendency to be a McCarthy supporter; with 62 per cent of the high-strain men being pro-McCarthy, in contrast with 47 per cent of those feeling a little strain and 39 per cent of those without any concern about the relative ranks of their statuses." These findings held within different analytic subgroups. While much more work remains to be done to analyze the relationship between status strain and political protest and between objective discrepancy and subjective strains, Sokol's research suggests that the general assumptions about the relationship of the status strains of an open society and the type of political protest represented by McCarthy may have some validity.

Another hypothesis is that McCarthyism also reflected strains inherent in the varying statuses of different ethnic and religious groups in American society. It was assumed that Catholics and other recent immigrant groups with relatively low status, or with ethnic ties to neutral or Axis nations, were disposed to favor McCarthy, while those of high status or with ethnic links to Allied nations opposed the Senator. These generalizations also tend to be supported by survey data. It is clear, as has already been noted, that Catholics as a group were more pro-McCarthy than Protestants, who in turn were somewhat more favorable to him than were Jews. The strong relationship between religious affiliation and attitude toward McCarthy among supporters of the two parties may be seen in Table 23, taken from the University of Michigan study.

TABLE 23   Attitudes Toward McCarthy According to Religion and Party Identification, 1954

Attitude toward McCarthy	Strong Democrat	Weak Democrat	Independent	Weak Republican	Strong Republican
			Protestants		
Pro	7%	6%	7%	11%	23%
Anti	55	45	35	33	28
Excess of Anti over Pro	−48	−39	−28	−22	− 5
Number	(184)	(213)	(173)	(128)	(123)
			Catholics		
Pro	18%	23%	19%	20%	39%
Anti	33	20	21	28	23
Excess of Anti over Pro	−15	+ 3	− 2	− 8	+16
Number	(51)	(58)	(55)	(25)	(18)

Source: Angus Campbell and Homer C. Cooper, Group Differences in Attitudes and Votes (Ann Arbor: Survey Research Center, University of Michigan, 1956), p. 149.

In the Protestant group, the ranking of the different denominations with respect to sentiment toward McCarthy corresponded on the whole to their socioeconomic status. As Table 24 shows, the higher the status of

TABLE 24   Protestant Denominational Support for McCarthy (Roper)

		Attitude toward McCarthy—Percent				
Denomination	Percent of Group High in S E S	Agree	Disagree	Don't Know	Difference between Agrees and Disagrees	Number
Episcopalians	40	29	44	27	−15	(157)
Congregationalists	32	33	44	23	−11	(89)
Methodists	19	29	33	38	− 4	(509)
Presbyterians	27	37	36	27	+ 1	(208)
Lutherans	23	33	31	36	+ 2	(207)
Baptists	12	28	24	49	+ 4	(471)

the members of a denomination, the more antagonistic the group was toward the Wisconsin Senator.

Methodists constitute an exception to this generalization; although a relatively low-status group, they were more anti-McCarthy than the Lutherans or Presbyterians. The rank order of denominations in terms of McCarthy support is, with the exception of the Baptists, identical with that reported earlier for Coughlin. Baptists ranked relatively high in opposition to Coughlin and in support for McCarthy. It is difficult to suggest any plausible explanation for this change in the position of the Baptists other than that they may have been particularly antagonistic to the Catholic church, and hence unwilling to approve the political activities of a priest, yet not deterred from supporting a Catholic Senator.

Both the INRA and Roper surveys contain information concerning the ethnic origins of respondents which permits an elaboration of the relationship between ethnic and religious identification and McCarthy support (see Table 25). Unfortunately, the two studies differed greatly in the wording of questions on ethnicity. Because INRA asked for the

TABLE 25   Relationship Between Religion and Ethnic Background and Attitudes to McCarthy

(Percent Difference Between Approvers and Disapprovers)

Roper—1952			INRA—1954		
	Number			Number	
Catholics			Catholics		
4th Generation, America	(198)	—11	No Answer	(252)	— 2
Ireland	(81)	+18	Ireland	(545)	+ 5
Italy	(61)	+16	Italy	(393)	+ 8
Germany	(54)	+13	Germany and Austria	(424)	— 6
Great Britain	(13)	*	Great Britain	(272)	+ 4
Poland	(36)	— 6	Poland	(246)	— 2
Protestants			Protestants		
4th Generation, America	(1,190)	— 2	No Answer	(1,037)	—22
Ireland	(29)	+ 7	Ireland	(487)	—21
Germany	(172)	+ 2	Germany and Austria	(1,266)	—19
Great Britain	(102)	— 8	Great Britain	(1,814)	— 5
Scandinavia	(68)	— 3	Scandinavia and Holland	(851)	—25
Negroes	(252)	— 7	Negroes	(438)	—13
Jews	(96)	— 6	Jews	(245)	—54

* Too few cases for stable estimates.

country of ancestors, while Roper asked for the country of the respondent's grandparents, the Roper survey reported many more Protestants as simply "American" in background. Among Catholics, too, the Roper survey reported a smaller proportion with German or British ancestry than did the INRA survey. On the other hand, INRA's request for country of ancestors produced a large "don't know" or "no answer" group. About 20 per cent of the whites did not reply to the question.

Differences in attitude among the ethnic groups were more pronounced among Catholics than Protestants in both the Roper and the INRA studies. In the Roper survey, Irish Catholics were 18 per cent more favorable to the Senator than unfavorable, while "old American" Catholics were 11 per cent more negative than positive. Among Protestants, on the other hand, those of German origin were the most pro-McCarthy (2 per cent), while those of British ancestry were most opposed (−8 per cent).

Results from both surveys show that Irish and Italian Catholics were among the most pro-McCarthy groups. The Roper data indicate that Germans, both Catholic and Protestant, were disproportionately in favor of McCarthy, but the INRA materials do not confirm this finding. The explanation for this seeming inconsistency may lie in the differing formulation of the questions on ethnicity. It may be that McCarthy appealed successfully to the "Roper" Germans whose families had emigrated to the United States within the past three generations and consequently retained emotional ties to Germany that made them receptive to McCarthy's isolationist appeal. "INRA" Germans are likely to have included many old-stock Americans who, like other "old American" groups, were predisposed to disapprove of the Wisconsin Senator.

The most recent effort, by Michael Rogin, to analyze the social sources of McCarthyism reiterates Polsby's suggestion that some interpretations of the sources of McCarthy's support are more clever than they have to be. To the proposition that anti-Communism was only a pretext for the release of personal anxieties, whether induced by status or other problems, he counter-proposed that Communism and the cold war were themselves the core of the anxiety which McCarthy dramatized. "To many Americans, especially those in the lower classes who were not actively in touch with events in the political world, McCarthy was simply fighting Communism. Support for McCarthy meant opposition to Communism."

Rogin's empirical findings, derived from ecological analyses of voting returns, however, basically agreed with most of the earlier efforts to locate the social bases of McCarthyism based on analyses of opinion surveys. Thus he also concludes that it is a mistake to see McCarthyite strength as rooted in the status-stricken or among the midwestern agrarian populists, and argues that it is to be seen more simply as a conservative Republican movement feeding on these prevalent anxieties about Communism and the Cold War. Rogin agrees with Nelson Polsby and the Michigan Survey Research Center in emphasizing Republican support of McCarthy and with Samuel Lubell concerning the strong relationship of McCarthyism to anxieties about Communism and the Cold War. He also finds evidence to sustain the objections raised by the results of the survey research to the ascription of a literally direct line between McCarthyism and agrarian radicals in the Midwest. McCarthy did not receive the electoral support of the La Follette stream in Wisconsin politics. He first defeated Senator Robert La Follette, Jr. in 1946, and continued to face the opposition of La Follette's followers in succeeding years. McCarthy did not receive the electoral support of agrarian radicals as such. His support in the Midwest came from the economic conservatives.

The agrarian radicalism of the Populist era had shifted, of course, to a dominant conservatism in the Midwest because of a change in the economic character of the area. This development underlines the split in the Republican party, a coalition of a certain kind of Republican conservatism in the Midwest and of a certain kind of Republican liberalism in the East. McCarthy's main support was among the conservative Republicans, though after the shock of Truman's victory . . . many liberal Republicans by and large were willing to tolerate him for the usual political reasons. After Eisenhower's victory in 1952, the liberal Republicans were the first to pull away from him. It is true that much of the midwestern conservatism and ethnic isolationism which entered the stream of McCarthyism was in areas which had historically been Populist and Progressive areas. But, as has already been pointed out, it is not so much a matter of an identity between the backers of these earlier agrarian movements or their ideological descendants and the supporters of McCarthy. It is simply that insofar as this midwestern political tradition was laced with such tendencies as opposition to the effete eastern elite, and attraction to the concept of direct democracy, it affected the nature of McCarthyism.

But, more important, the distinction must be made between support for McCarthy and for McCarthyism. Electoral endorsement for McCarthy and poll support for McCarthyism, which Rogin properly differentiates, are discrete entities. McCarthyism cannot be measured on an electoral basis. It was never a political movement; it was a political tendency, unorganized, activating certain impulses in a sympathetic audience, which had certain effects in areas of public life. McCarthy as an electoral figure appealed to Republicans, to barely enough of them usually to enable his election. His support of other politicians was no more potent than his own electoral appeal. The impulses of McCarthyism, which McCarthy indeed activated, were much more widespread. McCarthy, as the symbol of McCarthyism, had more appeal, but this did not necessarily lead to direct political support. McCarthy as an electoral figure never served the classic right-wing extremist function of uniting elite and popular support. But, for a time, and in a limited fashion, McCarthyism did. It united different segments of the population for their own reasons. Republicanism was only one of those reasons, although it may have been the main reason for voting for McCarthy himself. Anti-Communism, as a real reaction to the Cold War, was also just one of those reasons. There is no reason to believe that there was substantially less uneasiness about global Communism among those who opposed McCarthyism than among those who embraced it. As one observer notes:

> Communism was clearly more than an ideological and a symbolic issue to Americans in the post-war decade. Soviet Russia existed as a very real counterpoise to the extension of American power and values throughout the world, and presence of the Red Army in Europe and new communist states in Europe and Asia were undeniable. Yet it was the symbolic "Communism" . . . rather than the realities of international politics, that the McCarthyites chose to confront.

The point is that it was not *realpolitik* anti-Communism which McCarthyism traded in, but a kind of religious hysteria which was called anti-Communism and embodied a whole set of preservatist impulses. The two obviously were not unconnected; but among American anti-Communists, those subject to the latter hysteria were the most likely to become McCarthyites.

From a different vantage point, support for McCarthyism carried with it another significance: a certain tolerance for monism. It is not just that McCarthy supporters backed McCarthy, they did not react against his techniques. There is some indication that those who ranked high on an Authoritarian Personality Scale were more likely to support McCarthyism (See Table 26). But the largest differences in response to McCarthy, as related to the authoritarian scale, occurred among the college-educated. As various studies have indicated, this scale serves best as a predictor of attitude predispositions among the well educated. Among the less educated, a high authoritarianism score reflects in some part attitudes common to the group. However, in the context of these variables, and in the general context of opposition to Communism, the data indicate that some combination of three kinds of population groups were most prone to support McCarthy: (1) the economic conserva-

TABLE 26   Relationship Between Attitudes Toward the McCarthy Committee and Score on an "Authoritarian Personality" Scale Within Educational Groupings 1953 (NORC)

Education and Authoritarianism	Percent Difference between Approvers and Disapprovers	Attitude toward McCarthy Committee (Percent)			
		Approve	Disapprove	Don't Know	Number
Grammar School					
High authoritarian	42	56	14	30	(183)
Middle	43	57	14	29	(229)
Low	28	44	16	39	(57)
High School					
High	68	78	10	12	(139)
Middle	49	65	16	19	(252)
Low	37	61	24	15	(188)
College					
High	75	85	10	5	(20)
Middle	46	66	20	14	(84)
Low	10	49	39	11	(132)

Note: High equals an authoritarian response on at least four items; medium means an authoritarian score on two or three items; low indicates no or one authoritarian response out of the five items.

tives; (2) the status-volatile; (3) the uneducated. Insofar as they were different groups, McCarthyism was able to bind them together for a while under the banner of a moralistic, monistic, conspiracy-style anti-Communism, which had different significances for them.

23

The Structure of American Industry in the Twentieth Century: A Historical Overview

ALFRED D. CHANDLER, JR.

Much has been written about the concentration of industry in the twentieth century, but no one has been more precise in delineating the growth and organization of American business enterprise than Alfred D. Chandler, Jr. His *Strategy and Structure: Chapters in the History of the Industrial Enterprise* (1962) charted the stages of bureaucratic development of great business concerns. Building on that expertise and utilizing tables compiled by P. Glenn Porter and Harold C. Livesay ("Oligopolists in American Manufacturing and Their Products, 1909–1963," *Business History Review* 43 [1969]:282–98), Chandler shows which areas of American industry were most susceptible to concentration and suggests why oligopoly developed in these sectors.

In describing the industrial structure of their country, American economists have rightly focused on the concentration of production and distribution by a few large firms within individual industries, and on the growth of the large firm itself. Economists including Morris A. Adelman, A. D. H. Kaplan, Adolph Berle, Gardiner C. Means, Willard Thorp, Warren G. Nutter, Ralph L. Nelson, Michael Gort, and John Kenneth Galbraith have pointed out that American industry is highly

From *Business History Review* 43 (1969):255–63, 265–81. Reprinted with omissions by permission of the publisher. © The President and Fellows of Harvard College.

concentrated, that concentrated industries are dominated by large firms, and that concentration has not increased significantly in recent years. Only a few of these scholars, however, have emphasized that concentration came in some industries and not in others, and still fewer have suggested why these differences occurred. Nor have they studied, as a historian would, the changing developments within industries and within the large firm decade by decade since 1900. They have, for example, failed to analyze the ways in which multi-industry enterprises emerged from the vertically integrated companies. Moreover, these economists have used various industrial classification systems and different criteria in measuring concentration. Therefore, it is often difficult to make comparisons between their findings.

In an effort to provide more detailed and more satisfactory answers to the questions of when, why, and how certain industries became and remained concentrated and certain enterprises became large and remained unconcentrated, two of my students, Harold C. Livesay and P. Glenn Porter, undertook two related projects. One study developed measures of concentration for the industries listed in the four Censuses of Manufactures of 1909, 1919, 1929, and 1939 and in the concentration-ratio materials compiled by the Bureau of the Census for the years 1947, 1958, and 1963. In this study they defined a concentrated or oligopolistic industry as one in which six or fewer firms contributed 50 per cent, or twelve or fewer contributed 75 per cent of the total product value. Livesay and Porter used the two-digit and four-digit categories defined by the Bureau of the Budget in its 1957 *Standard Industrial Classification Manual.* The Standard Industrial Classification Code places the products of all American plants into approximately 430 industries which are assigned four-digit numbers. These 430 are then placed in twenty-one industrial groups which are given two-digit numbers.

Livesay and Porter's second study examined the product distribution of the largest eighty to ninety manufacturing firms in the United States (by assets) for the years 1909, 1919, 1929, 1939, 1948, and 1960. The names came from the list of the top 100 firms given for these years by A. D. H. Kaplan's *Big Enterprise in a Competitive Society,* first published by the Brookings Institution in 1954 and then revised in 1964. (Non-manufacturing companies were not included by Livesay and Porter.) The information on the products of these companies came from Moody's and Poor's *Manuals* and annual reports of the companies themselves.

This decade by decade review is condensed into two sets of tables. . . . One set shows for each of the seven different years studied the number of concentrated four-digit industries in each two-digit industrial group and the value of the output produced by the top six or twelve firms (termed the oligopolists in this paper) that was defined as concentration in those four-digit industries. The tables also indicate the percentage of the total of four-digit industries in a group which are concentrated and the percentage of the total product value in a group produced by the oligopolists in each of the concentrated industries in that group. The second set of tables lists the largest firms for the years 1909, 1919, 1929, 1935, 1948, and 1960 by these same two-digit industrial groups, and then shows the number of four-digit industries in which each firm operated. I will summarize very briefly the contents of these tables, and then by using these and other relevant data propose a historical explanation for the changing industrial structure of the twentieth-century American economy.

I

Livesay and Porter's tables show that concentration has occurred only in a minority of American manufacturing industries during the twentieth century, but that these industries include those which are most critical to the strength, continued growth, and defense of a modern, urban, industrial, and technologically advanced society. The data further indicate that large firms have occurred most often in concentrated industries, and that large firms have increasingly expanded their production lines into more and more industries.

Broadly speaking, concentration tended to increase through World War II and then to decline slightly. The number of concentrated industries was 32 per cent of the total in 1909, 31 per cent in 1919, 30 per cent in 1929, and down to 27 per cent in 1939. In 1947, it was 43 per cent and has declined to 42 per cent in 1958 and 37 per cent in 1963. The percentage of total product value produced by the oligopolists rose from 16 per cent in 1909 to 21 per cent in 1929, and then jumped to 28 per cent at the end of the depression in 1939. Since World War II the figure has remained stable, being 26 per cent in 1947, 25 per cent in 1958, and then up to 27 per cent in 1963.

Far more useful and significant than these cumulative figures are those for each of the different two-digit groups. These figures of number and percentage of concentrated industries in each industrial group and the product value produced by oligopolists in the four-digit industries in the two different two-digit groups are, as those in the previous paragraph, in no sense precise. Because of difficulties of specifically allocating value of products of firms to different four-digit industries and because of the changing definition of the four-digit industries themselves in suc-

cessive censuses, these data can only be used as indices of the broadest
of trends. Yet these trends do seem to be clear enough to be worth
describing and analyzing.

The two following charts best present these trends. Chart 1 shows
the percentage of the total four-digit industries in the two-digit industrial
groups which were concentrated. Chart 2 indicates the percentage of

CHART 1   Percentage of Concentrated Industries Within Industrial Groups, 1909–1963 [a]

Type A Groups—Rarely 25 Percent of Industries in Group Oligopolistic

	1909	1919	1929	1939	1947	1958	1963
31 Leather	13	8	8	0	0	25	10
27 Publishing & printing	20	10	10	7	6	12	7
24 Lumber & wood	18	14	7	6	38	28	8
25 Furniture	20	0	0	11	44	13	0
23 Apparel	18	23	16	8	14	17	6

Type B Groups—25 to 50 Percent of Industries in Group Oligopolistic

	1909	1919	1929	1939	1947	1958	1963
22 Textiles	35	44	38	21	38	38	31
26 Paper	22	27	27	18	36	33	35
34 Fabricated metals	44	32	25	27	29	37	29
35 Machinery	55	41	31	31	36	39	29
20 Food	30	20	30	26	40	48	43

Type C Groups—Over 50 Percent of Industries in Group Oligopolistic

	1909	1919	1929	1939	1947	1958	1963
32 Stone, clay, & glass	31	38	10	27	57	55	52
28 Chemicals	32	27	30	33	68	61	54
29 Petroleum	50	50	33	33	75	60	60
30 Rubber	100	50	50	100	75	75	60
33 Primary metals	33	40	41	33	65	53	54
36 Electrical machinery	67	29	80	50	76	62	73
37 Transportation equipment	25	33	36	50	57	64	64
38 Instruments	20	54	70	73	70	90	64
21 Tobacco	100	100	100	100	75	100	100

[a] "Industries" refers to the four-digit and "industrial groups" to the two-digit classification of the Bureau of the Budget's Standard Industrial Classification Manual (Washington, 1957). Specific classification numbers are given for each individual industrial group listed.

CHART 2   Percentage of Total Product Value Produced by Oligopolists Within Industrial Groups, 1909–1963 [a]

Type A Groups—Up to 3 Percent of Product Value Produced by Oligopolists [b]

	1909	1919	1929	1939	1947	1958	1963
31 Leather	<1(8)	<1(13)	<1(13)	0(12)	0(12)	2(12)	1(10)
27 Publishing & printing	<1(5)	<1(10)	<1(10)	<1(15)	<1(16)	2(16)	1(15)
24 Lumber & wood	<1(11)	<1(14)	<1(14)	<1(16)	3(16)	<1(18)	1(13)
25 Furniture	<1(5)	0(4)	0(4)	2(9)	8(16)	2(15)	0(12)
23 Apparel	1(18)	<1(22)	<1(25)	2(65)	4(42)	2(41)	3(33)

Type B Groups—Up to 25 Percent of Product Value Produced by Oligopolists

	1909	1919	1929	1939	1947	1958	1963
22 Textiles	<1(17)	<1(23)	2(21)	6(34)	7(34)	6(32)	19(29)
26 Paper	<1(9)	2(11)	2(11)	1(11)	4(11)	6(12)	14(17)
34 Fabricated metals	2(16)	3(28)	2(24)	5(34)	10(31)	13(30)	11(28)
35 Machinery	16(11)	20(17)	9(16)	18(29)	19(39)	24(41)	18(38)
20 Food	24(30)	28(36)	26(37)	25(50)	19(42)	15(42)	18(44)

Type C Groups—Over 30 Percent of Product Value Produced by Oligopolists

	1909	1919	1929	1939	1947	1958	1963
32 Stone, clay, & glass	2(16)	5(21)	<1(19)	14(33)	39(30)	32(29)	31(27)
28 Chemicals	9(25)	9(30)	17(27)	18(27)	44(41)	31(41)	31(28)
29 Petroleum	34(6)	44(6)	63(6)	66(6)	65(8)	62(5)	68(5)
30 Rubber	76(2)	69(2)	63(2)	83(4)	55(4)	47(4)	29(5)
33 Primary metals	35(18)	40(25)	42(17)	51(21)	49(20)	42(19)	46(24)
36 Electrical machinery	68(3)	40(7)	11(5)	23(16)	52(21)	36(21)	40(33)
37 Transportation equipment	9(8)	3(12)	20(11)	73(10)	53(14)	64(14)	63(14)
38 Instruments	10(5)	48(13)	48(10)	48(11)	48(10)	53(10)	45(11)
21 Tobacco	75(1)	80(2)	80(2)	76(3)	81(4)	84(4)	89(4)

[a] "Industries" refers to the four-digit and "industrial group" to the two-digit classification of the Bureau of the Budget's Standard Industrial Classification Manual. Specific classification numbers are given for each individual industrial group listed.

[b] Figures in parentheses beside the percentages give the total number of industries within an industrial group for each of the seven-year periods studied.

the total product value of the group produced by the oligopolists in that group. Of these two sets of figures the second would seem to be the most useful. Because the classification of four-digit industries often changes from census to census, I have given in Chart 2 in parenthesis the total number of industries in a two-digit industrial group for each of the seven-year periods studied. An increase in the number of industries in an industrial group from one census year to the next increases the possibility of a few firms handling a large share of the output of an industry and a decrease in the number would statistically decrease the likelihood of such concentration. Yet these statistical biases should not be over-estimated. The classification in the censuses are carefully worked out and do reflect realities of output and markets. They also indicate continuing technological and market developments within the industries and groups.

These data indicate that the nineteen two-digit industrial groups can be classified into three types: (A) those with little or no concentration; (B) those with some; and (C) those where concentration has become significant. In those groups listed under Type A, there has been very little indication of concentration throughout the twentieth century. In leather and leather products, publishing and printing, lumber and wood products, furniture and fixtures, and apparel and related products, the percentage of product value produced by oligopolists has always been low (Chart 2). It has normally been about 1 per cent of the total product value of the group and rarely has risen as high as 3 per cent. (The only instances of product value by oligopolists reaching more than 3 per cent was in furniture and apparel in 1947.) In these same two-digit groups the percentage of industries which were concentrated very rarely rose to 25 per cent (twice in lumber in 1947 and 1958 and once in furniture in 1947). In this type of industrial group the only trend toward concentration seems to have come in the years shortly after World War II and then only on a very small scale.

In the second type (B) of two-digit industrial group there have been more indications of concentration. In three of this type of group the increase came after 1940. Except for those three (textile mill products, paper and allied products, and fabricated metal products) during the years before World War II, the product value produced by oligopolists rarely went below 5 per cent and rarely above 25 per cent of the total value produced by the group. (Only one rose once above 25 per cent, food in 1919.) In these same groups the percentage of four-digit industries in the industrial groups which were concentrated were rarely more than 50 per cent and rarely below 35 per cent.

The third type (C) of two-digit industrial group can be considered the one in which concentration has been most prevalent in manufacturing in the United States during the twentieth century. In three of these (stone, glass, and clay, chemical and allied products, and transportation vehicles), concentration came only as the century moved on. Except for these three in the early years of the century, the percentage of product value produced by the oligopolists was rarely less than 30 per cent and usually more, and the percentage of four-digit concentrated industries in the group was rarely less than 50 per cent. Because of the importance of these industries to the growth of the modern American economy, it seems proper to review briefly the figures in Chart 2 for this type of group.

Of the four industrial groups whose processes of production tend to be more chemical than mechanical—that is, chemicals, rubber, petroleum, and stone, glass, and clay—the last (stone, glass, and clay) was the slowest to show signs of concentration. The increase in the indices of concentration in the decade of the 1930's may partially reflect the sizable number of industries added to that group; but from 1939 to 1963 the number of industries remained roughly the same, while the percentage of product value produced by the oligopolists rose sharply from 1939 to 1947 and then dropped back slightly in 1958, staying about the same in 1963. Also the most concentrated industries in this group tended to be those where the chemical and other processes of production were the most complex, as in the case of glass and gypsum, and the less concentrated industries in this group were those where the technology was the least complex, as in the case of brick, concrete, and cut stone products.

Somewhat the same pattern holds for the chemical group, although the indications of concentration come earlier than in stone, glass, and clay. In chemicals the percentage produced by oligopolists almost doubled between 1919 and 1929 and then remained about the same in 1939. The sharp jump during the war may reflect a large increase in the number of industries in the group. But a drop in the value of the output produced by oligopolists in the immediate post-war years is obvious. The significance of the changes between 1959 and 1963 are less certain, again because of a change in the number of industries in the group. Fortunately, information in the 1963 *Concentration Ratios in Manufacturing Industry* is quite complete for the years 1958 and 1963. It indicates a decrease in concentration in nearly all four-digit industries. In chemicals, too, the indices of concentration were higher in the more technologically complex industries, including dyes and pigments, industrial gases, alkalies and chlorines, and less in the less technologically complex ones such as fertilizer, printers' ink, and toilet preparations.

In the other two chemically oriented industries, rubber and petroleum, the indices of concentration have always been high. In petroleum the greatest increase in the value produced by oligopolists came in the 1920's when the new basic market—the automobile—became set. In rubber there appears to have been a slight decline in the value of the output of the oligopolists from 1909 to 1929 and then an increase in 1939, but how much the latter might be due to reclassification is not clear. There is no question, however, of the sharp decline in the value of the output of the oligopolists after World War II.

The other groups in Type C were, except for tobacco, in the primary metals (which might be properly called a chemically oriented group) and those involving the making of complex metal machinery and instruments. In the primary metals the per cent of product value generated by oligopolists was relatively high at the start, and it rose slightly from 1909 to 1939. It has declined somewhat since then. In the electrical machinery group this same index of concentration was high early in the century and then dropped quite sharply until World War II. It then rose to a high level to fall again, though not as sharply as it had in prewar years. The change in the value of the output of the oligopolists in industries in the transportation vehicles group reflects the swift growth of the automobile industry, and the elimination of the smaller passenger car firms during the depression. There may have been a slight drop in the percentage of product value produced by oligopolists since 1939. If so, such a drop reflects the importance of the less concentrated truck, trailer, and shipbuilding industries, for the growing aircraft industries have been as concentrated as the automobile. In the instrument group this same index of concentration indicates that it has been high since 1919 with a slight rise and then slight drop after World War II.

The final group is tobacco, which has been the most concentrated of any group throughout the century. It has the characteristics of several of the four-digit food industries which, like tobacco, have been concentrated for a long time. In distilled liquors, prepared cereals, canned specialties, and in tobacco, the heavy investment in advertising and distribution has always encouraged concentration. There has also been concentration in the food industries whose raw materials came in good part from overseas, including sugar, cocoa, and chicle. The first of these three, Porters and Livesay's studies indicate, has become less concentrated in recent years, but concentration in the chicle (chewing gum) industry has remained high.

II

Livesay and Porter's second set of studies on the distribution of the products of the largest firms during the six decades of the century emphasizes the close relationship between concentration of industry and size of the firm. Very few of the eighty to ninety largest companies have appeared in the groups where the indices of concentration are low. In 1909, there were only two companies listed in all five of the least concentrated of the industrial groups and in 1960 only one. There were none during the century in the apparel or the furniture groups. Only one appeared in the printing and publishing group (Hearst Consolidated Publishing Company, listed in 1935 and 1947). Only two firms in the lumber industry were on the lists. (One appeared only once in 1929 and the other, the Weyerhaeuser Company, emerged only after World War II.) Three leather companies were listed, but all disappeared from the lists after 1939. . . .

Livesays and Porter's tables not only place the eighty to ninety largest firms into two-digit industrial groups, but also show the number of four-digit industries in which each of these firms operated. This detailed study . . . indicates that the large firm moved into new industries first as management carried out its strategy of growth by vertical integration and as it developed a "full line" of products which were made by comparable production technologies for somewhat similar markets. Later expansion came by a diversification, that is, the making of products from roughly similar production processes for very different markets. These methods of expansion are suggested by the summary tables, if the number of industries in which a firm operates is used as a very rough gauge of integration and diversification. It seems safe to say that in most cases, if a firm produces products in two to four four-digit industries, it has become a full line, vertically integrated company; if it produces in five to nine industries, it has begun to diversify; and if it produces in ten or more industries, it has become fully diversified.

In 1909, the majority of firms already made products in more than one but less than five industries. Twenty-eight still operated in only one four-digit industry. Only three of the largest firms made products in more than ten. They were General Electric, Westinghouse, and United States Steel. Eleven produced in five to nine industries. So the majority, thirty-eight, produced in two to four industries. In 1919, the pattern was still much the same, but by 1929 eight firms were operating in over ten industries, while twenty-three large firms were in the five to nine category (most of these were in five or six industries). Before the depression, the diversified firms (in ten or more industries) were clustered in the chemical and electrical machinery industries, and those that were beginning to diversify were the rubber, metals, and some food companies. During the depression diversification increased. Three of the five chemical companies operated in more than ten industries by 1935; the others operated in five and six industries. During the 1930's, Allis-Chalmers joined the other two electrical firms with products in over ten industries, as did U.S. Rubber. Another rubber company, Firestone, operated in seven industries. General Motors was making products in more than ten industries and Ford in nine. Two meat packers, Swift and Wilson, had moved into the ten-industry category, while Armour was in nine. Three primary metals firms joined U.S. Steel on the over-ten list, as did one machinery company, American Radiator.

During World War II, the same trend continued, and then after the war came a great wave of diversification. By 1960, the large majority of the firms were operating in more than five industries and thirty-three were in over ten. All but one of the nine chemical companies operated in ten industries and that one, Procter and Gamble, in eight. All four rubber companies, all four electronics companies (plus Allis-Chalmers), two of the four paper companies, five of the eight food companies, one textile company, two of the new aircraft companies as well as Borg Warner and General Motors in the transportation vehicle category were all producing goods in ten or more four-digit industries. On the other hand, only two of the metals, none of the oil and none of the machinery companies except Allis-Chalmers and Borg Warner were in more than ten industries. By this date only two of the largest firms other than those in oil operated in less than five industries and fifteen of the oil firms were still operating in less than five. Among the country's top 100 firms, only four oil firms were producing in a single industry. Nevertheless, since the census does not consider the production of crude oil, the transportation of crude and refined and the marketing of refined as manufacturing activities, a petroleum company can be fully integrated and still have its products in one four-digit industry, and also can be beginning to diversify when it is operating only in two to four four-digit industries.

By 1960, the large American enterprise had become multi-industrial. The firms which were the first to diversify were those in the most technologically advanced industries—chemicals, rubber, electrical, and transportation machinery. They were followed by others with less complex technologies including food, metals, other machinery, and even oil. In the 1960's, the latter still remained less diversified than the former. As these large enterprises which began in concentrated industries started to diversify, they often went into unconcentrated industries. Just as often they moved into other concentrated industries and so made such industries more competitive.

III

These statistics have suggested the broad outlines of concentration and size in American industry during the twentieth century, but they only hint at the dynamics of these changes. By supplementing the data compiled by Livesay and Porter with information drawn from the studies by economists, I can suggest tentative answers to these essential questions: Why did some industries become dominated by a few firms and others not? Why did the large firm develop within concentrated industries? Why did it then become multi-industrial? Finally, why did firms in the most modern, science-based industries lead the way in formulating a strategy of expansion by diversification?

The industrial sector of the American economy, like that of any modern technologically advanced nation, grew out of two different types of industries. There were those industries with a history, those which had long been involved in processing goods for an older, predominantly agrarian economy. And there were the new chemical and machinery industries which, based on modern engineering and science, only began to develop in the late nineteenth century.

During much of the·nineteenth century American manufacturing was primarily involved in the processing of products of field and forest, with relatively small scale production of metals, chemicals, and stone, glass, and clay products. These older industries had long been characterized by small family businesses in much the same way as had agriculture, mining, and pre-railroad transportation. Even as late as 1909, the older industries produced the largest share of product value in American industry (65 per cent even if primary metals were excluded). The eight industrial groups in which there was very little concentration in 1909 were all in these older industries. On the other hand, by 1909 concentration was already significant in the newer machinery and chemically oriented, as well as many older metals industries whose production had been revolutionized by high-volume-output techniques based on modern metallurgical sciences (see Charts 1 and 2). And these metal, machinery, and chemical industries were the basis of the modern economy.

Before the great merger movement at the turn of the century, the large firm had made its appearance largely in those industries where manufacturers were required to develop extensive distribution networks. In the older industries based on agricultural products, this had been true for the processors of perishable goods like meat, beer, bananas, and tobacco which required refrigeration, quick transportation, or careful storage for high volume distribution. In the newer machinery groups concentration of production in the hands of a few large firms had occurred primarily where the manufacturers, using a complex technology, also needed a national or international sales organization in order to provide initial demonstrations, consumer credit, and service and repair. This occurred in such industries as agricultural machinery, sewing machines, cash registers, and electrical machinery.

During and after the price decline that followed the depression of the 1870's, the small, non-integrated manufacturers in most industries had joined associations or alliances which attempted to control price and production. Until the merger movement at the turn of the century, however, very few of these associations or cartels followed the example of John D. Rockefeller's Standard Oil Company, which converted the alliance into a centralized manufacturing organization and then integrated forward, to control partially its own marketing, and backward to control partially its own raw materials.

Only after the merger movement which began in early 1890's and culminated in the years 1897 to 1903 did the modern structure of American industry begin to appear. In those years mergers occurred more frequently and were more successful in the modern metals, and the new machinery and chemically oriented industrial groups, than in the older, longer established ones. . . .

In the more modern chemically oriented and machinery industries, the large firm could develop and improve complex technological processes and make the most of new administrative techniques. It could create an extensive purchasing organization for the buying of scarce and often distant raw materials in high volume and at lower costs, and in the case of some consumer goods, it could benefit from a widespread distribution network.

In these industries and in the primary metals, size of course provided its classic advantage. Heavy initial investment and continuing large operating costs were necessary to obtain the high volume production that would substantially reduce unit costs. The resulting lower unit cost made it difficult for firms with smaller output to stay in competition. At the same time, the high initial investment protected the company from the entrance of new firms into the industry. In much the same way, the creation of an extensive distribution network and heavy advertising expenses protected firms in some foods and tobacco and other consumer goods industries from new competitors.

For the makers of textiles, clothing, leather, and paper goods, and even the manufacturers of simple fabricated metals like structural steel, sheet metal, stampings, bolts, nuts, hardware, wire, and pipe, size did not provide these advantages. Nor did size offer significant economies to machinery and chemical firms which were not involved in complex production technology, did not have heavy fixed and operating costs, and did not produce for a relatively high volume market. For example, such industries as machine tools (including machine cutting, metal forming, and metal work tools), pumps and compressors, dies and patterns, paints, fertilizers, and certain acids and salts did not secure such economies. These industries remain unconcentrated, and in them the large firm was rarely a continuing success. So too in the food industries the successful large firms were those such as producers of meat, breakfast cereals, biscuits, and distilled liquors which could benefit from the establishment of large distribution networks and the extensive use of advertising; or those few high volume producers using relatively complex and costly refining techniques, as in the case of sugar and some corn products; or those like sugar and chocolate firms whose large buying organization gave them advantages in purchasing a raw material that came from overseas.

. . . In the first years of the century the successful mergers began quickly to expand by completing their lines and by vertical integration. Many of these horizontal combinations consolidated their factories into a single manufacturing department, created their own wholesaling and in some cases retailing organization, developed their own purchasing, and often moved back to take at least partial control of parts and accessories firms and of semi-finished and raw materials. Growth through integration helped preserve concentration. The cost, technological, and administrative advantages of size became even more pronounced. Entrance by new firms into the industry became even more hazardous and competition by existing small non-integrated enterprises even more difficult. At the same time it may have helped oligopoly replace monopoly or duopoly in some important cases; for, as different horizontal combinations controlling a large share of the production at one stage of an industrial process, integrated backward and forward, they gave new competition to the combination controlling the other stages in the process. This happened when primary steel manufacturers moved into fabrication and fabricators into making of sheet steel or gray iron, and when crude oil producers moved into refining and refiners moved into the production of crude oil, or when the cartridge makers decided to produce their own powder or the powder companies decided to go into chemicals.

For the successful mergers completed at the turn of the century, the primary strategy of growth continued to be vertical integration until the 1920's. Most firms developed marketing and purchasing organizations shortly after they combined manufacturing activities. The patterns of further integration differed, however, from industry to industry. Nearly all primary metals firms obtained some control of supplies of ore and fuel, and a number moved forward into the fabrication of simple metal products. Almost none, however, went so far as producing machinery, because this involved them in a very different technology of production and different marketing requirements. The machinery companies, on the other hand, particularly those using interchangeable parts manufacturing, moved back to obtain for themselves the parts and accessories needed to assure a continuous flow of materials for their assembly lines. Such backward integration, like that in metals, was essentially defensive. However, machinery firms only rarely moved still further backward into building their own blast furnaces once the supply seemed fairly assured, for the cost of such production was very high and the technology of production and the market needs were very different.

In the chemically oriented industries those making a single major product (such as gasoline or tires for the consumer market) tended to obtain some control of all the processes involved, from the production of raw materials to retailing to the final customer. By World War I, the leading rubber companies had already purchased rubber plantations in the Far East and had begun to build their own retail tire outlets. The story was more dramatic in the oil industry where the coming of the automobile, the opening of the new fields, and the breakup of the old Standard Oil Company in 1911 led to a spate of mergers in the second decade of the century. The old Standard Oil firms, which were largely refining and distribution companies, moved backward into the production of crude; those based in the new oil fields—such as Texaco, Gulf, and Phillips—moved forward into refining and distribution. In the chemical industry the large fertilizer and salt firms secured control of raw materials as did duPont. Unlike duPont, however, their processing techniques were simple, raw materials ample, and initial investment and operating costs were relatively low. These older industries, therefore, never became concentrated. After duPont moved into chemicals, and as Union Carbide and the other modern chemical companies grew, they tended to integrate backward to assure themselves of basic materials; but they rarely moved forward into the production of consumer goods, largely because of the very different marketing organization needed.

The prevalence of expansion by vertical integration from the beginning of the century until the 1920's was pointed out by Willard Thorp in his excellent analysis of the 1919 Census of Manufactures, entitled *The Integration of Industrial Operations.* Thorp analyzed the product distribution of close to 5,000 central office (that is multiplant) firms, listing joint products, by-products, complementary products, auxiliary products, dissimilar products from similar processes, dissimilar processes for the same market, and finally successive products. This last (which he properly defined as vertical integration) he found to be "the most prevalent of the complex forms of organization." With the exception of stone, glass, and clay, this form occurred most often in the more concentrated industrial groups. One half (51 per cent) of the central office firms which operated in more than a "single type establishment" produced successive products. Such integration occurred most often in the following industrial groups and in the following order: iron and steel; stone, glass, and clay; metals and metal products other than iron and steel (includes machinery); chemicals (which included petroleum and rubber); and vehicles. The industrial groups which had the fewest integrated firms were food, liquor and beverages, textiles, leather, and lumber. In the food industry those firms which were integrated appeared in meat packing and the refining of sugar and corn products.

Thorp's data also reinforces the conclusions that can be drawn from Livesay and Porter's statistics by emphasizing that, while vertical integration had become quite common by 1919, expansion by diversification was still a rare phenomenon in American industry. Of the 4,813 central office firms, only 0.9 per cent operated in more than five and 0.2 per cent in more than ten industries. The only industrial groups in which 2 per cent or more of the central office firms produced in more than five industries were vehicles (4.8 per cent), nonferrous metals and machinery (4.3 per cent), and iron and steel (2.3 per cent). Chemical firms (which included petroleum and rubber) were still largely undiversified, with only four out of 557 (0.4 per cent) operating in more than five industries.

By the 1920's the first stage of growth of the large enterprise in the United States was essentially complete. The large firm had come primarily in the newer and most technologically complex industries where size had real economic advantages, and where the necessity of assured supplies had encouraged vertical integration. These were precisely the industries which, as the century progressed, became increasingly critical to the continuing strength and growth of the national economy. In his recent book, *The Dual Economy*, Robert T. Averitt has identified such key industries by using eight criteria: technological convergence, capital goods production, industrial interdependence, price/cost effect on other industries, leading growth sectors, research and development, wage setting demand effect, and full employment bottleneck industries. Averitt identified forty-one such key industries. In 1919, the top 100 firms operated in all but two of these key industries. These two were machine tools and mechanical measuring devices. Furthermore, these key industries (with the exceptions of machine tools, measuring devices, construction machinery, and one or two of the chemical industries) had become quite concentrated by 1919.

IV

Since 1920, concentration in American manufacturing has remained relatively stable—growing in such industries as glass, paper, and textiles where the production and distribution processes became more costly and complicated, and declining, though not until after World War II, in those areas that were already concentrated. And since 1920, the large firms have increasingly followed a strategy of growth by diversification rather than by vertical integration. Indeed there are indications that, because firms found it difficult to both diversify and integrate, integration in American manufacturing may have declined since Thorp made his study. Diversification, that is the development of dissimilar products based on similar technological and production processes (or as in the case of the food industries, new products using similar distribution facilities) has made for the greatest change in the profile of American industry during the last thirty or forty years.

The pioneers in the new strategy of diversification were those firms which had the technological and research skills to develop new products and the administrative experience to produce and distribute them at high volume for national and international markets. Not only did technology give them a greater opportunity to develop new products and processes than had other firms, but in addition, their size and technological and managerial know-how continued to protect them from new competitors in their basic fields. Moreover, since their volume of operations tended to assure higher profits than those of smaller firms, they had more capital available (particularly during the years of the Great Depression) to carry on the costly research and development work required to bring the new products to market. Understandably, then, the large chemical and electrical machinery firms were the first to embark on a strategy of diversification, and understandably, too, they were followed by makers of automobiles, other machinery, rubber, glass, instruments, and some food industries, and to a lesser extent by primary metals and oil firms.

More than technological opportunity, however, was needed to bring most of these firms to a strategy of diversification. It took the economic pressure created by the slowing down of the economy in the 1920's and its miserable performance in the 1930's to turn these technically sophisticated enterprises to the new strategy of expansion. Precisely because these firms had accumulated vast resources in skilled manpower, facilities, and equipment, their executives were under even greater pressure than those of smaller firms to find new markets as the old ones ceased to grow. In the 1920's, the chemical companies, each starting from a somewhat different technological base, began to widen their product lines into new industries. In the same decade the great electrical manufacturers—General Electric and Westinghouse—which had concentrated primarily on the manufacture of light and power equipment, diversified into production of a wide variety of household appliances. They also entered electronics production with radios and x-ray equipment. During the depression General Motors (and to a lesser extent other firms in the automobile industry) moved into diesels, appliances, tractors, and airplanes. Some makers of primary metals, particularly aluminum and copper, turned to consumer products like kitchenware and household fittings, while rubber firms developed the possibilities of rubber chemistry to compensate for declining tire sales. In the same period food companies employed their existing distribution organizations to market an increasing variety of products.

Where the depression pushed firms into diversification, the war encouraged the adoption of this strategy by opening new opportunities for the production of new products. The huge synthetic rubber program, for example, caused both rubber and petroleum companies to make far greater use of chemical technologies than they had ever done before. Radar and other electronics equipment carried the electrical, radio, and machinery firms further into this new field. The production of tanks, high-speed aircraft, and new drugs all created skills and resources which large enterprises were anxious to put to use after the war ended. The post-war boom, which was characterized by pent-up demand and by a rapid expansion of the amount of government funds for research and development, gave an impetus to the great spread of diversification in the late 1940's and 1950's. Nevertheless, most makers of primary metals, some machinery manufacturers, and oil companies have remained less diversified than the producers of chemical, electrical, electronic equipment, and transportation vehicles (including aircraft engines and airframes).

Unfortunately, the studies made of American industry in the 1930's and 1940's (including those by Adolf Berle, Gardiner C. Means, and Warren G. Nutter) focused on concentration and said very little about the product distribution of large firms. Two recent analyses, however, help supplement and reinforce Livesay and Porter's tables by providing somewhat different and broader samples. One is Frederick M. Sherer's study of the product distribution of the 500 largest firms on *Fortune's* 1955 list. On Sherer's list, the chemical industry had the most firms (thirteen) with products in ten or more industries. Second was vehicles, with twelve (eight transportation vehicle firms and four aircraft firms) producing in more than ten industries, and electrical machinery was third with eleven.

More revealing is Michael Gort's review in his *Diversification and Integration in American Industry* of the product additions made by 111 enterprises after 1929. He showed that for the period 1929 to 1939 chemical companies made the largest number of additions, followed in order by those in electrical machinery; transportation vehicles; food; primary metals; rubber; stone, glass and clay; machinery; and paper. From 1939 to 1950, the order was chemicals, transportation equipment (now including aircraft), electrical machinery, rubber, petroleum, paper, food, and machinery. As time passed, food and metal firms tended to limit their diversification while the chemically oriented rubber (especially tire) and petroleum firms moved toward greater diversification. Gort also shows that when firms ventured into new industries they went primarily into the chemical and machinery fields. In the 1929 to 1939 period, the industries which the large firms moved into (as opposed to the type of firm making the additions) were in order, chemicals, machinery, fabricated metals, electrical machinery, food, and stone, glass and clay. In 1939 to 1950, they were chemicals, machinery, electrical machinery, transportation machinery, stone, glass and clay, food, and primary metals. As Gort stresses, "The industries which have become complex, and changing technologies which require relatively large numbers of technical personnel have proved the most attractive as diversification outlets.

Diversification has come primarily in those industries which make the greatest use of sophisticated scientific techniques, particularly those developed by modern chemistry and physics. Studies of men and money devoted by American industry to research and development further testify to applied science's importance to these same industries. One careful appraisal indicated that as early as 1929, 75.8 per cent of all research and development personnel were concentrated in five industrial groups. The largest number were in the electrical industry (31.6 per cent), followed by chemicals (18.1 per cent), machinery (6.6 per cent), metals (6.6 per cent), and rubber (5.9 per cent). Nearly a quarter of a century later (in 1952) five industries again accounted for 78.1 per cent of R & D personnel. The electrical industry (including electronics) still employed the largest number of R & D personnel with transportation vehicles (largely aircraft) next, then chemicals, machinery, and instruments in that order. (If the research personnel in petroleum and metals were added, seven industries in 1952 would have employed 87.4 per cent of the total.) By 1957, the same top five as in 1952 accounted for 84.2 per cent. Research and development costs followed the same pattern. In 1960, the same five industries incurred 88.0 per cent of all research and development costs in the industrial sector of the American economy.

The enterprises that followed the strategy of diversification in the most technologically sophisticated industries were also those that developed an effective new type of administrative organization, the decentralized structure. This form was initially fashioned by duPont to meet the needs arising from operating in several industries and markets. Its adoption in turn made easier the process of moving from one industry to another. The decentralized structure consisted of autonomous operating divisions and a general office. The operating divisions each handled all the functions involved in producing a line of products for a major market. The general office, manned by staff and general executives, evaluated the performance of the divisions and made the critical decisions as to the allocation of the enterprise's resources, including capital, plant and equipment, and technological and administrative skills. By 1960, the large majority of diversified firms had adopted this structure.

The decentralized structure effectively institutionalized the strategy of diversification. The research department of such an enterprise developed new products and tested their commercial value. The executives in the general office, freed from nearly all routine duties involved in the output of specific goods, determined whether the new product could use enough of the firm's resources or could aid in building enough new ones to warrant its large scale production and sale. If the executives agreed on its profit potential, they then decided whether to handle the product through an existing division or to create a new one.

The diversified and decentralized industrial giant has, since World War II, taken over an increasing share of American industrial activity. In 1947, the 200 largest companies, many of which had not yet become fully diversified and decentralized, accounted for 30 per cent of the value added by manufacturing. By 1963, when most of them had adopted the new strategy and structure, they accounted for 41 per cent of value added. At the same time these companies, by moving into new products for new markets also helped to decrease concentration in the critical science-based industries. The product value produced by oligopolies has decreased in the chemical, rubber, electrical machinery, transportation vehicles, and stone, glass and clay, as well as in primary metals and food. (There was, however, little decrease in the petroleum industry, for while petroleum companies could move into chemicals and synthetic rubber, rubber and chemical companies have not yet developed a synthetic gasoline.)

These giant multi-industry enterprises are of central importance to the American economy. They have generated the great share of the private funds used for industrial research and development and employ by far the largest number of people who carry out the technological innovation so essential to economic growth. Moreover, they spend the greatest part of the massive funds that the federal government has allocated to research and development since World War II. These are the same firms that, according to Europeans, have moved so successfully into the Common Market—more successfully indeed than many European firms themselves. These are the corporations that the government used as prime contractors for weapons production in World War II and again in the Korean and Viet Nam conflicts.

The modern diversified enterprise represents a calculated, rational response of technically trained professional managers to the needs and opportunities of changing technologies and markets. It is much less the product of ambitious and able individual entrepreneurs or of governmental policies. Early in the twentieth century the most successful large enterprises were in those industries which had the most complex and costly production and distribution facilities and where, therefore, the economies of scale were most obvious. These same firms had the technological capabilities as well as the necessary funds for the development of new products and processes when the economy leveled off and faltered so badly in the 1920's and 1930's. They were the enterprises that gained the most from the development of new technological skills and resources during World War II. They were, therefore, in the best position to benefit from the post-war boom and full employment that has continued through the 1960's.

The individual entrepreneur did play a part in the original creation of many of these giant enterprises. Early in the century, a breed of individual manufacturers and financiers, who resembled Joseph Schumpeter's creative entrepreneur, took an important role in their formation. Nevertheless, to be successful, a business empire builder had to pick his industry carefully, avoiding those like textiles, leather, lumber, or furniture and turning instead to those like steel, chemicals, electrical machinery, or automobiles. Even within the industries where conditions favored the enterprising empire builder, technological training quickly proved its worth. In the automobile industry, for example, it is instructive to compare the outstanding record of Alfred P. Sloan, Jr., educated at M.I.T., to the disastrous one turned in by the renowned financier William C. Durant, or even to the dismal performance of the untrained manufacturer, Henry Ford, after the industry began to reach maturity. In chemicals, a similar comparison can be made with the performance of M.I.T. trained duPonts to that of financier Orlando Weber of Allied Chemical.

Furthermore, strategies of diversification were rarely if ever carried out by individual financiers or owner-executives. They were undertaken by professional managers, anonymous bureaucrats whose names are not even known to the most conscientious student of American business history. These men were executives who precisely because of their educational background and their experience in the management of the large, vertically integrated enterprises, had developed the necessary technological and administrative skills to initiate and execute a new and complex strategy of expansion. Such skills were rare in the small-unit clothing, furniture, or lumber industries, or even in the textile or publishing and printing industries. Such skills, so vital to industrial innovation and economic growth, still appear to be in short supply in the rest of the world, even in the old industrial countries of western Europe.

Governmental policies appear to have had even less effect on the development of the large firm or the overall structure of industry than have had individual entrepreneurs. Before World War II the policies of the federal government that most affected American industry were those involving anti-trust regulation, taxes, and tariffs. Clearly the needs and requirements of changing technologies and markets rather than anti-trust policies have played the major role in determining changes in concentration in American industries. Anti-trust had nothing to do with keeping the clothing industry diffuse and transportation vehicles concentrated. It was research and development, not anti-trust that led to the lessening of concentration in the electrical machinery, chemical, and rubber industries after World War II. For a brief period the breakup of Standard Oil affected concentration in the petroleum industry, but the coming of a huge new market—the automobile—and the opening of new oil fields were equally significant. Tariffs and taxes may have played a more important role, but tariffs were generally as protective on products of industries that remained diffuse and operated through small firms as they were on the products of those industries where a few firms came to dominate. Tax policies in the 1930's undoubtedly influenced the reinvestment of profits for research and development. The undisturbed profits tax did not, however, prevent diversification in those industries where firms had technological opportunities for product development.

Since the 1930's, however, the federal government has played a larger role in the American economy, and while not directly affecting the structure of industry in any significant way, it has strongly influenced the environment in which industry operates. Committed to assuring full employment, the government has helped in maintaining aggregate demand and assuring a stable and even increasing market. Of more direct importance to American industry the government has made available vast amounts of money for research and development. Through its control of the allocation of these resources the federal government has and can continue to guide the direction which research and development of new products and processes takes. At the same time, the growing concentration of production of these technologically advanced products by a few hundred large, multi-industry enterprises would seem to facilitate the coordination of long range planning between the government and private enterprises. Such coordinated planning of the use of technological skills and resources, combined with effective policies for maintaining aggregate demand may ultimately make it possible for Americans to meet the continuing challenges of successfully managing the technologically advanced industrial economy. Even if such sensible cooperation fails, these giant enterprises will undoubtedly continue to play as decisive a role in the American economy during the remainder of the twentieth century, as they have during the years of this century that have already become history.

The Riot Participant

NATIONAL ADVISORY COMMISSION ON CIVIL DISORDERS

For the American people the 1960s was a decade of violence. Those years were characterized both by the tragic assassinations of John F. Kennedy, Robert F. Kennedy, Martin Luther King, Medgar Evers, Malcolm X, and George Lincoln Rockwell and by shocking riots in more than a hundred cities. The assassins were either irrational or evil men, but ghetto rioters represented a far more complex yet ultimately solvable problem. Seeking an answer to the question of why blacks rioted, the National Advisory Commission on Civil Disorders analyzed interview surveys made after the 1967 Detroit and Newark riots. These surveys indicate that common assumptions concerning rioters are invalid.

It is sometimes assumed that the rioters were criminal types, overactive social deviants, or riffraff—recent migrants, members of an uneducated underclass, alienated from responsible Negroes, and without broad social or political concerns. It is often implied that there was no effort within the Negro community to attempt to reduce the violence.

We have obtained data on participation from four different sources:

Eyewitness accounts from more than 1,200 interviews in our staff reconnaissance survey of 20 cities;

Interview surveys based on probability samples of riot area residents in the two major riot cities—Detroit and Newark—designed to elicit anony-

From *Report of the National Advisory Commission on Civil Disorders* (Washington: U.S. Government Printing Office, 1 March 1968), pp. 73–77. Footnotes omitted.

mous self-identification of participants as rioters, counterrioters or non-involved;

Arrest records from 22 cities; and

A special study of arresters in Detroit.

Only partial information is available on the total numbers of participants. In the Detroit survey, approximately 11 percent of the sampled residents over the age of 15 in the two disturbance areas admittedly participated in rioting; another 20 to 25 percent admitted to having been bystanders but claimed that they had not participated; approximately 16 percent claimed they had engaged in counterriot activity; and the largest proportion (48 to 53 percent) claimed they were at home or elsewhere and did not participate. However, a large proportion of the Negro community apparently believed that more was gained than lost through rioting, according to the Newark and Detroit surveys.

Greater precision is possible in describing the characteristics of those who participated. We have combined the data from the four sources to construct a profile of the typical rioter and to compare him with the counterrioter and the noninvolved.

THE PROFILE OF A RIOTER

The typical rioter in the summer of 1967 was a Negro, unmarried male between the ages of 15 and 24. He was in many ways very different from the stereotype. He was not a migrant. He was born in the state and was a lifelong resident of the city in which the riot took place. Economically his position was about the same as his Negro neighbors who did not actively participate in the riot.

Although he had not, usually, graduated from high school, he was somewhat better educated than the average inner-city Negro, having at least attended high school for a time.

Nevertheless, he was more likely to be working in a menial or low status job as an unskilled laborer. If he was employed, he was not working full time and his employment was frequently interrupted by periods of unemployment.

He feels strongly that he deserves a better job and that he is barred from achieving it, not because of lack of training, ability, or ambition, but because of discrimination by employers.

He rejects the white bigot's stereotype of the Negro as ignorant and shiftless. He takes great pride in his race and believes that in some respects Negroes are superior to whites. He is extremely hostile to whites, but his hostility is more apt to be a product of social and economic class than of race; he is almost equally hostile toward middle class Negroes.

He is substantially better informed about politics than Negroes who were not involved in the riots. He is more likely to be actively engaged in civil rights efforts, but is extremely distrustful of the political system and of political leaders.

THE PROFILE OF A COUNTERRIOTER

The typical counterrioter, who risked injury and arrest to walk the streets urging rioters to "cool it," was an active supporter of existing social institutions. He was, for example, far more likely than either the rioter or the noninvolved to feel that this country is worth defending in a major war. His actions and his attitudes reflected his substantially greater stake in the social system; he was considerably better educated and more affluent than either the rioter or the noninvolved. He was somewhat more likely than the rioter, but less likely than the non-involved, to have been a migrant. In all other respects he was identical to the noninvolved.

CHARACTERISTICS OF PARTICIPANTS

Race

Of the arrestees 83 percent were Negroes; 15 percent were whites. Our interviews in 20 cities indicate that almost all rioters were Negroes.

Age

The survey data from Detroit, the arrest records, and our interviews in 20 cities, all indicate that the rioters were late teenagers or young adults. In the Detroit survey, 61.3 percent of the self-reported rioters were between the ages of 15 and 24, and 86.3 percent were between 15 and 35. The arrest data indicate that 52.5 percent of the arrestees were between 15 and 24, and 80.8 percent were between 15 and 35.

Of the noninvolved, by contrast, only 22.6 percent in the Detroit survey were between 15 and 24, and 38.3 percent were between 15 and 35.

Sex

In the Detroit survey, 61.4 percent of the self-reported rioters were male. Arrestees, however, were almost all male—89.3 percent. Our interviews in 20 cities indicate that the majority of rioters were male. The large difference in proportion between the Detroit survey data and the arrestee figures probably reflects either selectivity in the arrest process or less dramatic, less provocative riot behavior by women.

Family Structure

Three sources of available information—the Newark survey, the Detroit arrest study, and arrest records from four cities—indicate a tendency for rioters to be single. The Newark survey indicates that rioters were single—56.2 percent—more often than the noninvolved—49.6 percent.

The Newark survey also indicates that rioters were more likely to have been divorced or separated—14.2 percent—than the noninvolved —6.4 percent. However, the arrest records from four cities indicate that only a very small percentage of those arrested fall into this category.

In regard to the structure of the family in which he was raised, the self-reported rioter, according to the Newark survey, was not significantly different from many of his Negro neighbors who did not actively participate in the riot. Twenty-five and five-tenths percent of the self-reported rioters and 23 percent of the noninvolved were brought up in homes where no adult male lived.

Region of Upbringing

Both survey data and arrest records demonstrate unequivocally that those brought up in the region in which the riot occurred are much more likely to have participated in the riots. The percentage of self-reported rioters brought up in the North is almost identical for the Detroit survey—74.4 percent—and the Newark survey—74 percent. By contrast, of the noninvolved, 36 per cent in Detroit and 52.4 per cent in Newark were brought up in the region in which the disorder occurred.

Data available from five cities on the birthplace of arrestees indicate that 63 percent of the arrestees were born in the North. Although birthplace is not necessarily identical with place of upbringing, the data are sufficiently similar to provide strong support for the conclusion.

Of the self-reported counterrioters, however, 47.5 percent were born in the North, according to the Detroit survey, a figure which places them between self-reported rioters and the noninvolved. Apparently, a significant consequence of growing up in the South is the tendency toward noninvolvement in a riot situation, while involvement in a riot, either in support of or against existing social institutions, was more common among those born in the North.

Residence

Rioters are not only more likely than the noninvolved to have been born in the region in which the riot occurred, but they are also more likely to have been long-term residents of the city in which the disturbance took place. The Detroit survey data indicate that 59.4 percent of the self-reported rioters, but only 34.6 percent of the noninvolved, were born in Detroit. The comparable figures in the Newark survey are 53.5 percent and 22.5 percent.

Outsiders who temporarily entered the city during the riot might have left before the surveys were conducted and therefore may be underestimated in the survey data. However, the arrest data, which is contemporaneous with the riot, suggest that few outsiders were involved: 90 percent of those arrested resided in the riot city, 7 percent lived in the same state, and only 1 percent were from outside the state. Our interviews in 20 cities corroborate these conclusions.

Income

In the Detroit and Newark survey data, income level alone does not seem to correlate with self-reported riot participation. The figures from the two cities are not directly comparable since respondents were asked for individual income in Detroit and family income in Newark. More Detroit self-reported rioters (38.6 percent) had annual incomes under $5,000 per year than the noninvolved (30.3 percent), but even this small difference disappears when the factor of age is taken into account.

In the Newark data, in which the age distributions of self-reported rioters and the noninvolved are more similar, there is almost no difference between the rioters, 32.6 percent of whom had annual incomes under $5,000, and the noninvolved, 29.4 percent of whom had annual incomes under $5,000.

The similarity in income distribution should not, however, lead to the conclusion that more affluent Negroes are as likely to riot as poor

Negroes. Both surveys were conducted in disturbance areas where incomes are considerably lower than in the city as a whole and the surrounding metropolitan area. Nevertheless, the data shows that rioters are not necessarily the poorest of the poor.

While income fails to distinguish self-reported rioters from those who were not involved, it does distinguish counterrioters from rioters and the noninvolved. Less than 9 per cent of both those who rioted and those not involved earned more than $10,000 annually. Yet almost 20 percent of the counterrioters earned this amount or more. In fact, there were no male self-reported counterrioters in the Detroit survey who eaned less than $5,000 annually. In the Newark sample there were seven respondents who owned their own homes; none of them participated in the riot. While extreme poverty does not necessarily move a man to riot, relative affluence seems at least to inhibit him from attacking the existing social order and may motivate him to take considerable risk to protect it.

Education

Level of schooling is strongly related to participation. Those with some high school education were more likely to riot than those who had only finished grade school. In the Detroit survey, 93 percent of the self-reported rioters had gone beyond grade school, compared with 72.1 percent of the noninvolved. In the Newark survey the comparable figures are 98.1 and 85.7 percent. The majority of self-reported rioters were not, however, high school graduates.

The counterrioters were clearly the best educated of the three groups. Approximately twice as many counterrioters had attended college as had the noninvolved, and half again as many counterrioters had attended college as rioters. Considered with the information on income, the data suggest that counterrioters were probably well on their way into the middle class.

Education and income are the only factors which distinguish the counterrioter from the noninvolved. Apparently, a high level of education and income not only prevents rioting but is more likely to lead to active, responsible opposition to rioting.

Employment

The Detroit and Newark surveys, the arrest records from four cities, and the Detroit arrest study all indicate that there are no substantial differences in unemployment between the rioters and the noninvolved.

Unemployment levels among both groups were extremely high. In the Detroit survey, 29.6 percent of the self-reported rioters were unemployed; in the Newark survey, 29.7 percent; in the four-city arrest data, 32.2 percent; and in the Detroit arrest study, 21.8 percent. The unemployment rates for the noninvolved in the Detroit and Newark surveys were 31.5 and 19.0 percent.

Self-reported rioters were more likely to be only intermittently employed, however, than the noninvolved. Respondents in Newark were asked whether they had been unemployed for as long as a month or more during the last year. Sixty-one percent of the self-reported rioters, but only 43.4 percent of the noninvolved, answered, "yes."

Despite generally higher levels of education, rioters were more likely than the noninvolved to be employed in unskilled jobs. In the Newark survey, 50 percent of the self-reported rioters, but only 39.6 percent of the noninvolved, had unskilled jobs.

Attitudes About Employment

The Newark survey data indicate that self-reported rioters were more likely to feel dissatisfied with their present jobs than were the noninvolved.

Only 29.3 percent of the rioters, compared with 44.4 percent of the noninvolved, thought their present jobs appropriate for them in responsibility and pay. Of the self-reported rioters, 67.6 percent, compared with 56.1 percent of the noninvolved, felt that it was impossible to obtain the kind of job they wanted. Of the self-reported rioters, 69 percent, as compared with 50 percent of the noninvolved, felt that racial discrimination was the major obstacle to finding better employment. Despite this feeling, surprising numbers of rioters (76.9 percent) responded that "getting what you want out of life is a matter of ability, not being in the right place at the right time."

Racial Attitudes

The Detroit and Newark surveys indicate that rioters have strong feelings of racial pride, if not racial superiority. In the Detroit survey, 48.6 percent of the self-reported rioters said that they felt Negroes were more dependable than whites. Only 22.4 percent of the noninvolved stated this. In Newark, the comparable figures were 45 and 27.8 percent. The Newark survey data indicate that rioters wanted to be called "black" rather than "Negro" or "colored" and were somewhat more likely than the noninvolved to feel that all Negroes should study African history and languages.

To what extent this racial pride antedated the riot or was produced by the riot is impossible to determine from the survey data. Certainly the riot experience seems to have been associated with increased pride in the minds of many participants. This was vividly illustrated by the statement of a Detroit rioter:

INTERVIEWER: You said you were feeling good when you followed the crowds?
RESPONDENT: I was feeling proud, man, at the fact that I was a Negro. I felt like I was a first-class citizen. I didn't feel ashamed of my race because of what they did.

Similar feelings were expressed by an 18-year-old Detroit girl who reported that she had been a looter:

INTERVIEWER: What is the Negro then if he's not American?
RESPONDENT: A Negro, he's considered a slave to the white folks. But half of them know that they're slaves and feel that they can't do nothing about it because they're just going along with it. But most of them they seem to get it in their heads now how the white folks treat them and how they've been treating them and how they've been slaves for the white folks.

Along with increased racial pride there appears to be intense hostility toward whites. Self-reported rioters in both the Detroit and Newark surveys were more likely to feel that civil rights groups with white and Negro leaders would do better without the whites. In Detroit, 36.1 percent of the self-reported rioters thought that this statement was true, while only 21.1 percent of the noninvolved thought so. In the Newark survey, 51.4 percent of the self-reported rioters agreed; 33.1 percent of the noninvolved shared this opinion.

Self-reported rioters in Newark were also more likely to agree with the statement, "Sometimes I hate white people." Of the self-reported rioters, 72.4 percent agreed; of the noninvolved, 50 percent agreed.

The intensity of the self-reported rioters' racial feelings may suggest that the recent riots represented traditional interracial hostilities. Two sources of data suggest that this interpretation is probably incorrect.

First, the Newark survey data indicate that rioters were almost as hostile to middle-class Negroes as they were to whites. Seventy-one and four-tenths percent of the self-reported rioters, but only 59.5 percent of the noninvolved, agreed with the statement, "Negroes who make a lot of money like to think they are better than other Negroes." Perhaps even more significant, particularly in light of the rioters' strong feelings of racial pride, is that 50.5 percent of the self-reported rioters agreed that "Negroes who make a lot of money are just as bad as white people." Only 35.2 percent of the noninvolved shared this opinion.

Second, the arrest data show that the great majority of those arrested during the disorders were generally charged with a crime relating to looting or curfew violations. Only 2.4 percent of the arrests were for assault and 0.1 percent were for homicide, but 31.3 percent of the arrests were for breaking and entering—crimes directed against white property rather than against individual whites.

Political Attitudes and Involvement

Respondents in the Newark survey were asked about relatively simple items of political information, such as the race of prominent local and national political figures. In general, the self-reported rioters were much better informed than the noninvolved. For example, self-reported rioters were more likely to know that one of the 1966 Newark mayoral candidates was a Negro. Of the rioters, 77.1 percent—but only 61.6 percent of the noninvolved—identified him correctly. The overall scores on a series of similar questions also reflect the self-reported rioters' higher levels of information.

Self-reported rioters were also more likely to be involved in activities associated with Negro rights. At the most basic level of political participation, they were more likely than the noninvolved to talk frequently about Negro rights. In the Newark survey, 53.8 percent of the self-reported rioters, but only 34.9 percent of the noninvolved, said that they talked about Negro rights nearly every day.

The self-reported rioters also were more likely to have attended a meeting or participated in civil rights activity. Of the rioters, 39.3 percent—but only 25.7 percent of the noninvolved—reported that they had engaged in such activity.

In the Newark survey, respondents were asked how much they thought they could trust the local government. Only 4.8 percent of the self-reported rioters, compared with 13.7 percent of the noninvolved, said that they felt they could trust it most of the time; 42.2 percent of the self-reported rioters and 33.9 percent of the noninvolved reported that they could almost never trust the government.

In the Detroit survey, self-reported rioters were much more likely to attribute the riot to anger about politicians and police than were the noninvolved. Of the self-reported rioters, 43.2 percent—but only 19.6 percent of the noninvolved—said anger against politicians had a great deal to do with causing the riot. Of the self-reported rioters, 70.5 percent, compared with 48.8 percent of the noninvolved, believed that anger against the police had a great deal to do with causing riot.

Perhaps the most revealing and disturbing measure of the rioters' anger at the social and political system was their response to a question asking whether they thought "the country was worth fighting for in the event of a major world war." Of the self-reported rioters, 39.4 percent in Detroit and 52.8 percent in Newark shared a negative view. In contrast, 15.5 percent of the noninvolved in Detroit and 27.8 percent of the noninvolved in Newark shared this sentiment. Almost none of the self-reported counterrioters in Detroit—3.3 percent—agreed with the self-reported rioters.

Some comments of interviewees are worthy of note:

Not worth fighting for—if Negroes had an equal chance it would be worth fighting for.

Not worth fighting for—I am not a true citizen so why should I?

Not worth fighting for—because my husband came back from Vietnam and nothing had changed.

25

Protean Man

ROBERT JAY LIFTON

What manner of person is the American of the 1970s? Delineating national character or personality is a difficult task, and in confronting that task, Robert Jay Lifton, a psychiatrist, does not limit himself to American material but draws on both cross-cultural experiences in the Orient and European literary examples. Lifton is convinced that the pressures of contemporary historical forces account for the constant shifting and changing of one's image, which has become a universally shared tendency.

I wish to discuss a set of psychological patterns that I believe to be characteristic of contemporary life and that I shall summarize under the concept of "protean man." I intend this to be no more than a preliminary statement of an idea I hope to pursue more thoroughly in the future, but I shall at least try to make clear what I mean by protean man. The essay is part of a long-standing attempt to combine depth-psychological and historical perspectives—an approach greatly influenced by the psychoanalytic tradition, notably by the work of Erik Erikson; by anthropological and sociological studies of national character, particularly those of [Margaret] Mead, [Ruth] Benedict, and [David] Riesman; and by work from various sources that emphasize man's dependence on the symbol and the image, including that of [Ernst] Cassirer, [William L.] Langer, and [Kenneth E.] Boulding.

My stress is on change and flux. I shall therefore not make much

From *The Psychoanalytic Interpretation of History*, edited by Benjamin B. Wolman (New York: Basic Books, Inc., Publishers, 1971), pp. 33–49. Reprinted by permission of the publisher. © 1971 by Basic Books, Inc.

use of such words as "character" and "personality," both of which suggest fixity and permanence. Erikson's concept of identity has been, among other things, an effort to get away from this principle of fixity; I have been using the term "self-process" to convey still more specifically the idea of flow. For it is quite possible that even the image of personal identity, insofar as it suggests inner stability and sameness, is derived from a vision of a tradition culture in which man's relationship to his institutions and symbols are still relatively intact—hardly the case today. If we understand the self to be the person's symbol of his own organism, then self-process refers to the continuous psychic re-creation of that symbol.

CROSS-CULTURAL STUDIES

I came to this emphasis through work in cultures far removed from my own, studies of young (and not so young) Chinese and Japanese. Observations I was able to make in America, between and following these East Asian investigations, led me to the conviction that a very general process was taking place. I do not mean to suggest that everybody is becoming the same, or that a totally new "world self" is taking shape. But I am convinced that a universally shared style of self-process is emerging. It derives from the three-way interplay responsible for the behavior of human groups: the psychobiological potential common to all mankind at any moment in time; those traits given special emphasis in a particular cultural tradition; and those traits related to modern (and particularly contemporary) historical forces. My thesis is that this third factor plays an increasingly important part in shaping self-process.

My work with Chinese was done in Hong Kong, in connection with a study of the process of thought reform (or brainwashing) as conducted on the mainland. I found that Chinese intellectuals of varying ages, whatever their experience with thought reform itself, had gone through an extraordinary array of what I then called identity fragments—of combinations of belief and emotional involvement—each of which they could readily abandon in favor of another. I remember particularly the profound impression made on me by the extraordinary psychohistorical journey of one young man in particular. He began as a "filial son," or "young master," that elite status of an only son in an upper-class Chinese family, with all it meant within the traditional social structure. He then felt himself an abandoned and betrayed victim, as traditional cultural forms collapsed amid civil war and general chaos, and his father, for whom he was always to long, was taken from him by political and military duties. He became a student activist in militant rebellion against the traditional cultural structures in which he had been so recently immersed (as well as against a Nationalist regime whose abuses he had personally experienced). This led him to Marxism and to strong emotional involvement in the Communist movement; then, because of remaining "imperfections," he participated in a thought reform program that advocated a more thorough ideological conversion, but that, in his case, had the opposite effect. He was alienated by the process, came into conflict with the reformers, and fled the country. Then, in Hong Kong, he struggled to establish himself as an anti-Communist writer, and after a variety of difficulties, found solace and significance in becoming a Protestant convert. Following this, and only thirty years old, he was apparently poised for some new internal (and perhaps external) move.

Even more dramatic were the shifts in self-process of young Japanese whom I interviewed in Tokyo and Kyoto from 1960 to 1962. I shall mention one extreme example of this protean pattern, though there were many others who in various ways resembled him. Prior to the age of twenty-five he had been many things. He was a proper middle-class Japanese boy, brought up in a professional family within a well-established framework of dependency and obligation. Then, owing to extensive contact with farmers' and fishermen's sons brought about by wartime evacuation, he was a "country boy" who was to retain what he described as a life-long attraction to the tastes of the common man. Then, he was a fiery young patriot who "hated the Americans" and whose older brother, a kamikaze pilot, was saved from death only by the war's end. He then became a youngster confused in his beliefs following Japan's surrender, but curious rather than hostile toward American soldiers. He became an eager young exponent of democracy, caught up in the "democracy boom" that swept Japan, and, at the same time, a youthful devotee of traditional Japanese arts—old novels, Chinese poems, kabuki, and flower arrangement. During junior high and high school, he was an all-around leader, outstanding in studies, student self-government, and general social and athletic activities. Almost simultaneously, he was an outspoken critic of society at large and of fellow students in particular for their narrow careerism, on the basis of Marxist ideas current in Japanese intellectual circles. He was also an English-speaking student, which meant, in effect, being in still another vanguard and having strong interest in American things. Midway through high school, he experienced what he called a "kind of neurosis" in which he lost interest in everything he was doing and, in quest of a "change in mood," took advantage of an opportunity to become an exchange student for one year at an American high school. He became a convert to many aspects of American life, including actually being baptized as a Christian under the influence of a minister he admired—his American "father"— and returned to Japan only reluctantly. As a "returnee," he found himself in many ways at odds with his friends and was accused by one of "smelling like butter" (a traditional Japanese phrase for Westerners). He therefore reimmersed himself in Japanese experience—sitting on *tatami*, indulging in quiet, melancholy moods, drinking tea, and so on. He became a *ronin*—in feudal days a samurai without a master, now a student without a university—because of failing his examinations for Tokyo University (a sort of Harvard, Yale, Columbia, and Berkeley rolled into one), and, as is the custom, spent the following year preparing for the next round rather than attend a lesser institution. Once admitted, he found little to interest him until becoming an enthusiastic Zengakuren activist, fully embracing its ideal of pure Communism and having a profound sense of fulfillment in taking part in the planning and carrying out of student demonstrations. But when offered a high position in the organization during his junior year, he abruptly became an ex-Zengakuren activist, resigning because he felt he was not suited for "the life of a revolutionary." Then, an aimless dissipator, he drifted into a pattern of heavy drinking, marathon Mah-jong games, and affairs with bar girls. Later, he had no difficulty gaining employment with one of Japan's mammoth industrial organizations (and one of the *bêtes noires* of his Marxist days) and embarking on the life of a young executive, or *sarariman* ("salaried man")— in fact he did so with eagerness, careful preparation, and relief, but at the same time had fantasies and dreams of kicking over the traces, sometimes violently, and embarking on a world tour (largely Hollywood-inspired) of exotic and sophisticated pleasure-seeking.

There are, of course, important differences between the protean life styles of the two young men, and between them and their American counterparts—differences that have to do with cultural emphases and that contribute to what is generally called national character. But such is the intensity of the shared aspects of historical experience that contemporary Chinese, Japanese, and American self-process turn out to have striking points of convergence.

I would stress two general historical developments as having special importance for creating protean man. The first is the world-wide sense of what I have called "historical (or psychohistorical) dislocation," the break in the sense of connection which men have long felt with the vital and nourishing symbols of their cultural tradition—symbols revolving around family, idea systems, religions, and the life cycle in general. In our contemporary world one perceives these traditional symbols (as I have suggested elsewhere, using the Japanese as a paradigm) as irrelevant, burdensome, or inactivating, and yet one cannot avoid carrying them within or having one's self-process profoundly affected by them. The second large historical tendency is the flooding of imagery produced by the extraordinary flow of postmodern cultural influences over mass communication networks. These influences cross readily over local and national boundaries and permit each individual to be touched by everything, but at the same time cause him to be overwhelmed by superficial messages and undigested cultural elements, by headlines, and by endless partial alternatives in every sphere of life. These alternatives, moreover, are universally and simultaneously shared—if not as courses of action, at least in the form of significant inner imagery.

THE PROTEAN STYLE

We know from Greek mythology that Proteus was able to change his shape with relative ease—from wild boar to lion to dragon to fire to flood. But what he did find difficult, and would not do unless seized and chained, was to commit himself to a single form, a form most his own, and carry out his function of prophecy. We can say the same of protean man, but we must keep in mind his possibilities as well as his difficulties.

The protean style of self-process, then, is characterized by an interminable series of experiments and explorations—some shallow, some profound—each of which may be readily abandoned in favor of still new psychological quests. The pattern in many ways resembles what Erik Erikson has called "identity diffusion" or "identity confusion," and the impaired psychological functioning these terms suggest can be very much present. But I would stress that the protean style is by no means pathological as such and, in fact, may well be one of the functional patterns of our day. It extends to all areas of human experience—to political as well as sexual behavior, to the holding and promulgating of ideas, and to the general organization of lives. I would like to give a few illustrations of the protean style, as expressed in America and Europe, drawn both from psychotherapeutic work with patients and from observations on various forms of literature and art.

One patient of mine, a gifted young teacher, spoke of himself in this way:

> I have an extraordinary number of masks I can put on or take off. The question is: is there, or should there be, one face which should be authentic? I'm not sure that there is one for me. I can think of other parallels to this, especially in literature. There are representations of every kind of crime, every kind of sin. For me, there is not a single act I cannot imagine myself committing.

He went on to compare himself to an actor on the stage who "performs with a certain kind of polymorphous versatility"—and here he was referring, slightly mockingly, to Freud's term "polymorphous perversity" for diffusely inclusive (also protean) infantile sexuality. And he asked: "Which is the real person, so far as an actor is concerned? Is he more real when performing on the stage—or when he is at home? I tend to think that for people who have these many, many masks, there is no home. Is it a futile gesture for the actor to try to find his real face?" My patient was by no means a happy man, but neither was he incapacitated. And though we can see the strain with which he carries his polymorphous versatility, it could also be said that, as a teacher and a thinker, and in some ways as a man, it served him well.

In contemporary American literature, Saul Bellow is notable for the protean men he has created. In *The Adventures of Augie March,* one of his earlier novels, we meet a picaresque hero with a notable talent for adapting himself to divergent social worlds. Augie himself says: "I touched all sides, and nobody knew where I belonged. I had no good idea of that myself." And a perceptive young English critic, Tony Tanner, tells us: "Augie indeed celebrates the self, but he can find nothing to do with it." Tanner goes on to describe Bellow's more recent protean hero, Herzog, as "a representative modern intelligence, swamped with ideas, metaphysics, and values, and surrounded by messy facts. It labors to cope with them all."

A distinguished French literary spokesman for the protean style— in his life and in his work—is, of course, Jean-Paul Sartre. Indeed, I believe that it is precisely because of these protean traits that Sartre strikes us as an embodiment of twentieth-century man. An American critic, Theodore Solotaroff, speaks of Sartre's fundamental assumption that "there is no such thing as even a relatively fixed sense of self, ego, or identity—rather there is only the subjective mind in motion in relationship to that which it confronts." And Sartre himself refers to human consciousness as "a sheer activity transcending toward objects," and "a great emptiness, a wind blowing toward objects." Both Sartre and Solotaroff may be guilty of overstatement, but I doubt that either could have written as they did prior to the last thirty years or so. Solotaroff further characterizes Sartre as "constantly on the go, hurrying from point to point, subject to subject; fiercely intentional, his thought occupies, fills, and distends its material as he endeavors to lose and find himself in his encounters with other lives, disciplines, books, and situations." This image of repeated, autonomously willed death and rebirth of the self, so central to the protean style, becomes associated with the theme of fatherlessness —as Sartre goes on to tell us in his autobiography with his characteristic tone of serious self-mockery:

> There is no good father, that's the rule. Don't lay the blame on men but on the bond of paternity, which is rotten. To beget children, nothing better; To have them, what iniquity! Had my father lived, he would

have lain on me at full length, and would have crushed me. Amidst
Aeneas and his fellows who carry their Anchises on their backs, I move
from shore to shore, alone and hating those invisible begetters who
bestraddle their sons all their lifelong. I left behind me a young man
who did not have time to be any father and who could now be my son.
Was it a good thing or bad? I don't know. But I readily subscribed to
the verdict of an eminent psychoanalyst: I have no superego.

We note Sartre's image of interchangeability of father and son, of "a
young man who did not have time to be my father and who could now
be my son"—which, in a literal sense refers to the age of his father's
death, but symbolically suggests an extension of the protean style to
intimate family relationships. And such reversals indeed become necessary in a rapidly changing world in which the sons must constantly "carry
their fathers on their backs," teach them new things that they, as older
people, cannot possibly know. The judgment of the absent superego,
however, may be misleading, especially if we equate superego with sus-
ceptibility to guilt. What has actually disappeared—in Sartre and in protean man in general—is the classical superego, the internalization of
clearly defined criteria of right and wrong transmitted within a particular
culture by parents to their children. Protean man requires freedom from
precisely this kind of superego—he requires a symbolic fatherlessness—
in order to carry out his explorations. But rather than being free of guilt,
we shall see that his guilt takes on a form different from that of his
predecessors.

There are many other representations of protean man among
contemporary novelists: in the constant internal and external motion
of beat generation writings, such as Jack Kerouac's On the Road; in
the novels of a gifted successor to that generation, J. P. Donleavy,
particularly The Ginger Man; and of course in the work of European
novelists such as Günter Grass, whose The Tin Drum is a breathtaking
evocation of prewar Polish-German, wartime German, and postwar
German environments, in which the protagonist combines protean adapt-
ability with a kind of perpetual physical-mental strike against any
change at all.

In the visual arts, perhaps the most important postwar movement
has been aptly named "action painting" to convey its stress on process
rather than fixed completion. And a more recent and related movement
in sculpture, "kinetic art," goes further. According to Jean Tinguely,
one of its leading practitioners, "Artists are putting themselves in rhythm
with their time, in contact with their epoch, especially with permanent
and perpetual movement." As revolutionary as any style or approach
is the stress on innovation per se that now dominates painting. I have
frequently heard artists, themsleves considered radical innovators, com-

plain bitterly of the current standards dictating that "innovation is all," and of a turnover in art movements so rapid as to discourage the idea of holding still long enough to develop a particular style.

We also learn much from film stars. Marcello Mastroianni, when asked whether he agreed with *Time* magazine's characterization of him as "the neo-capitalist hero," gave the following answer:

> In many ways, yes. But I don't think I'm any kind of hero, neo-capitalist or otherwise. If anything, I am an *anti*-hero or at most a *non*-hero. *Time* said I had the frightened, characteristically 20th century look, with a spine made of plastic napkin rings. I accepted this—because modern man is that way; and being a product of my time and an artist, I can represent him. If humanity were all one piece, I would be considered a weakling.

Mastroianni accepts his destiny as protean man; he seems to realize that there are certain advantages to having a spine made of plastic napkin rings, or at least that it is an appropriate kind of spine to have these days.

John Cage, the composer, is an extreme exponent of the protean style, both in his music and in his sense of all of us as listeners. He concluded a recent letter to the *Village Voice* with the sentence: "Nowadays, everything happens at once and our souls are conveniently electronic, omniattentive." The comment is McLuhanlike, but what I wish to stress particularly is the idea of omniattention—the sense of contemporary man as having the possibility of receiving, or taking in, everything. In attending, as in being, nothing is off limits.

CONSTRICTED SELF-PROCESS

To be sure, one can observe in contemporary man a tendency that seems to be precisely the opposite of the protean style. I refer to the closing off of identity or constriction of self-process, to a straight-and-narrow specialization in psychological as well as in intellectual life, and to a reluctance to let in any extraneous influences. But I would emphasize that where this kind of constricted, or one-dimensional, self-process exists, it has an essentially reactive and compensatory quality. In this it differs from earlier characterological styles it may seem to resemble (such as the inner-directed man described by Riesman, and still earlier patterns in traditional society). For these were direct outgrowths of societies that then existed, and in harmony with those societies, whereas at the present time a constricted self-process requires continuous psychological work to fend off protean influences that are always abroad.

Protean man has a particular relationship to the holding of ideas that has, I believe, great significance for the politics, religion, and general intellectual life of the future. For just as elements of the self can be experimented with and readily altered, so can idea systems and ideologies be embraced, modified, abandoned, and reembraced, all with a new ease that stands in sharp contrast to the inner struggle we have in the past associated with these shifts. Until relatively recently, no more than one major ideological shift was likely to occur in a lifetime, and this one would be long remembered as a significant individual turning point accompanied by profound soul-searching and conflict. But today it is not unusual to encounter several such shifts, accomplished relatively painlessly, within a year or even a month; among many groups, the rarity is a man who has gone through life holding firmly to a single ideological vision.

In one sense, this tendency is related to "the end of ideology" spoken of by Daniel Bell, because protean man is incapable of enduring an unquestioning allegiance to the large ideologies and utopian thought of the nineteenth and early twentieth centuries. One must be cautious about speaking of the end of anything, however, especially ideology, and one also encounters in protean man what I would call strong ideological hunger. He is starved for ideas and feelings that can give coherence to his world, but here too his taste is toward new combinations. Though he is by no means without yearning for the absolute, what he finds most acceptable are images of a more fragmentary nature than those of the ideologies of the past; these images, though limited and often fleeting, can have great influence on his psychological life. Thus political and religious movements, as they confront protean man, are likely to experience less difficulty convincing him to alter previous convictions than they do providing him a set of beliefs that can command his allegiance for more than a brief experimental interlude.

THE SENSE OF ABSURDITY

Intimately bound up with his flux in emotions and beliefs is a profound inner sense of absurdity, which finds expression in a tone of mockery. The sense and the tone are related to a perception of surrounding activities and belief as profoundly strange and inappropriate. They stem from a breakdown in the relationship between inner and outer worlds —that is, in the sense of symbolic integrity—and are part of the pattern of psychohistorical dislocation I mentioned earlier. For if we view man as primarily a symbol-forming organism, we must recognize that he has constant need for a meaningful inner formulation of self and world in which his own actions, and even his impulses, have some kind of fit with the outside as he perceives it.

The sense of absurdity, of course, has a considerable modern tradition, and has been discussed by such writers as Camus as a function of man's spiritual homelessness and inability to find any meaning in traditional belief systems. But absurdity and mockery have taken much more extreme form in the post-World War II world and have in fact become a prominent part of a universal life style.

In American life, absurdity and mockery are everywhere. Perhaps their most vivid expression can be found in such areas as pop art and the more general burgeoning of pop culture. Important here is the complex stance of the pop artist toward the objects he depicts. On the one hand, he embraces the materials of the everyday world, celebrates and even exalts them—boldly asserting his creative return to representational art (in active rebellion against the previously reigning nonobjective school), and his psychological return to the real world of things. On the other hand, everything he touches he mocks. Thingness is pressed to the point of caricature. He is indeed artistically reborn as he moves freely among the physical and symbolic materials of his environment, but mockery is his birth certificate and his passport. This kind of duality of approach is formalized in the stated duplicity of camp, an ill-defined aesthetic in which all varieties of mockery converge under the guiding influence of the homosexual's subversion of a heterosexual world.

Also relevant are a group of expressions in current slang, some of them derived originally from jazz. The "dry mock" has replaced the dry wit; one refers to a segment of life experience as a "bit," "bag," "caper," "game" (or "con game"), "scene," "show," or "scenario"; one seeks to "make the scene" (or "make it"), "beat the system," or "pull it off" or else one "cools it" ("plays it cool") or "cops out." The thing to be experienced, in other words, is too absurd to be taken at its face value; one must either keep most of the self aloof from it, or if not one must lubricate the encounter with mockery.

A similar spirit seems to pervade literature and social action alike. What is best termed a "literature of mockery" has come to dominate fiction and other forms of writing on an international scale. Again Günter Grass' *The Tin Drum* comes to mind, and is probably the greatest single example of this literature—a work, I believe, that will eventually be appreciated as much as a general evocation of contemporary man as of the particular German experience with Nazism. In this country the divergent group of novelists known as black humorists also fit into the general category—related as they are to a trend in the American literary consciousness that R. W. B. Lewis has called a "savagely comical apocalypse" or a "new kind of ironic literary form and disturbing vision, the joining of the dark thread of apocalypse with the nervous detonations of satiric laughter." For it is precisely death itself, and particularly threats of the contemporary apocalypse, that protean man ulitmately mocks.

The relationship of mockery to political and social action has been less apparent, but is, I would claim, equally significant. There is more than coincidence in the fact that the largest American student uprising of recent decades, the Berkeley free speech movement of 1964, was followed immediately by a Filthy Speech Movement. Though the object of the Filthy Speech Movement—achieving free expression of forbidden language, particularly of four-letter words—can be viewed as a serious one, the predominant effect, even in the matter of names, was that of a mocking caricature of the movement that preceded it. But if mockery can undermine protest, it can also enliven it. There have been signs of craving for it in major American expressions of protest such as those of black power and the opposition to the war in Vietnam. In the former a certain chord can be struck by comedian Dick Gregory, and in the latter by the use of satirical skits and parodies, that revives the flagging attention of protesters becoming gradually bored with the repetition of their "straight" slogans and goals. And on an international scale, I would say that, during the past decade, Russian intellectual life has been enriched by a leavening spirit of mockery—against which the Chinese leaders are now, in their current reactivation of thought reform programs, fighting a vigorous but ultimately losing battle.

NURTURANCE VS. AUTONOMY

Closely related to the sense of absurdity and the spirit of mockery is another characteristic of protean man, which I call "suspicion of counterfeit nurturance." Involved here is a severe conflict of dependency, a core problem of protean man. I originally thought of the concept several years ago while working with survivors of the atomic bomb in Hiroshima. I found that these survivors both felt themselves in need of special help and resented whatever help was offered them because they equated it with weakness and inferiority. In considering the matter more generally, I found that this equation of nurturance with a threat to autonomy was a major theme of contemporary life. The increased dependency needs resulting from the breakdown of traditional institutions lead protean man to seek out replacements wherever he can find them. The large organizations (government, business, academic, and so on) to which he turns, and which contemporary society increasingly holds out as a substitute for traditional institutions, present an ambivalent threat to his autonomy in one way, and the intense individual relationships in which he seeks to anchor himself, in another. Both are therefore likely to be perceived as counterfeit. But the obverse side of this tendency is an expanding sensitivity to the inauthentic, which may be just beginning to exert its general creative force on man's behalf.

Technology (and technique in general), together with science, have special significance for protean man. Technical achievement of any kind can be strongly embraced to combat inner tendencies toward diffusion, and to transcend feelings of absurdity and conflicts over counterfeit nurturance. The image of science itself, however, as the ultimate power behind technology and, to a considerable extent, behind contemporary thought in general, becomes much more difficult to cope with. Only in certain underdeveloped countries can one find, in relatively pure form, those expectations of scientific-utopian deliverance from all human want and conflict characteristic of the eighteenth and nineteenth-century Western thought. Protean man retains much of this utopian imagery, but he finds it increasingly undermined by massive disillusionment. More and more he calls forth the other side of the god-devil polarity generally applied to science, and sees it as a purveyor of total destructiveness. This kind of profound ambivalence creates for him the most extreme psychic paradox: the very force he still feels to be his liberator from the heavy burdens of past irrationality also threatens him with absolute annihilation, even extinction. But this paradox may well be—in fact, I believe, already has been—the source of imaginative efforts to achieve new relationships between science and man and, indeed, new visions of science itself.

AMBIVALENT FEELINGS

I suggested before that protean man was not free of guilt. He indeed suffers from it considerably, but often without awareness of what is causing his suffering. For his is a form of hidden guilt—a vague but persistent kind of self-condemnation related to the symbolic disharmonies I have described, a sense of having no outlet for his loyalties and no symbolic structure for his achievements. This is the guilt of social breakdown, and it includes various forms of historical and racial guilt experienced by whole nations and peoples, both by the privileged and the abused. Rather than a clear feeling of evil or sinfulness, it takes the form of a nagging sense of unworthiness all the more troublesome for its lack of clear origin.

Protean man experiences similarly vague constellations of anxiety and resentment. These too have origin in symbolic impairments and are particularly tied in with suspicion of counterfeit nurturance. Often feeling himself uncared for, even abandoned, protean man responds with diffuse fear and anger. But he can neither find a good cause for the former nor a consistent target for the latter. He nonetheless cultivates his anger because he finds it more serviceable than anxiety, because there are plenty of targets of one kind or another beckoning, and because even moving targets are better than none. His difficulty is that focused indignation is as hard for him to sustain as is any single identification or conviction.

Involved in all these patterns is a profound psychic struggle with the idea of change itself. For here too protean man finds himself ambivalent in the extreme. He is profoundly attracted to the idea of making all things, including himself, totally new—to what I have elsewhere called the "mode of transformation." But he is equally drawn to an image of a mythical past of perfect harmony and prescientific wholeness, to the "mode of restoration." Moreover, beneath his transformationism is nostalgia, and beneath his restorationism is his fascinated attraction to contemporary forms and symbols. Constantly balacing these elements amid the extraordinarily rapid change surrounding his own life, the nostalgia is pervasive and can be one of his most explosive and dangerous emotions. This longing for a golden age of absolute oneness, prior to individual and cultural separation or delineation, not only sets the tone for the restorationism of the politically rightist antagonists of history: the still-extant emperor-worshipping assassins in Japan, the colons in France, and the John Birchites and Ku Klux Klanners in this country. It also, in more disguised form, energizes that transformationist totalism of the left that courts violence, and is even willing to risk nuclear violence, in a similarly elusive quest.

Following on all that I have said are radical impairments to the symbolism of transition within the life cycle—the *rites de passage* surrounding birth, entry into adulthood, marriage, and death. Whatever rites remain seem shallow, inappropriate, fragmentary. Protean man cannot take them seriously and often seeks to improvise new ones with whatever contemporary materials he has available, including cars and drugs. Perhaps the central impairment here is that of symbolic immortality—of the universal need for imagery of connection predating and extending beyond the individual life span, whether the idiom of this immortality is biological (living on through children and grandchildren), theological (through a life after death), natural (*in* nature itself, which outlasts all), or creative (through what man makes and does). I have suggested elsewhere that this sense of immortality is a fundamental component of ordinary psychic life and that it is now being profoundly threatened by simple historical velocity, which subverts the idioms (notably the theological) in which it has traditionally been maintained, and, of particular importance to protean man, by the existence of nuclear weapons, which, even without being used, call into questions all modes of immortality. (Who can be certain of living on through children and grandchildren, through teachings or kindnesses?)

Protean man is left with two paths to symbolic immortality, which he tries to cultivate, sometimes pleasurably and sometimes desperately. One is the natural mode we have mentioned. His attraction to nature and concern at its desecration has to do with an unconscious sense that, in whatever holocaust, at least nature will endure—though such are the dimensions of our present weapons that he cannot be absolutely certain even of this. His second path may be termed that of "experiential transcendence"—of seeking a sense of immortality in the way that mystics always have, through psychic experience of such great intensity that time and death are, in effect, eliminated. This, I believe, is the larger meaning of the drug revolution, of protean man's hunger for chemical aids to expanded consciousness. And indeed all revolutions may be thought of, at bottom, as innovations in the struggle for immortality, as new combinations of old modes.

We have seen that young adults individually, and youth movements collectively, express most vividly the psychological themes of protean man. And though it is true that these themes make contact with what we sometimes call the "psychology of adolescence," we err badly if we overlook their expression in all age groups and dismiss them as mere adolescent phenomena. Rather, protean man's affinity for the young—his being metaphorically and psychologically so young in spirit—has to do with his never-ceasing quest for imagery of rebirth. He seeks such imagery from all sources—from ideas, techniques, religious and political systems, mass movements, drugs; or from special individuals of his own kind whom he sees as possessing that problematic gift of his namesake, the gift of prophecy. The dangers inherent in the quest seem hardly to require emphasis. What perhaps needs most to be kept in mind is the general principle that renewal on a large scale is impossible to achieve without forays into danger, destruction, and negativity. The principle of death and rebirth is as valid psychohistorically as it is mythologically. However misguided many of his forays may be, protean man also carries with him an extraordinary range of possibility for man's betterment, or more important, for his survival.

Three important questions about the over-all concept of protean man have been repeatedly raised and are worth considering a bit further. First, is protean man—with his continuous psychic movement and shifts in identity and belief—exclusively a young man? Second, is he really a new man or merely a resurrection of a type we are familiar with from many periods in the past? And third, despite his fluidity, just what in him, if anything remains stable?

I would, very briefly, answer these questions as follows. He is most prominent among the young—or to put the matter another way, the young are most protean—but it would be a great mistake for the rest of us to hide behind this truism, because no one is immune to the larger influences at play and, in greater or lesser degree, protean man inhabits us all. Similarly, such men have indeed existed in earlier historical times also out of joint because of extreme dislocation and rapidly changing symbols and ideas. But contemporary influences have converged to render him a much more clear-cut and widespread entity than ever before. About his stability, it is true that much within him must remain constant in order to make possible his psychological flux—among which I would mention certain enduring elements in the mother-child relationship (what I refer to elsewhere as the "emotional-symbolic substrate"), certain inner consistencies of style (including his sense of absurdity and mockery, his approach to individual and group relationships, and various aesthetic emphases), and even the continuous expectation of change itself. Surely the whole issue of stability amid change needs much more exploration within a specifically psychohistorical framework.